One Man's Chorus

❖

ONE MAN'S CHORUS

THE UNCOLLECTED WRITINGS

ANTHONY BURGESS

Selected with an Introduction by
BEN FORKNER

CARROLL & GRAF PUBLISHERS, INC.
NEW YORK

Editor's note:

In the interest of authenticity, the essays and articles in *One Man's Chorus* have been printed directly from the original typescripts of Anthony Burgess, thus preserving, deliberately, the occasional idiosyncracies of punctuation and spelling.

First Carroll & Graf edition 1998

Carroll & Graf Publishers, Inc.
19 West 21st Street
New York, NY 10010

Library of Congress Cataloging-in-Publication Data is available
ISBN: 0-7867-0568-X

Manufactured in the United States of America

TABLE OF CONTENTS

❖

ACKNOWLEDGMENTS

❖

Two years ago, in 1996, Liana Burgess suggested that I put together a collection of essays and articles written by Anthony Burgess during the last decade of his life. During these two years, Liana has followed and assisted in the preparation of *One Man's Chorus* at every step of the way. I would like to thank her, my wife, Nadine, my son, Benjamin, and the staff at Carroll & Graf, in particular Martine Bellen, for all their support and expertise. Knowing that a place can be as influential as a person, I would also like to thank the University of North Carolina, since it was there, on the campus of Chapel Hill, where I first met Anthony and Liana in the fall of 1969.

—Ben Forkner

ONE MAN'S CHORUS

❖

INTRODUCTION

❖

The paradox in our title *One Man's Chorus* can be easily unknotted when we consider the multitude of different voices Anthony Burgess could apparently summon at will, whatever the occasion or mode of expression demanded. Of course it is the singular resonance of the voice behind the voices that cannot be forgotten by anyone who ever heard the man himself speak in the flesh. And since the writing in *One Man's Chorus* is as much a vocal as a verbal performance, that voice deserves to be evoked before anything else.

I first met him thirty years ago when I was a young graduate student of literature, burdened by books, the toil of learning, and too many hours bent over works of scholarship that did not always make the blood throb with delight. The year Anthony Burgess arrived on campus, I was spending most of my time in the underground depths of the library. The sound of my own footsteps echoed behind me as I shut the door of a private carrel as impenetrable as a tomb. It was difficult not to feel buried in an ivory tower, with the fear that life and literature were now divided against each other for good. The fear would fade in the classrooms because I was fortunate to have excellent teachers who had crafty methods, and years of experience, in awakening the dead. During that same year I had been awakened too, and impressed, by several well-known writers invited to the university to read their works. But too often when these writers stopped reading and began answering questions their voices lost their vigor and assurance. They seemed worn out with the effort, relieved to relax from the strain of literary perfection and to fall back into the small talk of the ordinary stuttering world.

Anthony Burgess belonged to a different race of writer and speaker altogether. The voice that radiated creative fire and conviction while he read from his writing went right on radiating when he put the book down and addressed the present moment. He could not be worn out (as we were to learn one memorable day), and the

spell that the recital of his written words had cast during that first
reading continued unabated as he held forth throughout the hand-
shakings, receptions, official dinners, and late-night drinking ses-
sions that followed. The holding forth lasted not for a few days only,
but during the entire month of his stay. For most of us, certainly
for most of the tomb-stiff graduate students, this demonstration left
us dismayed and thrilled at the same time. We were dismayed because we knew we could never hope to match the tremendous energy
and erudition of the man, even if we buried ourselves in the library
for a lifetime, thrilled because this was the first time we had ever
experienced the sheer electric passion human speech can convey in
the mouth of a master. Here was the inspired eloquence his novels
are filled with, the immense culture, the outrageous wit, the oddity
and pithiness of phrase, the effortless improvisation on any theme
under the sun and moon. Places he had visited or lived in, the
world's languages, politicians of every stripe and smell, songs from
the whole history of Broadway and the English music hall, poetry
from any time and place, invariably illustrated from memory with
entire stanzas: the range of his interests and the depth of his knowledge seemed to have no limits.

The explosive shock of these displays might have left his increasingly captive audience not only filled with awe and envy, but
stunned into silence for good. Whenever he lectured in a classroom
this was in fact often the case. On the day that has now become a
legend on the campus, he had been invited to teach five different
courses, not on general matters of his choice but on the scheduled
topics of the required syllabus. These courses were given by five
different professors, each one a highly regarded specialist in his field.
The topics ranged from an account of Chaucer's scientific knowledge
in a specific passage from "The House of Fame" on up to the problem of Celtic myth in Joyce's *Ulysses*. A number of more arcane
mysteries were to be demystified in between. Whether or not this
was a plot by certain jealous professors is impossible to prove. Certainly it was not expected that he would accept all the invitations.
An ambitious graduate student would not have signed up for more
than two of these courses on the same day.

Burgess of course, without batting an eye, transformed what
would have been a grueling death march through a day of duty for
a normal academic mortal into a one-man parade of spectacular

virtuosity. A small group of us, joined by a few of the younger professors, followed him from class to class. We were dazzled, even the crusty old Miltonian whose eyes were moist when the lecture in his class came to an end with a long passage from *Areopagitica* quoted from memory (always from memory). We had all been given a valuable lesson. Literature did not mock the grave because it was printed on the page, but because it could be carried around alive in the brain. After five hours of uninterrupted brilliance, without a hesitation or a false note to mar the performance, no professor or student dared or desired to say a word. In a lesser man, this would have been enough. But we were to learn quickly that Burgess never talked for triumph, and that he took too much delight in the company of others to confine his energies to the classroom, or to allow the electroshocked captives therein to remain tongue-tied for long.

Above all he loved to please, to entertain. The mischief in his voice was contagious, and no table where he was sitting was allowed to grow glum or grim, much less dull. There was a great deal of the showman in his facial expressions and in the sudden gesticulations of his hands, and a great deal of theatrical skill in the ease with which he modulated tones and shifted accents. He parodied, he mimicked, and he joked. Charles Dickens and Groucho Marx joined the party. And he sang, in all the voices, choralling through time and across the ocean. He would break into Rodgers and Hart or Gilbert and Sullivan or a ribald Scottish ballad at the drop of a hat. He relished the thrust and challenge of free speech made freer by those who were willing to match him drink for drink. I learned later that this was the kind of jousting once prized in Dublin pubs, and that his upbringing in the Irish streets of Manchester before the war had helped hone his reflexes of sharp retort to a razor edge.

As graduate students, wary and often subdued, we were won over entirely by the hearty spirit of derisiveness, especially when the powers of the earth were evoked. If disrespect was considered by certain well-paid professors a weakness in a scholar and a gentleman, and they could well see he was both, it was a weakness we admired, especially since it was always based, verifiably, and amusingly, on the exact fact. Burgess never sneered, but he could not resist the pomposity-pricking anecdote about great men (and women), and we loved him for his lack of resistance. Laughter was the rule, the only rule to be taken seriously. Late at night there might be sudden flights of fury and wild plunges of pessimism, but these were part of the overall enchantment. I never detected much bitterness in his despair at the world's folly, and self-pity was not in his nature. Somehow even the darkest doomsday pronouncements were full of humor. The end result of human history might be tragic, but human nature itself was essentially comic. When Anthony talked the road to hell was strewn with banana peels.

For those of us who had the chance to hear him talk, *One Man's Chorus* is a tape recorder or telephone into the past; for those who did not have that chance, they can rest assured that the essays in *One Man's Chorus* capture the speaking voice, voices, to a syllable, or rather, I can hear him chide over my shoulder, to a phoneme, or is it allophone. Would that he were actually standing by my side to set me right. Still, we can be thankful that the learning and the exuberance of the living man are here on every page. There is more, however. Another quality of his speech that needs to be singled out has something to do with the underlying coherence of his thinking, whatever the subject: a tough-minded logic or reasonableness that can be found in everything he wrote as well, even when the writing was done once, in a hurry, and never revised. This is the greater miracle of the Burgess legacy, not so much that he possessed the gift of speaking in tongues, in person and in print, but the fact that the tongue-speaking was always intelligible and to the point.

Mr Enderby, the dyspeptic poet whom Burgess created but could not kill, once wrote a poem with the line "the thought that wove it never dropped a stitch." This was the case when Anthony Burgess spoke, though stitch-making is not the only metaphor that comes to mind. The words spilled out, but they spilled out in perfect order, in patterns with a purpose. The combination of reckless improvisation and lucidity of thought was, and is, astonishing. He had the gift of going at once to the heart of the matter, along with the rarer gift of making a single statement comprize a lifetime's philosophy. A five-minute comment over a glass of beer had the polish of a printed paragraph, and every line of *One Man's Chorus* bubbles up, champagne-like, with the freshness of the moment. It was said of Samuel Johnson's sentences that even in the heat of argument they left the tongue fully formed; they might glow with the heat, but they cooled at once into hard iron. Burgess admired Johnson, but unlike Johnson, he always stopped short of the oracular. Burgess was a committed individualist who had lived through World War II, and who had had his fill of causes and castes. He was a novelist, not a spokesman, and he shunned the robe of the pontiff like a poisoned shirt. Here too, the young graduate student would learn a valuable lesson. However well-rounded and definitive the sentences that un-rolled into the air, something in the sly sidewiseness of the eyes gave off the warning not to take things too seriously, and not to be taken in by false completeness. There was always more to be said, more to be written. Endless time was the essential condition of truth, and as long as there was time left, the final sentence would have to wait.

Time, however, in the busy life of Burgess was often more a prob-lem than a promise. He called his first collection of journalistic es-says *Urgent Copy*, a title that points to the pressures of writing against a deadline. The same title could apply to most of *One Man's Chorus*. Several of the shorter essays, in fact, were actually com-posed as they were dictated to newspaper offices in London and Rome on the spur of the moment over the phone. They were then typed up from the recording, and the typescripts mailed back to the Burgess home. More often, he would type up the essays himself. And here too the words apparently flowed straight from the inner mind (always at a high tide of activity) directly to the published page. I saw him work on one of these essays in the lobby of a hotel. I had come by to take him to lunch, and was supposed to meet him in the barroom. When I entered the lobby had been taken over by a tour group, and the barroom was closed. To calm the disgruntled tourists drinks were being noisily served in the lobby itself. I tracked him down quickly by the sound of the typewriter and by the smoke signal rising above the crowd from the eternal panetella. There he was in a corner, sitting at a small table. The keys clanged, the roller turned, the carriage slammed to the right, the bell rang, the smoke puffed upward. The Burgess engine was at work. A London news-paper had called him earlier in the morning and had reminded him of an article that had to go to press that very day. I fobbed myself off as a tourist, took a free drink, and waited while he typed. He seemed oblivious to everything but the rhythms he himself was mak-ing. The hammering on the keys was steady, sure, professional. He could have been a skilled carpenter nailing in a roof. As the pages left the typewriter, his wife Liana picked them up and put them into an envelope. The article was mailed to England on our way to lunch.

All in a morning's work, and like the carpenter's roof, made to last.

I insist on the vocal, or conversational element in these essays, and on the concentration Burgess could bring to bear on the task at hand, because he was often surprised when he was asked in interviews how he was able to write so much, and in so many different genres. The quality of the writing he was prepared to defend, if legitimately attacked, but how could he respond except with shrugs and chagrin to the charges of doing something well too often. The answer, I think, lies in his devotion to the craft he had chosen, a radical, almost puritanical devotion that made him exert all his powers whenever words were concerned. A carpenter will not mishandle a plank of good wood on or off the weekly job. For Burgess there was a mystical bond between the words he wrote and the words he spoke. To neglect or minimize either act was to somehow deny the entire faith. I once asked him if he thought Homer spoke Homerically. He answered that he could not have done otherwise. For Burgess the possibility was an absurd contradiction, as it was not for the other writers I listened to as a graduate student. I wonder, in fact, if the memory of his conversational voices will one day bring renewed attention to the wonders of his written work, or perhaps it will be the other way around. What other writer could have composed the novel-poem *Byrne* on his deathbed had not one of the voices in his head been in the habit for years of speaking every day to itself in wryly rhymed ironic verse.

One Man's Chorus obviously does not represent the full structural range of his verbal art, the expansive multilinear narration of *Earthly Powers*, or the complex architecture of *The End of the World News* or *The Napolean Symphony*. None of the essays in *One Man's Chorus*, nor those in his two earlier collections, *Urgent Copy* and *Homage to Qwert Yuiop*, were composed to hold the center stage. They were written quickly, for the day's purpose, as candid commentary on any odd subject of the hour or the week. Three solid thick volumes of shorter pieces, however, by the same Burgess who filled the longer works with brio and brightness in every line, cannot in any sense be thought of as less than a major part of the immense opera of living English he left to the world. This is one more reason why the word chorus strikes the right note, or chord, in our title. These essays are not by any means the whole work, but without them the whole work would be less than complete.

This said, we should not be surprised to find many of the preoccupations of the fiction echoing throughout *One Man's Chorus*: a serial chorus, if we like, of the main Burgessian themes: human life as a perennial dramatic action, propelled by the same old Manichean cycles of conflict; the power and pleasure of music, high and low (for everyone's "depth of brow" as he himself put it); the great creative, destructive dance of the sexes, on and off the stage; the necessity of moral judgment in a world of political doubletalk and journalistic cowardice; the willingness of the independent voice to address the ultimate purpose of civilisation; the pure existential joy of making use of the whole harmonic verbal register. Oddly, for all these choral manifestations, here and elsewhere, Burgess seldom wrote directly for the theater. And yet what other modern novelist has looked at humanity with more dramatic delight and theatrical expertise than Burgess in his prose fiction.

The delight, the expertise, the old energy, the full command of all the voices: these were still very much alive when I next saw Anthony Burgess and his wife Liana, some twenty years after the first encounter. I was then teaching in the state university in Nantes, France, where he had been invited to give two lectures, one on Gerard Manley Hopkins, the other on T. S. Eliot. On the same occasion the city fathers had asked him to attend an official dinner, and to speak on the history of film and literature later that evening. Due to a train strike, all three talks were forced upon him on a single day: Hopkins in the morning, the official dinner at noon, Eliot in the afternoon, film and literature for the general public in the evening. The Burgess dazzle had not dimmed, despite a program that would have drained many a good man half his age. The city fathers had forgotten to plan a meal after the evening speech, so I suggested that Anthony and Liana come home for supper with me and my wife, Nadine. This was a rash suggestion because by then even the late night grocery stores were closed, and all we had were fresh farm eggs.

Nadine is not easily flustered, and with her usual French (or Breton) flair, she whipped together a magnificent golden omelette within a few minutes. Coarse black pepper, *fines herbes*, and a bottle of wine did the rest. At the time I planned to make a short meal of it and to take Anthony and Liana back to their hotel to have at least one good night's sleep before the early morning train. It was soon obvious that neither of them had considered this possibility for an instant. Liana matched her husband in every way, in readiness and conviviality. They were both looking forward to a long evening of conversation and company, the longer the better. Burgess once explained that he wrote his special brand of journalism, the kind of essays in *One Man's Chorus*, as weekly lifelines back to England and English. He could accept geographical exile, but he feared exile from his native tongue like a deadly curse. He had been speaking French all afternoon, to journalists, intellectuals, students, and the various notables of Nantes. It was English he needed now; and even a French omelette in his eyes turned into a manifestation of Englishness, a sort of Hopkins epiphany of golden light spreading through the black depths of Nadine's cast-iron skillet. Hopkins, his favorite poet, was much on his mind that day. He had given a beautiful rendering of "The Windhover" in the morning lecture, from memory of course. After the omelette, and the third glass of wine, I asked him if he knew other Hopkins poems by heart. He began to recite the sonnets slowly. He knew them all. Before he began the much longer "The Wreck of the Deutschland" I asked if I could turn on a tape recorder. After two hours the tape ran out. Two hours later I finally drove Liana and Anthony back to the hotel. They were both wide-awake and Anthony was singing one of the songs from "Blooms of Dublin," the musical he made of Joyce's *Ulysses*. It is difficult to believe that so much life can leave the world at once, all in one man. Fortunately we can still hear the voice in the books, and in the essays of *One Man's Chorus*. And we can still celebrate the man. We had better, whenever we can, because there will never be another like him.

—Ben Forkner

Genius Loci

As one of the great world-travelers of modern fiction, Anthony Burgess never ceased to meditate on the power of place in his novels, setting them with absolute authority all over the world: England, France, Italy, Spain, Russia, Africa, Malaysia, Australia, the United States, and elsewhere. During the last decade of his life, he lived primarily in Europe, a fact that explains the concentration of the travel essays in One Man's Chorus on European cities and countries. Worth noting particularly are the three pieces on France (a country whose national idea of itself can inspire violent ambivalences in anyone who has lived there for long); the two pieces on Manchester, his birthplace; and "Never Again Again," the comical account of a trip to Puerto Rico, a classic Burgess situation wherein the hapless victim extricates himself from one disaster only to discover he is being led helplessly on to another.

THE BALL IS FREE TO ROLL

❖

Monaco io sono
Uno scoglio
Del mio non ho
Quello d'altrui non toglio
Pur viver voglio.

This means: "I am Monaco, a mere rock. I've nothing of my own. I do not take the goods of others. And yet I want to live." In the middle of the last century these lines kept chiming hopelessly in the head of Florestan, Prince de Monaco, Duc de Valentois, Marquis des Baux, Comte de Carladès, Baron du Buis, Seigneur de Saint-Rémy, Sire de Matignon, Comte de Torrigni, Baron de Saint-Lô, Baron de Hambye, Baron de la Luthumière, Duc d'Estoutville, Duc de Mazarin, Duc de Mayenne, Prince de Château-Porcien, Baron d'Altkirch, Marquis de Chilly, Baron de Massy, Marquis de Guiscard, Comte de Ferrette, Comte de Belfort, Comte de Thann, Comte de Rosemont, Grandee of Spain. He had many titles, but he had little else. The principality of Monaco was bankrupt.

There had been a time when the Grimaldi family, the oldest aristocratic family of Europe, had possessed Menton and Roquebrune, as well as the rock which was, and still is, the smallest independent state in the world. But with the post-Napoleonic settlement, the subsequent anti-feudalism that animated Europe, the death of so many of the old monarchies, the only way in which a tiny principality could keep alive was through that new and hateful thing called commercial exploitation of resources. The trouble with Monaco was that it had no resources—except oranges and lemons. The Monégasques hated work. They were content to live on their olive oil, citrus fruits, and dried figs. "Why don't you work?" you could say to a Monégasque, and he would

3

reply: "Je ne me sens pas." In the middle of the nineteenth century the future of Monaco looked black.

But Monaco had two commodities which didn't require much exploitation: the sea, and a healthy climate. The valetudinarian British had already discovered the virtues of Nice and Cannes. They had turned these two small coastal towns into healthful suburbs of London, spending the mild winter there, drinking in the good air and dabbling in the sea. Why should not Monaco follow the example of her two French neighbours? Prince Florestan didn't have the energy to pursue the idea, but his son, Honoré-Charles, went so far as to draw up a plan for a company to be called La Société de Crédit de la Région Méditerranéenne, which would build a sanatorium, various villas, and a bathing station. He needed capital, though—two million francs—and he couldn't raise it. Then he began to hear about Hesse-Homburg in Germany, a tiny independent state like Monaco itself, which had made itself rich through its casino. The trouble with casinos, however, was and still is an aspect of Christian morality. It is not exactly sinful to gamble, but there are better things to be done with money than staking it on the turn of a wheel. Neither Baden-Baden nor Wiesbaden nor Hesse-Homburg liked to call itself a gambling resort. It had to be disguised as a spa, bubbling with healthful spring water, with a casino as a kind of absent-minded distraction.

Nice, in 1849, had tried to open a casino and it had encountered immense moral and legal opposition. Monaco, being an independent state, made its own laws. In 1856 two French businessmen, Napoleon Langlois and Albert Aubert, were granted an exclusive concession to develop Monaco as a centre of civilised amusements, these being an ostensible sideshow to the main natural attractions of the principality—an excellent climate and mild sea water. The concessionaires were to provide

> . . . balls, concerts, fêtes, games such as whist, écarté, piquet, faro, boston and reversi, as well as roulette with either one or two zeros, and trente-et-quarante with the refait or demi-refait, all this at the discretion of the concessionaires, the whole being subject to the supervision of one or more inspectors or commissioners appointed by His Serene Highness.

To Langlois and Aubert all this meant one thing: install roulette wheels and start them spinning. On November 14 1856, a single mansion, the Villa Bellevue, opened as Monaco's proto-casino.

But there is little point in spinning roulette wheels if potential gamblers find it hard to get to them. Monaco had always been hard to reach. Indeed, the whole of the Riviera, to which the world now flocks by sea, air, and road, was virtually cut off from civilisation until Napoleon ordered a road to convey troops from France to Italy. The engineer Sigaud should have built his road by the sea, but he was fearful of British frigates; hence he followed the old Corniche footpath. After the end of the Napoleonic wars, the road, already a bad one, had been allowed to fall into neglect. The whole area reverted to a wilderness of overgrown footpaths and roving bandits. The only way to reach Monaco from Nice was by an irregular and uncomfortable omnibus service, which, in theory, could carry eleven passengers and achieve its journey in a single day. As for getting to Monaco by sea, there was only a wretched leaky steamer which preferred to rust in Nice harbour rather than to venture into the unknown waters which lapped the rock of Monaco.

And when you arrived at Monaco, what did you find? A bad inn and a filthy gaming-house. Gamblers came, but they were not the milords and ladies whom the Prince expected. They were seedy adventurers, their pockets stuffed with counterfeit coins and forged banknotes. Between 15 and 20 March 1857, only one visitor came to the casino, and he won two francs. On the 21st, two came, and they lost two hundred and five francs. This was not big business. Langlois and Aubert wanted to get out, so they sold their concession to Pierre Auguste Daval, a showy character who had been a member of the famous Paris club Frascati's before the 1838 abolition of public gambling in France. Daval did no better than his predecessors. He imported unemployed waiters from Nice and drinksoaked *décavés* and set them up as croupiers. He proposed building a fine new casino, but the workmen complained that they received no wages. The architect walked out in disgust. The Prince of Monaco seriously considered selling his doomed rock to the Emperor of Russia. But the Duc de Valmy intervened. He bought the concession and deputed the exploitation of the casino to François Lefebvre, chairman of the Valmy syndicate. He was a parsimonious and timid man, scared of losses, his eyes shut to the occasional gains of the casino. In 1860 the Prince's commissioner reported: "The disappointment of visitors to Monaco is considerable: everyone knows that there are no comfortable hotels, no bathing facilities, no amusements of any kind. Nobody goes there at all."

It was very nearly true. Gamblers came, but they were of the kind that could not afford the minimum two-franc stake. They would sit at the Café du Soleil and play cards for a few sous a hand until one or another of them had made enough to venture into the casino. The croupiers would climb the battlements and look through a telescope to see if any clients were coming along the hard road from Nice. The timid Lefebvre wanted gamblers to come, but he would not gamble himself. He would not put money into hotels, villas, even newspaper advertisements. The company's balance sheet for 1860 showed a loss of 80,434 francs. The Duc de Valmy, as exasperated as the Prince, removed Lefebvre and looked at the place that had never failed—Hesse-Homburg. There he found the men who were to make Monaco into the gambling centre of the world—the Blanc brothers.

François and Louis Blanc were twins. Born in the Provençal village of Courthozon on 12 December 1806, they were natural gamblers, and lucky ones. Their field of operations was Paris, where King Henri IV had long established a precedent of public gambling which, despite occasional interventions from the government, flourished like a fever until 1838, when a governmental fiat seemed likely to shut the gaming-houses forever.

Roulette itself, the queen of all games of chance, is a French invention, and it is attributed to no less a personage than the great austere theologian Pascal. Certainly Pascal coined the word *roulette*, though not in a gambling context: to him it meant merely the curve traced in space by a point on a rolling circle. But he conceived two basic elements in the game—the wheel and the ball—and he corresponded with his mathematical colleague Pierre de Fermat on the theory of probability in games of hazard. Whether his ghost wills it or not, he is the father of roulette, as of the public omnibus, the computer, and the wristwatch. Nor need his spirit reject the attribution, since roulette is, of all games, the most honest. Diderot said: "At roulette the player may risk his money in complete security." Roulette was Dostoevsky's game, and this Christian saint of literature has elevated it to a kind of wheel of martyrdom. With roulette we touch the hell of despair and live in the purgatory of hope. It is no ordinary game of chance.

Most government ordinances are unwise. When the French government closed the gaming-houses on January 1 1838, it deprived various charitable institutions of the revenue legally levied on the proceeds of the tables, and it lost an annual six million francs in gaming licence fees. Gambling was not stamped out; it merely moved elsewhere. The Paris entrepreneurs and addicts rushed to Baden-Baden, Wiesbaden, Ems, Schwalback, Kissingen, Pyrmont, Spa, and Aix-la-Chapelle. The Blanc brothers, now thirty-five years old, had had enough gambling experience in Paris to realise that they could make a fortune, not out of play but by holding the bank. They had as yet little capital: it was the comparative smallness of Hesse-Homburg that attracted them—a state miserably poor, its only resource a mineral spring that drew few visitors. They were granted an opportunity by the Landgrave to develop a gambling facility, but they went further than the failed entrepreneurs of Monaco. They publicised the spa, organised fêtes and concerts, improved hotel accommodations, turned Homburg into a profitable resort as well as a Dostoevsky myth. Their Homburg is caught forever as "Roulettenburg" in *The Gambler*, along with the mad aristocratic addicts who sat all day at the tables, fed distractedly on sandwiches.

Even that harmless and universal word *sandwich* springs out of gambling fever, though long before the time of the brothers Blanc. It was England's Earl of Sandwich who could not tear himself away from the tables for dinner. He ordered a slice of meat between pieces of bread to be brought to him as he played. His gaming mania modified the eating habits of the world.

The Blanc brothers ate large dinners in tranquillity. They never worried about the fate of their casino, even when it disbursed large sums to jubilant winners. "He who breaks the bank today," said François Blanc, "will without doubt come back to be broken by the bank tomorrow." Satisfied with his achievement at Homburg, he was nevertheless unhappy in Germany. He was a Frenchman, and yearned for a Francophone ambience. That is why he had his eye on Monaco even during the worst days of its failure as a gambling resort. When his brother died he was lonely. He was also hurt by the ingratitude of the small German town he had turned into a prosperous city, whose citizens now sought to limit his powers and profits as a concessionaire. Moreover, he foresaw the German future, with its achieved dream of national unification, the end of small independent states like Hesse-Homburg, new laws which forbade gambling as harmful to the national image.

Blanc made an offer for the Monaco concession. Valmy and Lefebvre turned it down. They were greedy: any sum that Blanc offered was immediately countered by a higher sum. Blanc lost patience. One day he took the boat from Nice, drove to the Monaco casino, laid down three bonds on the Bank of France worth 1,100,000 francs, and said: "You want to sell the concession. I want to buy it. I am having lunch in Monaco. The boat leaves for Nice at four o'clock. I shall be on that boat. I want everything settled one way or the other before then." He got the concession.

The Société des Bains de Mer et Cercle des Etrangers was founded with a capital of eight million francs. The Bishop of Monaco was a shareholder. So was Cardinal Pecci, who later became Pope Leo XIII. The aura of holiness helped the reputation of the new enterprise, but Blanc's name was more potent than God's. And Blanc's energy was remarkable. By the start of 1864 there was a much improved road to Nice, along with a regular, safe, and comfortable bus service. The restaurant of the Hôtel de Paris was open. A fine new casino building began to rise. The railway line from Nice had already reached Cagnes. By 1866 Monaco was a mecca for international gaming aristocrats, including the Duke of Hamilton, Lord Stafford, Princess Souvaroff, and Countess Kisselev—doyenne of the Homburg tables and an immortal character in Dostoevsky's *The Gambler*.

The response of the neighbouring coastal resorts to Monaco's new prosperity was a number of sanctimonious attacks, in which the sinfulness of gambling was emphasised. Jealousy finds many masks. The poor, said the carping voices, would be made poorer still by this terrible temptation of the casino. Blanc's response was to exclude the poor, that is to say "clerks, domestic servants, labourers and peasants." He also excluded the journalists of Nice and Cannes who vilified his venture.

This venture was, in effect, the building of a new city. The casino, with its surrounding shops, restaurants, and hotels, transformed a barren hill into a parnassus of play. It needed a name. Charlesville? Albertville? Perhaps it would be unseemly to call the source of Monaco's new prosperity after Monaco's monarch or his son. But Charles III did not think so. On July 1 1866 the hill was named Monte Carlo. From now on, Monaco was divided into three distinct townships: the old rock, or Monacoville, with its princely palace and government offices; the Condamine, once a garden of flowers and citrus fruits but now a growing commercial centre; Monte Carlo, the gambler's combined hell and paradise, garnished with soft beds, painted ceilings, and a Parisian cuisine. The threefold division remains. Strangely or not so, the whole principality has been swallowed up by one of its parts. Not everyone knows Monaco, but everyone knows Monte Carlo. You book a railway ticket to Monte Carlo, but you alight at the Condamine of Monaco. It is given to few men to build a city. Monte Carlo is wholly François Blanc's creation.

He died in 1877 at the age of seventy-one, leaving a fortune of eighty-eight million francs. This seemed to justify the old saying: "Essayez rouge, essayez noir. C'est toujours Blanc qui gagne." The week after his death the Casino (we must now capitalise the initial letter) lost 640,000 francs. It was taken as an indication that without Blanc's living presence the venture might die. But the profits returned, and the future was golden. All the casinos in Germany were closing. Monte Carlo ceased to be a mere minion of the Goddess of Chance: she became the Goddess of Chance herself.

The Golden Age of Monte Carlo came with the Belle Epoque in France and the Edwardian Era in England. Gambling had lost its aura of sin and acquired a large glamour. Who could associate sin with the elegant décor of the Casino and with its aristocratic habitués? Everybody who was anybody came to Monte Carlo— the King of Sweden, Prince Mirza Riza Khan of Persia, the Aga Khan, the prince of Denmark, Grand Duke Serge of Russia, the Duke and Duchess of Marlborough. . . . Queen Victoria of England never came nearer than Menton, never called on the Prince, indignantly returned a bouquet of flowers humbly, or cunningly, sent by the management of the Casino. But her son, Edward Prince of Wales, King Edward VII, graced the tables, though under a pseudonym. For him crèpes Suzette were invented at the Hôtel de Paris.

Royalty and aristocracy have never, till the present day, been associated with high morality. It is not surprising that filles de joie flocked to Monte Carlo, among them great courtesans of international repute, such as Liane de Pougy and La Belle Otero. A story, probably apocryphal, is told of these two. La Belle Otero appeared one night in the Casino with a décolletage that induced palpitations behind the stiff shirt-fronts, wearing her entire jewel collection, including pearl necklaces that had belonged to the Empress Eugénie and the Empress of Austria respectively, and a diamond bolero from Cartier that was valued at three million francs. Liane then appeared in classic white with a single pearl, followed by her pet poodle arrayed in all her jewels.

There was high art as well as gaming for high stakes. The Monte Carlo Opera outclassed Covent Garden in London and the Opéra in Paris. Caruso had his first triumph there in 1902, singing in *La Bohème* opposite Melba. For Melba the pèche Melba was invented, as well as its austere antithesis, toast Melba. Chaliapine first sang there in Boito's *Mefistofele*. What Monte Carlo paid in high artist's fees she got back in the Casino. She could not lose. There was glamour, but there was also tragedy. Failed gamblers shot themselves. Their bodies could always be moved across the Boulevard des Moulins into France. As for murders, there were only four in ten years. It was alleged that murderers were gently persuaded to cross the invisible frontier into Beausoleil and commit their crimes on French soil. We have no evidence of this. The immorality of Monte Carlo was confined to the sumptuous bedrooms of the Hôtel de Paris and the Hermitage, or at least that was the official story.

Monte Carlo has always been easily hit by wars. In 1914, someone dramatically wrote, gambling stopped as suddenly "as if death had struck the croupiers in the very act of spinning the white ball." But Monaco, being neutral, buzzed with a different game, that of espionage. Mata Hari was here, hired as a glamorous "oriental" dancer. She shot a Russian colonel on leave, and swore she was only defending her honour. The following year it was disclosed that the Russian was an agent of the Allies, suspected that Mata Hari was a spy, and left some papers in the villa where he entertained her, planted temptingly within reach of her white hands. She stole the papers, as expected, and he was shot in attempting to catch her with the evidence. The Deuxième Bureau watched her from then on; a year later she faced a firing squad.

The fortunes of Monaco in the modern era are associated with two very wealthy men, both gamblers in the widest possible sense. The first was Sir Basil Zaharoff, the armaments millionaire, who, by the end of the First World War, had been coming to Monte Carlo for thirty years with his Spanish mistress, the Duquesa de Marquena y Villafranca. Sir Basil had a demented idea—that of taking over the principality as his own province, deposing the Grimaldi family and installing his mistress as its nominal ruler. But first he had to be free to marry her. In 1924, at the age of seventy-five, he heard of the death of her husband, the mad Spanish duke, and entered the matrimonial state. Meanwhile, he had been feeding money into the Casino, treating it as a cold-blooded business concern, a kind of gambling factory, untouched by the paternalistic humanity of the Blanc family. Ruined men and women would approach him at his table in the Hôtel de Paris, saying: "Sir Basil, you're the richest man in the world. Please help me." And Sir Basil would invariably reply: "Go to hell."

Zaharoff never succeeded in ousting the Grimaldis from the princely throne. His ambitions and interests collapsed when his wife died. He sold out his shares to Daniel Dreyfus, the Paris banker.

The second of the wealthy gamblers was Aristotle Onassis, who entered the Monegascan scene in 1953. Monte Carlo had known the inevitable period of decline during the Second World War, when the Gestapo, and later the headquarters of General von Kohlermann's Panzer division, occupied the Hôtel de Paris. Kohlermann may be accounted a lover of the Casino and hence a friend of the principality. When the Gestapo suggested that the copper roof of the noble structure should be removed and sent to help the Third Reich in its hour of need of heavy metal, he declared the Casino to be a historical and cultural monument. But, safe as it was from military depredations on both sides, Monte Carlo had to struggle from 1945 on to recover its former glory. By 1951 it was running at a loss, while Nice boomed. Onassis saved the situation.

He began by making an offer for the premises of the old Sporting Club, no longer in use, and to his surprise the offer was refused. His scheme was a reasonable one: Monaco was a perfect base for a shipowner, and it did not levy taxes. The Sporting Club would have provided a useful "convenience headquarters": still, it was not for sale. All Onassis could now do was to buy shares in the company, increasing his purchases until he had control of its properties, and then the Sporting Club became his. His name had glamorous and adventurous connotations. People of the international jet set jetted to great parties at the Hôtel de Paris. Onassis would reorganise Monaco: he would make it his personal fiefdom.

He reckoned without Prince Rainier. Rainier, twenty-six years old but mature, conscientious, responsible, came to the throne in 1949. He regarded his principality as a sacred trust, not as a mere field for financial speculation. He approved of glamour, but not the tawdry glamour with which Onassis proposed to invest the place. After all, he made a glamorous marriage, with Grace Kelly, a Hollywood film star, but she had more than superficial celluloid allure: she came of a distinguished Philadelphia Catholic family, she had dignity, intelligence, the quality suggested by her first name. Rainier was more democratic than the successful boy from Smyrna. He saw that the age of the common man had arrived, and he saw no reason why the facilities of Monaco should be reserved to the monied. He wanted visitors with middle-class incomes to frequent the Casino, playing for low stakes and given drinks on the house. A symbol of the change in policy was the abolition, chiefly at the insistence of Princess Grace, of the old bloody sport of pigeon-shooting. Aristocrats were always great and casual spillers of blood; ordinary men and women felt differently about it.

Onassis wanted nightclubs; Rainier wanted culture. Annoyed at the prince's high-toned ambitions, Onassis once went so far as to say that there was no room for high tone in a ruler whose income was mainly derived from gambling. He even expressed the view that gambling was immoral. Rainier said that Onassis was in no position to lecture anyone on morality. Onassis said that it was monstrous that a company like the Société des Bains de Mer should be virtually, because of the princely right of veto, in the hands of one man. Rainier said that if Onassis didn't like the situation he should sell his shares and go away. Onassis did.

And so we come to post-Onassis Monaco, with benign princely rule and a diversification of facilities and, hence, of sources of income. There is something bizarre about the gambling of the 1970s. The glorious décor of the Belle Epoque looks down, along with the ghosts of old aristocratic gamblers, on a new generation of gamesters. There are occasional American business tycoons and movie stars, but for the most part there are women in slacks and men without ties staking their twenty francs or so. There are wrinkled old men and ladies, survivors of an earlier gambling age, who go to the Casino in the mornings as devoutly as if going to mass. Occasionally, as in one incredible week never to be forgotten, the Arab oil-sheiks look in, ready to win a quarter of a million francs on one turn of the wheel, as ready to lose thirty million. But of course the word "loss" hardly incurs in a petrodollar multimul-timultimillionaire's vocabulary.

There are other things in Monaco, and the other things are not a mere sideshow of the Casino. The Casino itself continues progressively to become the sideshow, a relic of a Golden Age that is irrecoverable. Monte Carlo is the place where the motor rally is held, where international conferences meet in the functional new centres, where Cousteau pursues his oceanographical researches. It is the place where people come to start businesses, unhindered by a crippling tax system that seems, to most of us, to represent a more terrible immorality than could ever be attached to merely spinning a roulette wheel. Monaco is a tiny pocket of good sense in a world that is becoming one unified fiscal tyranny. People come here to live, buying or renting an apartment or a studio in one or other of the highrise buildings that are eclipsing the decent rococo dignity of the Golden Age.

Why am I here? Not to gamble, not to offer the turtle-lidded eyes of old age to the sun. I am here to write in an apartment on the rue Grimaldi in the Condamine, a place tranquil in winter but noisy with endless streams of Nice-bound traffic in summer. The tax advantages are negligible for an author, who must pay his imposts in all the countries where his books are published. Prices follow the prices of France, and are high. But there is tranquillity here of a kind no longer to be found in Italy, from which country I emigrated on hearing the news that my son was about due to be kidnapped. The pressures of politics are not to be found here, as they are in our two great neighbours. The police are many but they are paternal rather than oppressive.

The best countries are the easiest ones to get out of. I walk for ten minutes up the hill and I arrive at the railway station, whence I can travel to Rome or Geneva or Paris or Barcelona, often in something like the old comfort of the Belle Epoque. I travel, and I am happy to travel back. In Rome one is burgled, in New York one is robbed and knifed; here there is law and order, protection for the person and his property. There is a lack of intellectual discourse, but Monaco, unlike Paris, has never made any claim to be a city of new philosophical movements or aesthetic fashions. But music flourishes here. I, who began my artistic career as a composer, duly enter my musical composition for the annual concours and expect to fail. The chief oboist of the very fine symphony orchestra comes to my apartment once a week and, for fifty francs, gives an oboe lesson to my son. Things could be a great deal worse.

I sometimes feel a little hampered by the tradition of bourgeois respectability that prevails here. Writers are not, by nature, respectable: their function is to be subversive. When I leave my writing for an hour or so and go out, unkempt, baggy-trousered, dirty-shoed, to a café or tobacconist, I feel that people are looking at me strangely, as though I do not fit into the townscape. I have a whitewalled motor caravan, and I feel that the police frown on this as, again, not sufficiently respectable in a state shiny with Cadillacs. But I hope to persuade the great Jean Miró to paint something on the white bodywork, and that may restore it to official acceptance.

What do I do after work? Very little. I have long ceased to be a great frequenter of bars, theatres, cinemas. I like to look at the old Monaco, especially now as the sun warms, but does not warm too much, and drink in its undeniable architectural charm. The great gift of the southern lands to our civilisation is the simple right to sit at an outside café table and look at things. But even from my little balcony on the rue Grimaldi I can take in an admirable vista of houses of the Golden Age, with trees planted about them and, beyond, the uplands of the Alps Maritimes. I regret the new skyscrapers, but I do not see how they could well be avoided. Monaco has become a little Manhattan of the Mediterranean. She can only expand upwards, and that upward expansion is a necessary condition of her growing prosperity.

Certain things are preserved here, despite the incursion of modernity. As in my own country, England, we have a hereditary ruling house with a tradition of courtesy, tolerance and, I may say, charm. It is a pleasure to be a subject of Prince Rainier and Princess Grace. They let me get on with my writing, and I let them get on with their wholly benevolent rule. I do not (forgive me, France) much care for republics; leaving a monarchy I had, sooner or later, to gravitate to a principality. The princely family set a standard of courtesy which the police are quick to follow. Functionaries are efficient but easygoing. One wholly misses the bad-tempered hustling of the great cities. It is good to be here.

I can say this despite the fact that I live less in a town than in the periphery of my own mind. Every morning I sit down to write. Every evening I rise, stiff, and start to cook the family dinner. I have so much work to do that I am the most conspicuous living contradiction of President Nixon's taunt about the Côte d'Azur being a province for the idle. I never set foot in the famous Casino; it is an event when I am seen even in the café across the street. But I am aware, through the open window of my study, of a circumambient benevolence. I look left up to the Rock, right up to the gambling hill. Everybody is getting on quietly with his own job, while I am getting on with mine. Politicians don't hector; drugged junkies don't sleep against the door; the thieves and muggers pursue their work in Nice and Cannes and leave us in Monaco alone. To be left alone is the most precious thing one can ask of the modern world. Monaco is perhaps the last pocket of the ancient civilisation which was built on respect of that right. While Europe condemned roulette, Monaco continued to promote its harmless solace. While Europe seems to condemn individual freedom, Monaco continues to uphold it. The ball is free to roll and find its own socket.

—1978

FRANCOPHONIA

❖

Some years ago I wrote a light-hearted piece for a British news-paper in which I lamented that, while the Latin word *aqua* had remained *aqua* (or *acqua*) in Italian and changed to the not very different *agua* of Spanish, it had undergone unbelievable meta-morphoses in the province of Gallia. The French word for *aqua* is a single vowel *eau*, and it is a very inefficient word. The great French linguist Martinet pointed out that you can't make an ad-jective from it and have to fall back on that original *aqua* to talk about *sports aquatiques*. The French seem determined to destroy their Roman inheritance by chopping up words until they become as short as possible, and as capable of being confused with other chopped up words as only a genuinely morbid condition of lan-guage can allow. Even when a French word or name bears some visual resemblance to its classical original, the spoken form sub-mits to the axe. I can never grow used to pronouncing *Jésus Christ* as *Jézu Cri*, and I feel that if the French could cut the holy name down to something like *Jé Cr*, they would.

The English are accustomed to being jeered at by foreigners for their impossible diphthongs, their tongue-biting *th*, and their de-mented orthography. They remain good-humoured about it. But dare to suggest that there is something wrong with the French language, and you have insulted national honor, trampled on the tricolor, and affirmed that all Parisiennes are whores (which they probably are, but I will not pursue the matter here). My little grumble about the reduction of the noble *aqua* to the trivial *eau* provoked a ten-page letter from the cultural attaché of the French Embassy in London, in which I was accused of the regular British crimes—philistinism, chauvinism, ignorance, hypocrisy, and a love of bad cooking—as well as a desire to destroy the good Anglo-French relations which the cultural attaché had devoted his diplomatic career to promoting. The French are a very sensitive people.

Their sensitivity, however, applies only to their image of themselves as a nation. They have a very insensitive attitude to other nations. They seem to like the Germans, whom they had the privilege of knowing well during the Occupation, but they totally distrust their old comrades-in-arms, or part-rescuers, the British. For the Italians they seem to have a profound contempt. This may be because those Italians working in France are in lowlier positions than their own and, very sensibly, attempt to make their adopted language conform more to Italian sound and structure than bourgeois French usage allows. They do not despise the Italian cuisine. They occasionally even imitate it, though they usually spell it wrong. But of their superiority to the Italians and, indeed, all other nations except the Germans (who gave them a brisk hard lesson on the theme of racial superiority), the French are in no doubt at all, and the great symbol of their excellence is their language.

The principle of *Francophonie*, or of the universal desirability of everybody speaking French, is frequently aired, trumpeted, and played on full Berliozian orchestra. The claims that are made for the utility of French are, as we all know, not merely chauvinistic but unrealistic. I have spoken English from my cradle, but I do not regard it as a particularly beautiful or rational language. If it has become a second language for many of the countries of the world (free, unfree, and third), it is because of a historical accident. Britain colonised North America; the language of North America is inevitably the language of the British; the Americans are a powerful people with a well-developed commercial instinct, technological talent, and capacity for developing surrogate foods and entertainments that have a universal appeal. English was bound to become a world language.

The French resent this and would, if they could, rewrite history. In a sense, they have actually succeeded in doing this, for the French-speaking province of Canada has at last broken away from its Anglophone neighbours, and one cannot doubt that Francophone propaganda from the mother country has had much to do with it. General de Gaulle visited Quebec and shouted, to some applause, *"Vive le Québec libre!"* The implication was that the tyrannical Anglophones were forcing the Francophones to eat hot dogs, drink Coca-Cola, and read "Peanuts" in the original English. It seems that all the Quebec French wish to do is to eat hot dogs, drink Coca-Cola, and read "Peanuts" in French. This they have been doing for some time; now they are doing it with all the patriotic verve of people who have destroyed their nonexistent bonds.

The French should be pleased. In a sense, part of the American empire which the British stole from them has now been restored. It is a pity, however, that the French despise the French Canadians just as they despise the Italians and the British. They despise their French, which had developed from seventeenth-century Norman and lacks the polish of the Parisian variety. A few years ago I was on the jury of the Cannes Film Festival, and a very fine film called *Les Ordres* was submitted by Canada. The French journalists on the jury complained that they could not understand the dialogue and, of course, they could not understand the English subtitles either. A British imperial conspiracy was afoot, unfair to France.

You will not find Canadian French fiction or poetry in the bookshops of Paris (you will not find much of it in the bookshops of Montreal either). The victory of the Quebec separatists is a purely linguistic victory, and it will not result in closer cultural ties with Paris. All that has happened is that hot dogs have become *chiens chauds*, although they are still hot dogs on the Côte d'Azur, and that the need to find a French term for hamburger grows more and more urgent. In other words, the culture of French Canada will remain much the same as that of British Canada—North American, with flapjacks and maple syrup for breakfast, and television series like *Dallas* imported not from Hollywood but from Paris, where they will already have been translated into French.

The situation is one which only French chauvinists can praise. A united Canada, in which English and French had the same status and were taught together in schools, has now become bitterly divided. When, in late 1977, I was in Toronto and the separatist Québecois were already replacing bilingualism with monoglottism, most Canadians of British stock told me that they were withdrawing their children from French classes. We have two Canadas now, but the big business interests of the United

States will increasingly concentrate on trading with the Anglophone part. With this they have at least a language in common. I cannot foresee them making a linguistic effort to accommodate the Francophones. Quebec may now glory in speaking the language of de Gaulle and subduing the language of Shakespeare, but they are opting out of the big North American entity, transforming themselves into a belated colony without a mother country. For their French mother has forgotten them now, as a bitch forgets her puppies, except for the yap and bark they share with her.

I have nothing against *Francophonie*. I have been speaking, reading, and writing French for the last forty-five years, but I speak the language with increasing reluctance. This is because the French are so unforgiving if one speaks their tongue badly. One dare not forget a gender or bend a grammatical rule. The Italians, sensibly and humanely, permit any foreign deviation from linguistic rectitude so long as communication is established and maintained. Even if I turned *acqua* into *eau* I might be forgiven. But in France everybody—taxi-driver, waiter, prostitute—is a schoolteacher, ready with a reproving rap: *"On ne dit pas cela, monsieur."* This kind of treatment strikes one literally dumb. Or, if you mouth "Oh" in rebuked embarrassment, you will be told: *"DE L'eau, monsieur."*

—1981

GOING NORTH

❖

I have just returned, with my wife, from Stockholm, where the days are already beginning to grow very short and the cold Arctic winds announce the coming of the endless nordic winter. I am a child of the North, though my native Manchester had a positively tropical climate compared with Sweden's capital, and to travel north is to engage once more the dismal skies of my youth. During the last war, the British War Office sent me south, to Gibraltar, where I learned to love the dirt, disorder, superstition, roguery, and original sin of the Mediterranean. In 1954 I went to live in Southeast Asia, where I was bathed in day-long sweat, cried out against the tyranny of the sun, and dreamed of the north as a paradise of cold houses, hot soup, and blazing log-fires. But my blood grew thin, and I knew that I could never again live in the north. For the last thirteen years I have wandered from one place to another on the Middle Sea of my traditional culture—Hebraic, Greek, Catholic—and have thought of Scandinavia with a shudder.

But various obligations of a literary nature have sent me to Oslo, Copenhagen, and Stockholm, though, if it was Stockholm in early November, it was Oslo in August and Copenhagen in May. I have been also to Leningrad in July, and I know all about the long white nights of the Baltic. Midnight sun seems to me to be as much an abomination as midday darkness—a natural extravagance which finds its human counterpart in the attempt to build extravagantly stable and just societies. What you notice in Scandinavia is the triumph of the social contract.

You notice particularly such social virtues as honesty. As a Catholic, or at least a member of an old and staunch Catholic family, I feel deep regret that the Church of Rome has never achieved that diffusion of moral integrity which you take for granted in the Protestant realms. The Lutheran Church is weak in Scandinavia. It provides ill-attended services in which women pastors officiate. But the Lutheran tradition still holds. You must not steal or cheat or run dubious businesses. You do not permit *scippatori* on Lambrettas without a *targa*. My wife had her hand-bag stolen three times in three weeks in Rome, and now carries her necessities around in a plastic shopping bag. In Stockholm, or Oslo, she can be sure that her car will not be Neapolitanly stripped or her camera snatched from a café table. Admittedly, among the bored young, there are various subversive Scandina-vian movements designed to bring the thrills of the violent South to the calm North, but the principles of honesty, obedience to the law, and the cult of personal integrity are deeply ingrained.

Sweden has its reward for integrity, and its recompense for a long, dull, dark winter, in a condition of prosperity so thorough that it can only invoke in the Swedes a profound sense of guilt. This guilt is palliated by hospitable immigration laws which per-mit Turks, Greeks, and Jugo-Slavs to take on the lowly jobs of the community. It is a kind of voluntary slavery typical of our age. Nobody believes that slavery has disappeared from the world: the conditions of slavery have changed, that is all. Slaves nowadays have passports and salaries, but they recognise them-selves as inferior beings lucky to be alive and not at all resentful of the privileges of their masters. In Stockholm the lowly work is done by people of dark hair and skin; the fair Nordics labour at the more exacting tasks of creation and administration. They earn much and they pay exorbitant taxes, in return for which they are granted all the amenities of the welfare state. They are not per-mitted to drive cars while drunk and thus injure themselves and others. If they are stopped arbitrarily by the traffic police and a blood test discloses that they have taken half a glass of wine, they are forbidden to drive and have to undergo the beneficial priva-tions of prisons indistinguishable from hospitals. Their streets are as clean as their houses. They do not resound with drunken song, as in certain southern capitals. Life is safe. Life is dull.

And yet safety is inseparable from dullness, and we would all accept, apparently, nordic dullness for the sake of not having to worry about being raped, robbed, or thrown into third-world in-digence. It is, theoretically at least, wonderful to have a pater-nalistic state which saves us from the consequences of our own original sin. You find that your hotel bar is not open until five in the evening and on Sunday not open at all. There are no raucous pubs as in London (which must count, for the Swedes, as a very southern city, a positive Naples). On the other hand there is a highly sequestered drink problem, the consequence of having the Dionysan element in all human nature suppressed by the Apollonian state. But the drinks which Swedes drink are not calculated, one would think, to breed addiction—thin beer and a toothachingly sweet punch. Even the television programmes are of a blandness evidently designed to forbid even domestic excitement: I watched, at peak viewing time, a highly instructive though sedative film on shoemaking in a remote Swedish village.

The old Spanish adage is true: take what you want and pay for it. The price you pay for the gaiety, garlic, sunlight, and exuberance of Naples is theft, unemployment, dirt, and poverty. The price you pay for the utopian conditions of Sweden is a sense that life is a puritanical burden whose awaited end is a clean hospital cot and every comfort short of euthanasia. In matters of art, the price is blandness and recognition that the greatest Swedish reward for literary attainment can rarely go to a Swede. As a Northerner (though, as you can confirm by looking at a map of England, not all that much of a Northerner) I was possessed in Sweden by a certain nostalgia for blandness and blondness, the comfort of a long firelight evening with the blizzard raging outside, the assurance that I would not be cheated in business nor attacked on the street. But as a kind of Northern Catholic I was tormented by visions of baroque Rome, insolent *scippatori* who would be mere dark-skinned slaves in Stockholm, the taste of amply flowing wine and the reek of garlic, and, of course, the warmth of the sun. We are never satisfied.

The trouble with the Swedes is that they think they are satisfied. What more could civilised humanity ask than this fine Northern Venice with its pretty houses, its opulent hotels, sugar in everything—even in the bread? Yet there is the Swedish unconscious which dare not speak and announce that life is probably better in Naples. In a great Swedish dramatist, August Strindberg, the unconscious spoke clear and loud, but it is universally recognised as the voice of madness.

—1981

Understanding the French

❖

I have been spending the summer in the Var, which, being in Provence, is not quite French, but it is French enough for an Englishman like myself. The Italians are not too happy with the French at the moment. The French, having long been the leaders of the European Economic Community (or they consider themselves to be the leaders; they were quick to tell the British they were not sufficiently "European" to join it), are now disrupting the whole notion of European economic unity by refusing to accept Italian wines. But if the Italians are not exactly pro-French at the moment, at least they understand the French—they are fellow-Latins, putative daughters of the same Church; they drink wine and cook with garlic. Englishmen do not understand the French at all.

Frenchmen do not understand the English either, although they consider that their intellectual equipment enables them to understand everything. It is strange that only thirty-three kilometers separate the coasts of the two nations, and yet France and England might as well belong to different planets. It is all a matter of philosophy, I think. The English are empirical. The systematiser of their attitude to life was the Scotsman David Hume, who taught that all knowledge comes from the external world and is bounded by the senses. According to the English, who are not only empirical but pragmatic, it is dangerous to lay down rules (except for games, which are the British substitute for philosophy); it is especially dangerous to think too much, and it is even perilous to formulate a political constitution. The French, on the other hand, pride themselves on being Cartesian. With them the processes of thought are more important than the objects of thought. Logic has its own reality, and it is a more powerful reality than the world of sensation.

This statement seems false. Surely there is no race more sensuous than the French, producers of exquisite perfumes, *la haute cuisine* and *la haute couture*? Yes, the French appreciate the senses, but only when they have passed through the filter of the intellect. A perfume, being the product of intellectual ingenuity, is superior to the scent of a rose in a garden. *Cuisine* and *couture* and intellect systems devised for improving on nature. The French did not invent nakedness, but they invented the nude, which is a means of looking at nakedness from the aspect of one who believes in clothes. Even wine, which should be a joyous sensuous experience, has to submit to intellectualisation. What is wrong with French wines at present is that they have turned into ideas.

We see this intellectualisation at work most typically in the system known as structuralism, which the English can't understand at all. The human mind is so constituted, according to the French, that it has to take over the spectrum or continuum of nature and reorganise it as a series of reflections of the brain itself. Both the *cuisine* and the *couture* are seen by French intellectuals as structures, and Claude Lévi-Strauss announced that the structure known as "synchronic sweet-sour" did not exist in the European *cuisine*. It was pointed out to him that the English regularly eat pork with apple sauce and mutton with red currant jelly and apple pie with cheese (especially in Yorkshire), but his response was to deny that the English were properly Europeans. This was a view held also, for different reasons (something to do with geographical structure) by the late General de Gaulle. If a rule or system devised by a French mind is contradicted by reality, then the reality itself must be denied.

A few months ago I was travelling to the United States by Air France. I requested a smoking area, but when I boarded the aircraft I found that I had been allotted a seat in the *défense de fumer* section. The plane was full and I could not change my seat. After a time I discovered that every passenger seated in my row had requested the smoking area and had, like myself, been made to submit to the no smoking structure. "*La solution est tout à fait simple*," I told my neighbours. "We will remove the etiquettes which say *défense de fumer* and convert this area into a smoking zone." They submitted uneasily, and we all smoked. Then the chief steward came along and said it was forbidden to smoke. But, I said, everybody is smoking so it cannot, by the rules of democracy, be forbidden. Oh yes, it can, he said. The reality, according to him, was the etiquette saying *No smoking*. My

French fellow-smokers, who had discreetly put out their cigarettes, did not support me. They wanted to smoke, but the abstract reality was more important than their need. So I, an
empirical Englishman, was unable to prevail over Cartesian logic.

The idea is more important than the reality in more than no-
smoking areas. I have been served some disgusting meals in
French restaurants, but if the dish is called *poulet Marengo* it has
to be good, even if the chicken is putrid and the sauce watery. It
has to be good (a) because it is called *poulet Marengo*, thus belonging to an intellectual category or structure, (b) it was eaten
by Napoleon, (c) it is French. Even French chauvinism is capable
of intellectual justification. I complained publicly some years ago
(although the complaint was not seriously intended) that, whereas
Italians had converted Latin *aqua* to *acqua* and the Spanish to
agua, both recognisable mutations of the original, French had
turned it to *eau*, which is not a word at all but a mere round
vowel. I had, according to the French, traduced the honour of
France. I received a ten-page letter from the cultural attaché of
the French Embassy in London, bitterly complaining that I was
rupturing relations between France and Great Britain. I cannot
see the logic in this, but the French undoubtedly can. Apparently
the way in which French has transformed Latin follows a line of
phonological logic ordained by God (whose major prophet is Descartes): it is an intellectual reality and therefore holy.

Everything French is holy, however bad. The God of the French
has ordained that mint sauce must not be taken with roast lamb,
and he should properly have transubstantiated himself, that memorable evening in Jerusalem, into French wine and croissants. It
has been the task of the French nation to improve on the way
God made the world and the manner in which the Italians cook
pasta. My Italian wife proposed yesterday, in a French restaurant,
throwing some ill-cooked *soi-disant* tagliatelle into the face of the
patronne as an insult to the Italian nation. This was resented and
also not well understood. After all, the French know better than
the Italians, even when it is a matter of making and cooking tagliatelle. For tagliatelle are an intellectual concept, and the French
are the acknowledged kings of the intellect.

—1981

NEVER AGAIN AGAIN

❖

I have said so frequently, since settling into old age, that I would do no more travelling, and I have done, since settling into that same old age, or something like it, so much travelling, that no reader is likely to take seriously what I say now—namely, that, after my forthcoming trip to Barcelona and Madrid, I will do no more travelling.

The magazine publishers of the United States arranged that their annual conference should, in 1982, take place in a luxury hotel in Puerto Rico. Well in advance of the date in early October, I was asked to address the gathering on the problems of mass communication. I said I would go if I were paid an exorbitant fee (which, to the organisers, probably seemed very moderate: I do not know how much General Alexander Haig, my fellow-addressor, was paid). I also demanded that I be permitted to travel by Concorde as far as New York. In other words, I required every comfort. No problem: an air ticket and computer-processed itinerary duly arrived at my flat in Monaco. I was to travel from Nice to Paris first-class and pick up the Concorde at Charles de Gaulle Airport.

Arriving at the Airport of the Côte d'Azur and checking in at the Air France counter, it was demanded of me that I book my single suitcase through as far, at least, as Kennedy Airport. Ah, I said, I wish to make various purchases at Charles de Gaulle and place these in my suitcase; then, surely, I may check my bag on to the Concorde. Not as easy as you think, monsieur: you will see when you get there.

At Charles de Gaulle Airport I discovered that there had been some expansive changes since my last flight thither. I walked from the National area of the airport to the International. The International sector turned out to be a kind of bus station. There there were only pert girls who expressed wonderment that I had not checked my bag in at Nice. Never mind, you must take it with you on the bus to the International Terminal. I boarded the bus and was taken to the Terminal, where my bag was severely examined. I lugged the bag up stairs and along walkways to the Duty Free Shop. There I chose two tins of Schimmelpenninck panatellas and joined the queue at the cash desk. There I was told, on showing my ticket, that I was on a kind of international flight not catered for in this particular terminal and that my purchase was illegitimate. But surely, I argued, air travel is dichotomous: there is only the division of National and International. Not so, monsieur; there are two international terminals and you have come to the wrong one. I found out, with some difficulty, how to get to the right one. My bag was once more severely examined, I mounted a walkway, went out by the same door as I had entered, found another bus. This took me through charming landscapes and pretty towns to the correct terminal. *"C'est très compliqué,"* admitted the driver.

In this new terminal I met my Monégasque postman, who is always travelling. This time he was on his way to Chicago. He was desperate to micturate, but the terminal contained only one vaysay, tucked in at the side of a low eatery, and the queues were long. I lugged my bag to the Concorde concourse and took a seat in rich October afternoon sunlight. I was aware that a dose of influenza was beginning, part of the syndrome of travel. I coughed bitterly and my throat was scratchy. I needed, of course, a drink. There was a white-coated disdainful barman, glasses, bottles. A drink, please. He said that the ice cubes had not yet arrived. A drink without ice cubes, please. That was not *convenable*. I waited. Shortly after the ice cubes arrived, we were told to board the Concorde. We boarded the Concorde. We were then told to get off the Concorde: a little strike had erupted. The strike was probably a poor workers' protest against rich people who could afford to travel by Concorde. They should have known better. No private person can afford to travel by Concorde. Only corporations can do that. We all went back to the bar. The barman told us that the glasses had all been sent off to be washed: we were not permitted to swig from the bottles. Moreover, all the *glaçons* had been used up. When clean glasses and *glaçons* arrived, we were told to get back on to the Concorde: the little strike was over. I now knew that I had missed my connection to San Juan.

As is well known, only Great Britain is now expert at the *cuisine française*. The British Concorde (note the final *e*, the imposition of the chauvinist French) serves, as I know well enough, an exquisite meal enclosed in cocktails, liqueurs, cigars, and little pocketable gifts. The French Concorde served great lumps of things, unnamed in any menu. The cabin staff knew that none of us had bought his own ticket: why then should we be cosseted? We were poured off at Kennedy at six in the evening: I discovered that there was a flight to San Juan at midnight.

I object strongly to the insistence of Kennedy's customs officers on examining everything. After all, at Heathrow you are treated in a more civilised manner: if you have nothing to declare you have nothing to declare. I have often, at Kennedy, marched through, handing over my declaration of non-declarability to a seated ethnic officer who does not always examine the document for its cryptic mark denoting that the bag or bags has or have been examined. This time the card was scrutinised. You get back there to customs, man. But I have nothing to declare. Makes no difference, man, you get back there. A couple of customs officers witnessed this exchange and were interested. Guy there with something to hide. My bag was rummaged through to the limit and my stomach tablets confiscated. Then they had a go at my raincoat pockets.

I was shocked when, out of the left-hand pocket, an automatic pistol was drawn. It was a toy one, bought for my son at a Motta stop on the Italian autoroute from Rome to Bergamo. He had kindly, knowing I was going to criminal America, stowed it as at least a simulacrum of defence. The police were now summoned. Aircraft had been hijacked with toy guns before now, brother. My name was entered in a book, later, no doubt, to be transferred to the great variorum volume of undesirables that is the American immigration officer's bible. But I was allowed to keep the toy pistol, probably in the expectation that I would meet further unpleasantness from airport officials as I continued my journey.

I caught a bus to the terminal of American Airlines. I was not only ill: I was fatigued. I drank several whisky sours, which did no good. I needed to lie down somewhere. Eventually I lay down on the floor of an upper gallery of ranged seats, all occupied. I tried to sleep but was leapt over and over by gleeful Korean children. When these had, with their parents, set off for Korea, I slept. I was awakened by the boot of a cop. This ain't no bedroom, friend. Near midnight I poured myself on to my aircraft and was transported to San Juan.

I arrived at San Juan at 3.35 A.M. The hotel, I knew, was some thirty miles away along the coast. It was hot and humid and my flu raged tropically. The hotel, naturally, had failed to send transport. I sat down and wept, then slept with my never-once-checked-in bag for a pillow. At last a drugged Puerto Rican shook me awake. He had, he said, a second cousin outside with a taxi, did I wish to go someplace? The taxi was kind of old but it would get me someplace if that place was not too far. The second cousin wanted sixty dollars. He did not know the hotel in question but we together would endeavour to find it. After all, we had much of the night ahead of us, and a great deal of the morning too.

Puerto Rico is a pretty large island, full, in daytime, of gasoline fumes and obscene hills. By obscene I mean humped and knobbed or of the shape of roughly licked ice cream cones. Not at all like the gracious parabolic promontories of dear distant Europe. But this was black night and we saw nothing except the wrong roads, which took us round the entire coastline without disclosing the presence of my hotel. Was I certain the hotel existed? Here, *amigo*, is the printed prospectus of the establishment. We met five times the same group of vigilantes prepared to shoot down dangerous drivers, bearing a board saying QUEREMOS NUESTROS NIÑOS. At 5 A.M. the outworks of the hotel arose from out of a swamp. Like a nuclear installation it had an armed guard at the gate of its endless pathway. At 5.30 A.M. I was in bed. Thanked be Almighty God. At 6 A.M. I was awakened by the activities hostess or go-go girl: did I want to go jogging?

I performed the task for which I had come. General Haig told the assembly about the world political situation into which the magazine proprietors would be emitting their products. I spoke of the newest theories of mass communication. But first I wakened my jog-drugged audience by flashing a toy gun at them. Even this, I said, is a device of communication, frequently the ultimate one. You don't want to do that, friend, a man said to me afterwards.

You can give some poor guy that's been jogging a heart attack that way. That way planes have been hijacked.

What, you will ask, are you grumbling about? You got from Nice to Puerto Rico without being captured by Palestinians or suffering engine failure. You travelled by the most sumptuous class available. You were fed and drenched and the servants of the State did not unduly molest you. You got your toy gun there and you got it home again. I am not really grumbling. I am merely saying that I am getting old and am no longer fit enough to cope with the rigours of luxury travel. I will not live long enough to experience the consequences of the delayed rational conclusion that travel is an illness and must be treated as such: the hypodermic in one's own living-room, the total anaesthesia dissolved in the predestined hotel bedroom. I merely ask for the moment that our travel services be placed in the hands of the very old and preferably arthritic. We need people who realise what an agony it all is. The pert young and fit are too much in charge. After my trip to Spain and, just after, to Korea I shall stay where I am. Mother Earth represents the only reasonable aircraft. She does not go on strike and she is always on time. On her you hardly know you are travelling at all.

—1982

Something About Malaysia

❖

I lived in Malaysia, which used to be called Malaya—or, in the Malay language, *Tanah Melayu* (Malay Land)—from 1954 to 1959. When I went back in 1980, I found various changes. Malaysia was no longer a British protectorate and there was an enmity between the constitutent peoples—Malay, Chinese, Indian—which had not existed in the old colonial days. There were discotheques, a high level of electronisation, evidence of small pockets of Muslim fanaticism learned from the Ayatollahs, stupid politicians—but it was still basically the country that I loved and for which I had worked and, more importantly for me, the country where I had started to write and to publish fiction. My Malayan novels are still around in English and in Italian, but neither the Germans nor the French, and certainly not the Russians, have shown much interest in the works, which argues, conceivably, a lack of interest in Malaysia itself. It is a long way away. Though it is technically part of the Third World, it has neither interesting poverty nor heartening revolutions. It is all too stable. That it learned its stability from colonial rule is a truth that, in these postcolonial days, few progressives would be willing to consider. Of the beauty of the land the camera provides sufficient witness. But few people travel these days in search of beauty.

Let us consider briefly what Malaysia used to be and what it is now. When the British had a free capitalist organisation called the East India Company (free in the sense that the British Government was not particularly interested in it), its import and export trade in India led, almost automatically, to the smaller peninsula futher east. British officials of the EIC (as we still tend to call it) found a number of river settlements governed, apathetically or corruptly but certainly inefficiently, by Malay sultans or rajas. The Malays they discovered to be a lithe, handsome, amiable, lazy, brown-skinned race who had been converted by Arab traders to the faith of Islam. Those who could write their own language wrote it in Arabic script. The natives called on Allah, not only in their converse but during their five times of daily prayer. There were mosques but there was no purdah for the women. The Malay women, delicate and elegant but self-willed, have never taken kindly to male domination and they will not cover their faces with the yashmak. In the sultanate of Kelantan on the northeast coast the women walk ahead of the men, heads high in the pride of their beauty. In Negri Sembilan (the name means Ninth State) there is a matriarchal system which obliges a man to live in the village of the woman he marries and which insists on inheritance through the female line. The country, though thoroughly Muslim, in no way resembles rigorous Iran. You can buy pork if you are not a Muslim, and you can drink whisky whether you are Muslim are not. On my last visit I got very heavily drunk with the Sultan of Perak and his entourage.

The British traders tried to keep out of Malay politics and set up their posts in the two fine harbours which looked west, Penang and Malacca. They did not have much to do with the hinterland. But with the silting up of Malacca there was need to look for another natural harbour, and this was found by Stamford Raffles—at first a mere clerk in the EIC—on an island called Singapore, right at the southernmost tip of the Malay peninsula. As the British became concerned with establishing a presence— chiefly at the request of sultans who could not discipline their rebellious and greedy river chieftains—they took to establishing British Advisors or Residents in the chief towns of the sultanates. They did not make any territorial claims on such states as Perak, Selangor, Pahang, and Johore, but they did regard Penang, Malacca, and Singapore as very much British property and they called them Crown Colonies.

If the primary concern of the British was with trade, the secondary concern was with developing the resources of the peninsula, chiefly the tin on which the wealth of the state of Peraks depends (*Perak* in Malay means silver; there is some silver there, and to the naked eye, tin rather resembles it). Later, the rubber became just as important. Rubber is almost synonymous with Malaya or Malaysia, but it is a British import. Rubber trees from

South America were planted in Kew Gardens, London, and it
was decided to take a few cuttings from London to Malaya to
see if the plant took kindly to the soil and the climate. It did
and does. You can see the first rubber tree in Kuala Kangsar in
Perak, the royal town where I worked. Malaya became a sym-
metrical series of forests of rubber trees. Tin mines were exca-
vated and dredgers went to work. But where was the labour to
come from?

Not, certainly, from the Malays. These sons of the soil, who
regard the land as their own, though they are immigrants like
everyone else (true, remoter immigrants than the others), do not
care for hard work. They are wise. Malaya is delightfully warm
and blessed not only by a benign sun but by rain, which falls
heavily in the monsoons and gently, at about tea time, in daily
shower-baths. The paddies yield three crops of rice every year.
The rivers are full of fish. Bananas grow in abundance. There are
pepper bushes and mangoes and papaya and pomelo trees. When
nature feeds one so lavishly, why work? The Malays are not
greatly interested in money. Place them in a cash economy and
they quickly fall into debt. Pay them a wage and, within an hour,
they have spent it all. The Chinese and the Indians are different.

So, following a benign British rule and a flourishing production
of rubber and tin, the Indians and Chinese have traditionally
flowed into Malaya to make money not only as workers in mines
and on the rubber estates, but in trade and services and administration. The Tamils from Southern India came to the rubber
estates but also entered the professions: medicine, veterinary sur-
gery, education. The Bengalis took to money-lending, but to
other, more reputable, trades as well. The Chinese, the race which
invented work, came to make money in everything. You will see
turbaned Sikhs running the railways and the post offices, but also
as police inspectors. The Cantonese run restaurants. There are
other races too, including the Eurasians—proud and beautiful
products of East-West miscegenation—and the Japanese, the Jav-
anese, the Bugis, the Sumatrans. In the jungles lurk the real ab-
origines—the *orang darat* or *orang hutan*, which means men of
the woods and must not be applied to the monkey we call orang
outang but should really call *mawas* or *maias*. Pygmies with blow-

pipes are at one end of the social scale, while at the other are the Chinese millionaires. The British never made much money out of Malaya. If they were civil servants or rubber estate managers they drew a salary and hoped for a pension, but they left the amassing of real wealth to the Chinese—especially to the Chinese who run Singapore.

The period of British rule was, it is generally agreed, a tolerable one. The white *tuans*, more red than white, sweated, changed their clothes three times daily, and did their work in their offices or, if they were administrators, going around the towns and villages in their little Ford cars. They came home to their bungalows at midday for their tiffin and a couple of bottles of Tiger beer. In the evening they would go to the club. The wives did not flourish as the husbands did. They grew dissatisfied or developed tropical anorexia or smarted under the bite of mosquitoes and sandflies. There was a lot of adultery, neurosis, jealousy. The husbands grew fat while the wives shrank to atrabilious ghosts. You can read of the lives of the expatriate British in William Somerset Maugham's Malayan stories, which are accurate if limited. In Maugham only the rather dull white people are real, while the brown and yellow Orientals are mere padding bare feet on the verandah. When I wrote my own Malayan stories I tried to restore the balance. I was not interested in the white men and women, who were philistine and not over-intelligent. I found the Malays and Chinese and Indians much more rewarding, and I put them at the centre of my books.

I spoke something of the languages, which Maugham never did. My job was that of instructor in government schools and it was necessary to take from my pupils as well as give something to them. I had to know what was going on in their minds, and this meant knowing their languages. I always had difficulty with Chinese, but Malay—which is now called *bahasa negara*, tongue of the country—became a second language to me. It is a language very different from German—no genders, no verb or noun or adjective endings—but its very lack of grammar makes it subtle. So much depends on the order of words. If you say *saya makan*, that means "I eat." If you say *makan saya*, that means "eat me," an improbable request, so it has to mean "my food." Malay has a fine and subtle poetry, usually expressed in the forms of four-line poems called *pantuns*. Here is one of them:

> *Kalau tuan mudek ka-ulu,*
> *Charikan saya bunga kemoja.*
> *Kalau tuan mati dahulu,*
> *Nantikan saya di-pintu shurga.*

This means roughly: If you, my lover, go up-river, find some fran-gipani for me. If you, my lover, die before I do, wait for me at the door of heaven. The subtlety lies in the sound and the imagery, as in all good poetry. I used to spend pleasant evenings with Ma-lays, men and women, improvising pantuns. It was more exhila-rating than playing bridge at the club.

The peaceful prosperity of the Malaya of the 1920s and 1930s resembled a ripe fruit ready to fall. The British administration was complacent and did not take seriously the threat of the Japanese demand for *Lebensraum*. In 1942 the guns of Singapore pointed the wrong way. The Japanese invaded the peninsula by a door no one had anticipated—the unimportant port of Kota Bharu in the northeast. With their maps and bicycles they stealthily made their way through the jungle, got down to Johore, killing and occu-pying as they went, then crossed the causeway into Singapore. It was considered that Eastern peoples like Malays and Chinese and Indians would take more kindly to the rule of an Eastern nation like Japan than to the exotic British. Unfortunately the Japanese were bigoted and cruel. The house I lived in in Kuala Kangsar had been the headquarters of the Japanese secret police, and there was not only indelible blood on the floors but, it was popularly thought, the wailing ghosts of the tortured and slain in the rain-trees of the garden. There was a Chinese underground which tried to fight against Japanese domination. When the Japanese surren-dered in 1945 they were still there. This time they geared them-selves to fighting against resumed British domination.

When I went to Malaya in 1954 there was a new war, although it was called, euphemistically, the *dzarurat* or emergency. There were Chinese in the jungle fighting on behalf of the new victorious ideology of the East: the Marxism decreed by Pekin. Their weap-ons were mostly left over from the previous war, and they survived through terrorising jungle villages. They called on the peoples of Malaya to rise against their British oppressors and proclaim the Marxist state, but not many of the Malay rice-planters or Indian rubber-tappers or Chinese shopkeepers were interested. A Malay regiment was formed, and young British soldiers were sent out to assist the natives in their struggle against these dissidents who lurked in the jungle. The British decreed that Malaya should be a self-governing independent state by 1957, which gave the lie to Communist propaganda about the British determination to cling to their Eastern possession.

Malayan independence has, in fact, been an accomplished fact for twenty-five years, but it is not certain whether the war against the Communists is really over. There are certainly armed terrorists in the north of Perak, on and north of the Thailand border, and the Malaysian army, which is manned mostly by young Malays, is on the alert for them. But there is another kind of war going on, though it is mostly bloodless, and this is between the Malays and the other peoples. The Malays, or *bumiputera*—sons of the soil—as they are now called, have most of the political power but they resent their lack of economic power. Whether they like it or not, it is the Chinese who are in charge of the country's economy, and the Malays or *bumiputera* are angry about it. They have become arrogant and have imposed their language on everybody, although, previously, the whole population got on very well with English as a *lingua franca*. There are no government English schools now, and the wise know that this is a mistake: English is still the key to Western trade, and Western culture is not to be despised. There have been restrictions on economic enterprise which favour the Malays. To take a very small example, a Malay may run a taxi but a Chinese may not. Yet Malays do not want to run taxis or anything else: they merely want to be lazy. So a Chinese runs a taxi while a Malay merely owns it. This is known as an Ali Baba arrangement, Ali being a popular Muslim, hence Malay, name, and Baba the term given to Chinese who live in the towns.

The towns have become prosperous, with ambitious business enterprises, modern skyscrapers, and luxury hotels, especially in the capital of Kuala Lumpur. This name means *muddy estuary*, but Jean Cocteau, thinking of opium and brothels, called the city *Kouāla l'impure*. You can stay, as I recently did, in an American-style hotel which would not disgrace Hamburg, but one feels that the substructure is not yet strong enough to support such ventures. When I was in the elevator all the electricity of the city was suddenly cut, and I was stuck in sweltering darkness for five hours. Needless to say, you will not find Malays doing the essential work necessary to maintain modern utilities such as electricity, airports, railways, and hotels. As ever, it is the Chinese and the Indians and the Eurasians who labour, while the Malays preen themselves on their national dignity and parade in the glorious uniforms of state ceremony.

But it is true to say that the true Malaya of the Malays is not to be found in the towns and cities. The Malays are a gentle and pacific people who are happiest in their villages, or *kampongs*, fearing the corruption of the towns and content with their fish, rice, bananas, peppers, games of chess, traditional poems, songs and dances, and visits to the mosque on Fridays. At least, this is true of the older Malays, who are polite, soft-spoken, hospitable, and fairly moral. There is a new breed in Malaysia, as there is everywhere, which has learned the joys of consumption and is drifting into the towns. The streets are noisy with Vespas and Lambrettas—the Malay emblems of youthful prosperity—but quiet with the older wealth of the Chinese Mercedes, Bentleys and Rolls-Royces. The Malay boys are aggressive, and will beat up a Chinese or an Indian for the fun of it. They smoke marijuana and go to discotheques. Their parents in the *kampongs* worry about them. It is a familiar worldwide pattern.

There are times, however, when one feels that things have hardly changed at all. This is particularly so when one goes to the club, traditionally the white man's domain. There are very few white men left, except for Americans on business, and the old white Malayans as still exist are moribund planters in retirement, unable to understand the new Europe they have occasionally visited and content to die under a familiar sun. The clubs are now in the hands of prosperous Chinese and Indians, and they run them as the British used to, on a basis of exclusivity. They come to the club at the day's end for a game of bridge, an English dinner, a cold beer in the bar, a couple of whiskies before getting into the Mercedes and driving home to the decent white-wooded house in the leafy suburbs. For the most part they keep the Malays out. Where there was a caste system based on race, there is now one based on income. Afternoon tea is served, cricket is played on Sundays, and the old British pattern persists. The language of the club is, of course, always English.

I must confess that the club is not my milieu. I am strongly drawn to the life of the *kampong*, and there was a time—in 1957, independence year—when I resisted repatriation and wanted to be accepted as a genuine Malayan. I proposed entering Islam, which would have entitled me to four wives but barred me from eating ham for breakfast. My name was chosen for me—Yahya bin Abdullah—and I started to study the Koran. It was an agreeable prospect. The weather is nearly always fine, like an English May, and the sweat flows delightfully. For some reason the tropics bestow on white men a great appetite for sensuality—food, drink, and sex—whereas white women dwindle and die. I would marry four Malay wives and beget a host of particoloured children who would respect me and call me *bapa*. I would make the pilgrimage to Mecca and come back wearing a turban with the title *Haji*. Haji Yahya bin Abdullah. I would be a known and beloved figure at the mosque meetings on Friday, and I would die, full of years, under that benign sun, among those green leaves. But one night in sleep I was admonished by the voice of Europe: this is not your world, go back to the cold lands where you belong. I still, in old age, wonder whether I made the right decision.

I have said nothing of Singapore, which many Europeans think, if they think of it at all, is a part of Malaysia and perhaps the only part worth visiting. It is important to remember that Singapore is very much an independent state, and a somewhat fascist one, with a one-party government, police who enforce conformity of behaviour and even of hair style (no long-locked hippies are wanted), and a tradition of Chinese money-making which is alien to the code of the peninsula to the north. Here the Malays are in a minority, and, when you see one wearing a *sarong* and the little black cap called a *songkok*, you respond to him as you respond to an abo in Sydney. The theme of the city is wealth and conspicuous consumption and, for sybarites, it is the most insidious city in the world. All the cuisines are available, and all the consumer goods. The Chinese women are chic and desirable. But there is no atmosphere of free thought or of a healthy culture. It is a stultifying life that is offered, and it can be blamed on a political system that, rejecting British colonialism and Chinese Marxism alike, is merely monolithic, repressive for the sake of repression, and concerned only with the abstractions of money-making and social stability.

Penang, that green island to the northwest of Malaysia, is a very different place. It is sometimes called the Pearl of the Orient and it is delightful with its raintrees, banyans, and cool sea winds. It breathes some of the spirit of the old easygoing times when the British ruled it as one of the Straits Settlements (the others being Singapore and Malacca), and it can break the heart with its love-liness and the friendliness of its people. Malacca breathes an older spirit still. It was here that St. Francis Xavier came to spread the blessings of that Counter-Reformation that his friend Ignatius Loyola had inaugurated. Here you will find Catholic Malays as well as Catholic Chinese in retirement, also old chapels and churches, a sun-fed sleepiness, traces of the Portuguese language, even remnants of Dutch architecture, for both the Portuguese and the Dutch were here before the British, trading with arrogance or, with equal arrogance, imposing a triune and alien God on a Muslim people.

But the Malaya I knew is still more or less preserved in two towns: Kuala Kangsar in Perak and Kota Bharu in Kelantan. In Kuala Kangsar the primary residence of the Sultan of Perak, is the *Istana* or palace and mosque, which is one of the wonders of the East. In Kota Bharu, or just outside it, is the *Pantai Chinta Berahi*, sometimes translated as the *"Beach of Passionate Love,"* though the Malay name properly means *Shore of Unlawful Passion*. Kelantan can boast the loveliest women in the world, as well as a bizarre culture which mixes Hindu gods with the one God, which is Allah. It is, I suppose, finally this capacity to mix race and culture which makes Malaysia unique. It is a tribute to the unifying power of a benign colonialism, which lets people go their own way, rejoicing, in the juxtaposition of mosques, temples, and wooden churches. Rejoicing, too, in the juxtaposition of languages, cuisines, kinds of folklore, but always regarding the political spirit which is the true breeder of dissent as an intrusive nuisance. Now Malaysia is all too political, and it is the worse for it. There was a lot to be said for that old Empire in which political ideologies were left to the intellectuals. But, of course, there were no intellectuals in that Empire, and the Empire was the worse for that. I, as a sort of intellectual, was alienated from the men of my own colour and culture, and I do not think I was the worse off for being forced into the company of the natives.

The animals too, for Malaysia is as rich in fauna as it is in flora and the efflorescenes of that strangest faun of them all, man. There was a time when I had my own private zoo: an *anjing ayer* or otter, a hamadryad (a highly intelligent snake, very long, very hungry), a *musang* or civet cat, a *pelandok* or mouse deer, a pair of *beroks* or rhesus monkeys, a snarling corral of jungle cats and, as a brief visitor, a *mawas* or *maias*. I would sit in shirt and shorts on my verandah at the end of the day, watching the swift descent of the *mata hari* or sun and listening to the wail of the distant *bilal* calling the faithful to the last *waktu*, or prayer, of the day. My houseboy Yusof would bring me another iced *stengah*, or whisky and water, or else a gin *pahit*, or pink gin. In the kitchen a *gulai* or curry of *ayam* or chicken would be in preparation, with *gula Melaka* or ground rice and molasses in the manner of Malacca, to follow. Exotic Wagner or Mozart would vie with the noise of my zoo, or the mewling of the fifteen domestic cats fighting for possession of the body of a snake which their mother had killed. It was a good life and it will never come again. Or perhaps it will. None of us knows how he will end up, and there are daily flights from London to Kuala Lumpur. *Barangkali saya balek ka-Tanah Melayu. Balek* means return and *barangkali* means perhaps. I need not translate the rest.

—1982

THE BRIGG

❖

At the end of the last war the British government, faced with a great shortage of primary school teachers, initiated a scheme short-lived but useful—that of giving to ex-servicemen and women a thirteen-month course in educational theory and practice, as well as potted studies in academic subjects. It was as a lecturer in Speech and Drama that, in 1948, I went to Bamber Bridge Emergency Training College in the Ribble Valley of South Lancashire, England. Though a Lancashireman, born in Manchester, I knew little of the rural portions of a largely rural county. The little town, or large village, of Bamber Bridge was on the railroad that linked the town of Preston with the Irish Sea, a place that had known cotton mills during the time of the great cotton boom but was now becoming a dormitory town—five pubs, one butcher, a cooperative store, a British Legion club—that slept workers and their wives who gained their bread from the industries of Preston and Chorley and Leyland.

Bamber Bridge, or the Brigg as it was locally called, might not have been chosen as a centre for teacher training had it not already been the site of a U.S. Army training camp during the war. The Ministry of Education took over this camp but did not modify either the prefabricated buildings or the signboards. Thus it was soon possible to stand up in a pub and recite, in the manner of Stanley Holloway (Mr. Doolittle in *My Fair Lady*, in case you have forgotten), a monologue beginning:

> *There's a place in't' Brigg called the College.*
> *It's the camp where the Yanks used to be:*
> *You can tell from the way they've spelt CENTRE*
> *With the R coming after the E.*

Note that Brigg, which means bridge, of course, points to an old Scandinavian verbal habit of opposing a hard sound to replace an Anglo-Saxon soft one (like kirk for church or, if we go back far enough, skipper for shipper and skirt for shirt). If you belonged to Bamber Bridge you were a Brigg lad or lass. One native of the town worked on the Ribble buses as a conductor and was in the habit of saying to riders: "Art a Brigg lad? Th'art? Raht, tha needn't pay." This was pushing local patriotism to the limit.

The linguistic aspects of the town and its district were to me, a teacher of English, of immense interest. There were old Norman remains in the names of local towns like Newton-le-Willows and Whittle-le-Woods, as well as Danish sounds in the local speech, but it was amazing how far a lot of the dialect had resisted the changes imposed elsewhere by the invaders. The common word *she* came into Old English fairly late, *heo* being the older form. Brigg lads and lasses used *oo* for she, and husbands would make their excuses for leaving the pub by saying "Oo's getten chip-pan on," meaning that dinner, which usually had French fries in it, had been prepared by oo or 'er or the missis or wife. "Art wit-shet?" meant "Art thou wet-shod?" or "Are your feet wet?" If your wife had a pain in her shoulder you said: "Oo's getten showder-wartsh." I used to travel wide at weekends with my Professor Higgins notebook, taking down variations in speech sounds. Here was a language with a number of dialectal variations which had had a literature at about the time of *Sir Gawain and the Green Knight* but, under the centralising influence of British culture, had lost it. The language itself could only be written down in the International Phonetic script; it was a tongue that had lost its alphabet.

The Brigg primarily interested me because it was an example of a community totally satisfied with itself and of a culture pretty well self-sufficient. It was easy enough to get to the cinema or theatre in Preston or Chorley by bus or train, but it was more satisfactory to make one's own entertainment in the pub or the British Legion hall (the British Legion being a society of ex-servicemen who kept alive the community spirit and accumulated sparse funds to help the needy). The whole of the Northwest of England is a source of national popular entertainment, though a lot of it stays home. The Beatles left Liverpool and Gracie Fields left Rochdale, but they took with them a Northwestern quality only a town like Bamber Bridge could properly appreciate. The richness of the talent in the region needs explaining.

I ascribe it to the fact that the Northwest resisted the Reformation and, maintaining its Catholicism, was cut off from the preferment that only high education can give. Proscribed by law until 1829 from going to a university, a Northwestern Catholic could not become a lawyer or a doctor; if he had talent and imagination, his only professional outlet was the stage, either classical or popular, usually popular. The seaside resort catering to the masses is a Northwestern invention—one of the fruits of the Industrial Revolution—and marine paradises like Blackpool and Clevelys and Southport have always had a large need for entertainers. You see this in the hinterland—Bamber Bridge, for instance—and there are few Lancastrians who cannot stand and give, however amateurishly, a song or dance or monologue. Coming from this same tradition—father a music hall pianist, mother a singer and dancer (the Beautiful Belle Burgess)—I fell back easily into it, playing the piano in pubs and clubs. Instructors, even in training colleges, were ill-paid in those days, and I was happy to be paid thirty-five shillings every weekend to play in the evenings in the Red Lion. On the lid of the piano pints of beer, far more than I could drink, were placed by appreciative customers. Singers got up to sing—"Best of order, please. The singer's on his feet"—and the crowd joined in the choruses. Things may be different now. After the war and postwar suspension of the BBC's television services Brigg lads and lasses, without doubt, began to stay home and watch soap operas. One of the ironies of the Northwest cultural situation now, and for twenty years past, is the popularity of the twice-weekly series *Coronation Street*, which shows a Northwest far less compelling than the reality.

Nearby Preston is a centre of the Catholic faith—the name used to be Priests' Town—but the outlying towns and villages are not wholly Catholic. Yet in various pubs you could find a statue of the Virgin Mary in the public bar and hear even Protestants swear "by 't' mass." The old Catholic ambience did not promote a more rigorous morality than elsewhere, and there was a fair amount of quiet fornication and adultery. But the Brigg used to look down on the looser morality of the town of Colne, at the foot of the

Pennine hills which separate Lancashire from Yorkshire, and say that there it was "all 'oorin' an't' bloody brush." The tradition there was for a married woman alone in the house to leave a sweeping brush outside the front door to show that she was free to give her favours. The sign in the Brigg that a woman was not so free or so willing was her appearing in the streets in curlers. Indeed, most women assumed that they were invisible during the day: it was no shame for a housewife to do her shopping with steel curling clips and no concealing scarf.

But the tradition of a woman not displaying daytime allure went back to the old mill days, when hardly a woman, married or single, young or old, did not work in the cotton mills. Women's fingers are delicate instruments and were very skillful at managing the looms. The mythical millgirl was incarnated in the impressions of Gracie Fields, who would appear on the stage with clogs and shawl and ready wit: a true lassie from Lancasheer. The tradition of working and, during the depression, supporting a household made these girls and women very pert and assertive and, in affairs of the heart, far more passionate—indeed, Sicilianly operatic— than the wives and daughters of the Southeast of England.

These Northwestern housewives never had the time to cook a weekday meal, though Sunday dinner was as ceremonious as Christmas (roast beef and Yorkshire pudding, apple tart and custard). Bamber Bridge, like other towns of the region, had its fish and chip shops and pie and tripe and cowheel emporia, and these fed the populace on working days. Add to these rough delicacies Lancashire specialities like black puddings, Eccles cakes, Bakewell tarts, jam puffs, and baked custards in crusty pastry and you had a cuisine not to be despised. The king of Northern dishes—Lancashire hotpot—was essentially a feast for the household, best end of lamb's neck, potatoes, and onions cooked slowly in stock in the oven, and it came into its own at the striking of the midnight which brought in the New Year. The day before New Year's Day—the Feast of the Circumcision—was traditionally a day on which meat could not be eaten, but the hotpot could be aproached on the first chime of the New Year bell. You missed committing the sin of non-abstinence by a mere second, and hence the meal was known as the Devil's Supper. The hotpot was always served with pickled red cabbage and washed down with beer and strong tea. No tea is stronger than that brewed in the Northwest. Only last week I was staying in the Parker Meridian Hotel in New York, and my breakfast tea consisted of a jug of tepid water with a couple of teabags on the side. This, to a Lancashireman, is rank heresy.

Chips, or French-fried potatoes, probably derive from Belgium, but Lancashire likes to believe that they are a Lancashire invention. Certainly the combination of fish and chips is pure Lancashire, but a dish of chips and nothing else but bread and butter is a product of the Lancashire depression, when nobody could afford either fish or meat. A chip butty—a hot chip sandwich—is a genuine coarse feast. The vinegar one sprinkles on the chips has to be made from good brewer's malt—none of your Frenchified sour grapes. Properly the vinegar of the North is alegar or ale-vinegar.

The almost incestuously ingrown social habits of Bamber Bridge and towns like it were best demonstrated when the time for the summer holiday came round. The wakes week is an institution going back to the beginning of the Industrial Revolution and would hardly be tolerable in an industrial situation which demands the perpetual turning of the machines. For when the annual week began, an entire town would die: the boilers would cease to boil and the furnaces would grow cold and be raked; the shops would close and the churches hold no services. Even household pets would have a change of scene. For the essence of a holiday—in Blackpool, Clevelys, Fleetwood, Southport, Scarborough or Bridlington—was not the seeing of new faces in new scenes but the temporary transplantation of an entire community to a bizarrely different environment. There would be seaside flirtations with people from other places, the taste of different brands of beer, but, in a sense, you had not left home at all. To see Jack or Ethel from next door in the Brigg temporarily transformed—lobster-hued, photographed under the Blackpool Tower (modelled on the Eiffel one but far more glamorous)—was the best kind of change, one in which continuity was asserted. Nowadays, without doubt, the Continental holiday has won out—fish and chips and British beer on the Costa de Sol—but the older tradition is still enshrined in the monologues of Graham Moffett, whose best exponent was Stanley Holloway:

There's a famous seaside place called Blackpool,
That's noted for fresh air and fun,
And Mr. and Mrs. Ramsbottom
Went there with young Albert, their son . . .

They didn't think much to the ocean,
The waves they was fiddlin' and small,
No wrecks and nobody drownded—
In fact, nothin' to laff at at all.

That second verse ascribes a peculiar sense of humour to the children of the Northwest. In fact, nobody laughs at the misfortunes of others—at least, not more than elsewhere—but there is an earthy grimness in Northwestern jokes which is highly distasteful to the refined Southeast. The best Lancashire jokes are about death. In these closely knit households where all the generations live together, the grandfather will say "I'll just take a walk as far as graveyard" (note the absence of the definite article, which never really caught on up there) and get the reply "Hardly worth thi while comin' back, is it?" Or there is the story of the lady who poured her cremated husband's ashes into an egg-timer instead of sand, saying: "Boogger did no work while 'e was alive, 'e might as well do some now he's deed." Or there was the man who, visiting a friend in the evening, missed the last bus home and was offered half of the bed where the friend's kid brother lay. In the morning the guest said he slept well enough but "Your kid's arse isn't half cold." The host said: "Aye, he's been dead three days." This is as Northwestern as chip butties.

In Bamber Bridge nearly everybody seemed to have the surname Bamber. "What's the name of your dog, missis?"—"Laddy Bamber." There was not much of an influx of strangers, except German prisoners of war who seemed to the Brigg lads and lasses to speak a kind of exceptionally broad Lancashire. The strangers who got on best there during the war were the American blacks "in't' camp," tough-minded soldiers who revolted against their white comrades and, with ample arms and ammunition, waged the Battle of Bamber Bridge, well remembered in the local annals but not, so far as I know, recorded in the bigger chronicles of World War II. When the local pubs were asked to initiate a colour bar, the innkeepers responded with notices saying "Black Yanks Only." A tough people who went their own way, kept a dour sense of humour in all circumstances, and always contrived to enjoy life, the lads and lasses of the Brigg have probably by now succumbed to the mondial plastic culture which is killing our old folkways and rendering travel to foreign parts a waste of time. I travel back to Bamber Bridge only in my head. Sometimes I wonder if I invented the place. But the name is still there on the map, a name denoting a locality which probably has more in common with Springfield Mass. or Trenton N.J. than what one used to think of as Merrie England. The Brigg folk have probably been supermarketed and computerised and televised out of merriment.

—1983

WINTERREISE

❖

In Munich I celebrated, if that is the right term, my sixty-seventh birthday. Klaus, my friend from Düsseldorf, gave me as a present a cassette of Fishcher-Dieskau singing Schubert's *Winterreise*. It was appropriate. I was making a winter journey across Germany and seeing, from the comfort of Germany's incredibly efficient trains, snow snow, everywhere snow. Cologne, Hamburg, Frankfurt, Stuttgart, Munich. And lastly, which is only historically and was very briefly Ostmark territory, Vienna. I had just published a book in Germany, a very long novel entitled *Der Fürst der Phantome*. The work had taken ten years to think out and two years to write. It seemed to my publisher that I ought to persuade the German public, through the medium of press, radio, and television, to attempt to read it. It is not pleasant for a writer to have the impression of having thrown his work into a great silence. That had previously been my experience with German translations of my books, except for the damnable *Uhrwerk Orange*, which had been made into a film and thus seemed to secure my temporary immortality at second-hand. It had also established me in Germany as a kind of godfather of violence. It was time to show the Germans that I was a very unviolent old-fashioned liberal, grey-haired, jowlish, totally harmless and indubitably old. It would also show the German world how badly I spoke their beautiful language.

I had been in Germany before, but in the wrong Germany. In 1938 I was in the Third Reich, which seemed to me a very well-run polity with too many uniforms. I had slept in youth hostels and been oppressed by ebullient members of the Hitler Youth. These objected to my playing jazz on the hostel piano: they said it was negroid and decadent. They themselves sang German folk-songs about sunrise over the glorious German mountains; it was their sunrise, their day. They showed how tough they were by sleeping out, even when it rained. I did not like them, but not because they were German. Even when I was young I never cared much for the young. They have too much misdirected energy. In 1939, in late August, I was on my way to teach English in a school in the Black Forest. Fortunately I got drunk in Antwerp, spent two days recovering from my hangover and another few days cultivating a new one. By the time I was ready to cross the frontier into the arms of the Reich, war had broken out and I took ship for England. From then on I was in very inimical contact with Germany.

My postwar ventures into Germany have, again, taken me to the wrong country. I was commissioned to write an article on East Berlin, which I found charming but very run-down. I was later commissioned by *Time* magazine to cover the World Football Cup. A football stadium has little to do with national culture, and such national culture as West Berlin represented was not to my taste. It was the month of May, and those gorgeous white asparagus were on all the menus. A waiter in the Kempinski Hotel served me with a portion of them and said: "Here you see, sir, how good can come out of evil. These asparagus have been nourished by the best Jewish bonemeal from the eastern territories." I sent my plate away and asked for cabbage.

One of the problems that any Englishman has to face when visiting Germany is linguistic. We know that German and English are cognate tongues, but, while English is bent on turning itself into Chinese—a grammarless language which depends on tonal variations and the position of words—German is still, so it seems to us, locked in an armour of accidence and syntax which forbids the piercing of the learner's lance. A thousand years ago, English was rather like German in possessing a formidable battery of grammar. This is from your *Hildebrandslied*:

> *Ik gihorta that seggen,*
> *That sih urhetten aenon muotin,*
> *Hiltibrant enti Hathubrant untar heriun tuem,*
> *sunu fatar ungo . . .*

And this is from our national epic *Beowulf*:

Tha waes on healle heardecg togen,
sweord ofer setlum, sidrand manig
hafan handa faest . . .

There seems little to choose between them. Dag, our word for your *Tag*, which is now *day*, used to be masculine, like yours, and liked to inflect itself into *dages* and *daga* and *dagum*, but in 1066 a terrible thing happened to the English people. They were faced from the East with Danish invaders and from the South with the Normans. The English tried to make a double contact through their own language and they instinctively simplified it. Genders were the first things to go, and they have never returned. Endings disappeared. There was no time to think out sentence structures ahead, ensuring that past participles were shunted, as they still are in German, to the end of the statement. English turned into a contact dialect—a pidgin—and then established itself as a creole. It is genderless and caseless. It must look to the average speaker of High German like a country dialect, not worthy to be a national language. When an Englishman tries to speak German he can never see the point of *der, die,* and *das.* Genders will not stick in his mind. Unfortunately or fortunately, he finds practically all Germans only too ready to speak English to him.

And, for the most part, very good English too. On my winter journey I heard far better English than I myself speak—idiomatic, expressive, learned, perfectly accented. Having married into Italy and settled myself in Southern France, I find my own English somewhat corrupted by Mediterranean elements. Educated Germans may well prove the ultimate guardians of the language of their former enemy. Hearing and seeing the dialects of Hamburg, Cologne, and Vienna, I felt that our educators were missing a great opportunity. An Englishman could best find his way into official or educated German through being allowed to learn some form of *Plattdeutsch.* But we still have to struggle with *der, die,* and *das* and, when speaking, make fools of ourselves. All the more so when our interlocutors speak such admirable English.

It is evidently taught *efficiently,* and it is efficiency that all foreigners expect to find in Germany. I was both delighted and annoyed when, after my winter journey, I made a brief spring trip by air to Hamburg and discovered that Lufthansa had lost my luggage. This had not happened to me before, not even in those unshaven siesta-taking countries where you expect luggage to be lost. To my satisfaction and disappointment my bags were eventually found and delivered, with maximal efficiency, to my hotel where, however, the telephone did not function. In a Munich hotel the management lost a parcel of *Toblerone* chocolate which was (inevitably) the gift of a Swiss friend. I was annoyed, but more pleased than annoyed: the myth of total efficiency had been exploded, and the Germans could be just as slipshod as the English are. It is not human to be too efficient. The Germans, thank heaven, are human enough.

They were human back in 1938, despite the Nazi régime; they were as pleasant then as they are now. This probably means that their livers function efficiently. The French suffer a great deal from their livers—they are a liverish race—and this morbidity is manifested in official beahviour, especially in the morning. They do not eat breakfast, and this makes them surly until they have had lunch. After lunch they are somnolent. The French drink wine adulterated with tannin, which gives them headaches. Their food is at its most French when it is richly sauced. The German cuisine seems to me to be better because it is simpler. There are great chunks of meat presented in honest nudity and there are root vegetables, which are good for the bowels. German beer is of an excellence which ought to be expressed in lyric poetry.

I did not think it possible to put down as much Munich beer as I did on my winter journey, and totally without hangover. I visited the monastery at Andechs where aproned monks draw the appropriately heavenly brew from their own Klosterbräuerei and serve it in mugs almost too heavy to raise to one's lips. The excellence of that beer is, I am told, all to do with the water. We may drink German beer in France and elsewhere and not remark any particular beauty in it. Like the Guinness of Ireland, it cannot properly be exported. It is worth visiting Germany if only to get sweetly drunk.

But, sitting in the Andechs beer cellar, surrounded by swilling men in Tyrolean hats and *lederhosen*, I saw which of the seven deadly sins might be attributed to the Germans (if it be allowed that the citizens of Munich are as *echt* German as any). They are not slothful and they are not quick to anger; they are not lustful and far from covetous, and they have, in the past, only had envy imposed upon them by their rulers. But they are gluttonous. They chew long sausages, grind at legs of pork, shovel in cabbage. They have a vast liquid intake. At Andechs I saw an elderly toper vomit out gallons in the Abort and, wiped clean, heard him announce his intention of starting again. This perhaps is a Roman virtue rather than a Teutonic vice, but it makes my puritanical British soul shrink. And the elation that beer produces—we may not call it drunkenness—can, I think, lead to that other deadly sin of pride. I remember, back in 1938, buying a packet of cigarettes called *Rassenstolz*. They don't exist any longer, but the capacity for national pride certainly does. When the British get drunk they sneer at their country and spit on their government. In the blue eyes of a well-soaked Tyrolean, mug in beefy hand, you see the stirring of the desire to sing about the glories of the fatherland. I can well understand why a particular national philosophy took hold in Munich beer cellars. The beer bids the freed cerebrum rise to heaven. Heaven is another term for a German Utopia.

I said above that the Germans are far from slothful, and here they differ from their English cousins. The English have become the laziest race on earth. This cannot be a matter of racial endowment, since the nineteenth century saw monstrous prodigies of energy expended in the building of the British Empire. It is a matter, rather, of the victory of syndicalism, hard fought for, which promotes the worker's rights to the end of his doing as little as possible for as much money as possible. These rights were jealously guarded even during the Second World War, when coal miners and munitions workers would go readily on strike while their uniformed brethren fought the Nazis for very little money. I get the impression from contemporary Germany that the power of syndicalism has still to be realised. Hitler effectively killed the trade unions and thus created a gap in a historical process. What I find most saddening in modern Britain is the death of pride in work well done. Musicians see the music they perform as less important than their union rights and are, at Covent Garden Opera House, prepared to kill a performance at the beginning of the third act because they would rather go to bed than earn overtime pay. I do not think this could happen in Germany.

I know that praise of a transport system is not necessarily the best tribute to a nation (we associate the efficiency of Italian railways with the tyranny of Mussolini's fascism), but it would be boorish not to tell the world, and the German people, how remarkable their trains are. They arrive and leave not merely to the minute but to the second; they are comfortable; they have remarkable dining cars; there is a plethora of printed and vocal information about the journey one is taking. There seems to be a pride in the running of the railway system which, to the employees of British Rail, would look like a shameful selling out to the consumer. The principle of the dignity of service, which socialism always seeks to destroy, is healthily alive in Germany. How much longer it will live is, of course, hard to say. The philosophy of how much you can get away with without too many cries of pain is on the march in Europe: it may be regarded as one of Britain's gifts to the world.

Let us, then, accept with satisfaction that the Germans continue to be hard-working and efficient. Let us accept that they enjoy life, meaning beer and boiled legs of pork. Let us accept that, if they have what is at present an unaggressive kind of national pride, they are justified in having it. There is no country more beautiful than Germany, even under the snow of a winter journey. Though the Allies bombed German cities to hell, they have been restored with a loving eye to their past glories. I need not enumerate the musical, philosophical, literary, and architectural achievements of the German race, though I deplore the ease with which some of them—Mendelssohn, say, or Heine or Thomas Mann—could be denounced as un-German during that diabolic régime now long ended. Germans have a lot to be proud of: they have always been a highly civilised people. The same thing, however, can be said of the French and the Italians. Yet the myth still persists that the Germans are the least easy of the civilised nations to understand, that they are unpredictable and dangerous; that they are prepared to throw their civilisation away for the sake of a confused racial mysticism. How different are they from their neighbours?

They are not physically very different. One looks in vain for a German "type"—the blond hero, the thick-necked Siegfried, or the crop-haired big-bellied paterfamilias with a stein in one hand

and a meerschaum in the other. These were always as much car-
icatures as the horse-toothed Englishman with a bowler hat or
the shrugging Frenchman with a Mephistophelian beard. All the
Germans I met on my journey looked like Irishmen, whatever
Irishmen look like. There are more blonds in Northern Italy than
in Hamburg or Cologne. The Nazi racialist philosophy was always false, but there is a modicum of sense in distinguishing between the colouring and physiognomy of the Baltic and those of
the Mediterranean. In Germany now the Mediterranean seems to
have married the Baltic. One can no longer laud particular physical types as essentially German. Youth in particular has become
internationalised—long-legged on the American model, tee-
shirted and jeaned, equipped with the same kind of mental furniture as you will find in Toronto or Tokyo. Such children, one
would think, could never follow a new Hitler.

Some theorists have traced Germany's reputation as the
naughty child of Europe to an event that took place in the reign
of the Emperor Augustus. The Romans had always had trouble
with the Germanic tribes—the Cimbri, the Teutones—and Julius
Caesar had had to drive Ariovistus back across the Rhine. When
Augustus tried to tame the Germans and introduce them to the
delights of Roman baths and taxes, Arminius, champion of the
Cherusci, strongly resisted and led a patriotic rising. Herman
Wouk, the Jewish-American writer, remains convinced that this
refusal to accept membership of a great civilised empire is at the
root of Germany's eccentricity. One can, of course, embroider the
theme, but whether to a useful end who can be sure? To evade
the embrace of Augustus was, potentially, to reject not merely the
Roman peace but Roman Christianity as well. Potentially, of
course. The Germans delayed too long in becoming Christianised.
So we are told. In 1517 Martin Luther failed to see how essential
was Roman centralisation to the health of Christianity and sowed
the seeds of a dangerous secular nationalism. And so on. And
so on.

On this winter journey I paid my first visit to Cologne. In a
sense I have always avoided going there because I did not wish
to modify the image I had of it from the Third Symphony of
Schumann—especially that last movement which seems to present
Cologne Cathedral in counterpoint. I preferred a Cologne of the

mind. But my visit reminded me to give the lie to the theorists who invoke the rebellion of Arminius. For Cologne was a great Roman city, home town of Nero's mother, whose name, Agrippina, is still commemorated in a great insurance company (with which, being superstitious and convinced that Agrippina's malevolence works from beyond the grave, I would never negotiate for the entrusting of my car or body). The Rhine was Romanised, and Germany became the Holy Roman Empire. Nor did Germany ever become thoroughly Lutheranised. The Reformation worked far more brutally in England, whose citizens have always been far more nationalistic than the Germans. Moreover, the English have always been a more violent race, and their history is the history of the taming of that violence. One cannot look to the history of the remote past to explain the triumph of Hitlerism and the shame of the Jewish extermination. One ought rather to look at the failure to produce a political revolution of the British kind (1688), which established an executive with limited power and a middle class powerful enough to dominate the legislature.

I don't know, and nobody knows, why the devil got into Germany in the nineteen-thirties. I don't know, either, whether that term *devil* should be taken as a mere metaphor. Sometimes it seems to me that certain phases of human history can only be explained in theological terms, that the *Fürst der Phantome* literally exists. Whether we like it or not, the German nation produced the most potent myth of our time and the most fascinating. Narrative art—particularly film—has been thankful for the Nazi disease and continues to exploit it. One can hardly switch on one's television set without being regaled with some new saga of the concentration camps or of the bestiality of the SS. A nation has a terrible responsibility—that of not playing into the hands of the sensational popular artists of the future.

That, I know, is facetious, and I apologise for it. But it is worth considering what precisely the Germans thought the future contained when Hitler brought dignity back to the Aryans at the expense of the lesser races. Clearly, there was no great capacity for looking very far ahead—beyond, say, the death of Hitler or even as far as that. The future tense in German, as in Anglo-Saxon is very close to the present and can be expressed by the present. Both Hegel and Marx looked towards a realisation of their prophecies in a not-too-distant future. The Germans must have believed that, when the supreme being exhibited himself at last in the Teutonically ruled World Island, time would have a stop. This seems to point to a lack of imagination, a quality with which both German art and German philosophy is crammed.

All nations have been guilty of the most frightful abominations, my own nation not least. British television viewers have recently been delighting in a series which showed how badly the British behaved in India; the Americans, with the series *Roots*, beat their breasts at the damnable history of black slavery. We are all to some extent collective masochists, but we are grateful to Germany for allaying our guilt by having proposed the extermination of an entire race—a project which exhibited imagination of a somewhat limited kind but which no other nation had as yet conceived. I put the proposal down to German efficiency and thoroughness and to the literalist willingness to pursue an idea to its limit. If a train can come in to the second, not just the minute, that impossible punctuality (impossible, certainly, to the British) can find a counterpart in other mathematical exactitudes. "Get rid of the Jews" was not just a pious aspiration; it was an arithmetical sum that had to be worked out to the bitter limit.

I do not enjoy expatiating on the bad past, but, unfortunately, I belong to a generation that lived through it and lost much—particularly years in which otherwise it might have been a pleasure to be young. Later generations have learned to interpret that bad past in a comforting way. I remember, when covering the World Cup in West Berlin, I sat down outside a *Bierstube* called *Der Moby Dick*. Nobody came to serve me, so, after a half-hour of waiting, I went inside and asked why. The young man who ran the place told me, in admirable English of course, "Because you are of the generation that started the war." In fact, it was the previous generation that had started it—my generation had merely fought in it—but I took the point and retired gracefully and beerless. Other more reasonable Germans I spoke to on my winter journey denied that they or their families had ever shown complicity in Nazi rule: they had added an *e* to the *Heil* in *Heil Hitler*; they had waited for "liberation." The responsibility for the ghastly régime rested with unidentifiable others. The very young, forced to sit through cinema film of loud exhortations from Nazi leaders, tell me that they find it funny, like Charlie Chaplin in *The Great Dictator*. The past has been interpreted and disposed of. There is no psychological link between the old Germany and the new.

One would like to forget that past totally, but it has too much macabre glamour, it has produced the sole memorable myth of our time. A month or so ago, I was a juror at the Monte Carlo International Television Festival, and my German colleagues complained that practically every film entry that we saw dwelt on the infamy of the Nazis and, by extension, was a source of embarrassment to German viewers. This was all too true. There is, in the Nazi régime, a wealth of easy brutality and sartorial elegance (we have all longed to try on an SS uniform) available for filmmakers who lack imagination. That time will not be forgotten; we have hardly begun to mine the theology of it. I insist on using the term, and I prefer to substitute compassion for useless hatred: the devil got into the German people and then was whipped out. Now he is at work, less spectacularly, in the kingdoms of Khomeini and Ghadaffi.

Before I entirely leave the subject, I think I have learned to exorcise my amazement at the willingness of the German people to destroy great monuments of German art because the Nazis said they were not German at all, merely Jewish. An entire nation that had enjoyed Mendelssohn's Violin Concerto was persuaded that it now abominated it because it was Jewish. There was a simple-mindedness at work there (one of the devil's opportunities) which could believe that certain tonalities contained Semitic plasm, just as ingenuous eyes could see special figurations for Jewish blood under the microscope. The fact is that there is no more intelligence, or erudition, diffused through the German people than in any other nation. Thoroughness and efficiency are not necessarily marks of intelligence. German universities, thanks perhaps to Humboldt's reforms, are models of scholastic brilliance, but their achievements have not rubbed off on to the entire nation. The Germans, for that matter, are no more musical than other people, though they have produced the greatest musicians, some of whom were Jews. The Germans, like the French, English, and Italians, are very ordinary.

National Socialism showed what can happen when very ordinary people get control of a state and the merely opportunist are regarded as the intellectuals. It was as though a gang of raucous and aggressive British football supporters had been turned overnight into statesmen. Adolf Hitler could draw very prettily, like a Victorian miss, but he elevated his small talent into genius misunderstood and, through the gift of the gab, avenged himself on the extraordinary. The ordinary are always very ready to believe they are God's chosen, especially if told this loudly and repeatedly, and, in our own age, Pope John XXIII affirmed that God loves the common people better than the uncommon, since he made so many of them (another indication that the devil can work even through the papacy). Hitler can happen anywhere; it was unfortunate that he came as the saviour and redeemer of ordinary people who, since their nation had produced so many extraordinary men, believed that they were the greatest of the earth. The post-Nazi epoch is the age of humility: Germany, and the rest of us, are merely members of the Common Market. But Hitler was right about the true enemy of Europe: he is there, unconquerable, breathing over the Berlin Wall.

I did not visit West Berlin on this winter journey, since there was an International Film Festival on and nobody could be expected to listen to a mere writer of books. But past visits have induced in me a hardly supportable rage. What, in God's name, will the rational future think of us that we could allow a great city to be split with bits of decayed building and slats of timber? What madness that a people that fought so long for unity should have a factitious ideological division forced upon it. And yet, ironically, East Germany is very different, except for the wearisome Marxist philosophy, from the Soviet Union which is its foster parent. As I have seen, the Germans, whether fascist, communist, or democratic, work hard, maintain discipline without being ordered to, and believe in efficiency. The Russians don't like too many Russian visits to East Berlin: they show up the inefficiency and improvidence of their own state. In a sense, the unity of Germany remains.

It is not necessary for me to say much about the free cities of the German West, except that they are clean, orderly, and (except for Stuttgart, with its heavily commercial obsessions) attractive. Let me now leave the national confines while still staying in the

country we may call Germanophonia. I ended my journey by travelling through the snow—the one black spot on my itinerary—to
Vienna. The German train was as ever, dead on time to the second, its shining galley ready all day and evening with anything
from a sausage to a carpetbag steak, its wine superb. In winter it
is perhaps better to travel than to arrive. It was not Vienna's fault
if the weather was chill and the *Danube* (which you have to get
outside the city to see, anyway; what you see in the city is the
Danube Canal) looked like grey slops. I had previously known
Vienna in spring and autumn, the right seasons for, respectively
Johann and Richard Strauss (*Voices of Spring*; the last act of *Der
Rose kavalier*). Now I had arrived just before Shrove Tuesday in
the bleak fag-end of a winter that seems exposed to the Russian
steppes.

It is, of course, unfair to Vienna to expect it to fulfill dreams
about love under the lindens, an open-air string orchestra dis-
coursing *schmalz* salted with the faint clang of the zither. There
is also the city of *The Third Man*, where it is too cold for pigeons
to brood on the head of a statue of Franz Josef. The winter city
looked grim, but it knew how to keep carnival, which had started
(as also in Germany) well before Christmas. I got to Vienna in
time for the sumptuous pre-Lent ball held in the Opera House.

This was an affair of white tie and tails, pearly exposed bosoms,
damnably expensive, with the whipped cream of Central European society sweating under the chandeliers as they jigged to rock
or swirled to Strauss. Yet there was something artificial and nostalgic about it. It evoked a dead empire, when the imperial me-
tropolis Vienna was a point of the triangle completed by Budapest
and Prague. It is not easy to get into Prague these days: in the old
days the élite thought little of going there for the prémière of
Mozart's *Le Nozze di Figaro*. Budapest, which is only a brief drive
away, opens ready enough gates and is perhaps the most tolerable
capital of the whole Soviet bloc. Nevertheless, one is aware of a
cold eastern wind blowing on to Vienna. Losing its empire, it
went into a decline. With the *Anschluss*, it participated in the
prospect of a world *Reich*. After Yalta it became, like the imperial
port Trieste, a door opening on to the Russian misery. Sightseeing
in Vienna is mostly snooping on the glorious past. The good ar-

chitecture is impressive baroque and wedding-cake rococo, and it all celebrates the Hapsburg dynasty. The modern age is typified by anonymous office blocks, which dimly glorify commerce, and by the statue to the Red Army, whose liberation of the city— meaning looting and raping—the Russians will not allow the Viennese to forget.

The Austro-Hungarian Empire, so some of us believe, was far superior to the Roman or the British. By its fruits shall ye know it: Metastasio Haydn, Mozart, Beethoven, Schubert, all the Strausses; Hofmannsthal and Rilke and Schnitzler; Freud and Adler; the uneasy Jewish atonalists. James Joyce's *Ulysses* was perhaps its last great product—started in Trieste, set in a Trieste which pretends to be Dublin, composed joyfully, though with hard labour, on the edge of a crazy elegant ambience where the secret police were omnipresent but inefficient. Vienna thrilled all Europe and was a staple of popular balladry. It jetted out the spicy aroma of goulash or Turkish coffee. The goulash is still there, flavoured with carraway, and the coffee houses are crowded, but you will find no new Freud at a *Stammtisch*, nor see a new Schubert scribbling a song on the back of a menu.

The Viennese cuisine is, of course, remarkable. It is too heavy, though: it renders Viennese evenings quiet and torpid: after the meal, the solider citizens climb slowly to bed. It's different for the young, who, more than in Germany, flock to Hamburger King and McDonald's. Soup, I found, was a meal in itself. *Brandteigkrappeln*—milk, butter, eggs, flour, semolina, nourishing floating bits of fat meat. *Brösel* and *Gries* and *Leberknödel*. A fine *Gulaschsuppe* which you can eat at five in the morning. Bits of *Strudel* floating in the soup; *Apfelstrudel* after dinner. Beefy *Tafelspitz*, which seems purely Austrian, while *Wienerschnitzel* comes from Milan and paprika from Budapest. I even met a dessert called *Powidldatschkerl*, which name turned out to be a corruption of "Poor Little Dutch Girl," triangles of pastry with jam in them, beloved of a resident English family. The restaurants I sampled were, I thought, good enough, though little better than obscure eating-hells in Munich and Hamburg. The Weisser Rauchfangkehrer in Rauhensteingasse; the Deutsches Haus near Saint Stephen's Cathedral; the Sacher with its *Sachertorte*; the

Drei Husaran, which is pure Hungary; the Zum Stadtkrug, with its light digestive music.

Vienna displays charm still, even in winter, though capitalist pragmatism and socialist dogmatism alike regard charm as decadent or time-wasting. This means, I suppose, that charm has something to do with flirtatious leisure, a property of the pretty ladies in Schnitzler's novels, and that Vienna, like Paris but unlike Munich, is a woman's city. The sharp aggressiveness of women's liberation (which puts them in the prison of an ideal) is not manifest here as it is in certain towns of Germany: women are women and aware of the reality of sexual magnetism. It would be dangerous to think of a *type* of Viennese woman, but they appear to be not quite Slav and not quite Italian. I saw them shopping in the boutique stores of Kärntner Strasse and in the Graben, and they bought frivolities. This is still a city where women buy evening gowns (and, by the way, it is the only city in the world which still manufactures top hats for men). It is also a city where strip-tease cabarets are not picketed by women's liberationists, and where the advertisements for escort services (some of them in Arabic) promise, probably, more than you will get. "If you wish nice company?" says one coyly. "Come and meet the most charming and elegant ladies of Vienna." (The telephone number is 45 31 25.) This is illustrated by the portrait of a charmer too nude to be elegant. This is not, despite the memory of the *Anschluss*, true German territory. With an Austrian ruling the Third Reich, the Viennese could feel they had a stake in it; now they joke about sending to Berlin an Austrian they did not particularly want. There is the kind of pert inferiority complex towards Germany—expressed as humorous contempt— that Australians feel towards England. The Austrians are not so efficient as the Germans, and they have a full awareness of the fact; but they consider that they have more charm, a more cultivated attitude to leisure, and they still feel touched by the breath of a great dead civilisation. But they know they are no longer in the middle of things, they feel that cold Soviet blast from the East. The native name for Austria, like the Nazi Ostmark, refers to an eastern empire, but the Latin name Austria, like Australia, refers to the south wind, which is warm and ripens the grapes. Incidentally, American spelling is becoming sketchy: too many letters intended for Australia end up in Austria, and the Viennese are getting tired of saying that they have no Alice Springs or Wagga Wagga. Perhaps there are so many Australians in the city because they have come for their mail. A lot of foreigners find Vienna lovable, an epithet hard to apply to Frankfurt or Hamburg. Or, for that matter, Zürich. Is Zürich German? Probably, because the southern Italian-speaking Swiss have the same attitude of vague fear and respect towards it as the Viennese have towards their former lords of the *Anschluss*. We all, whatever our country, have a respect for Germany tempered with a little fear. But I, returning to France, left it with an emotion I had not expected: homesickness.

This had much to do, I soon discovered, with my background. I come from Manchester, which, before the Luftwaffe knocked it to hell and subsequent economic change demoted it from being the cotton capital of the world, had many of the properties of a *Hauptstadt*. It had a Hanseatic solidity, and it had great German-Jewish families, like the Behrens and the Bünemanns. The conductor of its Hallé Orchestra had been Hans von Richter, who introduced Wagner to England. That great orchestra maintained its Wagnerian traditions: it sounded like a Wagner orchestra, not a Debussy one. I was brought up on Wagner, and also on Hegel and Kant and Schopenhauer. The university of Manchester, where I studied, looked north. My subject was Germanic philology. The rise of Hitler induced in many of us an agony which still stabs occasionally. We felt that the Germany which had given us so much, and which had partly formed my mind, was dead, perhaps forever.

The Jewish writer George Steiner believed, even long after the war, that irreparable damage had been done to the German sensibility, and even to the German language. We could never, he said in one of his jeremiads, use a word like *spritzen* again, because it was impossible to cleanse of associations of Jewish blood spurting under the knife. He was wrong, of course. Eating a chicken Kiev in West Berlin, I was warned not to let the warm butter *spritzen* on my shirt. The German language recovered, with the help of Günter Grass, who hurled the whole rich German lexicon at his readers and exorcised the mean limited tongue of whines and barks imposed by the Nazis. Germany cannot lose its greatness of soul; a Nazi bonfire could only have a Phoenix func-

tion. The German sensibility I knew in my youth has been modified only by American consumerism.

Tristan und Isolde opens with a sailor singing:

> *Frisch weht der Wind*
> *Der Heimat zu . . .*

That wind still blows me towards Germany, but what I have to
avoid is a strange siren voice borne on it, a quality of the German
temperament that I find in myself and have always tried to subdue. This may be termed the sentimentality of the death-wish,
which the end of *Tristan* succeeds in ennobling, but, in less tran-
scendental forms, has always subtly qualified the German delight
in making, building, constructing—whether a *Ring* or a *Critique
of Pure Reason*. Behind the shouts of glee that heralded Hitler
there was a desire, quite inarticulated, for destruction—the betrayal of Siegfried, the burning of Walhalla. It is the other side of
the German coin, and we can all, at times, respond to its seduc-
tiveness. It can be countered only by irony, by Voltairian wit or
English humour. What, with my books, I have tried to bring into
Germany on my winter journey is a self-deflating quality which
has nothing to do with self-destruction. Germany, in a word, must
not take herself too seriously. Nor must any of us.

The self-pity is at the end of an Austrian song-cycle, bought for
for my birthday in Munich, and it is dangerous:

> *Barfuss auf dem Eise*
> *Wankt er hin und her;*
> *Und sein kleiner Teller*
> *Bleibt ihm immer leer . . .*
>
> *Wunderliche Alter,*
> *Soll ich mit dir gehn?*
> *Willst du meinem Liedern*
> *Deine Leier drehn?*

After all, the ice melts and the Germans probably invented spring.
I look forward to a summer journey through a lovely land.

—1984

THE ART OF LIKING ROME

❖

Liking is, perhaps, not really the point, nor disliking either. It seems that some cities excite violent emotions in the visitor or temporary resident, others leave them indifferent. I am indifferent about Zürich, Vienna, London, Nice, Adelaide. I have towards New York, Leningrad, Barcelona, and Rome an ambivalent attitude which I cannot easily classify. It is compounded of physical lust, loathing, possessive passion, affectionate exasperation, jealousy—all the attributes of a sexual relationship. Cities being feminine (except Moscow and Chicago and probably Sydney), men feel more strongly about them than women. To a woman a city is an emporium, something to use. A man is used by it, bought, sold, sometimes enslaved.

The cities of the New World are the cities of the second chance. Boston and Washington are good examples: the religious intolerance and tyranny of the Old World drove certain strong but simple Europeans to cross the Atlantic and start again. Naturally, since human nature does not change, they failed to produce Utopias. They grew disappointed: America is the land of disappointment. In Rome there is no disappointment; no false expectation mars the stoicism of its citizens. For over two thousand years Rome has been ill-governed. It has been ill-governed twice over, by Church and by State. Some Romans dream of a Communist revolution unlike the bloody one of Soviet Russia—equality, efficiency, justice—but the majority of them are philosophical and take life as it comes—the thimbleful of espresso, the trestle tables of the open-air *trattoria*, the robbers on their motorcycles, the bribable police, and the corrupt politicians.

Rome is a casual work of art, planned, re-planned, too organic to yield to planners. There is no coddling of the past; the past just happens to be there. The ancient Romans had as their city motto SPQR: *Senatus Populusque Romani*, the Senate and the Roman

People. SPQR is still around on lamp standards and public buildings, but to the cynical Romans it means *Sono Pazzi Questi Romani*, They're mad, these Romans, or *Soli Preti Qui Regnano*:
Only the Priests Rule Here. This is the centre of Catholic Christianity, but the Romans are as pagan as they were under Nero.
A prostitute will make the sign against the evil eye when she sees
a priest: he is a dangerous anomaly, a man in a skirt. The Pope
is treated with amused tolerance as a useful tourist attraction;
John Paul II is affectionately called *lo s..... polacco*—a term too
obscene to translate. The Jewish stallholders on the Gianicolo—
one of the seven hills—regard themselves as the real Romans (they
were here before the Christians) and, though they respect Peter
and Paul as Jews who made the trip and got killed for their pains,
they will not accept Christ, a village lad who was unambitious
and got himself killed in Jerusalem.

The Romans are resigned, but they are not humble. *La bella
figura* is part of their way of life: pride in the flesh, in an ancient
citizenship, in a trade honourable or dishonourable. You see them
walking around in the evening *passeggiata*, looking and being
looked at—slim girls and paunchy fathers of families, crones and
kids. They are aware of the scenic allure of their background—
broken pillars and baroque statues, fascist grandiloquence and
eighteenth-century elegance—and they enact films without cameras or directors. Everything moves into the open air, family
quarrels and shy juvenile love. Life is civic. Everybody has a title:
you call the barman *dottore* and the streetsweeper *capo*. Pride in
being a Roman has nothing to do with great historical achievements: it has more to do with having survived.

Beyond the Ponte Garibaldi, where the ancient district known
as Trastevere begins (the Tiber is the Tevere, and Trastevere
means across it), there stands a statue of the Roman poet Belli, a
contemporary of Keats and Shelley (honorary Romans because
their graves are in Rome) but no romantic. He wrote nearly three
thousand sonnets in the Roman dialect, mostly obscene, all of
them cynical in the Roman manner. Belli, a man of culture and
a Vatican censor of plays, impersonates the typical Roman, but
the impersonation is so good that we take him still as the native
voice of the Roman gutters. If you want to know Rome you have
to read him. In his poems the whole world is reduced to the city,

with the Tower of Babel being built near the Vatican and the Ark on the Tiber. Jesus Christ is acceptable because he is ragged, half-starved, lashed, and killed, but also reviled for leaving his blood to the rich and mere lymphatic water to the poor. Here is rock-bottom realism. Here is Rome without illusions.

It is a dangerous city to visit in a spirit of romantic expectation. There is glamour enough, and also the comforts proper to a place dedicated to making the best of things. There is always somewhere to sit; fountains offer a release from thirst and heat; the eyes are always flattered, even by laundry on the line. This city could not be ugly if it tried: slums merely look like film sets, cripples like character actors. But the moment of deciding that one has at last come home is the moment for the *scippatore* on his Vespa to snatch your camera or handbag. The people are kind enough, but they are also rogues. American ladies who say "I *love* Rome" are destined to be in trouble.

Rome is not, despite Fellini's already dated "*La Dolce Vita*," the Via Veneto, where a Campari costs the earth and the *poules de luxe* parade with their little dogs. Rome is not the *luxe* restaurants but the little *trattorie* of the pasta-stuffers and the white acid wine of Frascati. For me personally Rome was the Trastevere district guarded by the statue of Belli. It was the Piazza Santa Cecilia, where I had my fourth-floor apartment and could look out on the Basilica of the patron saint of music. Working as a writer, respectfully called *professore* by the shopkeepers, I felt myself one with the bad sculptors and fakers of antique furniture— an artist of sorts, of the company of Dante, Michelangelo, and Leonardo. The noise—and only the Chinese love noise more than the Romans—was a sign that life was going on outside—honking Fiats, plangent complaining voices, the eardrum-shattering loud-speakers of the local festival *de Noi Antri* (translated from Trastevere dialect into good Italian as *di noi altri*—we others, i.e., the real Romans). I did not become a Roman: I was already one. My city of Manchester used to be Mancunium, a fort of the civilising invader. Living in Rome was a mere confirmation of an ancient citizenship.

So liking or disliking does not really come into it. Rome awakens in most of us an appetite for life which, in Oshkosh or Grand Rapids, too often lies dormant. It is, supremely, the life of the city, whose beauty of stone and water expresses human ideals sometimes capable of fulfillment. Despite the beauty and the history, Romans do not feel dwarfed by their city, as New Yorkers do. The Romans are about the same size as Rome. Even their neuroses are acceptable as part of the civic condition. The poet Blake wrote:

> *In a wife I would desire*
> *What in whores is always found:*
> *The lineaments of gratified desire.*

He never visited Rome, but he could have had Rome in mind.

—1984

FRANCE AND MYSELF

❖

France needs no defining, but *myself* does. I am a subject of her Britannic majesty who lives outside her territories, of mixed Irish and Anglo-Norman stock, brought up in the Northwest of England, a citizen of the ancient Roman city of Manchester (Mancunium, the adjective being Mancuniensis), the faith of my family—despite dispossession and persecution by the Protestant state—staunchly Roman Catholic. There are items in the above list of attributes which explain why, in allegiances and affections, I tend to leap over the Southeast of England, which is culturally foreign territory, and find myself at home in France, as far as the French, who employ a very limited interpretation of the term *English* and don't know the term *British* at all, will permit me to feel at home. Alternatively, I am drawn to Ireland, which is close to the Northwest of England. To a product of this region, Dublin and Paris are more sympathetic and meaningful capitals than London is.

In my youth, secondary education took France so seriously that the French language was a compulsory item in the curriculum. We learned Latin, Greek, and French as the major languages of civilisation, and if we wished to study German or Spanish, as many of us did, we had to have private lessons or pore over primers in our spare time. As the way into France is by way of her language, this early linguistic indoctrination implied a concern with the country itself, not just *Phéóre* and *Zadig* as examination texts. Our first trips abroad were inevitably to France or to Belgium. We regarded Belgium—wrongly and with gross unfairness—as an annex of France. On the other hand, the French spoken by Belgians was more intelligible to us than the Parisian variety, the use of *actante* and *nonante* seemed more logical than their periphrastic French equivalents, and the Belgians possessed Flemish as well as French, a language cognate with our own. Moreover, the Belgians seemed to be more amiable people than the French. The French have never seemed to the British to be an immediately likeable nation.

What precisely, in the view of the British, is wrong with the French? They have always seemed to be an irritable people, sharp-spoken and disdainful, their politeness suggesting the desire to wound more than the urge to please. Their unlikeable qualities, especially in centres of bureaucracy, have always been more man-ifest in the morning, after an insufficient breakfast and before a heavy luncheon. The British have always believed that the French would be more pleasant if they ate an English or American break-fast and consumed a smaller lunch. In other words, French irri-tability has something to do with the liver. They are a hepatic nation given to *crises de foie*. That the French sometimes call the French "frogs" has never had anything to do with their appear-ance or their leaping abilities: it is a reference to an item of diet which the British think to be more popular than it is. In other words, the British are horrified by the variety, bizarreness, and richness of the French cuisine, and they blame it for French he-patic behaviour. The English have no livers at all. Instead they have bad teeth and sour stomachs.

Despite this horror at the French disdain for strong tea and steak and kidney pudding, the British have always come to France in order to eat well. They recognise that the French are able to do something quite impossible to the greater part of the British: they treat the preparation of food as a great art. The culinary visitations of the British are made eagerly but also with a certain sense of guilt. They used to sneak into Paris restaurants as they sneaked into Paris brothels, ashamed of indulging their senses— which, to the French, is so natural an enjoyment that it demands to be augmented and subtilised through the devices of art. I still feel a twinge of Puritanical embarrassment when people say loudly *Bon appétit*. There is an air hostess on British Airways whose valediction to passengers alighting at Nice is that same *Bon appétit*, as though the whole of the Côte d'Azur were no more than a well-laid table. This makes many people, including myself, cringe with shame.

It is their awareness of the Puritan heritage left by our own brief republic under Oliver Cromwell that makes the British both resentful and envious of the epicurean traditions of the French. There is—at least in literature and popular culture—an attitude toward sex which is far more open, more ingenious, less guilt-ridden, possibly less moral than is permitted to the English (and even more to the Irish and the Scotch. The Welsh are different). The French have always treated marriage—or so the British believe—more cold-bloodedly than the Puritan tradition permits. Marriage has always seemed, in the British view of the French, a cynical matter of dowries; it is assumed that love is a different matter and can be conducted only extramaritally. This, anyway, we have learned from Guy de Maupassant. It is the British who are the great married people of Europe. Their Protestant Puritan heritage commands them to take marriage very seriously and to regard unmarried fornication as a heinous crime. The situation is even worse in America, where the Puritanism of the Pilgrim Fathers made adultery a capital offence and, in consequence, inaugurated the modern age of easy divorces or serial polygamy.

To the British, France is readily acceptable as the great country of logic, which the invocation of the name of René Descartes santifics. The French are Cartesian, though they do not always know what the term means. The British think it means that they consult the claims of the head more than the heart or the rest of the body (though French hedonism does not seem to confirm this). Those of us who know the Chinese are inclined to the view that the French resemble them in having a species of logic which does not conform to any Hellenic pattern. The Chinese will taxonomise according to what seem to the West to be irrelevancies, finding a cat more like a table than a female biped because both have four legs. The French gift, in British eyes, is the clarity of thought which we always associate with the syllogism. This makes French literature, music, and painting luminous. There is no luminosity in British art, which seems to the French to swim in a London fog. There is too much detail in deficiency of logic. The admirable Mediterranean property of an uncomplicated but not unintelligent joy in the external world is, par excellence, to be found in Renoir and Debussy. It is not found where you would most expect it—in Spain or Italy, both of which got bogged down in the baroque. This light and sweetness of French art, which is an idealised image of French life, is what the British admire.

The French, as I realise, have much to be proud of, and this makes them chauvinistic. Chauvinism is always, to use a term from French linguistics, diachronic: the French see France spread out in time as well as space, and they are always ready to invoke history. They are prepared to be very selective about this history, ignoring the Terror while they retain a sharp image of *le Roi Soleil*. The British have no objection to foreign chauvinism so long as it is not turned into a weapon and directed against themselves. The aggressive chauvinism of the late General de Gaulle is remembered with great British displeasure. Here was a man who called himself a soldier but only fired shots as a politician, which was cowardly. He enjoyed British hospitality and help during the war years, but then he turned against the British when they tried to enter the European Community, averring that they were not Europeans. In Canada he indiscreetly shouted "*Vive le Québec libre*," which was foolish and based on a bit of Cartesian illogicality which assumed that the French language is always a kind of French territory. This is a kind of Frenchness hard to accept. On the other hand, de Gaulle spoke French very slowly and clearly, which endeared him to such of the British as spoke French.

French readers ought to know that there is in Great Britain a very large body of extreme Francomanes. Most British intellectuals love France somewhat better than they love England. My old history professor, A. J. P. Taylor said publicly some years ago that there was no intelligent Englishman living who would not prefer to have been born French. These would have meant a very small addition to the French population, since it is generally admitted that there are very few intelligent Englishmen. Intelligence is not a quality greatly esteemed in England, and intellectuality is a very unpatriotic endowment. There is no *Club des Intellectuels* in London as there is in Paris. Walter Bagehot once said that the salvatory quality of the British was their stupidity. A stupid nation would not have continued to fight Nazi Germany in 1940 but, like the rational French, would have asked for an armistice. The British nevertheless consider that they need the intelligence of the French—as they need the French cuisine, *haute couture*, and sexual laxness—to explain the world to them. God, according to Charles Peguy, also needed the French to make sense of his universe. The British are sensible enough to recognise that the English language is half French, thanks to the Norman invasion of 1066, and the French are the people to explain certain hard words to them—like existentialism and structuralism and poststructuralism and deconstructionism and even parliamentary government and the separation of the powers.

The British who are genuine Francomanes don't live in France: they merely visit it as often as they can. I live in the independent principality of Monaco, which is controlled by French fiscal laws and has the benefit of French trains, gas, electricity, and post offices. The French would dearly like to capture this enclave and incorporate it in Metropolitan France, just as the Spanish would like to retake British Gibraltar. This makes myself, like other Monaco residents, rather suspicious of France. But the suspicion is something I have been taught to cultivate by my native country, long before I came to live on the borders of M. Mitterand's republic. The French and the British probably meet in a mutual suspicion. Neither has any longer a fear of the territorial ambitions of the other—the days of Henry V and Napoleon Bonaparte are long over—but each fears that the other will perform some treacherous act or other—abandoning NATO, becoming too friendly with the USSR, imposing tariffs on cheese or sausages. The French do not like the British. On the other hand, the British love France. There is a difference between "France" and "the French." Henry V of England said that he loved France so much that he would not part with a single French province. There was once an English milord who, after his first experience of sex, declared that it was too good for the common people. There are ordinary Englishmen who say that *bouef à la bourguignonne* and *profiterrolles* are too good for the French. Unfortunately we need French chefs to cook these delicacies, just as we need Frenchmen to write the works of Baudelaire and Mallarmé and compose the music of Berlioz and Ravel. We can't do without the French. Meaning that I can't.

—1985

Farewell (and Hello Again) Manchester

❖

"Farewell, Manchester, sadly I depart" is the first line of a song that Bonny Prince Charlie is supposed to have sung. The occasion was his leaving the city (and a number of pregnancies behind) after a recruiting drive for the 1745 rebellion. Manchester at that time had not yet become the Queen of the Industrial Revolution. It was more Catholic and Jacobite than filled with the Protestant work ethic. After all, it was near the Irish Sea and attracted Irish Catholic immigrants, like my grandmother's people and my stepmother. It had its indigenous Catholics, for the Reformation had difficulty in pushing so far northwest. As for its Jacobitism, my father insisted that the only monarch I was to honour was the disgraced and exiled James II, the last Catholic king of Great Britain.

My father made his second marriage into an immigrant Irish family, a member of which became the Catholic Archbishop of Birmingham. So the Manchester of my youth had a strong sectarian and immigrant flavour. I broke out of the Irish net when I married a Welsh Protestant. I broke away from Manchester itself when, having taken my degree at Manchester University, I joined the army. At the end of the war, like most of the demobilised, I went where the jobs were. They were in the Midlands and in the dwindling British Empire, not in Manchester. When I became a writer London was the heart of my culture. The vast Irish family of which I was a kind of offshore island stayed in the Manchester suburbs, prospering in their shops or drinking in their presbyteries. I said "Farewell, Manchester" in my early twenties.

In my late sixties I said "Hello again." A Belgian television team insisted on my returning to Manchester and, under the eye of their camera, looking for my past. The house in northeastern Manchester where I was born had long been demolished. The entire district of Moss Side, where I had spent my childhood and adolescence, had turned into a green wilderness set with posters promising redevelopment. While I stuttered bemused into one microphone, the Prince of Wales spoke into another for a reconstituted Moss Side. But there was no hope of reconstituting the three houses I had lived in. There is something almost surgically devastating about the loss of one's physical past. On the other hand, what among those jerry-built structures was worth preserving? So much of Manchester was thrown up hastily and ineptly to cope with the rapid growth of an industrial workforce.

Two solid monuments of my extreme youth were still around: the Xaverian College in Victoria Park, Rusholme, and the Holy Name church on Oxford Road. But Rusholme had turned into a Muslim ghetto. The old repertory theatre, which trained Wendy Hiller and Robert Donat, had long gone, and the rather dainty shops with their aura of county-town refinement had given place to Pakistani emporia. The Holy Name, a stronghold of British Jesuitry, would soon have to be deconsecrated for lack of a sufficient Catholic congregation. Islam was growing, Irish Christianity disappearing. And the university, in my day a small and manageable academy, had become expansive and American and would soon engulf Catholic church land.

Change, so Evelyn Waugh was always saying, is evidence of life, and we all have to register unconditional surrender to history. But it is hard to be philosophical and unresentful when, on racial grounds, one is thrown out of the Moss Side pub one's father frequented. I was politely, or not so, told to get out of what had become a West Indian preserve. The house on Moss Lane East where I used to live had turned into a shebeen before it was demolished. Very good—accept change: the Friday call of the muezzin instead of the Sunday summons of the bells, an Asiatic Manchester instead of the European one of my youth.

The cosmopolitanism of the city used to provide its own piquancy. The German Jewish element was strong, so was the Italian, and both forced Manchester into being a centre of the arts, particularly music. The Hallé Orchestra is well regarded today, but before the war it could claim preeminence in Britain. My father heard it give the first performance of Elgar's first symphony, and I myself heard the first performances of *The Rio Grande* and *Belshazzar's Feast*. I heard Schnabel and Rachmaninov play concertos and saw Stravinsky conduct. When the BBC formed its symphony orchestra it stole all the section leaders of the Hallé, eliciting a cry of pain from our Irish conductor Sir Hamilton Harty—"Amiable bandits." It was a great orchestra but very conservative. The cosmopolitan core of its audiences was content with Bach, Beethoven, and Brahms. Also Berlioz, whom Harty adored. Also Wagner, whom Hans von Richter had implanted in Manchester during Victoria's reign. Stravinsky only got in when Harty died. Early Shostakovich was tolerated because it was considered to be Tchaikovsky and water. Mossolov's *Music of Machines* earned a good laugh.

The conservative audiences supported a great Liberal newspaper. Some of us can never forgive the *Manchester Guardian* for deregionalising itself. I remember it under T. P. Scott's editorship, when it was all stern news, no frivolity, no headlines on Page One. It followed a Liberal tradition that was Manchester's own; it transcended party. Its musical and cricketing columns were the best in Britain and, when Neville Cardus took over, intelligible only in terms of each other. It published me when I was twelve and paid me five guineas. As the *Guardian* it turned into printer's pie and irritable radicalism. It certainly lost dignity.

The old city was far from beautiful: beauty was something to discourse in the Free Trade Hall or study in the Whitworth Art Gallery. Much of the old architecture has gone—the Luftwaffe helped—but the Town Hall remains to remind us of the messy neo-Gothic that was a kind of reflection of the mercantile mind. The city was concerned with trade, not Ruskinian aesthetics, though Ruskin used to be much read. I once ran a class in literature there, and a middle-aged man who attended read his *Manchester Guardian* from front to back while I taught. "Why do you come?" I asked him after the fifth session. "Lad," he said, "I'm waiting till tha gets on to John Ruskin." The progressive conscience sometimes stirred in the grim city. But it was primarily concerned with cotton—the proud nickname was Cottonopolis—and engineering. Mercantile enterprise cut a canal to the coast and turned Manchester into a port. "Manchester goods for Manchester Docks," read the slogan in the trams.

Well, that's over, and Manchester is like any other city. The climate which made Lancashire ideal for cotton-spinning is now probably a reminder to the Asiatics that the tropics can occasionally invade the Gulf Stream. The myth of Manchester's rain probably got into the non-Mancunian mythology because the monsoon season always coincided with the Test Matches at Old Trafford. I never found Manchester unduly rainy, though the chesty humidity could not be denied. Rain, anyway, was preferable to the sudden palls of blackness that struck even in summer weather. With the industrial smog came the opportunity for the nuns who taught me to suggest that this might be the End of the World and we'd all better join fingers and pray just to be on the safe side. The smog has gone and I've seen, even in winter, skies of Mediterranean azure. Manchester is distressingly clean.

But one thing has not changed: Manchester still eats well. The Mancunian contempt for London was expressed as much as anything in disdain for what were considered Southern eating habits. High tea down there meant half a hard-boiled egg and a limp leaf of lettuce. They could not make tea in the South; true, they didn't, and don't, have our soft water. Southern girls had inferior complexions (hard water again). But it is solid nourishment that Southerners lack. You can, you always could, eat food with Continental sauces in the French restaurant of the Midland Hotel (now a Holiday Inn, though it still looks like the old Midland), but the roasts of the main restaurant are what Manchester food is about. I do not, alas, see much tripe and cowheel eaten now, but I may have failed to look, or sniff, hard enough. Lancashire hotpot and meat and potato pie are still around. Fish and chips, as elsewhere, seem to be in the hands of the Chinese, but the Chinese, when not busy with tong warfare, are prepared to turn into decent Mancunians. I have not, in the last few visits, eaten better anywhere than in Manchester.

Change is evidence of life, and some of the changes are good: surely Deansgate is one of the most handsome shopping streets in Europe. The Central Library and the Town Hall Annexe, which I am old enough to remember being built, preside over what used to be St. Peter's Fields, where the Peterloo massacre took place (it is still bitterly remembered) and are as elegant as anything in England. But the more one looks for evidences of urban distinction, the less one finds it in brick-and-mortar solidities. The distinction is all in the people. Mancunians built the industrial world, they are the creators as well as the fruit of international modernity. Marx and Engels (and Engels was himself a kind of Mancunian) wrongly predicted that the communist revolution would spring out of Manchester's industrial strife. They thought in abstractions, ignoring the character of a people whose conservatism could be tempered by liberalism but not replaced by political innovation. Manchester's innovations have all been within the cadre of capitalism—railways, seaside resorts for the workers, workers' organisations promoting music (brass bands and choral societies)—rather than strategies of revolt. Mancunians have always been tough enough to accept oppression within limits and to soften the hard life with the amenities they made for themselves—cricket at Old Trafford, the annual performance of Handel's *Messiah*.

The river Irwell divides Manchester and Salford, the first an Anglican archbishopric, the second a Catholic one. They may be regarded as one people, and the millions who watch *Coronation Street* twice-weekly cannot be sure whether they are meddling in the lives of Mancunians or Salfordians. On the whole, this continuing soap opera reflects adequately the speech and dispositions of the urban Northwest, but it's a pity that no bigger art has done justice to them. We writers from Manchester have shamefully neglected our city, though I have tried to make amends in my latest, thirtieth, novel. If we want fiction about Manchester, we have to go to Mrs. Gaskell's *Mary Barton*, Louis Golding's *Magnolia Street* (which is about Jewish Manchester) or Howard Spring's *Shabby Tiger* (not a bad description of the city itself). As James Joyce's *Ulysses* has glorified Dubliners in spite of the Dubliners who go on neglecting or reviling the book, so there was need, at the height of Manchester's finest flowering, for some fictional genius to capture its essence in a great novel. This never happened. The Ibsenian drama that sprang out of Miss Horniman's patronage—plays like *Hobson's Choice* or *Hindle Wakes*—was trivial, and she herself was to assist in the establishment of a truly great regional theatre in Dublin. Manchester's talent—in drama, music, and fiction—migrated south. London, in spite of the immense differences in civic temperament, has always found it easy to absorb the best of Manchester, but only when that best has already been proved. "What Manchester thinks today, London will think tomorrow."

My native city, then, is not what it was. Napoleon was defeated by the lessons he taught other armies, and Manchester, teaching the cotton technology to nations without trade unions, ceased to be Cottonopolis. Manchester used to be European before the concept of a united Europe existed; now, while all England prepares to join Europe by a land-road, Manchester has become Asiatic. But this northwestern Asia speaks with a Manchester accent. If I regret the disappearance of the shabby tiger I used to know, I am proving myself stupidly resistant to the current of history. But memory preserves reality, and my own memory will not permit that greater Manchester to die.

As for the future, we must accept a kind of homogeneity that makes one English town very like another. London is the great exception, but London is not a town but a country. England, with Manchester and Birmingham in the forefront, led the world into the industrial age, but that age of great smoking chimneys is over. England delivers "services," whatever they are, and is cautiously interested in tourism. Industry has become industrial archaeology, cleaned-up, dead, apt for the photography of foreign visitors. The towns grant evidence of small commerce—neat shopping malls and plants in tubs, reasonable restaurants whose chefs are young and have been trained to produce an adequate ratatouille. Manchester is bland, and the old industrial filth and strife have been transmuted into sporadic gang warfare and the mugging of old age pensioners. This is the pattern of the European future. At the turn of the millennium, when you will be able to drive from Strasbourg to Manchester without even an awareness of the tamed choppy Channel (granted that you should want to drive to Manchester at all), the homogeneity of England, close to that of Europe, will be taken for granted. But, despite the centralising force of radio, film, and television, there will still be a Manchester temperament, expressed in Manchester speech, that will have resisted the bland levelling. The vowels will be close to Shakespeare's and epithets like "gradely" and "champion" will express cautious approval. Old men will still say "Oo's getten chip-pan on" instead of "My wife's cooking the dinner," and if your feet are wet you will be "witshet." You will go to Manchester to meet Mancunians, the fiercest and friendliest foreigners in the world.

—1988

Life (of a Sort) in Venice

❖

That film of Nicholas Roeg called *Don't Look Now* was about Donald Sutherland and Julie Christie in off-season Venice—all closed hotels, rain, chill, chunks of decayed church falling on people, funeral gondolas, sudden death in dark alleys. The Venice I know best is (except so far for the sudden death) rather like that. Indeed, it was only last summer, drawn by the film festival on the Lido, that I became involved at all in touristic Venice, for the first and, I hope, last time. The gorgeous water-city is affronted by fat matronly bottoms in shorts, it shudders at the clicking Leicas, it wistfully puts money in its purse, serves bad food, and waits patiently for the advent of bad weather and a resumption of heavy drinking.

The Italians in general don't get drunk. Drunkenness to them is an infraction of social grace, a crumbling of the *bella figura*. The Venetians, especially in winter, down their drams dourly. The rain teems on to the canals, they wince at their rheumatic chills, and they either try to swill the pain away in cold black wine or prick it with shots of grappa. The gondoliers have put their striped shirts in mothballs and hung up their ribboned hats. They dress in creaseless pants and porridge-coloured torn jackets and they drink. W. S. Gilbert, in *The Gondoliers*, made the tippling ways of an old boatman of the canals the very root of a plot about doubtful identities. The Venetians get drunk. Of this there is no shadow of doubt, no possible doubt whatever.

How, in winter weather, does one get to Venice? How, specifically, does one get to Venice's best and cheapest hotel, which is the Casa Frollo on the island known as the Giudecca? Whatever one's point of arrival, there's no evading the long water-taxi ride, or trip by *vaporetto*, across the canal that separates the Giudecca from Venice proper. That canal is wide and deep, and on it ply huge ships of the container variety making their way to Istanbul.

The water is choppy, and getting out of the *motoscafo* is perilous. One's main aim in arriving at the city at all is to avoid water as much as one can. Come by plane, and you have to travel, like Thomas Mann's Aschenbach, over the huge lagoon. That lagoon in Visconti's film of *Death in Venice* is serene and is set to the serenest of Gustav Mahler's music. In, say, February it is always promising tempest. Arrive at the railway station and you cut down on the water. I prefer to travel by road, parking the car on the Piazzetta di Roma, and deciding whether or not to be sick in the *motoscafo* that takes me to the Casa Frollo.

I mention the Casa Frollo because people are always seeking a good hotel in Venice and usually failing to find one. The Casa Frollo is a gardened palace of immense aging elegance, now split up into bedrooms of large size. There is no need to take a book to bed; you can beguile sleeplessness by analysing the complex fresco on the ceiling. This hotel is in danger. Its owner, who lives in Rome and rarely visits Venice, is ready to sell it to the Japanese, who will then demolish it and raise a touristic horror on the ruins. Those of us who love the hotel have been trying to save it with subscriptions to a fund and heavy propaganda. But I fear it may already be too late.

Working in Venice proper, as I have been doing on and off for years, has meant taking the *vaporetto* from just by the Casa Frollo over the canal (one stop at San Giorgio) to the landing-stage near San Marco. To summer tourists the *vaporetto* is mostly a great joke. Americans chugging up the Grand Canal towards the Rialto make corny quips about the next stop being 42nd Street. I'm sure there's a belief that water-travel is a kind of Disneyland attraction and, if you looked for it, you'd find perfectly normal land transport lurking somewhere. It's in touristless winter that you become aware of how much this boated city is a grim product of history, of how the gondola and the municipal shiplet are a logical way of life to the Venetians. Grim weather reminds you of a grim purpose. When Attila and his Hun hordes were raging in northern Italy, certain sons of the Adriatic decided that the only way to evade these murderous land invaders was to get off the land. And so the Adriatic islands were built upon, populated, linked, and turned into Venezia, Serenissima, queen of Eastern trade. History is always a nightmare, and Venice is the spawn of a nightmare.

It is the most absurd thing in the world to build a city on water and to force its citizens to do their shopping, go to their offices, visit their sick, celebrate their marriages, and bury their dead by gondola or *vaporetto* or water-taxi. The nightmare becomes manifest, appropriately enough, at night, when the municipal water-fleet is becalmed and the *motoscafi* take over. High charges and difficulties of embarkation and disembarkation reinforce the nightmare element. Let us walk home? Walk? We are not, say the Venetians, Jesus Christ. Well, not all of us.

If we are drunk, we may even think we are in on the last act of a tragedy, for the municipal water service is called ACTV. This, I think, means *Azienda Comunale Trasporto Veneziana*, but that is a typically Italian bureaucratic mouthful. It is certainly not Venetian, which is its own language and turns *Veneziana* into *Venexian*. Anyway, waiting for a *vaporetto* in winter on the drunkenly swaying landing-stage labelled ACTV, you're aware that waiting for a boat is no more than waiting for a bus. Handsome moustached men with briefcases are going to their offices. There is no touristic joshing. This is a way of life and not a piquant roller-coaster ride for the clicking camera bearers.

What and who are these Venetians, besides being waiters and gondoliers? Italians, yes, but that means little. An Italian is someone who lives in Italy, or emigrates from it, and speaks a dialect derived from Latin, unless he is from Calabria, when he is likely to speak a kind of Greek, or from Alto Adige, when he speaks German. Italy is and always was an abstraction. To talk of the Italian language is as inaccurate as to talk of the Italian cuisine. The Italian of the television announcers is likely to be the dialect of Tuscany, which is what foreigners are persuaded to learn. Venetians learn it too, but they're happier with Venetian, which is glorified in the comedies of Goldoni. Florentines will say *"Quando ho finito"*—when I've finished—but Venetians *"Quando go fini 'o."* The dead aspirate turns into a *g* in the manner of Russian, whose homosexuals are gomosexuals who perhaps read Yernyest Gemingvay. There is a Slav influence from across the Adriatic which travels even further west: in the Marche I have heard *Europa* turn into *Evropa*. But the Venetians are fundamentally Celtic: the pre-Christian Veneti seem to have migrated as far as northwestern France. The stock image of the Italian as

swarthy, small, and garlic-redolent won't really do: it derives from
the history of emigration, and the major immigrants into our
northern countries have all been from the south. Garlic, tomato
sauce, and pasta make up the diet of the dark and oppressed and
end up as the cuisine of Mamma Leoni's in Manhattan. The Si-
cilians and Calabrians are Italian, true, but it is wrong to call
them typical Italians.

Indeed, in Venice there is a historic resentment at being a province of the united Italy which Garibaldi fought for with posthumous success. Venice, now a *comune*, was once a republic. Think
of Venetians as a race and an independent people, and you won't
be so likely to see them as just another lot of Italians. Titian hair
was not an invention of Tiziano: blondness and bronzeness are as
common as raven locks and flourish as far north as Trieste. American film critics were astonished that the actor who calls himself
Terence Hill (Terenshe Eel in Italy) should be Italian. Fair hair
and blue eyes? Impossible. But Veneto produces such essentially
Celtic types. How do we expect Desdemona to look? Blonde,
without a doubt. The Elizabethans knew in advance that she'd be
smothered for a fancied sexual crime, only to them it would not
be fancied. Venetian women always had the reputation of sexual
looseness. And, indeed, on sheer topographical evidence, Venice
is the city of sexual intrigue, for the *palazzi* are labyrinths with
innumerable doors for quick exists. Was not Casanova here?

Carnival time was traditionally, what with sartorial disguise
and the trickery of the mask, the season for promiscuity, but nowadays all sex is licit: this is not Palermo, where bridegrooms paint
their penises purple and murder their brides if they express astonishment. The Venetian carnival is now wearily commercial, and
you know that it is on its way when the opera season starts. I
was involved in Venetian opera a couple of years ago.

The great opera house is called the Fenice, or Phoenix, and in
my time it was run by a South American named Gomez. Habituated to distant travel, he had been up to Glasgow to see the
Scottish Opera perform my version of Weber's *Oberon*. Weber
first conducted this work in London in 1828 and died a few weeks
later. It has not been performed much since, for the libretto is
insufferable, though the music is ravishing. All most people know
of the work is the overture. My task was to write a new libretto.

This I made very contemporary, with a couple of American airmen (tenor and baritone) rescuing from Khomeini's Tehran (rechristened Naraka, Arabic for hell) a couple of embassy secretaries (soprano and contralto). The opening scene has an aeroplane making a crash landing, piercing the paper cyclorama with its nose. Gomez imprudently imported this production from Scotland. It was interesting to see the reactions of Venetians better used to *Rigoletto* and *La Traviata*.

To say that the Venetians are musically conservative is to assert a truth which links them with the rest of Italy. The outrage expressed in the audience when the aviators crawled from their aircraft and started to sing was considerable. "*E un' operetta,*" they growled, "*non un' opera.*" The magic horn of the original libretto, which, being sewn into the score, could not be omitted from my version, strode onto the stage as a Glasgow dwarf, all serpentine metal and valves. This the Venetians could not stomach. They booed the American tenor, since, very appropriately, he did not indulge in oleaginous *bel canto*. This reaction could have been expected all over the peninsula, but this was winter, the Venetians drank, and in the bar next to the Fenice I heard the mutters of impending violence against my person. I was responsible for sullying their Fenice with improper art. The Venetians are a proud people.

And conservative, not only in music. It is difficult to reconcile conservatism with the bizarre geography of a water city, in which, when not rocking on a canal, one is going up and down over little bridges over canals. ("*Su e zo*" is the Venetian version of "up and down"—it sounds more like it than the Tuscan "*su e giu.*") But conservatism is an aspect of profound devotion to commerce. Venice has always been concerned with making money. *The Merchant of Venice* is a pleonastic title: it is like *The Film Star of Hollywood*. Money meant Jews and a ghetto: Shakespeare got it right. Big business—factories at Mestre, marine insurance—keeps in the background; small business is all around you—glass, textiles, fine printing. Venice has produced a lot of great art, but for no primary aesthetic motive. It has produced great architecture too, apparently in a fit of absent-mindedness. Palaces with their roots in deep water—if the architects had thought about it too much they couldn't have done it. We still need Canaletto to show us the beauty of the city. For the average Venetian it's just something that happens to be there.

And, of course, you have to be somehow outside the city to be aware of its beauty—outside physically and temperamentally. Being inside the city, especially in winter, is to be aware mainly of slopping around on waterlogged piazzas, making a wrong turn in deep night and finding oneself ready to plunge into a canal or a *rio*. With the chill in one's bones and varieties of grappa warring in one's stomach, Venice can deeply depress. One needs to get onto very dry land, which means taking a real, not water, taxi to Mestre, there to eat in one of the restaurants that Ezra Pound patronised. You are in northeast Italy, so you will eat *polenta* (a kind of maize pudding) with stewed rabbit, or else seafood, some of which has no English name and hence is suspect—things with legs and wiry whiskers, pulpy bodies enclosed in a hexagonal casing. There, in deep gloom alleviated by the grappa of the house, the landsmen (and there are more and more of them, former inhabitants of Serenissima who have got out) will foretell Venetian doom or demand that the Grand Canal be paved over. That Venice is decaying and will need national money to be patched up is a fact too well known. The one-third of the population that relies on tourism is resting from the American flux and getting ready to welcome it again. But these visitors are there for the old and the quaint, not for the thriving modern. The knowledge that one is old, not to say ancient, induces gloom.

I was strongly conscious of the impropriety of imposing plans for a great new modernistic Europe (dry land from John o' Groats to Syracuse) in a February Venice some four years ago. In the great baroque building of San Giorgio, a relic of the past *in excelsis*, I had to speak at a conference organised by the European Parliament on the problem of a common language for Europe. I intended to plead the cause of Latin, and the malignant spirit of modernity was determined to punish me for this. I appeared on a television programme in Hamburg, flew to Munich, and then, in a flimsy buffeted craft, got to rainy, squally Venice. Lufthansa, with unheard of inefficiency, lost my bag on the way. I was sick in the *motoscafo* crossing the lagoon, lost my lire stepping out at San Giorgio, and then had to type out my speech with carbons (the copying machine having broken down) for the benefit of the simultaneous translators. I had no hotel booking, and only a ramshackle bughouse was willing to take me. I had no money for dinner, so I starved.

The next day, breakfastless, I spoke as eloquently as I could on behalf of a resuscitated Latin. The French were appalled. They had no doubt about what was already the pan-European language. I was cold-shouldered and ate my buffet lunch in an enclosure of human backs. With difficulty I got a rail ticket back to Monte Carlo via Milan. On the train I saw my photograph in the Venetian papers, looking crapulous or lagoon-sick, with ribald comments on my demented linguistic proposal. Reconstruction work at Milan's main station entailed changing trains somewhere in the remote suburbs. I got to Ventimilia too late for a Monte Carlo connection. I had no money for a hotel so slept in the vast cold fascistic concourse. I got home, aware that I had been soundly scolded for daring to talk about a European future in a city that looked towards the European past. In Venice you must not take the future seriously at all. I had learned at least that lesson.

The great city is an astonishing monument to human imagination and ingenuity. But these are properties that belong to a civilisation long gone, deeply buried under the filth of the lagoons. It is no accident that great men go to Venice to die, not to be reborn. Thomas Mann's Aschenbach (ash and water) is their archetype. Wagner died there, so did Ezra Pound, so does the military hero of Hemingway's *Across the River and into the Trees*. They die surrounded by dreams of ancient glory that sprang out of a historical nightmare. The hero of *Don't Look Now*, having foreseen his own water funeral, is stabbed by a dwarf in the winter dark. It is perhaps best, after all, to be assured of the continuation of life somewhere else among the fat-bottomed camera-clickers of the tourist season. Off-season Venice is full of ghosts, and perhaps one of them, sidestepping time, is one's own.

—1989

MANCHESTER AS WAS

❖

I was born in Harpurhey in 1917, on the day when food rationing very belatedly came into force. Then I lived in a pub in Miles Platting before emigrating to the area that I consider to be very much mine—the place where I suffered pubescence, learned about sex, dimly descried my future as a writer. I mean Moss Side. Alas, it has ceased to bear any trace of my occupancy. The small tobacconist's shop at 21 Princess Road, the larger wholesale one up the street at No. 47, the off-licence at 261 Moss Lane East (which became a West Indian shebeen)—all are gone. This wiping out of one's youth is intolerable, but so is the conversion of a once leafy commercially prosperous district into what has been termed the Bronx of Manchester. The law of life seems to be that things don't get better, that deterioration is an eternal fact. But, looking at other aspects of Manchester, I see that this is not true. A great deal has improved since my youth. But, for the moment, I'm gloomily stuck in Moss Side.

When I lived at the corner of Moss Lane East and Lincroft Street, I used to catch the bus to Rusholme at a stop called Holy Corner, since there were three churches there. These, naturally, have disappeared, along with the trees that waved about them. Rusholme was a very respectable area. Here was the Repertory Theatre where Wendy Hiller and Robert Donat learned their craft; here were decent shops and tea-rooms with refined waitresses. Here was my school, the Xaverian College in Victoria Park, and also the Catholic church I sometimes attended, St. Edward's. This was very much a cut below the Holy Name, on Oxford Road, near to the University, where the priests had Noel Coward accents and the May Sunday crowning of the May Queen was a triumph of floral paganism. The Muslims have taken over Rusholme. The shops, which blazon names like Muhammed Ali and Omar Saifuddin, are indistinguishable from the ones I knew in Malaya. Ought one to regret this building of a multicultural society?

Manchester in my youth was very selectively cosmopolitan. There was no flaunting of the banners of Islam. At the University and in the technical institutes there were Japanese and Indians learning the useful arts of the West, medicine and cotton spinning. On Oxford Road, just opposite the University, an Indian restaurant opened called the Koh-i-Noor. This was rare, and girl undergraduates were frightened of going in unaccompanied by rugger players. Foreigners were not expected to be permanencies. An old lady who came to our off-licence for a noggin of gin once saw a black man on the street—collared and tied and scholarly—and said, "They scare the daylights out of me. They ought to be kept in their own country." Manchester was not really xenophobic, but in the Cheetham Hill area there could be sporadic antisemitism. It is all there in Louis Golding's *Magnolia Street*. But to be antisemitic was a lower-class disease; the educated element of the city knew how much, in terms of music, drama, and the upkeep of libraries, Manchester owed to the Jews.

It was, I suppose, an ugly city, and the aesthetic blindness of the prosperous Victorians is still preserved in the Town Hall. This blindness, and a concomitant deafness, did not apply to the arts. I remember the Hallé Orchestra and cannot believe that its present bisexual virtuosity has made it more outstanding than when it was beery, all-male, and desperately conservative. I was ashamed when Pierre Ansermet, as a visiting conductor, had to make it begin Debussy's *Images* again after a false start. The Hallé was always promising us Stravinsky's *Le Sacre du Printemps*, but its heart always failed when it approached that difficult score. Nowadays, of course, any youth orchestra can perform it yawning. But nothing could surpass the Hallé when it came to the traditional repertoire—the three B's, to which a fourth, Berlioz, had to be added because of Sir Hamilton Harty's immense love of the wayward Frenchman. I can still smell the pungency of the old Free Trade Hall, the odour of whose heating vents was reproduced for me in the aroma of Frazer and Neave's tonic water in Singapore.

If the Alley Band, as Joe Toole, Manchester's greatest Lord Mayor, used to call it, was flawed by a fear of the new, this could

not be said of theatregoers either at the Opera House or the Rusholme Rep. It was well known that Manchester could be trusted
with expensive, and possibly dangerous, premieres. Noel Coward's musicals always had their try-out at the Opera House; some
songs of Rodgers and Hart, and of Cole Porter, were heard in
Manchester before they got to Broadway. At the Rusholme Rep
I remember seeing—perhaps for three pence, certainly for no
more than sixpence—Eugene O'Neill's *Strange Interlude*, Elmer
Rice's *The Adding Machine* and Karel Capek's *R.U.R. (Rossum's
Universal Robots)*. Manchester had, of course, heralded the birth
of a new English drama, much influenced by Ibsen, in Miss Horniman's productions at the Gaiety Theatre. The tradition of dramatic novelty continues, but the venues have changed.

In my youth I saw the erection of what is still an astonishingly
elegant monument to culture: the Reference Library in St. Peter's
Square. This, to many of us struggling students of the pre-war
age, was the provincial equivalent of the British Museum Reading
Room. Here I wrestled unsuccessfully with Sanskrit, read books
on James Joyce (*Ulysses* was not yet available), and found cribs
for my Latin unseens. Opposite there stood, and still stands,
though under a different name, one of the finest hotels in Europe.
The Midland has become, God help us, a Holiday Inn, but it has
not yet been rationalised and Americanised. The French restaurant is still there. Coming out of the Reference Library, I would
express blasphemous envy of those who could afford to enter in.

As I remember, the Mancunians of the 1930s were a blasphemous and envious lot. This was the time of the Great Depression,
no mere recession, when malnutrition forbade physical violence
but provoked profound hopelessness. The unemployed fulfilled
T. S. Eliot's prophecy: "In this land there shall be one cigarette
between two men" (if they were lucky). But a theatrical instinct,
natural to the North, would sometimes prevail. The workless
would march in tattered pierrot costume, blowing popular tunes
on kazoos (a kind of refined comb-and-paper instrument shaped
like a miniature submarine), while a girl from a school of acrobatic dancing would turn cartwheels in the van. You could see
the signs of near-starvation in the hollow cheeks—half an egg a
week, a fourpenny tin of Japanese salmon, a loaf of the day before
yesterday. You can see the difference now, especially in the clear-

complexioned daughters of Manchester, long-stemmed when they used to be stunted.

Mancunians would, as I remember, eat well when they could afford to. There was always a tradition that the South ate badly, that tea meant a weak pot and half a tomato. The restaurants of my youth, especially those of the U.C.P. or United Cattle Products organisation, provided dishes you never saw in the South, mostly based on tripe, cowheel, and bull's blood. The South would faint at the sight of black puddings lovingly polished with olive oil. There was never any dish like the Lancashire hotpot, which we old Catholic families used to eat as soon as the clock struck in the New Year (December 31, a vigil before the feast of the Circumcision of the Lord, was a day of enforced abstinence from meat). It is still worth travelling to Manchester merely to eat of the roasts of the buffet in the Midland. Hotpot is reserved for the Lowry Bar. Manchester is not quite the city I knew as a boy. It is prouder, cleaner, more elegant, and it is quite certain that it has a future. In my youth there were philosophical doubts; but optimism kept breaking in. The Luftwaffe tried, but Manchester has proved unkillable.

—1993

In Our Time
(and Other Reflections)

These dozen representative articles and essays prove Burgess to be an incisive and original chronicler of the world he lived in, ready to speculate on any topic that crossed his mind, or on any challenge or question a newspaper or magazine editor happened to toss in his direction. Though the essays range freely through a number of miscellaneous subjects, certain dominant Burgess themes will be recognized by any reader familiar with the major fiction: exile and the modern writer; the nature and need of comedy (including the odd prejudices and fashions that all too often absurdly rule the day); and the fascination most of us share concerning those men and women we find constantly in the public eye because of the enormous wordly power and influence they wield or exemplify ("The Royals," "Thoughts on the Thatcher Decade," and "God and God's Voices").

CUT OFF

❖

When, as now, I sit down to write, I know I'm living abroad. My typewriter is a Continental one. I don't have to ink in accents on words like *café* and *rôle* and expressions like *plus ça change* and *tête à tête*. If I could understand the French or Italian instructions for activating a word processor I would not be using a typewriter at all, however. Living abroad locks me into the technological past. It also imprisons me in another kind of past—the Britain I knew when I left it in 1968. When I pay brief visits to London I come as a foreigner, unhandy with the coinage and angry at licensing hours. But I also come as an Englishman fossilised in 1968. Everything is too expensive and women swear too much. On one of my visits last year I heard a very young girl on television asking a very old man what it was like living in the sixties. (Thinking she meant the 1860s, he politely disclaimed direct knowledge.) I could have talked to her for hours about that tinselly decade; it is the seventies and eighties that cause me trouble.

When I see commercial hoardings like MILK DELIVERS BOTTLE, then I know I have become a Martian. I do not know TV personalities and minor politicians. I am totally unqualified to purvey the kind of gossipy journalism that assumes acquaintance with names like Terry Wogan and Anna Ford, whoever they are. But, remembering that Virginia Woolf said that the novel-form was more gossip and tittle-tattle than art, I have to wonder how qualified I am, in my exile, to be a novelist. Novels, which I have to write in order to live, are supposed to be brief or not so brief chronicles of the novelist's own time, society, culture, manners, and, above all, speech. Cut off from these, how can I practise my craft?

Well, I can always write in French, which is what the Irishman Samuel Beckett does, and make my locale France. But I cannot cope with either the language, the ambiance, as well as the French.

95

I could turn myself into a historical novelist and write about lust in Restoration England, but that is a kind of cheating. We rely on novelists to tell us, more truthfully than newspapers, what it was like living in a particular epoch and how people spoke then, and the epoch and speech must be what the novelist's eye and ear were able directly to record. I can write about those fabulous sixties, of course, but the sixties are history and demand historical reconstruction. It is now, this moment, two o'clock in the afternoon of January 12, 1984, that demands to be turned into fiction and, through the magic of the craft, to become more real than reality. I can take the place where I am at this moment—a point on the Côte d'Azur—but they don't speak English here and I write for what the Francophones call Anglophones. The real British 1984, as opposed to the Orwell one, has to be a closed book to me.

On the other hand, one of the reasons why I went to live abroad in the first place was to put distance between myself and my subject matter. Only distance can help you to learn what is worthy of being recorked and what is not. Some things are worthy of the journalistic record, but the journalistic record is itself ephemeral and passes as Terry Wogan (whoever he is) must pass. The novel demands something more substantial, and there is much to be said for letting distance—both spatial and temporal—sift your material for you. It will always be unwise to put a scene in a novel in which the characters watch *Coronation Street* or go to the theatre to see *The Mouse Trap*. Probably *Coronation Street* will still be going on when the novel itself has been long pulped, but that is not the point. You have to think of a vague posterity in which only things like *Hamlet* and Beethoven's Ninth have lasted and *Coronation Street* has to be explained in anthropological terms. It is best to invent something for your characters to watch on television. It is best, sometimes, even to invent the kind of colloquial your characters speak. That can date terribly.

I was aware of this in 1960 when I was writing a squib called *A Clockwork Orange*. This was a kind of horrific confession of crime and punishment put in the mouth of a teenager of the period. But, writing it, using the teenage slang of the time, I saw how terribly ephemeral that slang was. It takes a year to convert a typescript into a book, and my slang would be dead by the time the book appeared. So I invented a slang that, being an invention, would not be subject to time's ravages.

Graham Greene lives in Antibes but insists on writing about life in contemporary England. In *The Human Factor* he placed an ABC tea shop on the Strand, which research discloses not to be there; he also put carrots into a Lancashire hotpot; he also made a bigger thing of Maltesers than contemporary tastebuds might allow. These are errors of exile. James Joyce, whose exile started at the beginning of his artistic career and lasted till his death, was wise to place the events of *Ulysses* in 1904, a year in which he directly knew the Dublin which is the setting. He couldn't deal with the Dublin of 1914, the year he started writing the work. He could only get away with presenting the Dublin of 1922 by making a dream out of it and calling the dream *Finnegans Wake*.

If it is safe for the literary exile to write about the past, it ought to be even safer for him to write about the future. The trouble is that the future springs out of the present, and the present is what the expatriate novelist does not know. A few years ago I produced a brief novel called *1985* that is hopeless prophecy because it is so ignorant about what was going on in 1976—the year of writing it. I even put the Cherry Blossom Boot Polish factory in a future Chiswick, even though it was then already destined for liquidation. I married Prince Charles to a brunette, and I gave them a son named William (the first is a venial false prognostic, the second a mere lucky guess) and I made hopeless howlers about the way British workers now live, feeding them fish and chips when they now eat blinis and paella. And my 1985 dialogue has a fine antique 1968 ring. The fiction of hypothesis—the alternative present—is safer, but it is safer to leave it to Kingsley Amis, whose *The Alteration* has done the job once and forever.

While I envy Margaret Drabble's capacity for getting into fiction the world as it is now, or that portion of it which is at this moment, if not forever, England, and while I know that I will not bring out in 1985 a perfect fictional realisation of life in Hampstead in 1984, I think I was right to distance myself from the country which gives me my novelist's material. What I felt was happening to the British novel in 1968 is, I think, still happening: it is cosy and parochial, and it assumes that what is happening on Primrose Hill is of breathless interest to the rest of the world.

To judge from the best-seller lists, adultery among BBC producers does not appear to be all that fascinating even to those who buy novels in Primrose Hill bookshops. The novelist needs a bigger world than contemporary Britain; living abroad, he had a chance of finding it.

But living abroad is a kind of elected hardship for the writer: it is precisely the English cosiness he wants to avoid in his work that he misses in his daily life. He wants English sausages, Cheddar cheese, the benisons of British television. He does not evade income tax: no writer ever does, since tax is imposed wherever he publishes. Worst hardship of all, he misses his own language. Though he may think and write in English, he cannot avoid the corruption of that English by foreign elements. Talking to London today on the telephone, I was horrified to find myself using terms like *cadre* and *écarté*, not being able to find the English equivalents quickly enough. I have to think very hard these days before I write an English sentence on my Continental typewriter. But this desire to serve English literature by getting out of England is not well regarded by British authority. I note that exiled writers are not entitled to money from library loans. It's assumed that we have yachts and butlers, and don't need the odd extra copper.

There are good grounds for supposing I was mistaken when I opted for permanent expatriation in 1968. If, like Great Britain herself, I thought it a good idea to get into Europe, I might have reflected that insularity may be one of the conditions of British strength—cultural or otherwise. Chaucer, Shakespeare, Milton, and Dickens were content to dip into British-made ink; why can't the rest of us? The rest of us mostly do; we expats are the eccentrics. But it's no use either boasting or whining. It's the work that counts, and whether it's produced by the Thames or the Mediterranean is neither here nor there. The author's agonies or elations are impertinent, like the make of writing machine that he uses. Where I get my cedillas and circonflexes is my own affair.

—1984

THE ROYALS

❖

The monarchies are, if we ignore sultans, rajas, and ayatollahs, these days concentrated in the North. This may have something to do with Nordic good sense, or the cool reactionary spirit, or the cold-bloodedness that abhors revolutions. But revolutions often produce dictators, who are nothing if they are not monarchs. More frequently they end up with liberal constitutions, or oligarchies, or republics with elective presidents. The essence of monarchy, so we are taught to believe, is familial continuity, figurehead rule, nominal headship of the executive, the mystique of very blue blood.

Holland, Britain, and Scandinavia have royal families and, while Franco ruled Spain, the generalisation about cool blood and blue blood was a plausible one. Now that Spain has a king again, it has to be scrapped. It was always scrappable anyway, since the Principality of Monaco has consistently resisted the republicanism of its great neighbour France, and that tiny monarchical enclave is southern enough. It will only be swallowed by France when it ceases to produce heirs to the throne. There's a provision for that eventuality in the complex codes which tie the two states together—but there is no evidence of sterility in the Grimaldi family.

I live in Monaco, which is not only a monarchy but a Catholic monarchy. The British Catholic family to which I belong has always been staunchly monarchist, but in a somewhat unreal and romantic manner. My father gave retrospective allegiance to James II, the last Catholic British king, supplanted in 1688 by a Protestant Dutchman, and he honoured the Stuart cause that, with the defeat of Bonnie Prince Charlie at Culloden, foundered in 1745. He, and his only son with him, have anomalously accepted the Hanoverian usurpation, chiefly because we have never been able to stomach the idea of a republic. A republic has overtones less of protestantism than of atheism, and it is better to have an illegitimate monarch than no monarch at all. I have in my time lived in republics—Malta, France, Italy, the United States—but always with a sense that I was betraying a family principle. I should properly live in Spain, but the same element of anomaly creeps in there. I am patriotic enough to have absorbed the English tradition of a Spanish tyranny presiding over an invincible Armada, of a Spanish king being more of an enemy than a Spanish Caudillo. This is unfair, but it is the way the Catholic English mind works. I am better off where I am, the adoptive subject of a small Catholic prince. And my Celtic blood goes on paying homage to the ghost of an admirable Irish Catholic princess from Philadelphia.

Still, Irish princesses seem to belong to operetta, and Latin Catholic monarchs are something of an anachronism. Royal blood goes with northern blood, and it presides most typically over states which have long accepted the Reformation. Scandinavia is royal. I have just returned from the three Scandinavian capitals and heard no whisper of republicanism. I have seen decent bourgeois royalty waving in a friendly manner to the decent bourgeois citizenry. You see no crowns or ermine, hear no silver trumpets. Assimilation of blue blood to red blood is total. Ordinariness is mandatory for today's royals. In Copenhagen I saw the altogether handsome and charming Margrethe II, Denmark's first reigning queen for 500 years, so popular that there is talk of converting the monarchy into a republic so that she can be its first president. In Oslo King Olav V was, perhaps for my benefit, keeping a low profile. But in Stockholm I saw King Carl XVI Gustaf, a mere boy of thirty-nine years, with his lovely wife and three adorable children, typical middle-class Swedes (though the family springs from Napoleon's General Bernadotte). King Carl Gustav has been explicit about his function—the mere figurehead of a ship, he says, a little obscured by the sea-mist of a traditional mystique.

I flew back from Stockholm to Nice via Amsterdam, to confirm that the royal family of the Netherlands is still around. I remember well the old queen, Wilhelmina, and recall her successor, Juliana, as a mere golden-haired princess visiting London for one of our royal weddings. Juliana abdicated in 1980. There was some dissatisfaction about the mercantile machinations of her consort

Prince Bernhard, and she herself was said to be obsessed by the occult. Her daughter Beatrix has a sunny smile and an unobtrusive personality. Holland's neighbour Belgium looks back to a certain murkiness in its recent royal record. Leopold III surrendered to the Germans in 1940. After the liberation of the country in 1944–45, he became the centre of controversy (could he be regarded as a collaborationist?) and abdicated in 1951. His son Baudouin took over his constitutional powers in 1950 as *le Prince Royal* and became king, at the age of 21, the year after. He married Fabiola de Mora y Aragòn in 1960, a Spanish aristocrat who was that royal rarity a noble intellectual. She wrote stories for children, which may be considered a literary pursuit.

If these northern territories can look back on uninterrupted royal lines—first genuinely monarchical in the sense of absolute rule, later limited and constitutional—the kingdom of Spain has a different story. Franco took power in 1939 as Caudillo or Head of State but in 1947 announced that Spain was once more a monarchy, with himself acting as regent till death or incapacity overtook him. This was wise. In Britain Oliver Cromwell had tried the experiment of passing on the dictatorial office to his son Richard, who was so incompetent that he was called Tumbledown Dick. A dictator is *sui generis*: rule may not be in the blood. It was sensible to prepare Spain for the resumption of monarchy, but the early days of his reign were turbulent for King Juan Carlos and disturbing for his queen Sophia. On the whole it may be said that he managed the time of transition well and has been discreet in his handling of Catalonian and Basque truculence. Spaniards tell me that he came to maturity early after his accidental shooting of his brother: an emotional crisis was very sensibly resolved. He remains a constitutional monarch with considerable personal power. But, knowing Spain as an ever potential hotbed of political turmoil, we can never say, as we can of her sister monarchies, that regal Spain is secure.

The securest throne seems to be that of my own country, the United Kingdom of Great Britain and Northern Ireland. It is secure now, but it was not always so. In the seventeenth century, with Cromwell's Commonwealth, an imperial greatness began which owed everything to the spirit of a vigorous Protestant republicanism. The German-speaking Hanoverians were notable for losing, rather than gaining, empire: George III threw America away. With the accession of Victoria, and especially with her marriage to a German prince, republican voices were heard again in the land, and, paradoxically, the Queen's popularity was only promoted by her withdrawal from public life throughout her long widowhood. She became a numinous absence who, in a multitude of minutes and memoranda and letters, controlled a growing empire and kept much of Europe in order. A dozen years after her death, as Bernard Shaw pointed out, Europe became a hell. She was a constitutional monarch, but, an archetypal mother, she had her own way. She demonstrated that, despite the restrictions placed on monarchical power in 1689, the British constitution was elastic enough to accommodate a benevolent matriarchal tyranny. That she had a long reign was much in her favour. To some of her subjects it must have seemed that Britain had always been Victorian and always would be.

Her descendants have been loved. The faults of her son Edward VII—wine, women, gorging, gambling—were accepted as manly traits. In 1935 George V was astonished at the burst of affection that greeted his jubilee. Edward VIII's abdication over a passion for an American divorcee, the accession of a brother, George VI, ungroomed for rule and hampered by an incurable stammer, hit the British in their tenderest sensibilities. The elected government seemed remote to the people, the Archbishop of Canterbury was shown up as a sanctimonious fraud, but the royal family was human, vulnerable, and, though it did little to be loved, claimed a great deal of love. Elizabeth II, coming to the throne as a mere girl, both excited the protective instinct of the British and seemed to stand for a new renaissance of energy. This last was illusory, and talk of a new Elizabethan age was mere pathetic sentimentality, but there was no longer any doubt about the value of the British monarchy.

The British have produced a superb literature but they are not very articulate. Unlike the French, they are not intellectual, and they trust feeling more than thought. Walter Bagehot said that the British are stupid, meaning that muddle and a kind of animal instinct have proved more reliable than Gallic intelligence. The French in 1940 followed the path of reason and gave in to the German invaders; the British stupidly fought on until the Russians and Americans both saved and destroyed the old Europe. The British Constitution is a good example of salvatory muddle. It has never been written down, and nobody knows—as Queen Victoria was shrewd enough to recognise—how far the monarchy can legitimately go in the government of the country. What the British are murkily aware of is the advantage of having a head of state who is not involved in politics. They know that their true rulers are a prime minister, a cabinet, and a party with a majority in the House of Commons, but they also know that parties come and go, while the monarchy goes on forever.

Presidents, they recognise, are at the mercy of party. The election of the head of state is part of a democratic process which entails the regular swing from one ideology to another. A president is committed to a one-sided philosophy, that of his party. Being a politician, he is corruptible. There was a time—that of the Georges—when the monarch was sweatily into politics, when the Tory party ensured the survival of the crown, and the Church of England—defined as the Tory party at prayer—sanctified a king who was nominally its head. That situation no longer exists. The Queen will, at the annual opening of parliament, refer to a Socialist government as "my government" and theoretically be willing to dissolve not only her House of Lords but her own office. This is the acme of incorruption.

What precisely is the job of the Queen? In the first place she has to hold the British Commonwealth together. Mrs. Thatcher has authority in the country that elected her to power, but her writ does not run in Canada, Australia, or New Zealand. They have their own elected governments, but they share a common nominal head of the executive—the Queen of Canada or Australia or New Zealand as well as of the United Kingdom. There have been republican movements in both Canada and Australia, but the level-headed have seen no advantage in adding the burden of an elected president to the existing mess of party politics. On her home ground, that of Buckingham Palace in the capital of the Commonwealth, the Queen has the duty of regular consultation with her prime minister, which can also mean the giving of advice. She has seen governments come and go and is highly qualified to speak out of her political—but non-party—experience.

But she has other, vaguer, functions which she shares with the rest of the family. Among these is the maintenance of moral standards which can roughly be termed Christian—though her subjects include Jews, Muslims, and atheists. Scandal must not touch the monarch, and it is a good thing not to allow scandal to touch her subjects either. Her family sometimes lets her down. The Queen's sister, Princess Margaret, has had turbulent love affairs, a notorious divorce, and an unseemly liaison with a man the country would deem unsuitable. The Queen's cousin, the Earl of Harewood, has had a divorce that involved scandal. And he, being a musician and an intellectual, confirmed something that the British have always suspected—that cleverness and immorality go together.

The British fear of cleverness set into a permanent political attitude at the beginning of this century, when the Tories, finding intellectuality in their opponents the Liberals, kept writers and thinkers away from their country house parties and London dinners. British intellectuals have ever since felt themselves to be shut out from the centres of power, and George Orwell saw that they cherished dreams of power in dangerous directions. A lot of our intellectuals, in fact, identified their fortunes with Soviet Russia; some even defected. Orwell's novel *Nineteen Eighty-Four* is a fantasy about disaffected journalists, novelists, poets, professors, and schoolmasters imposing an idealistic philosophy on the countries of the West—amalgamated into the superpower Oceania—which is no more than a notion of the nature of reality forged in an Oxford or Cambridge common room. Intellectuals are dangerous and are consistently left out of the royal honours list, that twice-yearly index of whom the establishment considers acceptable. Jockeys, disc-jockeys, footballers, and orchestral conductors get knighthoods, but very few writers or academics.

All royal families—not just the British one—have to be philistine. This is because the majority of their subjects are philistine too. The British Queen may go to an occasional opera, but only to doze off in the second act and be shaken by her consort whispering "Wakey wakey." She reads little except *Sporting Life* and Ruff's *Guide to the Turf*. This is regarded as proper, thoroughly democratic. Intellectuals may grumble about this, recalling the age of the first Elizabeth, a true intellectual but one with her feet on the ground. They must nevertheless accept that a democratic society can never feel safe with a royal family that discusses Kant and Hegel or reads Goethe and Henry James. It is better that they watch *Dallas* and *Dynasty* and go to the races. If one or two members of the family can be extroverted and athletic, so much the better. Princess Anne is a professional horsewoman. The fact that she has started writing articles for *Punch* need not disturb anyone too much. If she starts reviewing works of sociology for the *Times Literary Supplement*, then we will be right to smell danger. The ideal princess is she of Wales, the blonde Diana, who did not do too well at school but can be charming to coal miners and schoolchildren.

How much power is vested in the royal family? Hardly any true political power, but a great deal of social clout. When I was serving in Brunei as a colonial officer, the Duke of Edinburgh came to visit us. A garden party was held to which my wife and I, and the rest of the British community, were invited. The Duke asked how things were going in the protectorate, and most of the ladies simpered and said "Fine, your highness." My wife, being Welsh and given to truculence, said "No, things are not bloody well fine" and gave a list of discomforts and injustices. The Duke smiled at her naval language, but I knew our tenure in the territory was at an end. I was eased out of Brunei on medical grounds, and my wife went with me. When Princess Margaret visited Danny Kaye in his dressing-room at the London Palladium, he greeted her with "Hi, sugar." He never came to Britain again.

Democratic Americans, who would never dream of addressing President Reagan as Ron, seem to imagine that royalty is only a kind of fancy dress that it is a democratic duty to strip off. Princess Grace was still Grace Kelly to American visitors. Frank Sinatra, her friend and colleague, used to get into fights in Monte Carlo bars and telephone her with "Grace, ya gotta get me outa this." He said at her death that she was a born princess, but he didn't understand how she fitted into the constitution of the principality. Royalty has a subtle social function and demands that we be mature enough to play the great game of protocol. The British Queen, talking to one of her estate stewards at Sandringham, noticed that he leaned his arm on the mantelpiece. "I don't think you should do that in my presence," she said. She was right. On the other hand, when university students implausibly complained that her official visit was disrupting their studies, she offered no rebuke, sweetly smiled, and said she was glad they took their work so seriously. She recognised that there are some people who will never learn.

My view of the monarchy—that it is safer than republican democracy, that it sustains national continuity, and that it satisfies a hunger for glamour and charisma—is considered reactionary and old-fashioned by young revolutionaries and even by old Americans, but I notice that democratic journalism is not averse to playing up princesses rather more than politicians. This is especially true of the magazines of France, the mother of revolution, which cannot leave the Princess of Wales alone and has a whale of a time with our Monegascan *famille princière*. The paparazzi long to snap Princess Stéphanie bare-breasted or discover scandal in the decent marital life of Princess Caroline. Journalists love to invent scabrous sagas about failed royal marriages, always without evidence, relying on the tradition of royalty's neither confirming nor denying. It worries the republican press that royals should be less corrupt than politicians, and it will do anything to present them as worse than common clay. But the charisma holds. A kingly feast is better than a presidential one, and New York is full of Jewish princesses. Popular musicians and film stars are called Earl and Duke: you will never purge hereditary titles of their strange magic. America is, of course, welcome any time to return to the royal British embrace it so wantonly spurned. The hollow at the heart of republicanism is everywhere being disclosed. There is no shine like the shine of a royal crown.

—1985

ENGLAND IN EUROPE

❖

The history of England, from the time of the Roman occupation until twenty years ago, has been about the insistence of a very insular people on cutting itself off from the huge and dangerous continent that lies to its east and is separated from it by a mere twenty miles of sea. It has been invaded by Europeans—the legions of Claudius, the Danes, the Anglo-Saxons, the Normans—and its response to these invasions was always the attempt to Britannicise the invaders. England succeeded in turning the Danish king Cnut into a kind of Englishman; even the Normans brought by William the Conqueror forgot their native French and, with the help of the conquered Anglo-Saxons, created a hybrid language called English. Since 1066 there have been efforts at dragging England into Europe. The Spanish Armada, in the name of the Counter-Reformation, tried to restore a heretic people to the Catholic fold but failed. Napoleon failed too to weave England into the fabric of a continental system. Hitler's was the final failure. When England then perversely tried to enter Europe on its own initiative, it was Europe itself—in the person of General de Gaulle—that objected. But now England is regarded as European, and nearly two thousand years of resistance to the continental merger have come to an end.

A question that must be asked is: how European is England? I, as an Englishman, would reply: Hardly at all. The traditional enmity with France continues, and no country can be called European if it does not love France. The English drink French wine and enjoy the French cuisine but have no further knowledge of French culture. At Christmas they raid the supermarkets of Calais, using not one word of French. The French may be exploited, but they must not be trusted. When English football supporters raid Europe, as we saw in Brussels last summer, they leave a trail of corpses and drunken vomit. Europe to the English is despised foreign territory. This traditional attitude is endorsed by Mrs. Thatcher's government, which sees England's friends as residing across the Atlantic and not in Europe at all. Travel eastwards across Europe and you will eventually come to the Soviet bloc. Travel westwards and you will meet a powerful people that speaks English and has adopted an English form of democracy.

The problem of turning England into a European territory lies precisely in the truth that England has colonised huge tracts of land and sea far from Europe. America was an English colony, and now England is an American colony. Australia, Canada, and New Zealand and even the distant Falklands speak English, acknowledge an English queen, subscribe to a parliamentary system of government. England looks at Italy, Spain, and Germany, remembers that they abandoned democracy or never really knew it, and is wary of the rise of a new Hitler, Franco, or Mussolini. Even France, home of liberty, equality, and fraternity, failed to resist a totalitarian system and settled on becoming part of a Germanicised Europe. Meanwhile, the Soviet hunger for territory has swallowed half of Germany and the whole of the Balkans. Europe is not a unity: it is half Catholic and half communist. England likes neither faith.

The great English martyrs like Thomas à Becket and Sir Thomas More died for Europe. They wanted the centre of power to subsist at Rome. They did not like the prospect of an English church, mainly under the domination of the secular power, that should be cut off from the rest of Christendom. England became important and wealthy because it turned its back on Europe and sent out its ships to found English-speaking colonies. The imperialist ambition did not accord with the continental view of life. Protestantism itself—in both its Anglican and Puritan forms—was an aspect of the mercantilism that built an empire. The empire no longer exists, but the English language has been sown widely, and it is not a European language. Lacking grammar, it is closer to Chinese than to French or German. The English think they have enough literature of their own without having to seek it in Europe. It is the plenitude of their literature that helps to keep them insular.

The spirit of England is insular still. That is decreed by geography as well as history. When the Channel Tunnel—which has been discussed for at least a century—is eventually built, there will be plenty of Englishmen around to see in it an easy road for Napoleonic or Hitlerian invasion. The distrust, and even fear, of Europe continues. More than that, there is a conviction, typical of English pragmatism, that Europe is not a real unity and never will be. It can be unified by force, as by Napoleon or Hitler, but it can no longer claim a common culture. Part of it is Lutheran, part Calvinistic, part Catholic. And a very large part is communist. The situation of Switzerland, both European and not European, reminds the English that not even the continentals are sure about unity. Scandinavia, which has its own modes of unity, feels historically and temperamentally closer to England than its closest neighbour France. A common market is only one aspect of unity and it does not seem to work well. The real unity should be linguistic, religious, and cultural, and there is no hope of that coming about.

If Europe shares a culture with England, it is through America, with its supermarkets, its fast-food chains, its rock music, Coca-Cola, films, and television series like *Dallas* and *Dynasty*. Europe has to find its unifying systems outside Europe, and if it does not, rightly, wish to choose Soviet Russia it must go to America. But the notion of an internal unity is a mockery.

That unity once existed. It existed before Martin Luther nailed his ninety-two theses to the cathedral door of Wittenberg and John Calvin began to undermine the principles of free will. Mediaeval Europe was Christendom. Its territories were united by faith and the systems of faith—the monasteries, the Latin of the Mass, even modes of ecclesiastical architecture. Even the humanists of the early days of religious reform walked freely through Europe, speaking scholarly Latin and exchanging international ideas. There was, in those days, no strong sense of the importance of a nation. Bernard Shaw was perhaps right when he saw in Joan of Arc—rightly burned by the Church and wrongly, if belatedly, canonised—the first stirrings of nationalism and, with it, protestantism. It is hard to think of France abandoning her chauvinism or Germans in Munich beer cellars not drinking to the Fatherland.

We shall only see a united Europe when the whole continent subscribes to a common faith that is not consumerism and is willing to speak a common language. The English know this as well as any. They continue to play the game of being Europeans while buying Japanese electronics and American television serials. But— and who should know better, since they invented the games that Europeans play?—they know that it is no more than a game. Like all games, it will cease with the blowing of a whistle. Then the unruly crowds will erupt on to the pitch and start killing each other. For the history of Europe is the history of Europeans killing other Europeans.

—1985

AFTER THIS OUR EXILE

❖

This title comes from a prayer we used to say every day in the Catholic elementary school in Manchester. The prayer was addressed to the Virgin Mary: "Hail, Holy Queen, Mother of Mercy. Hail, our life, our sweetness and our hope. To thee do we cry, poor banished children of Eve; to thee do we send up our sighs, mourning and weeping in this vale of tears." Not a bad prayer, never forgotten, still capable of turning on the taps of a mixed emotion (self-pity, yearning, hope, despair). The prayer went on: "And after this, our exile, show unto us the blessed fruit of thy womb. . . ." We were told, by our teaching nuns, precisely what exile meant: being cut off from our real home, sent out into an alien world. Though born and living in Manchester, England, we were not supposed to feel really at home there. Nor, indeed, anywhere else. There was only one country we ought to feel loyal to, and, poor children of Eve, we'd been cast out of it.

Anybody brought up in England as a Catholic used to find it easy to accept the secular implications of this theme. England had broken away from Rome under Henry VIII, but some of us, especially those Catholics living in the Northwest, had remained loyal to Rome and hence, for a long time, were a sort of traitors. To honour the monarch was to honour the Church of England, which we could not do. My father accepted no king or queen later than James II, who'd tried to reimpose Catholicism on a Protestant England and ignominiously failed. In a sense we were exiles from a dead time which couldn't be restored. Historically we could accept that England had done the right thing in asserting its island nature and cutting itself off from the Continental system, but, in terms of the true faith, it had damned itself. Our patriotism was highly qualified. Our capital was not London but Rome, and our provinces were cities like Dublin and Paris, where you could hear the Angelus at noon and make the sign of the cross in public.

I say all this to exhibit the roots of a physical exile which, for me, began in 1968, when I sold everything up in England and went to live abroad. I was reviled for this in, I think, the *Daily Mirror*, which accused me of being a rat leaving a sinking ship. Rats, of course, are right to leave sinking ships if they can, but I was not a rat and Great Britain was not sinking any more than usual. The hypocritical thing is that it used to be not merely acceptable but even heroic to get out of Britain in the days when the Empire existed. England was a reasonable country to die in, but you were supposed to do your working and living in Tanganyika or Kuala Lumpur. When the Empire collapsed, everything changed, and going to live abroad meant avoiding income tax and bad weather, things which you can't, in fact, get away from wherever you go.

Before I made my painful decision to leave England, England had already habituated me to getting out of it. There was, first, World War Two, in which a vast number of young men and women were exiled to foreign theatres of war. There was, after that, the period in which the Empire was running down and it was regarded as meritorious to assist colonies and protectorates on the road to independence. I went to Malaya in 1954 and to Borneo in 1957 and, though I lived under the sun and did not pay British income tax, I was not thought to be evading mandatory hardships. It was only when I came back to England and tried to get a job that I discovered that there was, after all, a price to be paid even for expatriation in a noble cause. For experience overseas was not regarded as a qualification for a job at home. Home from Malaya in 1957, I had to go abroad again almost immediately. Home again in 1960, I had made the situation worse as regards trying to get another job. I failed, joined the unemployed, and have, in a sense, been one of them ever since. A free lance writer is, almost by definition, one of the jobless.

I stayed in England from 1960 on, writing furiously and trying to make a living out of words. I paid my taxes and my national insurance contributions. I probably worked too hard to have a good time, but I saw that a good time was possible in the swinging sixties. England, in retrospect, seems always to have been sunny then; sexy, too—the epoch of the miniskirt and the Profumo scandal. "You've never had it so good," said Harold Macmillan, and, by God, he was right. If I left England towards the end of the decade, it was not because I had a foreboding that the good times could not last. It was because, with the death of my first wife and remarriage to an Italian contessa of progressive views, I felt it was time to change my life. England had been too cosy, too easy to live in; I had been drowning in honey. The writer's life requires the jolts of fresh experience, and you can't get these from an occasional holiday on the Costa Brava. You have to get out altogether.

I'm speaking as a professional writer, not as a remittance man or a Gauguin revolting against the bourgeoisie. A lot of professional British writers manage to strike fire out of a British environment with great success, but that success is usually recorded by readers and critics who share that environment. The job of the serious writer is not to confirm readers and critics in their prejudices about what is or is not important. I saw the narrow insularity of British life when I got back from Borneo. People I met in pubs, when told where Borneo was, used to ask what kind of television programmes we had there. It struck me that you couldn't make literature out of suburban adultery, the mythology of television entertainers, or the assumption that certain sports and political figures are of shattering world importance. If I wanted to go on writing, I had to get out.

Of course, I'm prepared to be told, by those who read my work at all, that I wrote better when I was living in England. Possibly, but my own view was that I wasn't writing well enough to satisfy myself. My own view was that I needed exile—not exile to, but exile from. Exile I saw as essentially a negative condition.

Exile is not possible for most writers living in the Soviet bloc. Exile has always been theoretically possible for writers living in the Western democracies. Practically possible too, for people like Byron—just a matter of transporting a strongbox full of gold over the Channel. But we have learned to live in a world of currency restrictions that Mrs. Thatcher wisely got rid of but will undoubtedly come back with the next socialist government. In 1968, leaving Britain meant going to another kind of Britain—a place in the sterling area. I could choose between Malta and the West Indies. I chose Malta.

It was an unwise choice for a writer. I couldn't doubt that, in the manner of a good cradle Catholic, I had homed to a place where the Angelus clanged at noon and saints' days were celebrated with violence and fireworks. There were two archbishops and two cathedrals. Pope John XXIII had presided over a church reform which had killed the old universality of worship, and so, far from being at home, I found myself in very foreign territory when I went to mass for mass was said in the vernacular, meaning Maltese, a dialect of Arabic. God was called Allah and the season of Lent was known as Ramadan. This wouldn't do. I discovered also that a very oppressive kind of Catholicism ruled. I couldn't read the books I wanted, because there was a very rigorous censorship. Newspapers arrived with swimsuit advertisements cut out. I couldn't even correct my own proofs, which were regularly confiscated by a couple of ancient near-illiterates in a dark room in the post office in Valletta.

There ensued a very interesting phenomenon—exile from exile. Malta became a mere address. I lived and worked in Chapel Hill in North Carolina, Princeton in New Jersey, Minneapolis, New York. I travelled to New Zealand and Australia in order to get away from the place of exile I had deliberately chosen. I even visited England, meaning London.

On these visits I made a sad discovery. I was a stranger in the country that had begotten me. I knew the language well enough, except for new slang terms that had crept in during my absence, but I had forfeited the right to a home. I was a hotel-dweller. I had no local pub. Decimal coinage had come in, and I fumbled over my change. I didn't understand what people were laughing at when I watched a television comedy show. The newspapers were full of the names of politicians which meant nothing to me. I had turned into a foreigner who spoke English astonishingly well.

Back in Malta, I had to plot techniques for getting out of the damned place. I had become a *persona non grata* because of my complaints about censorship. I gave a lecture on pornography to what looked like a thousand nuns and priests, all of whom listened attentively but none of whom asked questions. I was a marked man. But, if I wanted to move, I could only move to some other place in the sterling area. My idea was to leap into Italy, but I couldn't buy lire. By smuggling dollar royalty cheques into the peninsula and paying them into the bank account of an ex-patriate American sculptor living near Rome, I somehow managed to set myself up on the lake of Bracciano. The Maltese government wouldn't allow me to sell my house: this was so they could more easily confiscate it. They confiscated it, and I screamed aloud in the international press. They deconfiscated it. But the house remains unsold, unlet, unlived in.

I lived for a time in the house in Bracciano, and also in a flat in Rome. This was fine. This was what exile should be all about. Writers are not easily acceptable to the great British public. When the proposal to give them a public library lending right came up, Miss Jennie Lee, Minister of Culture, said she would not countenance a scheme whereby rich authors became richer still (undoubtedly thinking of scribbling exiles in Rome). Another MP said that writing was an ignominious trade, scrawling away over the fire. The Romans did not consider it ignominious. They regarded the writer's trade as an honourable *mestiere*, like that of the faker of antique furniture or the illegal vendor of Etruscan pottery. So highly was I thought of as a writer that an ex-mafioso, former colleague of Lucky Luciano, came to me and asked me to ghost his autobiography. I did not dare refuse; I said I would think about it. Later he came along and warned me that my son was next on the kidnapping list, and that we'd better get the hell out. So we piled into the car and made our way over the border to Monaco. That is where I have been for the last ten years. That is where I am writing this.

I find that I have certain signposts of exile stuck all around the Mediterranean—the Malta house, the house in Bracciano, a little cottage in the Var, a house in Lugano in Switzerland, this third-floor flat. At this moment my wife is investigating the possibility of renting something on the *rez de chaussée* of an apartment block opposite: climbing three flights of stairs is becoming too much for me. All this sounds like wealth, but it is really improvidence. No serious writer these days makes much money, and Somerset Maugham, who lived up the road at Cap-Ferrat, was probably the last of the great exiled money-spinners. No writer can evade tax: he is taxed wherever he publishes, and I have poured money enough into the fiscs of the French, German, American, and Japanese governments. But I pay nothing to Great Britain, which has the good sense to see that it is wrong to pay anything to a country that is giving you nothing in return.

I look back now on eighteen continuous years of exile, and I wonder whether it has been worth it. Writers need light to write, and I have been granted more light by the Mediterranean sun than by the perpetually overcast skies of England. That certainly has made expatriation worthwhile. This writer likes to smoke, an infantile habit but unbreakable, and smoking is marginally cheaper here than with you. Drink is expensive everywhere, and the wine you buy in a British supermarket is probably better than the Provencal vinegar I get here. Gin and whisky are best bought at airports. The meat and vegetables are better in England than here, and you have two things which I miss inordinately—British cheeses and British sausages. I can get draught beer of a sort. It's no good saying I miss British pubs, because a pub is essentially a social centre, a locality where you're known, a *local*, and there's something to be said for sitting at an outdoor table over a coffee and cognac. But these are small matters. Living is for our servants, if we have any. How about work?

My work consists in the manipulation of the English language, and I have to admit that I labour under a considerable disadvantage there. For I don't hear much English these days, except over the telephone, and then it is usually American English. My wife speaks Italian and French, so does my son. When I write I'm always in danger of using an Italian or French word because the English one doesn't come quickly enough. I'm not in touch with the various ways in which British English is changing. I was puzzled by the London poster stating that "Milk Delivers Bottle," and I don't quite understand the new meaning given to "wanker." I have to rely, like any foreigner, on dictionaries of slang. The television I watch is in French and Italian (and pretty bad it is, compared to what you get over there). I have to hear Groucho Marx wisecracking in Tuscan and Humphrey Bogart speaking impeccable argot without a lisp. Gary Cooper comes into the Wild West saloon and says "*Ciao, ragazzi.*" Benny Hill, whom the French for some reason love, speaks something that sounds like Marsellais. So I no longer, when I write, feel able to tap the current of British speech. I can only write about the past and the future. On the other hand, I'm not tempted to think that Hampstead is the centre of the world and that the Booker Prize is important.

England seems to me to be rather provincial. And when Englishmen come over here on holiday, they exhibit a provinciality which makes me ashamed of my own country. Kids come into the cafés with motorcycle casques on which a swastika is painted large—it means nothing to them that they're whizzing through a country which knew Nazi occupation. The murderous Liverpudlians at Brussels are not typical: they're merely a spectacular exaggeration of the ignorant British tourist abroad. When I hear the obscenity, witness the vomiting, take in the British contempt for Europe, then I become very European. But I'm tied to a great insular language, am divided, not quite sure where I am. But, as a Catholic youth in Protestant Manchester, I was even less sure. I don't think I'll be coming home.

—1985

THOUGHTS ON TIME

❖

Writers like myself who dwell in Europe are sometimes awakened at three or four in the morning with calls from New York or Los Angeles. The caller rarely apologises, though he knows that it is broad daylight with him and interrupted sleep for the called. Americans, who contest the rule of the world with the Soviet Union, assume that they are in charge of Time. American Time is the only time. But there are at least three American Times, and the two great temporal contenders within the United States are the time of the East Coast and that of the Western seaboard. California wars with New York on the issue: 9 a.m. Los Angeles is true time, and 12 noon New York a pale imitation. New York time is also Washington time, if we mean the city of Washington. But the state of Washington, up in the Northwest, follows Pacific time. Time in America is a great nuisance. The states are united, but time is not and never will be. If you want to telephone for the right time in New York, you must dial NERVOUS. In Los Angeles you dial ULCERSS. Those codes indicate what time is doing to Americans.

In the nineteenth century the situation was worse. In 1870 a traveller from Washington D.C. to San Francisco would, if he set his watch in every town he passed through, have to set it over two hundred times. The American temporal chaos was mirrored all over the world. Each French city had its own local time, taken from solar readings. Time bowed down to space. The prospect of a united world, made possible with fast trains and steamships, was defeated by man's inability to have confidence in his pocket watch. The family clock on the wall told the time for the family. The town hall clock told the time for the town. But the clocks in other towns were strangers, even enemies. Something had to be done about universal time. Something was done in 1884.

In that year twenty-five countries sent representatives to the

Prime Meridian Conference in Washington D.C. Heated discussions were eventually resolved in a proposal that Greenwich, just outside London, should be accepted as the zero meridian. The length of the day was fixed—twenty-four hours for everyone—and the earth was carved into twenty-four time zones one hour apart. As we travel east we keep adding an hour. As we travel west we keep subtracting an hour. There comes a moment, in the blue Pacific, when we find the whole system crumbling into an anomaly. We lose a day or gain a day, depending on the direction in which we are travelling. Men may be rational, but time is not. Time still makes us nervous and gives us ulcers.

But the 1884 conference destroyed some of the grosser contradictions of time. It was intolerable that, in the world of the railway and the wireless telegraph, St. Petersburg should be one minute and 18.7 seconds ahead of Greenwich. Naturally, the chauvinistic French objected to the chronic hegemony of a British suburb and enthroned Paris time (which was the same as GMT) as the king of all clocks. Joseph Conrad wrote a novel entitled *The Secret Agent*, in which anarchists attempt to blow up the Observatory at Greenwich. This represented the anger of all who rebel against centralist enactments. Why should my cheap Ingersoll watch be considered wrong and the big clock at Greenwich be regarded as correct? The answer, which was slow to be universally accepted, was that time is a public institution, and we must all—whether we are kings, presidents, or garbage disposal operatives—bow down to it. Time, being above kings and presidents, must be God. The secret agents who wanted to destroy Greenwich were atheists.

Nevertheless, in time time was more or less accepted as an orderly world structure which the world had, for its own sake, to obey. What everybody agreed on was that time was an objective reality—something out there, not a ticking personal truth in the waistcoat pocket or a variable flow oozing through each individual brain. The subjective attitude to time is contained in such contradictory statements as "Time flies" and "Time hangs heavy." Time is the enemy: the British still say, when they want to know the time, "How's the enemy?" Time is also a friend: "Time heals all things." Such subjective fancies, it has always been felt, do not relate to real time but to an inner time which is a mere ghost. The real public objective thing out there has been accepted ever since the invention of the mechanical clock in the fourteenth century. Isaac Newton defined time in 1687: "Absolute, true, and mathematical time, of itself, and from its own nature, flows equally without relation to anything external." The enactments of the late nineteenth century confirmed this less in terms of science than of expediency.

And yet the great age of the world clock was also the age of the discovery that internal time, subjective time, was quite as real as what was decreed at the Greenwich Obervatory. Literature had always known about this double reality, but it had never been taken seriously. In the eighteenth century the mad Irishman Laurence Sterne produced the novel *Tristram Shandy*, still the most avant-garde book ever written. This is an exploration of private time. Time expands and contracts like a rubber band. A minute's thought can occupy thirty pages. But in that same century Immanuel Kant presented fixed and rigid time as one of the *a priori* categories of his system of thought. He seemed to speak for common sense as well as for metaphysics. It was the artists, trusting intuition, who saw how private time conflicted with public.

In the first great flush of the establishment of universal public time, there were certain works of the imagination which could not be dismissed as mad fantasies like Sterne's boisterous anti-novel, and these said something about the double reality of time. Oscar Wilde wrote *The Picture of Dorian Gray*, in which the hero transfers public time, as well as public morality, to his portrait while himself residing in a private time which is motionless. This private time is on view to the public, which is awed by the mystery of a beautiful young man who never grows old or ugly. Real or objective time, which is a record of decay and sin, is hidden away on a painted canvas. This may be considered a metaphysical novel, though a minor one. The true fictional philosophy of time appropriate to the new age is to be found in Marcel Proust.

A la recherche du temps perdu states in its very title that time is not a flow but a solidity. We seem to travel through time and lose the past as we approach the ever-receding future, but, says Proust, the past, though lost, is recoverable. We cannot recover it by thinking. It is there, hidden in the memory, waiting to emerge in the present through the operation of physical magic.

The young Marcel eats a cake dipped in tea, and a former occasion when he did the same thing returns unbidden, not with the faded flavour of old history but with the freshness of a present reality. Intangible experiences—a smell, a taste, the sound of a piece of music—will unlock the door to real time, not the evanescent flow of the philosophers or the clock-winders. In that lost time recovered paradise is to be found, and it is the only reality that matters.

Time is very much the material of the modern novel. Franz Kafka's heroes are psychotic, and much of the psychosis springs out of the sense that the clocks don't agree. The inner one rushes along at a demonic pace, while the outer one marches steadily. But both private time and public time are inhuman—one is a property of the devil, the other a mechanical abstraction. Time has nothing to say to humanity. James Joyce, who had the Irish humour of Laurence Sterne, made a joke out of time. In his *Ulysses*, the sixteen hours of 16 June 1904, in which Leopold Bloom wanders through Dublin, are at the same time the twenty years of the journey of Homer's Odysseus. The nine months of gestation are compressed into an hour of medical students' drunken banter, but the narrative, presenting a conspectus of English prose styles from Alfred the Great to Thomas Carlyle, expands them into a thousand years of history. When Bloom's wife Molly commits adultery, Bloom's watch stops: public time becomes irrelevant in the face of private ecstasy and family sin.

Nobody has to take literature as a guide to the nature of reality (though it might be better for us if we did). We prefer to listen to the philosophers, when we can understand them, and the early days of this time-oppressed century produced Henri Bergson, who attacked French Cartesianism with its logic and its solidities. He declared that nothing was solid or fixed, that duration—*durée*—is the sole truth, and, because it will not stay still, it is not to be analysed by techniques derived from space. What are our clocks and watches but solid chunks of space, daring to measure what is not spatial? Time was certainly subjective, a thing attached to an observer, but nonexistent outside that observer. This, of course, had its counterpart in the physics of Albert Einstein. Everything was relative, though the speed of light was a constant. If there was no solidity in time, there was none in space either.

Time and space were perhaps the same thing, and both were mysterious.

But there were men in newly made Soviet Russia who were very angry about the new concepts of time and space. In 1908, nine years before the Russian Revolution, Lenin prepared for the new Soviet materialism by writing a book about them. While the new scientists and philosophers were speculating that these were merely subjective phenomena, or aspects of human physiology, Lenin had to shout that time and space were objective realities, eternal realities. The nineteenth-century physics that underlay Karl Marx's politico-economic philosophy demanded this. Soviet Russia is thus, with an out-of-date system that interprets everything, including the nonexistent God, committed to living in the past. Its clocks are massive and its watches are heavy, and it fills space with the boots of the Red Army. It has cut itself off from the subtler realities.

But the subtler realities of time are inescapable. They are there in the cinema. Film can show time speeded up, slowed down, stilled into an eternal present, even reversed. We have to regard all this as reality, since to see is to believe. And the invention of the internal combustion engine was also a time-obsessed innovation, since it produced the modern preoccupation with speed, which may be defined as the traversal of maximum space in minimal time. Time was precious (the Americans said it was money) and it had to be saved. The obsession with time wrecked the *Titanic*. It produced new urban rhythms, it promoted new neuroses. New dynamic arts were needed. In 1912 Balla started to paint movement: he showed a dachshund scurrying after its mistress and looking like a centipede. But the cinema could show the real thing. Static art had to go the way of multiple perspective, which meant Cubism.

The American Professor Stephen Kern has called the Great War of 1914–1918 the Cubist War. Picasso claimed, when he saw a procession of camouflaged tanks, that the Cubists had invented camouflage, and he was right. The inventor of camouflage admired the Cubists and acknowledged his debt. Gertrude Stein said of the Great War: "Really the composition of this war, 1914–1918, was not the composition of all previous wars, the composition was not a composition in which there was one man in the centre surrounded by a lot of other men, but a composition that had neither a beginning nor an end, a composition of which one corner was as important as another, in fact the composition of Cubism." This was the answer of space to the new conceptions of time. Time itself could not afford to be subjective. Public time become a vital instrument of coordination. It was a war of railway timetables. For the first engagements in August 1914, about two million Frenchmen were deployed in 4,278 trains, and only nineteen ran late. The wristwatch, which before the war had been considered effeminate, became the badge of masculine leadership. "Synchronise your watches." And then over the top.

The Great War was a war of new viewpoints, including the air, and it seemed to justify the breakdown of the old public syntax of time and space. Only Cubism could show what war looked like: Picasso had the technique ready long before the events of Sarajevo. The technique was more valid than ever, twenty years later, when Guernica was bombed from the air. Art and war express the same *Zeitgeist*, but art is always well ahead. The experience of time during both the First and Second World Wars was of a new kind to the average participant, but painting and literature had foretold it. The start of battles had to rely on public time, but soldiers lived on inner time—the eternities of apprehension that were really only a minute long, the deserts of boredom, the terror that was outside time.

It was between the two world wars that thinkers and artists tried to recover that old philosophical view of time which had prevailed at the beginning of the century. Present time was a burden, and it might be possible to escape from it into past or future time—not with the uncontrollable magic of Proust's tea-soaked madeleine, but through techniques of meditation and intellectual manipulation. Nobody now took seriously H. G. Wells's Victorian fantasy *The Time Machine*, in which physical exploration of past or future time was possible on a kind of sophisticated bicycle, but the Wellsian explication of time as merely another dimension of space seemed plausible to some. Time was the fourth dimension. An object extends itself through three spatial dimensions—up, down, laterally—but it does not have instantaneous existence: it needs time to exist in. The notion of treating time as if it were merely another aspect of space was fascinating. One could time-travel, but not like Wells's hero. Time-travel was to be an experience of the mind.

British philosophy, which has always tended to the idealistic, seemed to confirm that public time was the illusion and mental time the reality. Professor McTaggart had taught this and had even propounded that there were three kinds of mental time—the dual, whose components were before and after; the triple, with yesterday, today, and tomorrow; and a kind of modified dual time, in which what comes after is altered by what comes before. The best example of this last is to be found in music. The last part of a Beethoven first movement is the same as the first part, but our experience of it is changed by what has happened in the middle. McTaggart did not, like Proust, teach that past time was recoverable. To him time was merely a point of view.

But the literal, physical, recoverability of past time seemed to be confirmed when a couple of respectable ladies from an Oxford women's college visited Versailles and found themselves transported back into the France of Louis XIV. They wrote a book about it called *An Adventure*, and a wide public took it seriously. It turned out eventually that the ladies had intruded on a historical pageant, and that the France of Louis XIV was merely being enacted by costumed amateurs, but the notion of travelling into the past was too fascinating an idea to let drop. Much more fascinating, however, was the conviction by the mathematician J. W. Dunne that one could travel into the future. He wrote a book called *An Experiment with Time,* in which he presented the theory of time as a kind of spatial landscape which we could not see as a whole because we lacked the cerebral aircraft for flying over it.

His view was that we could not see the future because we did not want to. Seeing the future is dangerous, as any fortune teller who uses the Tarot pack of cards for divination will confirm. Our deaths lie in the future, and it is better that we do not know the day or the hour. But, said J. W. Dunne, we sometimes see the future whether we like it or not. We see it regularly, though often in a distorted form, in our dreams. He got into the habit of noting his dreams in a bedside notebook, and concluded that many of them used future material as much as fragments of past experience. In dreams, he said, we were not constricted by the temporal habits of daily life, which insists that we keep our eyes on the past and walk into the future backwards. In dreams we are mentally free, and part of this freedom permits us to see the future.

His theory is not to be lightly discounted. Not all our dreams are Freudian. Indeed, I sometimes dream that Dr. Freud is explaining to me the dream of which he is a component. Often our dreams, which are baffling to us when we awake, can be explained only by waiting for the future. If I may give what I think is a cogent example from my own experience, I dreamed some months ago that I was giving a lecture on John Ruskin and I concluded by affirming that Ruskin's great tragedy was that he turned literally into an elephant. The dream was vivid, brightly lighted, and full of circumstantial detail. But it was only explained a month later when, in the apartment of a friend in Milan, I saw engravings of Siamese elephant gods on the wall and, on a table, a new biography of John Ruskin. Two images had coalesced and turned themselves into a dream narrative. But both the images belonged to future time. I can give other examples. J. W. Dunne's book gives enough to convince the reader that there is something in his theory.

It was a theory that had some influence on the British literature of the 1930s, especially the drama. The play *Berkeley Square*, based on Henry James's story "A Sense of the Past," was about a modern young man finding himself transported to the eighteenth century. J. B. Priestly wrote three "time plays"—*Time and the Conways, Dangerous Corner* and *I Have Been Here Before*—which play with time entertainingly but not, to the common-sense mind, convincingly. The important thing about this aspect of the transient culture of the post- and pre-war period is that there was a hunger to get away from the present—to fly from the wrath to come either into the past or the remote future. But we now accept that time is not, after all, capable of such manipulation.

But it remains a mystery. We live happily enough with our two modes of time—the inner one, flexible and fantastic, and the outer one of the digital clock—and we recognise that both have their own forms of validity. We recognise too that the time of the urban world is not the time of nature. Nature is cyclical, and spring returns. But the digital clock proclaims that time is linear and goes on and on till the death of mankind. That time is not a unity and not a philosophical necessity (as with Kant) is a truth we have learned to live with. Once there was a Big Bang, and time began, along with space. Time was born, as we were, and it is no more immortal than ourselves. Even Shakespeare said "Time must have a stop." But, long before Shakespeare, St. Augustine examined the triple time of tradition and concluded that it had no real existence. He said that the past did not exist, the future had not yet come into existence, and the present had no duration. Therefore time was a sham, and we had better start thinking about eternity.

Good advice. Listen to Beethoven and we enter eternity, though the playing time of the Ninth Symphony is given as fifty-five minutes. Make love and, as Cleopatra said, eternity is on our eyes and lips. Time is not the enemy. It does not make us grow old, and it does not kill us. Marilyn Monroe spoke a great truth shortly before her death: "Gravity gets us all in the end." Not time. Time merely looks on, indifferent. We should reciprocate by being indifferent to time. Except when we have an important appointment.

—1985

THE JEW AND THE JOKE

❖

No Jew would have the *chutzpah* to assert that the Jews actually invented humour, but, on the evidence of the names of the great modern comedians, they seem to have been preparing for several millennia to claim a monopoly of it. Look at some of these names: the Marx Brothers, Jack Benny, Eddie Cantor, Milton Berle, Sid Caesar, Shelley Berman, Danny Kaye, Lenny Bruce, Mort Sahl, Phil Silvers, Peter Sellers, Jerry Lewis, Mel Brooks, Bud Flanagan, Marty Feldman, Woody Allen. There are grounds for supposing that the great Gentiles—Charlie Chaplin, Buster Keaton, and Harold Lloyd—were funnier, but they were funny in a way that puts comparison out of order. For these were silent stars, not men of the word. When sound broke into the cinema, the first words— "You ain't heard nothing yet"—were entrusted to a Jew named Al Jolson. This was appropriate. The Jews are verbal to the point of being verbose.

The Jews wrote the best book of all time, still more of a best-seller than the Koran or the Book of Mormon, to say nothing of John le Carré's latest piece of overpraised nonsense. Not even the most ridently labile of its readers would claim that it is a funny book, but it is not always serious. It cannot resist wordplay, its rollcall of characters reads like the *dramatis personae* of a stage farce—Slitnose (Harumaph), Weasel (Hulda), Flea (Parosh), Mouth (Puah), Bent (Toah)—and it is crammed with irony. Hebrew loved puns, and the paranomastic tradition of the Old Testament sometimes gets into the New, though the more rigid Greek tries to fight it. The Church was founded on a pun. The greatest joke in all Christian history was the destruction of Jerusalem so that the Church could found its headquarters in the capital of paganism. It was a black and bitter joke, not untypical of Jehovah, who refuses to become a God of fair play despite all our deistic rationalism.

An American-Jewish musical based on Plautus, starring the late Zero Mostel, was called *A Funny Thing Happened on the Way to the Forum*. We are still waiting for a Broadway success called *A Funny Thing Happened on Mount Sinai*. We will probably never get an extravaganza about the funny thing that has happened since, belatedly, the Jews settled in their national home. Humour has disappeared from the Hebrew language. Israeli writers are not funny, whether they are writing novels, plays, or film scripts. The language, waving a national flag, takes itself seriously and also reminds its speakers that it is too holy to be messed about with. And the circumstances of Israeli daily life are so hilarious—meaning you have to laugh so as not to cry—that they upstage the art of the comedian. The following story is not, I think, meant to be funny. A contractor showed his friend a house he was erecting in Tel Aviv. "Do you know," he said proudly, "I've already let the third floor." The friend said: "But you haven't even finished building the second." To which the reply was: "I know, but it's the rental for the third which is paying for that."

Real Jewish humour belongs to the diaspora generically to the Ashkenazim, specifically to the *shtetl* and the *shtat*, the little poverty-stricken towns and villages of Poland and Russia. Its language is not Hebrew but Yiddish. With the Russian, Polish, and German pogroms and the mass emigrations to America—*die golderneh medineh*, later renamed *die gayische medineh*—the humour of Yiddish, found at its best in the work of Sholom Aleichem, travelled to New York, but Yiddish itself began to disappear. You can go to expensive schools in Manhattan to learn Yiddish as you learn Spanish, but English, the pale Galilean, has become the tongue of the prospering Jews. Yet English is always eager to be raped by other languages, and it has welcomed an incestuous coupling with Yiddish, incestuous because Yiddish, being a dialect of Low German, is a cousin of English and has the same family face and the same habits. The great humour of our day is the work of speakers, or writers, of Yidglish.

The humour is laconic and depends on stress and inversion. "My son-in-law he wants to be" is not meant to be funny, far from it, nor is "So go fight City Hall," but such Yidglish tropes reveal what was always latent in English and cause a shock of surprised recognition expressed in laughter. But the humour is not just a matter of language. It is mostly ironic, born of long tribulation, and its capacity for paradox and nonsense has, as Joseph Heller recognises in his *God Knows*, deep roots, Heller has Moses saying that some of God's commands don't make sense.

"Whoever said I was going to make sense?" answered God. "Show me where it says I have to make sense. I never promised sense. Sense, he wants yet. I'll give milk, I'll give honey. Not sense. Oh, Moses, Moses, why talk of sense? Your name is Greek and there hasn't even been a Greece yet. And you want sense. If you want to have sense, you can't have a religion."

"We don't have a religion."

"I'll give you one."

There is a story of a lady on a bus in Tel Aviv scolding her son in Yiddish. "Why don't you talk Hebrew to him?", says a fellow-passenger. "I talk to him in Yiddish," says the lady, "so he won't forget he's a Jew." Though Jewishness can get through, even, (though with some difficulty) in French, it is happiest with Yiddish or, failing that, Yidglish. But Yidglish has to be fed not merely with irritable stress and disdainful inversion; it has to be a home for the Yiddish untranslatables, of which already about five hundred have settled comfortably on the host-tongue. Erica Jong has one of her heroines suggesting to a reluctant boyfriend that they make love in a ship's synagogue, saying: "Anyone who stumbles in will think we're *davining*." That word, derived from Hebrew, means praying, but *praying* does not have the right connotation. Gentile prayer is usually bland, quiet, and essentially private. Jewish *davining* can be noisy, disruptive, orgiastic. It can be rather like the act of sex.

We expect our comedians, Jewish or Gentile, to be male. But while God, tolerating Abraham's laughter, was not too happy about Sarah's, it is Jewish women, not *gaysiche* ones, who have asserted the right to challenge the male comedians on their own ground. Italian readers will be aware of the wit of the *New Yorker* writer Dorothy Parker, who called her pet canary Onan, because he spilled his seed on the ground. Her true name was Rothschild. She was writing in an age not favourable to the disclosure of Jewishness (Herbert Gold was asked to change his name to Gould when he offered his first book to a publisher, but he refused).

Then there was Fanny Brice, *née* Borach, reincarnated by Barbra Streisand in *Funny Girl*, and there is, though nobody is too happy about her, Joan Rivers, a comedienne who indulges in stomach-turning obscenity far worse than the well-remembered filth of the late Lenny Bruce. And how, apart from the endowment which enables Erica Jong to speak of "the rubber *yarmulke* of the dia-phragm," are these ladies Jewish? In possessing *chutzpah*, a pio-neering spirit, and a capacity for excess. There could have been, if Miriam had not been so grave an example to the Israelite women, a lot of comediennes to lighten the pain of the exodus. Nevertheless Miriam sang a good song, in belting Streisand style, on the safe side of the Nile.

Italians who want to master New York English had better learn the tropes and tricks of Yiddish. They should try expressions like "I need that like a *loch in kop*" (a hole in the head) or *Gewalt!*— the uttermost expression of disaster (obstetricians will ignore the screams of expectant mothers: it is only when they shout "*Ge-walt!*" that they will leap into action). Most of all they should learn the curious Yiddish trick of duplication, whereby Chianti is despised by being turned into "Chianti-shmianti—I prefer whisky." The best illustration of the usage is to be found in the response of the Jewish matron who was told by a psychiatrist that her son had an Oedipus complex. Her comment was "Oedipus Shmoedipus—what's it matter what he has so long as he loves his mother?"

—1986

THE BRITISH TEMPER

❖

I do not mean bad temper or good temper. I mean mental quality, mixture of elements, national disposition—all very vague terms. It's impossible to make an abstract summary of a race, even more so of a nation. The British used to be a sort of race, but now they're a nation of many races—Irish, Cornish, Welsh, Anglo-Saxon, Jute, Norman, Manx, West Indian black, Tamil, Bengali, Singhaiese, Sikh, you name it. The Nazis made the mistake of trying to identify race and nation. This meant killing off the Jews, many of whom were more genuinely German than Hitler, who was an Austrian. The strength of a nation, as America shows, lies in its capacity to bind racial diversity into a cultural unity. And by cultural we don't mean Covent Garden and Virginia Woolf. We mean what we eat, how we respond to stimuli, how we behave, the games we play—the whole pattern of social existence.

I was going to suggest that one could define a Briton as someone who has set up his home in Britain, but, considering my own situation, I find that will not do. I was born in Britain and have a British passport, but I have been living outside my native land for the last nineteen years. I don't have to excuse or explain this. A lot of Britons have lived outside Britain. Some were sent away in prison ships; others emigrated to earn a living or avoid religious persecution; yet others, in the days when we had an empire, were expected to go out and rule the natives. I had my own personal reasons, which are not historically significant. It is something of an advantage for me to able to assess my own people while living away from them. I see them more clearly when I come home on a visit through the mere fact of not being with them all day and every day. And, living as a guest of other nations—especially the French and the Italian—I am able to judge the British against the foil of peoples spectacularly, even comically, different.

The difference between the French and the British tempers is

almost too well known to recapitulate. The French call themselves
Cartesian rationalists, though many have never read René Descartes. This means that their approach to problems of politics,
economics, even *amour*, is highly logical. If an imported institution, such as a supermarket, seems to them reasonable and capable of being approached in mathematical terms, then they will
claim to have invented it. If patrons of a lunch counter are not
to be encouraged to stay too long and a degree of discomfort in
the bar stools helps to this end (a piece of American ingenuity),
then the French will make those bar stools excruciating, like an
operation for hemorrhoids. Things must be pushed to their logical
conclusion. It was logical, in 1940, to give in to the Germans.
The British, not being logical, did not think so. The British are
pragmatic, empirical. They do not like to think too much: too
much thought is dangerous.

It was Walter Bagehot who said that the British are stupid, and
that stupidity may well be their salvation. They blundered on im-
possibly from 1940 on against a superior enemy, to the amazement of logical occupied France, and they won through because
stupidity is, in real life as in fairy tales, often rewarded by the
goddess of luck, who despises the gods of reason. The British are
not intellectual, and they despise intellectuals who, in consequence, are careful not to call themselves that. The French admire
intellectuals. In Paris I have seen people, head high, walking into
the *Club des Intellectuels*. That could not happen in London, Edinburgh, Belfast, or Cardiff. We may find a kinder synonym for
stupidity and find it in reliance on instinct, an unconscious endowment of national wisdom, the lessons of history having sunk
in to the very bone. The French know their history in their heads;
the British in their fibres.

There is a very British quality known as fair play. This is almost
impossible to translate into French. It has nothing to do with
reason. A Swedish friend of mine, who lives in France but makes
television films for Stockholm, recently made a sixty-minute feature on this very theme. He interviewed Frenchmen who, though
they knew enough English at least to have met the term, could
not say what fair play was. They thought that, whatever it was,
it had to something to do with the failure of logic. It is logical to
kick a man when he is down, since he can't kick back. It is logical

not to feel compassion for condemned criminals. The logic of the law has put them behind bars: let them stay there; forget about them. Fair play has a great deal to do with feeling that law, meaning logic, cannot adequately deal with the human situation.

One sees fair play in action on British television, at the end of the local news. An old man complains, though without Gallic vigour, that he is going to lose his back garden because a new road is to be built in the vicinity. At once the advocates of fair play take up his cause and, with luck, the road-builders are compelled to make a costly deviation. The old man's chrysanthemums are saved. It was also on television, some years ago, that I met another aspect of fair play. I was on the panel of a word-game in which I had to guess the meaning of the term "trank." Unfortunately I knew the word and, perhaps stupidly, said so. I was shunned in the hospitality room afterwards and was never invited again. I had not played the game. Ignorance is a prized British virtue, though not a French one. Fair play ignores dictionaries as it ignores the law. There is nothing in the rules of cricket that says you may not catch the ball in your cap, but it is not fair play, or playing the game, to do so.

It may seem ironic to extol the British virtue of not kicking a man when he's down at a time when the British young are becoming notorious for putting the boot in. We do not like to think that the British are a violent nation, but there are historical grounds for believing that the prized British institutions—parliamentary democracy, the right to privacy, decency and gentleness—are the hard-won fruits of a struggle to control the violent impulses that once ravaged the British islands. When the British young become drunk or frustrated, they expend energy they have not been taught to use constructively in acts of aggression. It may, of course, be better to see this force at work in the private sector rather than harnessed by the state or by reactionary political parties anxious to take over the state. There is not much political violence in Britain. Even the mindless violence of Northern Ireland has more to do with lost and romantic historical causes than with the reality of politics.

It will not please radicals to be told that the great British virtues are best exhibited in the behaviour of the middle class, the major sector of British society and perhaps eventually, as in Scandinavia, to be identified with the nation itself. Even poets and painters belong to the middle class. I am always surprised, on visits to England, to see the good manners of queues at the bars in theatre and concert intervals. There is a fund of patience and philosophical resignation in the British that keeps them cool and makes them the best soldiers in the world. But there is a limit to patience. John Dryden rightly said "Beware the anger of a patient man." British anger is usually aroused by some manifestation of unfair play. They scent in bureaucracy a commitment to the rigid application of the law. In consequence British bureaucrats watch their step, go easy. Italian and French bureaucrats are different. Their police forces have not produced an analogue to the British bobby, who himself, alas, is increasingly becoming tainted by the Continental example. But he is still unarmed.

George Orwell, writing about the British in the late 1930s, saw no reason to neglect the trivialities of the life of the islanders, since these were part of the national culture and might have a deeper significance than was at first apparent. On coming to Britain and staying in hotels, I am glad to eat a British breakfast (one of the major importations into American culture). A Continental hotel offers me coffee and croissants, as does a Continental home, and I see in this insubstantial start to the day one of the reasons for French forenoon irritability. Starved all morning, the French taxi driver or post office clerk vents his liverishness on the clients. He then eats a too heavy lunch and his liverishness is enhanced. The British do not seem to have livers.

The British drink too much. This is one way of excusing ventures into aggression or even harmless theatricality which their normal demeanour, imposed by the habit of privacy of an island people, does not easily permit. The British seem cold to foreigners because coldness, which protects privacy, is the way of dwellers on a crowded island. The coldness is dissipated in the drama of drunkenness or in the sobriety of the drama. The British have produced the best plays and players in the world. At the moment French television is presenting weekly the BBC's integral Shakespeare series, in English with *sous-titres*, and the French I speak to are amazed at the skill and passion which actors no one has ever heard of consistently display. They might, on their visits to England, look with equal amazement on the acting abilities of

Britons who have never trodden a stage. For the British, being such a racial mixture, are unsure of their identities and have to find them by playing parts.

One reason why the British, for all their radical play-acting, do not wish altogether to be rid of the class system is because, as Bernard Shaw clearly saw in *Pygmalion*, that system expresses itself in the superficialies of speech and manners which, to the competent actor who lies below the surface of every Briton, are fairly easy of imitation. The class system has no longer a firm economic expression, it has little to do with castles and wide acres, and it presents mostly a fine opportunity for social comedy. Britain has the best con-men in the world.

Orwell saw that the British despised art but loved flowers. The French, being intellectuals given to dealing in abstractions, do not know the names of flowers, but they can give you a lecture on botany. Orwell saw in the middle-class cultivation of gardens a manifestation of love of the private life. It is eccentricity in the sense of getting out of the public circle. It is one of the British hobbies. The Anglo-Irishman I recently met outside Dublin who was papering the walls of his mouldering mansion with pages of *Finnegans Wake* (a book he did not propose reading) was in the British tradition. Hobbies, not art. Britain produces fine writers and is a haven for fine Continental musicians, but it does not call its artists *maestro* or *cher maître*. This is an aspect of its anti-intellectualism which may also be glossed as anti-professionalism.

We invent hovercrafts, jet propulsion, compact discs, and the Dolby system. We split atoms in the Cavendish laboratories with bits of string and sealing wax. When it comes to boosting our discoveries or selling our products a terrible shyness comes over us. On American television recently there was a news item about the quiet throw-away humour of British television commercials, highly praised by the presenter, who nevertheless had to say, "The British hate selling things." Government exhortations to British industry to display German or Japanese or American aggressiveness fail to understand the national temper. The British would rather disparage than praise their own products. They are committed to understatement. We may laugh sadly at wartime films about RAF heroism, soft-pedalled with "a potty little show but good fun really," but we are ruefully recognising the way we are.

Our aggression is reserved to the young who put the boot in but eventually grow up into exemplary law-abiders.

Those of us Britons who work in the arts, and find it is easier to do so in countries where we are called *maestro* and *cher maître*, have to deplore both the anti-intellectualism and anti-professionalism of our countrymen, but we realise that we can do little about it. I have sometimes inveighed against the Royal Family, which sleeps at the opera but is wide awake at Ascot, but it might be embarrassing to have a Queen who reads Kafka or a prince consort who can knowledgeably discuss early Schönberg. We will get no lead in what might be termed the continentalisation of Britain from either our legislature or our titular executive. We remain insular—Sikhs, Celts, Chinese, Anglo-Saxons, and all.

I see that I have presented the British temper from a very negative point of view. It seems that must be so, for it is easier to define a Briton in terms of what he is not—namely a Frenchman—than through positive attributes which he is not terribly willing to flaunt. The French, naturally, do not dwell on British virtues. In television commercials which, in advertising Twining's tea or somebody's brand of whisky, call for a representation of the provenance of these goods, they prefer venerable caricature of the officer class—a dinner-jacketed aristocrat sipping his tea while the house falls down or a bonny Scotsmen in kilts. They cling, as we do, to national stereotypes. They recognise a quality known as the British sense of humour, and they present every Sunday the Benny Hill show, translated into Parisian argot, which they doggedly try to appreciate. They do not understand the Donald MacGill logo which precedes it. But they think they understand British hypocrisy.

My wife, who is Italian but, like most Italians, loves England, affirms at least once a week that I, being British, am a hypocrite. I have to explain to her, with British patience, that hypocrisy is an aspect of both our theatricalism and our insularity. We have to present a front of virtue to the world while practising a secret life of mild vice in order to preserve our privacy. In other words, we're aware of the necessary division between the world of public values and that world of the individual which no moral system can define. We pretend to love animals but we hunt foxes. We pretend to be humane but we are the only nation that needs to have a Society for the Prevention of Cruelty to Children. We get readily drunk but we are moral enough to have licensing laws. This means that we recognise the necessity for public morality but, in our inner hearts, we know that this is always a sham. Nevertheless, we're too shyly taciturn to want to admit it. Without hypocrisy, however, we would not have been able to produce the greatest literature in the world. Think that over, and I don't just mean my wife.

—1987

THE WORLD DOESN'T LIKE GIPSIES

❖

It is a little over twenty years since my wife and I bought a Bedford Dormobile. This was the trade name for a vehicle of British manufacture meant to serve as a mobile home. The bodywork was of fibreglass, plain of appearance, not lacking elegance, giving the vehicle the look of a large ambulance. The interior was equipped for driving, cooking, eating, sleeping, living. By an ingenious adjustment of stout screens, the whole could be turned into two bedrooms which collapsed to form a dining room with a bar at one end. There was a cooker fuelled by butane gas, a sink into which water could be pumped from concealed tanks, and a secluded chemical toilet. There was ample cupboard space and a genuine wardrobe. The whole was a miracle of economy. My wife, son, and myself left England in this in the autumn of 1968 and travelled through France and Italy in it, coming finally to rest in Malta via Sicily. It was home. In some ways, it is the only home I have ever seriously acknowledged.

But it was not an address. Letters could not be delivered to it. To live a highly mobile life in it—Sicily to Malta to Africa: why not?—was to disobey the fundamental rule that is imposed on contemporary Western Man—the rule that insists we be static, findable, taxable. To live in a moving home was to sink to the level of the gipsy, and the world, however much it may poeticise the gipsy life and sing romantic songs about it, doesn't really like them. Hitler did not merely dislike them; he considered them a kind of Jew, despite their unimpeachable Aryan blood, and slaughtered them. They disobeyed all the Nazi laws, being free, not easily visited by the Gestapo or enrolled into the *Wehrmacht*, and hardly at all amenable to the tax authorities. A gipsy caravan carrying a swastika flag is hard to envisage. Their mobility and lack of the larger patriotism were their true sins.

The mere possession of a Bedford caravan turned my wife, my

son, and myself into lesser breeds, into honorary gipsies. No country in Europe has, to my knowledge, promulgated a law against the possession of a caravan, but there is no need of laws when the unwritten rules of social conformity prevail. There are garages, usually troglodytic, in all towns, but these are so constructed that they will not admit a vehicle of the height of a Bedford caravan. The caravan-owner is expected to drive his vehicle to a country site crammed with other caravans, the equivalent of the gipsy encampment. Caravans must not be seen among the parked Mercedes and BMWs. They are redolent of picnickers with brown bare legs and crumbs adhering to their beards. They sing unnervingly of the untidy *Wandervogel* and not the shaven citizen. They are not welcome in Milan. They are prohibited in Monte Carlo.

The saga of our Bedford Dormobile in the Principality of Monaco, where I carry a *carte de séjour* proclaiming me to be a privileged resident, is one of a mostly passive struggle against bourgeois conformity. There is no place in the territory where it can be parked; nevertheless we have parked it, since it is inconvenient to be driving it for twenty-four hours round and round a principality of highly limited space. There is no alternative to parking it illegally. It has been regularly towed away and reclaimed on the paying of an exorbitant fine. It hardly existed without an entourage of Monegascan police. Eventually, in despair, we drove it to the Var and parked it in the square of a French village. Placing it there entailed the somewhat expensive acquisition of a small house to justify our right to park. The right was, naturally, contested.

The poor vehicle has suffered from caravan-haters in the private as well as the public sector. In Italy sugar or water or a mixture of the two has been poured into the fuel tank. The virginal surface has been defaced, the doors forced open, pieces of clothing stolen, as well as books and highly personal correspondence. In despair we determined to give it up. But it is not possible to cast an imposing vehicle like the Bedford Dormobile on the garbage heap. Like any living citizen, perhaps more so, it is documented, and computers are always ready to regurgitate its considerable statistics. We left the caravan in a garage and stole away in our all-too-conformist Mercedes-Benz, hoping various conflicting things:

that it had found a good home, that it would be waiting for us some day, that it would be cannibalised to the limit, that it would disappear. But the data base of the Monaco Department of Motor Vehicles will not permit it to disappear. It exists as an agglomeration of numerical codes and, most importantly, as a number plate. Monaco number plates are, in the more barbarous regions of Europe, frequently stolen as souvenirs. This gives them a mystical value, and the Monaco Department of Motor Vehicles is fanatically devoted to them. It wants the number plate of our sequestered Dormobile. It will not license our conformist Mercedes for the new year without the delivery of that number plate. The trouble is that I have forgotten which garage holds it. Thus we, who were once so mobile, have been reduced to the utter limit of stasis.

This is a good example of the sly victory of conformism. It seems impossible nowadays to live the eccentric, or gipsy, life. And yet I look back to the autumn of 1968 as one of the healthiest, most productive, most essentially human episodes in my career. I was not wholly free, for I had the duty of hammering away at my typewriter every day, but what I wrote carried the breath of the open road. I woke early and retired with the sun. I had been reduced to something more elemental than a gipsy, to, in fact, an animal with claws that could write. Now I conform, cope with correspondence, am statically fixed at an address where the police and the tax-gatherer can find me. I cannot escape anymore, for I am denied the documentation by which the state accords a limited mobility. Hitler, so we are beginning to realise, merely enacted melodramatically what post-war democracy fulfills through the merely attritive techniques of the bureaucrat. Once the gipsies were brutally liquidated; now they are merely disappearing.

—1988

WHAT MAKES COMEDY COMIC?

❖

The film of Evelyn Waugh's novel *A Handful of Dust* is faithful to the original in its ending, which was seen some time ago in a brief television version which reminded us that Waugh originally intended it to stand on its own as a short story. The story of Tony Last, the small English squire who loses his wife to a nondescript bounder, finishes in great horror. Tony, lost in the Brazilian jungle, spends his days reading Dickens aloud to an illiterate halfcaste named Mr. Todd. There is no escape: if he refuses to read he starves. So horrible is this ending that some critics have imagined a reasonable sequel: Mr. Todd (whose name means death) is an old man and Tony is a young man, and some day the course of nature will spell release and a homeward trek. Indeed, since Waugh had already published this macabre episode in the United States as a separate story, he had been compelled to contrive a different, tamer, end for the American version of the book. Tony goes home to his estate and his wife and they live out mediocre loveless existences on their decaying country estate. Naturally, we all prefer the Todd horror, and there it is in the film.

It is a comic horror, and the reading of Dickens aloud forever is the product of an ingenious comic imagination. One is reminded that *comedy is more of a technique than a genre,* and it can square well enough with the macabre, or even the tragic. Not that tragedy as the Greeks knew it is a form much in evidence in today's literature or enacted drama. We use the term tragic very loosely, and our newspaper headlines are too ready to call a car accident, a plane crash, or the eruption of a nuclear power station a tragedy. The Greek word *tragoedia* properly concerns the sacrificial slaughter of a goat, and by extension it came to mean the downfall of a human being, usually of high estate, as a kind of sacrifice to divine justice. The downfall is not altogether imposed from outside, as death in an air crash is; there is an over-

141

bearingness, a lack of restraint, a failure to achieve self-knowledge in the tragic hero. The Greeks used the term *hubris*, defined as pride or arrogance, as the tragic human quality: it could properly only exist in a man of power, like Oedipus or Othello, and, since so few of our modern heroes are in positions of authority, they cannot suffer a tragic downfall. Theodore Dreiser's *An American Tragedy* was ill-named.

We cannot speak of tragic qualities, only of tragic careers, but we can use the opposed term comic to designate a quality in art, or in life for that matter, which induces a kind of shock, sometimes expressed in laughter, at the vision of incompatibilities in the world. The reading of Dickens is intended for pleasure, but Tony Last sees it as the main component of his jungle hell. The shock may produce a shudder in us, but it is a comic shudder. As a product of Lancashire, a county in the northwest of England which contains Liverpool and Manchester (despite the new administrative boundaries introduced by a British government with no sense of tradition), I was brought up on a kind of humour which can take death in its stride. I once had a female cousin who had been engaged to be married for twenty years (long engagements are not uncommon in Lancashire), and I wrote to felicitate her when she and her fiancé plucked up enough courage to tie the knot. I received a letter from her telling me that unfortunately her dear husband had died of a heart attack on the wedding night. The situation was not tragic (her dead husband was a dentist) and I conclude that it could only be comic. Unfeeling young man as I was, I even had to laugh. It was a question of the shock of incompatibles, the joys of the marital bed converted into their opposite, or a consummation turned into *consummatum est*. Many Lancashire jokes are about death, and, in some lower-class households, the decrepit great grandfather who proposes taking a walk as far as the churchyard is told: " 'Ardly worth yer while comin' back, is it?"

Sigmund Freud said that the comic was a great feature of the Jewish diaspora because it was the only way of reconciling a wretched life with the hope to which all mankind is entitled. The Jewish child who was sick of hearing about the children of Israel and asked "Didn't the grown ups do anything?" imparted a shock, the shock which always occurs when the metaphorical is stripped away to disclose the literal. Sometimes the shock is induced by a kind of logic that would have shocked Aristotle. The burdened wayfarer who was given a lift in a traveller's cart insisted on carrying his burden on his knees instead of throwing it into the cart-well: "It's good of you to schlepp me without schlepping my bag as well." The same logic is to be found in Irish situations which strike the outsider as comic. I was in a Cork hotel taking a bath when a knock at the door was followed by the announcement that there was a telegram for me. I asked that it be pushed under the door, but the hotel servant said this couldn't be done because the telegram was on a tray. He saw, rightly in a sense, that the telegram and the tray comprised a single object which had been entrusted to him, and the two items couldn't be separated.

Such situations are comic but they are not comedy. Comedy is a genre which may not contain the comic at all. There is not much of it in Dante's *Divine Comedy*, which is aptly titled because it has the happiest possible ending. I can think of only two comic lines, and one of them is absurd rather than comic. The terrible dog Cerberus barks *"Pepe Satan, Pepe Satan, aleppe,"* which means very little. The line *"Ed egli avea dal cul fatto trombetta"* is perhaps too disgusting to translate, very coarsely comic. The main plots of Shakespeare's comedies are not laughable, though the sub-plots are, meaning they are intended to provoke laughter. When the comic appears in Shakespeare's tragedies, it is not always recognised as such. The bloody sergeant at the beginning of *Macbeth*, who orates about Bellona's bridegroom, is near-fainting from his wounds and the incompatibility between his words and his condition must either convince the audience that the playwright doesn't know his job, or else excite them to laughter, which is probably in order. When we hear the lines "This my hand will rather/ The multitudinous seas incarnadine/ Making the green one red," there has to be intended comedy deriving from the rapport between actor and audience. The duller members of the audience don't quite understand the sesquipedalian line, so, in the next one, it's explained for them. We may have lost the capacity for this sudden switch. Finding the comic scene in *Antony and Cleopatra*, where the clown brings on the suicidal asp, rather tasteless, we have to reflect that Shakespeare is trying to let us down to the limit in order to elevate us to the utmost with the dénouement of his tragedy.

As that thundering line from *Macbeth* reminds us, there is a great deal of comic potential in the English language itself, and this is due to its juxtaposition of incompatibles or, to make it simpler, the consequence of the Norman Conquest of 1066. When English was pure Anglo-Saxon, with an admixture of Scandinavian elements that came from earlier conquests, it was not easy to be comic in it. Our earliest literature, which we have to read with a grammar book and a dictionary, is pretty grim, though there are some charming riddles. Once two disparate languages—one of Latin origin, the other Teutonic—began to jostle each other, it became possible to write the novels of P. G. Wodehouse. "My son likes to go round kissing girls" is not a comic statement, but "My son specialises in promiscuous osculation" may raise a titter. The conflict between the simple idea and the orotund rendering of it is the source of verbal comedy, or at least one of the sources. The elements of the mock epic begin to stir when the language of Cicero fecundates the tongue of the cowshed and the pigsty.

I think this mock-epic approach serves to explain the comedy of, say, Fielding's *Tom Jones*, where the very ordinary personages of the plot are often treated as if they were Homeric heroes. It is, of course, the essence of Joyce's *Ulysses* that there should be a relentless exploitation of an ordinary Dublin day in terms of epic. And, to return to Evelyn Waugh, the fun of his trilogy *Sword of Honour*, which is about the military snafus of World War Two as they strike the ordinary subaltern, is conveyed through language which, heavily Latinised or else drawing on the classical literary heritage which came in when Romanised Europe conquered Teutonic England, is rich in incompatibles. Or else there is a Gibbonian elegance, in itself classical, which raised the very ordinary to a kind of sublimity. Thus, Guy Crouchback, with Ian Kilbannock, enter Bellamy's Club at the height of the London blitz:

> In the front hall Job, the night-porter, greeted them with unnatural unction. He had had recourse to the bottle. His was a lonely and precarious post, hemmed in with plate glass. No one at that season grudged him his relaxation. Tonight he was acting—grossly over-acting—the part of a stage butler.

Jeeves, in other words. Jeeves, a mere servant, is the repository of the classic heritage, while his master is a kind of dispossessed nincompoop. You have to have, as in Evelyn Waugh, the aristocratic Norman element confronting the lower orders, but Wodehouse reverses reality. In America the opposed elements don't exist (in other words, America is democratic) so the comic has to be sought somewhere else. You find it frequently in the impact of an immigrant tongue on English (which one has to forget is itself an immigrant tongue). The fertilisation of English by Yiddish, which produces Yidglish, is perhaps the best source. But I don't think the class element comes into it. The assimilation of the Norman-Latin into British English has always been imperfect, which means that there can be a humour based on class-conflict. Americans do not seem to be aware of the conflict within the language itself, so that politicians can use big words without the fear of being laughed at. And there is nothing funny in the mingling of slang with technological language, as in "Now we zero in on the nitty-gritty of the problem of the differentiation between the phonemic and the allophonic."

But humour, or the comic, does best without language, as reshowings of Chaplin, Buster Keaton, and Laurel and Hardy movies continue to remind us. Why is Chaplin funny? Partly because of his recognition of class conflict, a very British importation into the United States. He carries the symbols of gentility—the bowler hat and cane—while living the life of a tramp. Buster Keaton, on the other hand, has no gentlemanly pretensions: he wants to succeed in the American way but is foiled by very un-American maladroitness. When he succeeds in succeeding, it is because his unconscious is allowed to take over (it is symbolised in the monkey of *The Cameraman*). Stan Laurel's British maladroitness confronts Oliver Hardy's desire for efficiency and order, which is very American. Italian versions of their talking films don't recognise the cultural difference and turn both into Englishmen talking Italian with a British grammar-school accent. Some of the point is thus missed, but Italians laugh just the same.

—1988

Thoughts on the Thatcher Decade

❖

In April 1979 I was privileged to receive from the fair hands of Mrs. Margaret Thatcher a cheque for £200 and a plastic plaque nominating me as Critic of the Year. This was at the Savoy Hotel in London, and, in a vigorous speech about the importance of freedom of the press, the new prime minister quoted liberally from one of my articles. That was the beginning and end of any contact between myself and the Iron Lady. I was living in Monaco at the time and still am. The political life of my native country has, for twenty years, been a somewhat remote and exotic affair. I have no political stance and can view the progress, or retrogress, of ten years of Thatcherism with a terrible objectivity.

Of course, it is dangerous to relate directly to Mrs. Thatcher's rule various phenomena I see on my infrequent visits to Great Britain. The advertisements on the hoardings are aggressive and vulgar. There is a good deal of physical aggression too. In 1979 Mrs. Thatcher's party complained that "the number of crimes in England and Wales is nearly half as much again as it was in 1973." Since then it has risen by another 40 per cent. The number of armed robberies has trebled. It is not Mrs. Thatcher's fault that supporters of the Liverpool football team have been responsible for two spectacular disasters. But violence is in the air and the stadia, as well as on the streets, and it can, perhaps fancifully, be considered an aspect of a philosophy of aggression. Get ahead, make money—that is the slogan of the prosperous Southeast. The unprosperous Northwest, where unemployment is the only thing that flourishes, feels frustrated. Liverpool is the major decayed city of the Northwest. Frustration has to find an outlet somehow.

While I, and others of my generation, were fighting Hitler, we were encouraged by a coalition government with a strong radical element in it to look forward to the building of a Welfare State. This was, at the end of the war, built slowly, painfully, and expensively. Mrs. Thatcher's aim has been its total dismantling. The State is not there to look after people. People must make money and learn to look after themselves. For those wretched citizens who cannot make money the outlook is bleak. The old, who are increasing in numbers, are a useless element in a society dedicated to the free play of the market. They cannot exactly be thrown on the scrapheap, but they can, and are, frequently blamed for indulging the wild dream that the State would look after them. If they die of malnutrition or hypothermia they are merely the unfortunate victims of a market economy.

In 1979, Mrs. Thatcher's party said: "The State takes too much of the nation's income. Its share must be steadily reduced." It is true that most British families now pay less in income tax than they did ten years ago, but they pay more in local government imposts, value added tax, and national insurance contributions. The total tax burden of the average family has risen from 35.1 per cent in 1978–1979 to 37.3 per cent in 1988–1989. But let us not talk of equality in this area. Incomes have risen faster in the South than in the North, and the rich have had far bigger tax outs than the poor. This is in accordance with a philosophy that rewards the makers of money. There is something criminal about being poor.

Some things cannot be considered in terms of a market economy, and the chief of these things is education. A recent report from Her Majesty's Inspectors of Schools laments that "many teachers feel their profession and its work are misjudged and seriously undervalued." This is inevitable when the ruling philosophy is utilitarian. Education is of little value unless, directly or indirectly, it leads to the expansion of the Gross National Product. Of what use is the study of history, philosophy, archaeology? There is a distinction between "training" and "education" that Mrs. Thatcher does not acknowledge. Education, we know, has always been useless in utilitarian terms. Training makes people into business executives and computer engineers, but it does not make them better educated. Mrs. Thatcher presumably sees no use in the teaching of moral values. There is little evidence in contemporary British life that it is considered better to help the sick and suffering than to kick them in the face.

Mrs. Thatcher is herself a notorious philistine. She is never to be seen at concerts, plays, or operas. She reads best-sellers. She recently confided with a kind of pride that she had just re-read *The Fourth Protocol* by Frederick Forsyth. Re-read, note. She is unintellectual. There is no poetry in her, as there was in Disraeli and Churchill. She has no music, unlike her predecessor Edward Heath. She has absolutely no sense of humour. She has no eloquence, only the capacity to rebuke and rail. But she thinks so highly of herself that she instinctively pluralises from "I" to "we." "We are a grandmother," she said. To a BBC reporter in Moscow she boasted: "We are in the fortunate position, in Britain, of being, as it were, the senior person in power." She promises to become a megalomaniac and, like all who are so afflicted, to have few grounds for this self-augmentation.

For how, with the Thatcherian philosophy, does Britain stand in the comity of industrial nations? When the Iron Lady came to power, the British inflation rate was 10.3 per cent, lower than that of America, France, and Italy. Ten years later it is eight per cent higher than that in any other industrial country. In 1978, Britain had a five billion pound trade surplus. Last year there was a fourteen billion pound deficit. As an industrial producer, Britain is just not competitive. Unit labour costs are too high. In 1986, productivity was 73 per cent higher in Japan, 106 per cent higher in West Germany, and 167 per cent higher in the United States.

I look back wryly, and so do many of my journalistic colleagues, to that April day in 1979 when Mrs. Thatcher was, in borrowed words, so eloquent in her laudation of a free press. In April 1989, the International Federation of Journalists accused her of a "systematic and extensive" effort to limit free reporting and free comment. It is probably in the area of televisual independence of governmental control that the grosser danger signals are being recorded, but this perhaps has less to do with the desire to muffle or muzzle than a manic devotion to the market. For the BBC is in peril, and the BBC, a free corporation that depends on a licensing system and not on the subvention of advertising, is the sole voice of all the media that sustains a responsibility to the arts, to learning, and to total freedom of comment. Mrs. Thatcher would prefer to see the BBC disappear and be replaced by yet another network of banal programmes commercially subsidised, obeying market forces, giving the people what they think they want. If Mrs. Thatcher could abolish in Britain such pretensions to intellectuality as exist, she would be glad to do so. The bulk of the citizens would not care. This is sometimes known as democracy.

I have painted a somewhat black picture of the Iron Lady and the decade named after her, and yet the fact that she has maintained herself in power for so phenomenally long a period must point to the country's ready acceptance of both her personality and her philosophy. In fact, the citizens of England and Wales (if not necessarily of Scotland) seem to approve of the getting and spending policy associated with her rule. There is no great love of socialism, chiefly because socialism has been tried and has been seen signally to fail. The socialist leaders of the country are no gentler, no more humane, than their powerful enemy. They posited a class struggle based on an outworn image of the working man that no longer applies. Working men are joining the middle class if they are prosperous enough; if not, and especially if they are young, they are becoming a violent but inarticulate *Lumpenproletariat*. The killers and rioters at football matches are expressing resentment at not getting their share of the Thatcherian cake. They are not demonstrating on behalf of a return to socialism. And yet, with a moribund liberalism unable to hope for power, socialism is the only viable alternative to Thatcherism. But what is the nature of this socialism?

It can only be a diluted form of capitalism, with heavier taxes to pay for enhanced state services, especially in the area of health. It cannot reassemble the structure of nationalised industries that the Conservatives are at such pains to dismantle. It may offer a greater sense of social responsibility, as opposed to the smash and grab opportunism of the Conservatives, but it will not offer the people what they really want: more and more goods to consume. In Eastern Europe, where the full, rich, thick cream of socialism used to be purveyed (there was no other nutrient), the people want a capitalist system in which, once bread and sausages are freely available, a flood of washing machines and videocassette players will follow. Nobody wants ideology anymore. The mild socialism, especially of the Christian kind, that Western Europe offers is really a kind of capitalist liberalism. But it is concerned with the market and the magic of conspicuous consumerism. This is what the world wants, and it is a kind of Thatcherism.

Of course, to call this monetarism or marketry after the lady with whom it is associated is to give her credit for an inventiveness and originality she does not possess. She is a typical product of the shopkeeping class that sings hymns but abhors ideas as pure subversion. She speaks with a painfully acquired bourgeois accent that sounds affected. She is, and this I have virtually failed to mention except through necessary grammatical accidence, a woman. She is not a sloppy unkempt woman of the bluestocking kind but a snappy dresser (far more elegant than her Queen) who looks after her coiffure with care. She has still a measure of sexual allure which she knows how to use.

Of course, sex and politics have always gone together in a manner which is best explained by invoking the great word *power*. Henry Kissinger, who was no sex-object, saw power as an aphrodisiac. But, with Margaret Thatcher, ten years of power are having the effect of nullifying her native potency as a woman. If we regard the Queen as a mother, we have to regard her prime minister as a mistress, not as a surrogate wife. Men, unless they marry them out of sheer weariness, always discard mistresses, often in something under ten years. For mistresses usually turn into shrews, demanding more than they have a right to, pouting if they do not receive enough love.

Mrs. Thatcher, who is only the wife of Denis Thatcher, has been usurping the power of the Queen by turning herself into the nation's mother, or, if you like, stepmother. She is not the caressing, loving, feeding head of the family. She scolds, raises her voice, administers raps and smacks and hard words. She has relied too much on the fancied glamour of her sex. As a grandmother (who, incidentally, is seen to be not very handy in dandling her new grandchild) she is assuming almost ancestral rights in dealing with her national flock. It is as though she has always been there, like Queen Victoria, and even aging statesmen are no more than her naughty brood.

There is a piquancy in seeing the most successful politician of the age as a member of the sex traditionally downtrodden. The trouble with her is that, despite the allure and the purposefulness, she is not likable. Churchill, with all his faults, was even lovable. So was the cuckolded Edwardian dandy Harold Macmillan. But we have had ten years of a lady who chills the heart and stultifies the national imagination.

She has called into being, almost as by a law of opposites, a kind of independent statesman who has nothing to do with politics. This is Charles, Prince of Wales, who has been demonstrating a genuine concern for the welfare of a nation which will soon acknowledge him as its monarch. He has efficiently inveighed against the wretched architecture which is typical of a utilitarian age. He is against ugliness, and he is all for compassion. Naturally, he has no power except the power of example or persuasion. But he stands for the decent, tolerant, concerned side of the British—the Orwellian side, if you like. If we associate Mrs. Thatcher with George Orwell at all, it is in a sense that goes too far. For the vision of *Nineteen Eighty-Four* was of a genuinely intellectual autocracy, in which an idealistic philosophy (reality exists only inside the collective brain) was imposed on the people. Mrs. Thatcher may see herself as Big Sister, but she is not all that fearsome. She will be there only so long as the people want her there. That, too, is what is sometimes known as democracy.

—1989

DIRTY PICTURES

❖

The Benny Hill Show has been censured in its country of origin as vulgar and sexist. In France, every Sunday at 20.00 on the *troisième chaine*, it sustains its popularity. It gives the French a chance to tap their own vein of vulgarity while pretending to be morally and aesthetically superior to the British. Its content is prefigured on the title frame with a couple of images taken from the picture postcards of Donald MacGill—fat-bottomed leering women of a certain age in bathing costumes—but the French are not able to catch the reference. They have produced their fair share of dirty pictures, but they are beyond the innocent obscenity of those seaside postcards with which, scrawling "Wish you was here" on the back, the British working class confided that it was enjoying its holiday.

George Orwell, in a notable essay, took Donald MacGill's work seriously as an index of the proletarian attitude to life. If the pictures were obscene, it was only in the vague sense that they dallied with sex either as a nightmare or an impossible dream. They were not obscene in any legal sense, or they would not have been allowed to pass through the mails. They all told the same story. Youth ends early and it ends with marriage. Lissom girls soon become steatopygous monsters. Men pine, grow thin but pot-bellied and have red noses. They get drunk and a wife in curlers waits with the rolling-pin. Ruined males sigh after pretty seaside girls while fat wives look thunder. There is nothing tragic about all this frustration: this is what life is, and the sooner you settle into a deprived middle age the better. As for sex, beer, football, and carrier pigeons are an adequate substitute. Orwell prized all this because it was a genuine proletarian culture. Donald MacGill, who appeared briefly on television in the sixties, was not himself a prole. He spoke with a patrician accent and condescended cheerfully to his art. He knew very well what he was doing.

He was clearly aware of a certain ambiguity in his depiction of the prototypical working-class wife, who, thin and vinegary when punitive, grew fat when she paddled at Blackpool or Margate. The fatness may have been gross, but it represented a kind of sexual ideal more civilised than not. A decadent society usually prefers its women thin, like the chic skeletons at the Park Avenue dinner parties of Tom Wolfe's *Bonfire of the Vanities*. Chinese *towkays* advertise their prosperity with fat wives; Indians like plumpness; the icons of the picture postcards took fatness too far but were on the right lines. The men in the pictures tended to be thin and phallic; the women were, in the vulgar phrase, something to get hold of. In a sense, too, they were a fulfillment of boyhood wet dreams, often primed by the Fat Lady of the sideshows.

But in no way were these pictures pornographs. Pornography has never been much in the British line. The dirty pictures sold by hissing touts in pre-war Paris, or on the quays of Port Said, were far from innocent. They could not be sent nakedly through the mails; they were for furtive study. They might be postcard-size, but the communication they promised had nothing friendly about it. And they were not usually art, like the Donald MacGill pictures, but crude camera studies, reminding us that the photo and the porno began at the same time. To certain members of Victorian high society, the camera granted the chance to be recorded naked. I doubt if there was a strong pornographic intent on the part of the subjects, rather a reaction against wearing too many clothes. The child photographs of Lewis Carroll are certainly pornographic, but there was not a hint of paedophily in his nature. It is probably the twentieth-century viewer who is corrupt.

The Greek word *porne* means a prostitute, and the basic dirty picture is of a desirable female partner, partly or wholly disrobed. It is a masturbatory instrument, as is the modern centrefold or third page. The young Stephen Dedalus, in Joyce's *A Portrait of the Artist as a Young Man*, has a bundle of shameful photographs stuck up the chimney, covered with soot. Their subjects probably simper and hold up their skirts: in Victorian Ireland or England, when the sight of a well-turned ankle would provoke lust, naked-

ness was never essential. And there is something about nakedness—chiefly its association with municipal art galleries—which
leaves the viewer cold, unless he happens to be H. G. Wells. Wells
learned to love the female form through allegorical statues of Industry and Commerce. The rest of us have always required a little
titillation, and that is what clothes, especially underclothes, used
to be for. Not now, regrettably. There is nothing less aphrodisi-
acal imaginable than panty hose. A Donald MacGill picture
showed a leering man in a bookshop asking the salesgirl if she
had any thrillers. That meant, I think, camiknicks. It was women
themselves who, recruited into the wartime ATS, called issue
pants passion-crushers.

The women we see enticing us from advertisements are, technically speaking, performing a pornographic job (they are
desirable and nameless, hence a kind of whore), but they are
clearly doing it within the law. The true forbidden pornograph
has no enticement in it: it shows some aspect of the act itself; the
enticement stage has long passed. I first came into contact with
this kind of picture when I was a soldier in Gibraltar. It came
from Spain and had to compete with the American importation
known as a nooky ration card. The first specimen I saw was not
a photograph but a detailed drawing of a wedding ceremony, in
which everybody was pedicating everybody, choirboys included,
and the bride was fellating the officiating priest. It advertised itself
as Hispanic because bride and bridesmaids and busy mothers of
bride and groom wore mantillas. All Spanish pornographs insisted, with a pathetic kind of patriotism, on their land of origin.
A dour man with a burro's equipment stood to gloomy attention
while indifferently performing the act (the equipment might as
well be bestowed there as anywhere else) in ill-fitting torero's costume. The female element had the inevitable mantilla. A most
intricate multiple session showed no shortage of sombreros. On
the Rock we were all sexually frustrated, but these Spanish in-
ducements to passion had the effect of a cold shower. Were they
then properly pornographic?

The reason why pictures showing the sexual act are condemned
by law has never been sufficiently clear. The thing that turns you
on and the thing that puts you off are treated in much the same
way. Obscenity is a fine catch-all word, in which the appetising

and the disgusting are subsumed. Generally, when we have got
beyond the enticement of lingerie advertisements in *Vogue*
(blessed by commerce and hence by law), we will find that most
sexographs work along with extreme puritanism to make the
erotic the emetic. The photographs offered by touts at the Gare
de Lyon before the war were very tough going—nun assaulted by
monk, naked necrophile leaping on to lily-strewn corpse in coffin,
multiple pedicants on, as it were, the march. The total taxonomy
of the brothels was exploited, save for bestiality. And none of it
was very attractive.

Bestiality was the speciality of the southern ports, especially
Port Said. And the classical coupling, straight out of the ancient
world, was from Apuleius's *The Golden Ass*. In Aldington's fine
Elizabethan version, the hero, transformed for his sins into a don-
key, is made to copulate in an Alexandrian arena with a lady who
coaxes him with "I have thee, I hold thee, my nops, my cunny,
give me all thy love." This is too charming to be disgusting, and
one was aware of the literary aura purifying the crude snapshots
offered by the fezzed polyglot hucksters on the quay. (A chapter
in Aldous Huxley's *Point Counter Point* reminds us how polyglot
they used to be.) If one wanted a perversion that went beyond
bestiality, it had to touch blasphemy. I don't know what the new
militant Muslims who want to burn Salmon Rushdie would do
about a muezzin being fellated while he cries that there is no god
but Allah.

It seems that the day of the dirty picture—postcard-sized,
pocket-size for speedy disgust or stimulation—is all over. The kiosks of the Côte d'Azur sell views of palms and hotels and mild
jokes about family hatreds (owl and cow, with "*Je suis chouette
mais ma femme est vache*"). In France we get our pornography
animated, on Canal Plus after midnight on Saturday. The old
healthy furtiveness is gone, and there is nothing for the pocket.
André Gide called pornography one-handed art, but the chronic
onanist must have difficulty in coping with a centrefold or a page
of the *Sun*. The old dirty picture was of the right size.

We've all lost our innocence. I have not been to Blackpool since
my pre-war youth, and I have no idea what kind of postcard is
now sent back to Oldham or Bolton by the operatives who have
been elevated to the middle class. The Donald MacGill picture

belonged to its time, like the Rector of Stiffkey in a barrel and Epstein's Genesis (both on exhibition on the Golden Mile). It fitted in well with a time of sexual naiveté, when the scandal of the early thirties concerned Colonel Barker and her bride (Colonel Barker was a woman, the bride took a long time to find out, and people speculated as to what they did together) and *The Well of Loneliness* was one of the unknown books (along with *Ulysses* and *Lady Chatterley's Lover*). The sexual act was an act of darkness, and the light thrown on it was thin and intermittent. The wink and the snigger were the right response to what one did, or hoped to do, on the wedding night. I'm not sure, however, that we are sexually healthier now than people were then. Dirty postcards have been driven out and we can see both necrophily and animalistic sodomy on television. There is no room for icons of the forbidden, and the hissing touts now sell heroin.

To look at the museum of postcard pornography housed in Hounslow and sedulously tended by an ancient friend of mine is to see how sex, the great eternal impulse, is as subject to change as dress or locomotion. It's not just a question of corsets, handlebar moustaches, tumbling cascades of hair, nor indeed of the shape of bodies—the women's legs as short as life, the pigeon toes, the obligatory (and civilised) fleshiness. It is the absence of light (for light and lust, says Shakespeare, are deadly enemies). It is also the implied presence of non-metaphorical dirt. Light is dim, bed sheets are in need of changing, there is a shortage of hot (or cold) water. Today sex has become, as they say, squeaky clean, and there is a lack of the murky and furtive. No sense of sin means a weakening of libido. When we were most innocent we felt most guilty.

—1989

GOD AND GOD'S VOICES

❖

Friedrich Nietzsche killed God somewhat prematurely. God, of course, is willing to be killed so long as he can rise again—the old fertility myths join with Christianity in accepting that doctrine—but Nietzsche, along with Marx, Durkheim, Lenin, Wells, Shaw, and other rationalistic pundits, assumed that God was a fiction for weak brains. True, God's existence can't be proved, but it depends what we mean by existence. If a human need presupposes the thing that satisfies that need (hunger and thirst would not exist without food and drink) then man's need of God posits his existence enough for all practical purposes. From that point let the organised religions take over.

Secularism and militant atheism belong to the last century, and the Soviet Union's now dismantled Anti-God Museums and professorships of Scientific Atheism once had the antiquarian charm of a steam engine or a mechanical computer. Orthodox and Catholic Christianity are very much alive in Russia, and the secular alternatives are revealed as shamefully hollow. But it is in Russia's next-door neighbour, Poland, that the unkillable vitality of organised Christianity can best be observed. It is no accident that Poland produced a world leader of the faith, but it is only now, in the ruins of East European Communism, that the appositeness of his election can be clearly understood.

Karol Wojtyla is the 263rd Roman pontiff, the first non-Italian to be elected since 1522, the youngest since 1846, the only one in history to emerge from Slavonic Eastern Europe. John Polack, as he is irreverently or affectionately called, is a product of Europe's Catholic heartland, and why Poland should be this is not hard to explain. The ethnic unity of the country helps to ensure a cultural unity, abetting an indefensible antisemitism, and the 95 per cent ethnic Poles are nearly all baptised Catholics. The faith flourished best, as faiths often do, under persecution, and its

157

core—free will, the right to choose—could not be separated from the political aspirations of the persecuted. Solidarity was driven by the Catholic faith. Lech Walesa was a devout Catholic. When a non-Communist government was elected, Tadeusz Mazowiecki, the editor of a Catholic newspaper, became Prime Minister. John Paul II had no active part to play in the building of what we may call a Catholic state, but his example and world authority were behind it.

Jesus Christ made it clear that religion should have nothing to do with politics. He would not join the Zealots who wanted to overthrow the Roman rule in Palestine: Caesar was Caesar and God was God, and their kingdoms could not be reconciled. But Christ lived under a colonial power that was concerned only with taxes and the keeping of civil order; with consensual government the gap between politics and religion is bound to diminish, since both lay down the law on how people should behave. That is why it is sometimes difficult for us to see our religious leaders—of whatever faith—as cut off from the world of secular enactments. That is why ordinary people, who need religion, become upset when it seems to impinge on what they think of as their secular rights. Our spiritual heads have to sail seas, or fly airways, turbulent with anomalies.

Pope John Paul II is an anomaly in himself. He is an intellectual, a genuine philosopher who tried to Christianise existentialism, but at the same time he is full of the populist faith that worships at shrines, looks for miracles, fingers rosary beads. He was active in the Second Vatican Council, called by Pope John XXIII in 1962 to modernise the Church. This *aggiornamento*, as it was called, seemed to offer Church members a new freedom from ancient rigidities that were very repressive. They expected hell to disappear and women to cease to be child-bearing machines. On the distant horizon there was the possibility of married clergy and women priests. But Paul VI put paid to the great expectations of the world's Catholics by reaffirming the old doctrines, particularly, in his encyclical *Humanae Vitae*, the inseparability of sex and procreation. When Wojtyla took the name Paul he was warning the Catholic world that he was not prepared for the kind of compromise that lets the secular erode the spiritual. Aristotle had said that sex was for making children, and the Church fathers followed Aristotle. Posters approved by government tell us to use condoms; the Church says nothing because it has said it all already. As for hell, Wojtyla blandly confirmed its continued existence one summer before going off to Castel Gandolfo. And yet he fills stadia with devotees. By the end of 1990 over 200 million had attended his masses. In Latin America and Africa there have been congregations of more than a million. Half of Ireland turned out to see him.

He has charisma, which need not have anything to do with the acceptability of the doctrines he embodies. There is an interesting split in the attitude of the faithful towards him: they take him as their undoubted spiritual leader but are ready to use common sense to confute his conservatism. Hell's a fable, no one can help being homosexual, it's manifestly absurd not to limit one's family. John Paul II stands for an orthodoxy which he wears as a high court judge wears a wig—so many seem to think: he's the voice of the orthodoxy, but it's all a pretence. Graham Greene's Catholicism, complete with God's infinite mercy and an empty hell, is the real thing. Nevertheless, John Paul II is a solid reassuring symbol of something or other, a world leader without the power or vindictiveness to punish the errant. And when people temporarily tire of his incessant blessings from the popemobile, there's always Mother Teresa or the late and still unsainted Padre Pio waiting to be worshipped.

The truth behind the papal symbol of massive Catholic unity is, from the angle of the faithful, disquieting. Catholicism has spread in black Africa—25 million in 1950 but 125 million in 1990—and risen with the birth rate in Latin America, but in the advanced nations it is declining. In the U.S.A., for example, the issues of contraception, homosexuality, female clergy, and marital annulment face a papal blank wall, and the dissatisfaction at John Paul II's conservatism is reflected in a drop in church attendance. In Britain we have statistics from the English Church Census of March 1991, which show that, in the last ten years, there has been a loss of half a million regular Sunday worshippers. The Catholic Church has lost 14 per cent, the Church of England 9 per cent. The Baptists have lost nothing, and evangelical Christianity generally is on the rise. The missionaries of the latter movement are mostly American and are backed by large American money which has taken them not only across the Atlantic but, once unthinkable, south of the Rio Grande.

We know these vigorous fundamentalists chiefly from television. With some of them Mammon prevails over God, but the large handsome figure of Billy Graham—74 this year but still ebullient—represents unshakable Baptist orthodoxy untainted by lust or greed. His showmanship is extravagant but not gaudy, and his calls for human regeneration are based solidly on the Bible. Of course, here lies the primal distinction between Catholicism and Protestantism: the authority of ecclesiastical tradition versus that of the holy printed word. Graham's power, like that of the other congregation-rousers, lies in his capacity to relate an ancient text to the sins of the present, to find AIDS in Deuteronomy and heroin in Exodus, to thunder and lightning, but also to pin down with chapter and verse. His followers know the Bible, but he knows it better. There is not very much more that he needs to know. His Biblical literalism can be dangerous. Manson and his killers learned from him when they found the Beatles in the Book of Revelation (four archangels with breast-plates, to be glossed as electric guitars) as a sign that the time for holy massacres had come. All fundamentalism is frightening, but Christians do not have to choose it. With Islam the situation is very different.

The possession of a sacred book, read by all Muslims who can read and not notably ambiguous, has not disposed Islam to a sense of unity. Islam split in the seventh and eighth centuries, and the existing division between Sunni and Shi'ite, to say nothing of the Druzes, the Ismailis, and the Alawites, is only given a film of unity in a common hatred of Israel. The Jewish faith has never required a universal leader on the analogy of the Pope of Rome, but Islamic fundamentalism is probably responsible for the rise of a new Jewish extreme orthodoxy under the Rabbi Meir Kahane, who probably sees himself as the true guardian of the faith. For that matter, Muslim extremism in India gave rise to the Janara Dal Party, which broke into violence in northern India with an attempt to assert the holiness of Hindu shrines in territories where mosques had been built. A militant Islam provokes opposing militancies, but there is no likelihood of a return to the Christian crusades. Nevertheless, the reasonable voices of Muslim intellectuals—in the press, in books, in pamphlets, though not much in the mosques—are still made inaudible by the memory of the Ayatollah Khomeini, who, in Western eyes, is the archetypal religious leader, meaning that he is fanatical, intolerant, and murderous.

The Islamic Republic that was established in Iran in February 1979 was, like Calvin's Geneva, a theocracy. There was no distinction between the secular and the spiritual; there was no awareness of the true nature of political rule, which controls through compromise. In the first two years, 8,000 people were executed as "enemies of Allah." As Paul Johnson puts it in the revised edition of his history of the modern world:

> From the start it organized the execution or murder of leaders of ethnic and religious minorities, killing over 1,000 Kurds, 200 Turkomans, and many Jews, Christians, Shaikhis, Sabeans, and members of dissident Shi'a sects as well as orthodox Sunnis. Its persecution of the Bahais was particularly ferocious. Churches and synagogues were wrecked, cemeteries desecrated, shrines vandalised or demolished. The judicially murdered ranged from the Kurdish poet Allameh Vahidi, aged 102, to a nine-year-old girl, convicted of "attacking revolutionary guards."

Khomeini was not some distant, near-mythical, Arabian Nights tyrant: he put a British subject, Salman Rushdie, in fear of his life, and the fatwah goes on from the grave. He has given the whole concept of religious leadership a bad name.

We have to cool ourselves with a look at the Dalai Lama in his fourteenth incarnation. Tibetan Buddhists accept him as Avalokitesvara brought back to earth, the embodiment of compassion, one of the attendants on Amida Buddha, known as Guan Yin in China and Kwannon in Japan. He was enthroned in 1940 at the age of five, but he fled Tibet ten years later when the Chinese overran the territory he ruled temporarily as well as spiritually. He was back after a year's absence, but in 1959 he left Lhasa for India after the suppression of a local uprising against Chinese rule. He settled at Dharmsala in the Punjab, but the Chinese are willing to have him back so long as he does not agitate for Tibetan independence. His deputy, the Panchen Lama, has cooperated with the Chinese but done little for the protection of the monks. The

Dalai Lama visited Britain in 1988, but the government was not willing to let him plead the cause of Tibet. He is a religious leader whose significance has become painfully political.

Such religious leaders as we have glanced at at least embody ancient traditions; they are not spiritual upstarts. But our century has seen the appearance of new faiths which claim credence not out of the operation of the spirit but from scientific or pseudo-scientific theory. L. Ron Hubbard in the United States began as a writer of science fiction but then developed a system of psychotherapy called dianetics. All mental and some physical illnesses are caused by "engrams," defined as "incompletely assimilated traumatic experiences, both pre- and post-natal." They could be exorcised through therapy. But the introduction of the religious term "exorcism" encouraged a theological view of the human mind. Behind each mind is an immortal being, the "Thetan," which has become imprisoned in a complex of engrams during cycles of reincarnation. Exorcise all these engrams and you become an Operating Thetan, with the probable power to work miracles, whatever miracles are. Scientology has its adherents, and Hubbard and his followers have been aggressive in their defence of what amounts to a new religion. The same is true of the leader and members of the Unification Church, who are termed Moonies.

Sun Myung Moon was a Korean industrialist but is now the father of a faith. He founded his church in Korea in 1954, giving it a Bible called *Divine Principles*, whose main theme is the formation of the perfect family, which shall have a special relationship with God. There's an attempt to synthesise Christian and Taoist ideas, the *tao* or "way" being based less on the moral life than on the discovery of a harmonious relationship with the environment. Marriage is a symbol of harmony, and marriage is the main ritual of the church, with marital partners chosen by Mr. and Mrs. Moon. The movement has been in trouble. There have been accusations of manipulative methods of recruitment, and Moon himself was convicted of tax fraud in the U.S. in 1982. But accusations of incest and cannibalism were made against the early Christians, and a membership of 200,000 thinks that the sun, or the moon, shines out of their leader's spectacles.

There are other leaders about—gurus and swamis who rise or

fall, TV evangelists who drop into carnal sin—and one has to ask whether we need them or not. The "we" in question excludes the feeble-minded who will follow any Führer or Duce or Caudillo of the spirit in the hope of not having to think for themselves. The ideal leader for lukewarm Protestants is the present Archbishop of Canterbury, who is educated, liberal, flexible, non-thundering, but history shows, alas, that the believing herd loves threats of hellfire. Savonarola did well in fifteenth-century Florence, not by promoting Christian love but by denouncing pleasure. Any self-elected leader who rose in Britain today to attack indiscrimate sex on moral grounds and to preach eternal punishment for fornication would be assured of an audience: his hot gospelling would add a new zest to transgression. Religious leaders do best on a local level, like old Starkadder in Stella Gibbon's *Cold Comfort Farm*, who condemns the Church of the Quivering Brethren to endless burning and whose choirmaster beats time with a poker. When a wave of suicides begins in Wales, it can only be cured by an injection of revivalism. The great reformers of this island, such as the Wesleys, began in a small way. The superstars of faith are in the position of rock singers and television luminaries—the heroes who remind us of our own lowliness. They are less real than the tyrants of the chapel.

It is probably not enough for us underlings to say that we can get along well enough with our rectors and rabbis. Jesus Christ made the first pope, and that pope denied him thrice. John Paul II, in claiming to trace his authority back to a repentant Peter, despite the mix-up of Avignon and the antipopes, stands, or rides in his armoured car, as a symbol of continuity. He is not there, any more than the papacy Savonarola hated was there, to give his Church an example of virtue other than the virtue of celibacy (the Borgias failed in this respect). When I lived in Malaysia, under an Islam that was becoming vaguely Anglican in its tolerance, the Sultans were spiritual leaders but not noticeably more virtuous than their subjects. The lack of virtue in Khomeini has not invalidated his brand of the faith. Figurehead status is all that believers require of their spiritual heads. When they think they need holy wars, they are not true believers.

Those of us who are Christians revere none of the popes of the past. John XXIII was supposedly greatly loved, but more as a beefsteak-eating saintly clown than as a director of doctrine. Paul VI dithered. John Paul II is what he is. The figures we revere are the theologians like St. Augustine or St. Thomas Aquinas or Duns Scotus, the eccentric saints like St. Francis of Assisi, the mystics like St. John of the Cross or St. Teresa. The popes come nowhere. The Church of England reveres a martyred archbishop who was Catholic, not Anglican, and a Scottish king who was beheaded for, among other things, his Erastianism. The Muslims should get back to studying the great commentators on the Koran, not listening to ignorant imams. The Jews provoke no spiritual complaint, whatever our view on the politics of the Middle East. The philosopher A. N. Whitehead said that "religion is what a man does with his own solitude." No pope, bishop, or hot gospeller will intercede for us on the Day of Judgment.

—1991

ARS POETICA

*Along with the shorter newspaper assignments ("All About Alice"
and "Flann O'Brien"), several longer, substantial essays are included in this section. The piece on Wagner ("Ring") is a brilliant
example of the Burgess gift for precise synthesis. As should be
expected, literature and music prevail, though the other major arts
are well represented: cinema ("Orson Welles: the Artist as Bricoleur"), architecture ("The Gaudiness of Gaudí"), and painting
("The Brotherhood"). I have always admired one of the emphatic
tenets of the Burgess aesthetic, the demand for the authentic note
of originality. For Burgess, no artist has a right to complain that
everything has already been done: "There is still an infinitude of
books to be written out of the twenty-six letters of the alphabet,
and there is still an infinitude of melodies to be generated out of
twelve notes and the innumerable rhythmical combinations of
these which want to be exploited."*

SUCCESS

❖

The other day I picked up the latest edition of the *Pelican* survey of contemporary British fiction and found that I was still missing—along with, I think, John Fowles—from the index. I have never felt any particular chagrin about this neglect, but I would feel happier if the index indicated total neglect in the text itself (there's disgruntled dysphony for you). I mean, when you're totally ignored you know where you stand: you're too totally good for the ignorer. But in this survey my name turns up over and over again, not as a novelist but as a critic of novelists. "Mr. Burgess (who has himself written the odd novel) says of Iris Murdoch . . ." That's how it goes, and I don't like it. Last spring I received, from the exquisite but powerful hands of Mrs. Thatcher herself, an award as Critic of the Year. I had to take the award and smirk at the cameras, but I felt the wrong footing had led her and me and everybody to the wrong plateau, the one from which there is no descent. It was never my intention to be known as a critic. Criticism, or reviewing, is something done to pass the time or pay the gas bills. It's not really a vocation.

I regard my vocation, which I came to very late (at the same age as Conrad, but he had to learn English first), as that of novelist, and I have to consider now whether I have had any real success in it. The trouble with fiction is that there are two ways of looking at it: as a business and as an art. Just up the coast from me at Cannes, sitting glumly but royally on his yacht, is a man who has succeeded indubitably with the novel as a business. His name is Harold Robbins. He is, however, not satisfied with having sold a great number of copies of books about sex and violence: he wants to be regarded, on the strength of his evident popularity, as the greatest writer alive. Nobody will so consider him (he is not in any index of any survey that I know of) and this makes him somewhat sour. It does, of course, sometimes happen that the most popular novelist is also the best—Dickens, for instance; perhaps even Hemingway—but the one doesn't follow from the other. We expect great fiction to be too subtle or complex for popular acceptance. A good writer will often worry if his work goes into too many impressions: he will feel that he has not been subtle or complex enough. He will feel that he has been inattentive to his craft and turned out something like John Braine.

From the business angle I can point, though cautiously, to some small success. In twenty-five years of professional writing I have been able to make a living. Even if this means no more than being able to afford an egg for one's breakfast twice a week it is still a matter for pride: one has called no man *sir*, except perhaps a New York black cab-driver, and one has been able to telephone from one's bed at eleven in the forenoon and tell someone to go to hell. This living, however, has come from steady application to the craft, a determination to write at least one thousand words a day, and not at all from the kind of *réclame* that greets a *Catch-22* or a *Princess Daisy*. A lot of the money has come from journalism and from writing scripts for films that were never made. A fairly exiguous trickle has come from fiction. If there is any money in the bank it is there because I have gone on bullying a fairly small public into buying a Burgess book every year. I have had, in other words, to keep at it.

The trouble with me is that I provide evidence of affluence to the superficial reader of works of reference. I have three or four addresses, but that means only that I have had to leave one and move to another because of becoming *persona non grata* or discovering that the kidnappers are interested in my son, and certain governmental regulations (as in Malta) have forbidden my selling property. A colour supplement recently listed me with Ringo Starr and the tennis-player Borg as a typical tax-evader of Monaco. But low income is as good a reason as high for going to a taxless zone. If I could afford it, I would probably live in England. For every artist there is the fear that sooner or later he will be unable to produce art. He has no state pension and he has to look to a future without income. He must save what he can while he can, and the British tax system, which would be happier without self-employed artists, does not permit saving.

If I have a little money in various banks (I am not sure how little it is: this may well be a signal of affluence) I cannot point to a financial success commensurate with that of a Beatle or a Karajan or any other pop-musician. No millions, for God's sake. Success, then, must, if I *am* successful, lie elsewhere. If not in fiction as business, then in fiction as art? Who can say? Certainly not the fictional artist. I have produced about forty books, most of them novels or novellas, and I am not really satisfied with any of them. When critics express a like, or even greater, dissatisfaction, I can only nod glumly in agreement. The horrid truth, though, is that one cannot really make oneself any better. The faults in one's work are less faults of artistic application than inbuilt and inextricable flaws in one's personal make-up. We would all write like Shakespeare or V. S. Naipaul if we could: not being Shakespeare or Naipaul rather hampers us.

The glow of the sense of success comes, when it comes at all, if somebody has read one of my books (it is usually when that person is in a weakened state, typically in hospital), has found a fresh revelation of the nature of life in that work, and is willing to express pleasure and admiration. Books, after all, are not written for critics but for people, especially when they are in a weakened state. That is real success, the feeling that the task of entertaining and enlightening at the same time has been adequately fulfilled. The kind of book that sells by the million rarely imparts to its readers the sense of epiphany: it has a different function and a good one—that of beguiling time and then inviting oblivion, a thing consumed with pips to spit out, no more. No matter how poor a writer is, if he has written a book which changes someone's life he has achieved the only sort of success worth having.

If a writer feels he is a success—he is known and read and even bought; American scholars write books about him; the reception clerk at the Algonquin knows his name—then he has a horrid sense that he is no longer travelling hopefully but has arrived. He has, in fact, reached one of those damned plateaux; he cannot climb any further and he certainly cannot go back to his old fearful and delectable struggles. I am thankful that I am not eligible for the Nobel Prize or the O.M., the kind of success which says: "You've made it. We don't expect you to do any more. Now for heaven's sake leave it to the next generation." How can anybody—prize committee or critical synod—estimate what a writer is still capable of doing? Shakespeare got his critical accolade from Francis Meres when he was successful as a writer of sugared sonnets and romantic comedies; there he was, placed on the nation's Parnassus, finished, a success. How disappointed Meres must have been when *Hamlet* and *King Lear* appeared. Success is a kind of death sentence.

The success of being known, which is success enough for many people, is not nowadays a thing to be honourably sought, since it is conferred instantaneously by a television appearance. Fame is neither here nor there. I have never yet been known to a British hotel receptionist or an airline agent. Giving my name to one of the latter, especially in America, I am usually genially asked: "Same as in Burgess Meredith?" or, in Britain, "Same as the chap who went over to the Russians?" Fame can be an aspect of success, but many of the most successful ventures of history have not brought fame. Milton accepted fame as the spur for writing well, but he meant fame for his books (and then only in the limited field of the learned and tasteful), never for himself. The great Murray, father of the Oxford English Dictionary, repudiated fame with terrifying dignity.

Success, then, in the somewhat inflated sense which I'm imposing on it here, means a more than adequate reward for producing something that doesn't belong to the world of subsistence. A soufflé may be successful, but not in the way that a sonnet or a symphony is (both, as Oscar Wilde would say, equally useless). The man or woman who has produced successful work is himself or herself a success. The rewards, if financial, are not merely impertinent but injurious. Money means consumption, and consumption gets in the way of work. Shoals of letters of admiration have to be answered, and this means that there's less time for writing books. No wonder success brings depression.

To every artist who considers himself successful (as, with many reservations, I consider myself) there remains a prick of doubt about the road chosen. Perhaps the true sense of achievement was waiting in some other métier, the one that beckoned and was neglected. When I was young, before I decided that my métier was fiction, my ambition was to be a great composer of music. I worked moderately hard at the art and failed. Since becoming

known as a writer I have been able to go back to my first love
with some hope of having my work performed. But it is too late
now to resume the old dreams of nine symphonies and five operas
(although the next task I envisage for myself is a choral and orchestral setting of *The Wreck of the Deutschland*). I didn't work
hard and long enough: if Polyhymnia (if that's the right muse)
doesn't turn her back on me now, she grins rather than smiles at
my music. But it is as a great British composer that I should like
to have figured in the reference books, not as a critic who writes
occasional novels, or as a novelist who helped to father a violent
film, or (it happens occasionally) as someone who has achieved a
moderate success with a large number of novels. What success
has taught me is the extent of my failure.

—1980

THE CELTIC SACRIFICE

❖

In England we have seen for many centuries the side-by-side subsistence of two impulses we may call the Celtic and the Teutonic. These designations have more to do with culture, meaning ultimately imaginative endowment, than with blood. Shakespeare, so the mother of Shaw's O'Flaherty VC believed, was born in Cork: he writes like an Irishman, is capable of bulls, and believes in fairies. The Teuton mind believes in good roads, sanitation, and a curb on fancy. But occasionally it is betrayed into imagination and even immorality, which is one of the fruits of imagination. Ashamed of the betrayal, it seeks to blame some outside demon. It finds its demons among the Celts.

I am always being corrected when I call Oscar Fingal O'Flahertie Wills Wilde a Celt. He was, I am reminded, an Anglo-Saxon of the Dublin British ascendancy, received the best possible Anglo-Saxon education, spoke like an Englishman, gained his fame and eventual notoriety in the theatres, drawing-rooms, and pederastic beds of London. I still say he was a Celt, as was Jonathan Swift, Dublin's great dean. No one can have a Dublin upbringing or a Dublin living without absorbing imagination, wit, fancy, the spirit of paradox, inspired illogicality, and the rest of the Celtic gifts.

Wilde, as we know, was punished by the Anglo-Saxons and very brutally punished. He lost everything: liberty, money, health, wife, children, home, even genius. Ostensibly he was punished for indulging in sodomy, an aberration not unknown to the British aristocracy of the time, since it had been educated in British public schools. His real crime was to be witty, subversive, an intellectual aristocrat among aristocrats of horseflesh and pudding. He put on the stage Anglo-Saxon aristocrats suffused with his own gifts of irresponsibility and wit. He suggested that there were forces at work beneath the code of the empire-builder which were subversive of empire. The Anglo-Saxons did not like this and sought a means of punishing him for evoking this image. The Marquess of Queensberg provided them with a first-class pretext. Wilde was a Celtic sacrifice to the Anglo-Saxon gods of dullness.

He was the most spectacular of the sacrifices, but he was not the only one. There are, at least in our own time, two vivid memories of Celtic sacrifices, one Irish, one Welsh, one of a playwright, the other of a poet (both together might have made half a Wilde), which dourly pleased the Anglo-Saxons indicating to them the lethal dangers of irrationality, imagination, and convivial excess. Brendan Behan, like Dylan Thomas, accomplished his own end, but he was given a rope and encouraged to hang himself. He was not a great playwright—rather more of a blarneyed improviser; his political convictions were liquidated by compassion; in the borstal in England to which he was sent for being an IRA man, he learned to love fair-skinned English boys. Moreover, he drank and was encouraged to drink. In London pubs he played the bard and was good free entertainment. If one of his plays was not doing well, he would leap drunk onto the stage and participate in the action. He was always ready for a street fight, like his brother Domenic (whom I once tried to rescue from himself by putting him in a taxi, but all the London taxi-drivers knew him and none would take him). He was good copy and a fine *memento mori*. This was his function among the Anglo-Saxons, and the Anglo-Saxons loved him for it, as they might love a pet rabbit they propose in time to turn into a pie.

Dylan Thomas was the great original of whom poor Brendan was a kind of copy. A genuine poet whose meanings were Celtically obscure he could drink but he could not hold on to money. He too was good Soho entertainment. Known in London as a drunk, in America, to everybody's astonishment, he turned into a lecher. A great masturbator who liked women mostly to cuddle to on a winter night, he was made to fit the priapic role by an American poet and academic, John Malcolm Brinnin. He was being fattened for sacrifice on both sides of the Atlantic, but it was Britain, with a fiscal ICBM, that struck the blow. Dylan had left money with his agent to pay the private school fees of his son Llewelyn. In New York he learned that the Inland Revenue had pre-empted the money and that his son had been expelled for his father's non-payment of fees. Dylan went out and got very drunk on whisky. He died of what the papers called an alcoholic insult to the brain, a very unceltic phrase. Middle-class Britain and middle-class America were shocked and quietly pleased. Once again a Celtic scapegoat had been found: beware of imagination, avoid the disease of poetry, two of whose symptoms are drunkenness and improvidence.

Since Brendan and Dylan, the Anglo-Saxon world has been rather short of Celtic sacrificial victims. How to designate Hugh MacDiarmid, the great Scottish poet who died at a great age, unhonoured by the British state, poor, a convinced Communist, the only possible candidate for the presidency of a republican Free Scotland, is uncertain. He drank much whisky but it did not kill him, rather the opposite. He was canny, and a good angel within him whispered of the dangers of the proffered rope. There was another, earlier, Scotsman, the magnificent Murray, father of the superb *Oxford English Dictionary* which has been termed the epic poem of the nineteenth-century British. He worked fourteen hours a day, was scorned by the very syndic that promoted his work, was ill-paid but, keeping himself fit on porridge, philoprogenitiveness, long walks, and Calvinistic abstinence, he survived to a great age, if not to X, Y, and Z. To the Anglo-Saxons, the Welsh and the Irish are more suitable sacrificial fodder than the Scots.

I have sometimes romantically seen myself as one of the potential Celtic literary victims. My grandmother was a Finnegan, I am a compound of Irish and Scots and Lancashire Catholic genes. I do not like the Establishment and it does not like me. But I have evaded the butcher's knives by going into exile. Even here in Monaco though, eleven years after leaving my native land, the tax authorities are after me for several thousands of pounds. I refuse to drink much. The doctor the other day, conducting an examination for insurance purposes, said that my body was not merely not *abusé*, it was not even *usé*. I will beat the Anglo-Saxons yet. But what the Anglo-Saxons really require is an incoming Celt, like Oscar or Brendan or Dylan, someone bemused by London, innocent about Anglo-Saxon deviousness, not knowing the ropes—or rather not recognising the noose that is politely handed to him.

On the other hand, perhaps, by a process of attrition, the victory over the Celts, with their dangerous imagination and radiant illogicality, has already been won, and not just in England. I feel that Dublin has been Anglo-Saxonised into sense, discipline, and a liking for reason, that it is just one more Western beehive. The mists have dispersed, and drink is out of everybody's reach. Irish playwrights, poets, and novelists require an American audience that will pay dollars. The IRA, whose organisation and technology will yet "beat the Brits," would not nowadays accept Brendan Behan. The London pubs would not welcome him, nor Dylan Thomas: their Celtic voices would get in the way of the jukebox. As for Oscar Wilde, his vice has become, if not a virtue, at least an accepted neutrality. The Celts, with Finn MacCool, lie buried under the concrete city till doomsday.

—1980

SHAW AS MUSICIAN

❖

At last, in Britain and America, Bernard Shaw's collected writings on music have been published—three volumes of very nearly one thousand pages each. I have read every page and am less fatigued than I expected. After all, the company of a man whose abstention from meat and alcohol makes him excessively energetic, a man, moreover, who is always right, cannot well be sustained through a week of solid reading without inducing exhaustion. But I have read all that Shaw wrote about music and end in a state of elation. This is because of a candour, wit, and insolence, as well as a lightly carried erudition, which the craft of journalism does not often encourage. It comes to us as something of a shock that the nineteenth century should be so genuinely liberal a period. Nowadays journalists are frightened of their editors, and editors are frightened of their proprietors, and everybody is frightened of the terrorists who are frightened of truth. Moreover, we have never enough newspaper space to enable us to speak the truth at length. The England of Queen Victoria, into which Shaw was born (properly he was born in Dublin, but Dublin was a cultural and political extension of London) was an age when men dared to tell the truth. Charles Dickens was the greatest of the truth-tellers, and Bernard Shaw followed his example. He had all the journalistic space he needed, and he had, thanks to a diet of wholemeal bread, fruit, and nuts, more than enough energy to fill it.

You may object that music is not politics, and that it is not hard to be candid in criticising the voice of Jean de Reszke or the orchestration of Dvorak. It was not like rebuking Dsraeli or Gladstone or the widowed Queen herself. Nevertheless, there were several dangers in speaking the truth about the mediocrity of cantatas and operas and oratorios, and these dangers had to do with religion.

Consider the musical situation in London, when Shaw first began to write criticism under the pseudonym of Corno di Bassetto. England had once been a great musical country, but that was in the seventeenth century. The last of the great British composers had been Henry Purcell, who died in 1695. The eighteenth century was dominated by Italian opera, and then it was the turn of German influence, which was initiated by George Frederick Handel. Throughout the reign of Victoria and the Prince Consort, who were both German and never spoke English in the home, the dominant voice was that of Felix Mendelssohn a German Jew converted to Christianity. Mendelssohn attempted to please the bourgeois British by composing Christian oratorios on the theme of Elijah or St. Paul, and any British composer who wished to make his name had to imitate Mendelssohn.

This was the position when Shaw began reporting the musical life of London. Professors and students of the royally established College and Academy of Music composed oratorios based on the career of Ezekiel or Jeremiah or Habbakuk, and they were very bad. The composers had no melodic or orchestral gift, but they were adept at constructing academic fugues, which served as a substitute for inspiration. Shaw hated fugues and he hated the academies, and he affirmed that St. Paul and Elijah were terrible bores, while Siegmund and Sieglinde, the loud incestuous lovers of Wagner's *Ring*, were interesting and attractive. This was dangerous, but Shaw, like Oscar Wilde, that other irreligious Dubliner, spoke out sturdily for the rigorous morality of art and denied that bad art could be ennobled by dealing with God and his prophets.

Shaw was a Wagnerian, and he wrote a little book called *The Perfect Wagnerite* in which he presented *The Ring* as an allegory of the decline of capitalism. *Götterdämmerung* was about the death of the moral and theological superstructure that had been raised to support the capitalist system. To promote the cause of Wagner in Victorian England was to advocate anarchy, atheism, free love, and universal discord. The discord was all too literal to many concert-goers, placed their hands over their ears when an orchestra played the Overtune to *Die Meistersinger*. But Shaw said that Wagner pointed to the future. He as good as foretold the coming of Schoenberg before Schoenberg was born. In the opening bars of *Tristan und Isolde* Shaw heard the breakdown of an old musical order and, with it, the end of a hierarchical social order. No new music offended him. He saw the point of Debussy's whole-tone scale and, dying in 1950, he felt that the experiments of the Moog synthesisers and the aleatorists were merely the fulfilment of the Wagnerian prophecy.

I met Shaw briefly when I was a very young boy. I asked him for his autograph and he said I could never afford it. It was impossible to take his discourtesy seriously, either in his writing or in his behavior, for it was an aspect of his life-long candour. There was no bile in him, perhaps because of his good vegetarian digestion.

Having spoken to him as a boy I feel he was a man of my own epoch. It is surprising to remember that he was already a mature man when Wagner, with his unsteady beat and his neuralgic scowl, came to London to conduct the Philharmonic Orchestra, and that he could be writing a celebration of the fiftieth anniversary of the death of Beethoven. He is the one writer we know who synthesises two centuries, and this is especially true of him as a writer on music.

As a young man in Dublin, Shaw was exposed to a great deal of Italian opera, which may be taken to include *Le Nozze di Figaro* and *Don Giovanni*, the Austrian Mozart being the true fulfillment of the Italian operatic ideal. Dubliners would expect to hear even English language operas like *The Bohemian Girl*, which no Italian knows, translated into Italian. Italian was the great second language of cultivated Dublin. It is important to stress the influence of the Italian opera on Shaw's dramaturgy. Although he taught himself harmony and counterpoint, Shaw never became a musical composer. He reserved musical structure for his plays. His *Back to Methuselah*—a dramatic cycle which takes five nights to peform and deals with the science fiction possibility of mankind becoming more intelligent by learning to live longer—is his equivalent of Wagner's *Ring*. It has duets and quartets and endless arias, all in English prose, and its climaxes are operatic. In a play like *Candida* (recently presented by RAI) he insisted that the actors be cast in the manner of operatic singers—soprano, contralto, tenor, baritone, basso cantanne. In the central episode of *Man and Superman* (it was Shaw who popularised *superman* as a rendering of Nietzsche's *Übermensch*) he takes the characters of *Don*

Giovanni and makes them present a kind of metaphysical opera in which music would be supererogatory. It is important that Shaw's plays, when performed in Italy, should be directed by men skilled in the direction of native opera.

Shaw, among other prophecies, foresaw that, despite the mediocre academic imitations of Mendelssohn, England would eventually enjoy a musical renascence. That such a renascence did come about few English musicians will deny, but it is hard for other countries—especially France—to take England seriously as a musical land: *Das Land ohne Musik* is the continued gibe of the nation that produced Karl Orff and Horst Wessel. Italy, to its credit, has performed Elgar's Symphony No. 1 in A flat on television, and very well too, despite the almost perpetual yawning of the first trumpet. But the truth is that orchestras play well in London and Manchester, that composers abound, and that solo instrumentalists win international prizes. All this is due to Shaw's three thousand pages of good-humoured nagging at the musicians of England to forget God and Mendelssohns and recover their own national genius. And while British music began to grow up, so did the British theatre. This, too is the achievement of that bearded vegetarian who dominated nearly a century of British intellectual life and has not failed to leave his mark on Europe.

—1981

RING

❖

Bernard Shaw translated *Das Ring des Nibelungen*, quite correctly, as *The Niblung's Ring*, while others, very inaccurately, have called the work *The Ring of the Nibelungs*. True, the Nibelungs are a whole race of dwarfs, but Wagner's massive foursome of music dramas is concerned with a ring belonging to one dwarf only. The titles of the two middle dramas—*The Valkyrie* and *Siegfried*—are pretty well in English what they are in German, but the first, *Das Rheingold*, goes better in English as *The Gold of the Rhine* rather than as *The Rhinegold*, which is too Germanic, and the last, *Die Götterdämmerung*, is more dramatic as *Night Falls on the Gods* (again, Shaw's title) than as *The Dusk of the Gods* (James Joyce's version) or the commonest translation of all—*Twilight of the Gods*, which suggests a cosy tea with muffins round the fire while the lights are low. When we talk of Wagner's *Ring*, nearly everybody knows what we refer to, but not everybody knows why such an enormous expenditure of time and music paper—twenty-five years and thousands of pages, all covered with exquisite penmanship—should have been devoted to the telling of a Teutonic fairy tale which is better fitted to the nursery than to the inadequate machinery of the nineteenth-century theatre.

First, let us consider what the fairy tale is about. It is not, of course, really a fairy tale, since there are no fairies in it, but there are giants and dwarfs and deities, as well as a dragon, a magic sword, and a helmet of invisibility. It looks, on the surface, like children's stuff, but, if we look more deeply, we shall discover a very powerful political allegory. *The Ring* is about the corruption of money and power and the need for revolutionary action in a world dominated by cynical tyranny. It is closer to Karl Marx and Bakunin than to a children's tale at twilight.

What happens? Three mermaids or naiads are swimming in the

river Rhine. They have a huge piece of gold there, which they love as a thing of beauty and never dream of putting on the market. An ugly little monster called Alberich comes slithering along the riverbed and he begs for the love of the three girls. They merely laugh at him, being elementals who have not learnt the social art of discretion, and, in his anger and humiliation, Alberich decides to abjure love and live for wealth. He steals the gold and sets up as a capitalist, making hundreds of other dwarfs, or Nibelungen, toil for him in a subterranean factory. Out of the gold they fashion two objects very useful to a capitalist: a ring which bestows supreme power and a helmet which confers the gift of metamorphosis. Wearing this *Tarnhelm*, as it is called, Alberich can assume any shape he wishes, or even no shape at all.

High above the world of the dwarfs is the world of the gods, whose head is Wotan. He has a wife named Fricka and a cunning intellectual henchman called Loge. He has commissioned certain giants, decent hardworking hardhatted creatures of little intelligence but much muscle, to build a palace called Valhalla, agreeing to give in payment the goddess of love and beauty and eternal youth—Freia, after whom the sixth day of the Northern week is named. Now that the time has come for fulfilling the bargain, Wotan is unhappy about it: without Freia the gods will wither and grow old; they need to feed on her golden apples. But Loge, who can suggest no tricky or cheating way out of the contract, has heard the complaint of the maidens of the Rhine—their gold has been stolen by the dwarf Alberich. The giants say they will take the gold instead of Freia, so Wotan and Loge trick Alberich into tarnhelming himself into a toad, and off they go with the wealth. The giants now grow greedy, and Fafnir, the greediest, commits murder for it. He turns himself into a dragon and spends his life guarding the hoard, the ultimate miser, not even a capitalist. Loge's magic makes a rainbow bridge, and over this the gods proceed into their new magnificent home.

So much, briefly, for the plot of the first of the four music dramas. Clearly, the gods are immoral, the giants stupid, the dwarfs ugly and avaricious (there is another named dwarf—Mime, kinsman of Alberich, whose villainy is reserved for the story of Siegfried). We need another kind of being, revolutionary, brave, of shining moral integrity. We need man and woman. Better, perhaps, we need what Nietzsche called the *Uebarmensch* and Shaw the Superman and Wagner was content to think of as the Hero. We need Siegfried, but we shall not meet him until the third music drama of the cycle.

In *Die Walküre* or *The Valkyrie* we meet Brünnhilde, whom it is best to think of as Brynhild (it saves the trouble of looking for an umlaut). Brynhild is Wotan's daughter, but she is begotten of the Earth Mother, not his wife Fricka, and is outside the realm of dynasty and alliance and trickery: she is as pure as a god's offspring ought to be. She is one of a group of warrior maidens who carry the bodies of slain men from the battlefield to Valhalla, and they have a fearsome cry which, in *Apocalypse Now*, Mr. Coppola unleashed over the napalm-stricken forests of Vietnam. From Brynhild and a chosen mortal man a new breed of heroes may come forth, but Wotan has to ensure that the divine seed dwells in these heroes, and he goes forth among the mortal women of the world impregnating them that they may produce potential heroic fathers. The father and mother of the hero who is to mate with Brynhild are named Sieglinde and Siegmund, and both are children of Wotan (who has been going round in a cloak and hat as the Stranger or the Wanderer, and in a wolfskin as a wolf). When they fall in love with each other they are ready to commit not only incest but adultery, since Sieglinde is married to a warrior called Hunding. Siegmund is a brave man but very unlucky; and he expects to be slain by the man he proposes to cuckold. In fact, he is, despite Brynhild's magical help, for Wotan, whose wife has told him she is on the side of the marital law as well as the dynasty to which Hunding belongs, steps in to enforce the law and see that Siegmund duly dies. Brynhild has not cared a damn about the law, and she is put to sleep like a fairy princess, surrounded by a wall of fire which only the coming bridegroom-hero can safely pierce. Sieglinde is pregnant with this hero, so that is all right.

In *Siegfried*, the young hero, eponymous hero I should say, is being reared by the dwarf Mime. Sieglinde died in giving birth to her son, bequeathing him a kind of broken birthright, the fragments of the sword called *Nothung* or Needful, which Wotan had thrust into a treetrunk for Siegmund, like King Arthur with Excalibur, to pluck forth. Mime does not like his adoptive son, and

Siegfried detests Mime; otherwise, they get on well enough together in the forest where they live. Mime wants one thing only
from Siegfried: that he should slay the dragon Fafnir and take his
gold; Siegfried will then be conveniently slain himself with a bowl
of soup seasoned with poison. The trouble is the forging of the
sword: every sword that Mime forges Siegfried breaks with ease,
jeering nastily at the poor swordsmith. There is only one unbreakable sword in the world, and that is *Nothung*, but *Nothung* is
broken. Why and how? Because it met the invincible spear of
Wotan in that fight between Siegmund and Hunding. But Siegfried
takes the fragments, melts them down, then lets the molten metal
run into a sword-mould. *Nothung* is refashioned, and Siegfried
goes off to meet the dragon—not out of love for Mime, but in
the sheer love of dangerous adventure. He kills Fafnir and takes
his ring and *Tarnhelm*; the rest of the gold he leaves as worthless.
While his hand is in, he kills Mime, to the joy of Alberich, who
is lurking in the background. Then, licking off some dragon's
blood that has got on to his finger, he discovers that he can understand the song of a bird that is evidently trying to tell him
something. There is a beautiful maiden waiting behind a wall of
fire for a hero's releasing kiss. Siegfried goes off joyously. At the
foot of Brynhild's mountain, Siegfried meets Wotan, in his earthly
disguise as an old man. He invokes the generation gap and insults
him. Wotan raises his spear, but this time it is powerless: *Nothung*
snaps it in two. We are ready for night to fall on the gods and
for the race of heroes to take over the governance of the world.

All Wagnerians agree that *Die Götterdämmerung* does not gear
well with the other music dramas of the tetralogy. There is something very operatic about it—duets, choruses, recitatives, and
arias—and the Siegfried and Brynhild we have already met change
their characters and become less than heroic. The music, however,
is glorious—the tone poem that describes Siegfried's journey to
the Rhine, the death march of Siegfried, the fire and water finale.
This is the sumptuous Wagner of his orchestral maturity, but the
libretto itself belongs to a much earlier period—the time when he
planned a genuine opera (not a music drama) called *The Death
of Siegfried*. What happens on the plot level follows logically
enough from what we have already heard and seen; it is the psychological treatment that upsets us.

Most of the action of *Götterdämmerung* takes place in the hall of the Gibichungs, who sound villainous and are. Gunther, the head of this Rhineland clan, is cowardly and foolish but thinks highly of himself. He and his crafty henchman Hagen know all about Siegfried and Brynhild and the ring and the *Tarnhelm*. Hagen, though not a dwarf, is the son of the dwarf who started all the trouble, Alberich, and he has inherited from his father a powerful, and very operatic, avarice. So he wants the ring while Gunther wants Brynhild. By the use of a magic potion they make Siegfried (who, still being in search of adventures, inevitably finds his way to the hall of the Gibichungs) forget his love for Brynhild and fall for Gunther's sister Gutruna. He will, in his changed and implausible state, do anything for his prospective brother-in-law, so he captures Brynhild, who is wearing the ring he gave her, and brings her in a flash, by virtue of the *Tarnhelm*, to the Gibichung court. Hating Siegfried now, she joins in a plot to kill him but eventually finds out the truth about his strange disaffection. So she lights a funeral pyre for the dead hero, rides into the flames herself, and presides, before being consumed, over the end of everything. The hall, having a pyre in it, goes up in flames and so does Valhalla, around which the self-destructive Wotan has arranged the dry wood of the World Tree. The Rhine obligingly overflows its banks and puts out the fire, though belatedly. The ring returns to the river and thus can do no further harm. The age of capitalism is dead, but so are the gods and the planned race of heroes. It has all been rather a waste of time.

That is a very bald summary, and it says nothing about the subtlety with which the music helps to delineate character, motivation, and place. But it may serve to show, for those who have picked up their knowledge of the great work from Nazi propaganda, how pessimistic Wagner was about human, or German, destiny. The Superman does not triumph: he dies. Hitler ought to have seen in his beloved *Ring* how accurately Wagner had foretold the end of the *Reich*. If Siegfried became the prototype of Nazi manhood—muscular, blond, and innocently cruel—he remained even more the type of the failed hero. He had no hope of redeeming the world. Such a task had to be left to Wagner's next and last hero, Parsifal, a holy fool in search of the Holy Grail. Wagner liked to think that *The Ring* was an illustration of Scho-

penhauer's philosophy, which found no virtue in striving and tried
to seek in passive resignation relief from the machinations of the
Universal Will. Very Germanic.

But Wagner was himself no man for passivity. He was energy
incarnate and in many fields—not only music but also the love of
women, aesthetics, sociology, ethnology, politics. It is his partic-
ipation in the revolutionary politics of Europe which began with
the Parisian turmoils of 1848—the year of revolutions—that
makes us see *The Ring* as a political allegory. In 1843 he became
opera conductor at Dresden and might have remained there, producing other men's operas as well his own, settling into the bourgeois life of a provincial capital, if he had not become excited by
the anarchic ideas of Proudhon and Bakunin. He wanted a break
with the past—not only socially but musically—and the works he
began to sketch in 1848 and 1849 combined the desire for a reformed society with the ideal of a new, freer, kind of dramatic
music. Thus, he proposed a work called *Jesus von Nazareth*, in
which Christ should be a political revolutionary, and began to
write the libretto for *Siegfrieds Tod* (Siegfried's Death—the original *Götterdämmerung*)—an opera, or music drama, fit for the
new age which seemed to be dawning.

In 1849 there was an uprising in Dresden, and Wagner joined
in it. He did not fight at the barricades, but he expended inflam-
matory words which made the authorities issue a warrant for his
arrest. Liszt helped him to escape to Switzerland. King Johann of
Saxony—whom Wagner had unrealistically begged to drop the
postures of traditional power and help inaugurate the new era—
later said that, had he not escaped, he would certainly have been
tried and sentenced to death. In Zürich he had operatic visions
which, he knew well, could never be realised in the opera houses
of the old régime—a régime, alas, which did not yield to the forces
of revolution. Though *Siegfried's Death* was to have most of the
features of the old opera, with recitatives, arias, duets, quartets,
and choruses, it was to demand orchestral forces and stage machinery (consider, for instance, that final conflagration) which
could not be found in the resources of the time. Wagner began to
dream of his own opera house.

In 1850 he drafted the music for *Siegfried's Death*, but, hopeless about the possibility of production, dropped it and began to

work on the dramatic poems which, logically, led up to the in-
cineration of his hero. He wrote *Der Junge Siegfried*—*The Young
Siegfried*, eventually just *Siegfried*—and *Die Walküre*, which
should describe the begetting of the hero, then finally the first
poem of the cycle *Das Rheingold*. By the end of 1852 he had
completed the entire *Ring* poem. He was drawing on the old
German epic called *The Song of the Nibelung*, but he was imposing his own ideas. The most startling of these ideas is the
highly democratic one that man is potentially greater than the
gods, and that the gods, or monarchs of the kingdoms of Europe,
unconsciously harbour a death-wish: they *want* to be overthrown.
When he started writing the music of *Das Rheingold* in 1854, it
was the need for gold—or any kind of financial security—that
was uppermost in his mind. It was not until ten years later that
King Ludwig II of Bavaria, who was a fanatical adorer of his
work, paid all his debts, offered him a fee of 30,000 florins for
completing *The Ring*, and granted him an annual allowance of
8000 florins. Wagner wanted more than that. He wanted a Wagner theatre in Munich, but Ludwig's cabinet used this extravagant
proposal to raise public feeling against him. They had other things
against him too: his adulterous relationship with Cosima, the wife
of Hans von Bülow and daughter of Liszt; his debts; his damnable
love of luxury. Of course, what they really resented was his influence with the king. They made him flee Munich, but he came
back again.

Das Rheingold was first produced in that city in 1869, twenty
years after the initial conception of the final drama of the cycle.
Die Walküre was first heard in the following year. But the Munich
opera house and its musical resources were not good enough, and
the dream of a theatre of his own began its realisation, with Ludwig's help. By 1874 Wagner had set himself up in Bayreuth, living
in the villa called *Wahnfried*, watching the theatre take shape. It
must not be supposed that Ludwig paid for it all. Wagner gave
concerts, started subscription lists, floated loans. If Hitler was to
make the Bayreuth theatre a charge on the Third Reich (first
having purged the enterprise of Jews, which angered Toscanini
and drove him away, thus depriving Germany of the finest Wagnerian conductor of all time), neither the State of Bavaria nor the

Reich of Wagner's own day cared a twopenny damn about the enormous musical vision and the home which was to enshrine it. The annual Wagner festival was a long time paying its way.

The entire *Ring* cycle was given, three times, in the summer of 1876. This parturition was the culmination of a gestation period that had lasted from 1849. (Though Wagner wrote other music dramas—*The Mastersingers, Tristan and Isolde*—as well as a large number of books and pamphlets and such exquisite trifles as the Wesendonck songs and the *Siegfried Idyll* during a time which, like all his times, was turbulent.) In the Bayreuth theatre Wagner had all his own way, as, until 1930, his widow was to have her own way also, a way that threatened to turn Bayreuth into a museum until her son Siegfried, and his son Wieland, found new ways of solving the staging problems which have bedevilled all Wagner producers. For the trouble with *The Ring* is that it is based on an epic and remains an epic. Epic takes kindly to dragons and magical swords, as well as universal conflagrations, but the stage is unhappy about them. What *The Ring* has always needed is cinematic adaptation, but the cinema, even in Nazi Germany, was always too popular a form to accommodate Wagnerian grandeur. Television, in the hundredth year after Wagner's death in Venice, has to be forced into accepting *The Ring*. This cycle of drama, music, myth, and social allegory is one of the great human achievements, and we ought to commit suicide rather than deny it to the small screen.

Let us consider briefly the nature of Wagner's artistic achievement. *The Ring* is (with the inevitable qualification concerning its final segment) not opera but a new form called music drama. Opera thrives on set numbers and, except for its recitatives and dialogue, comes closer to the four-square structure of song than to the flow of an Aeschylus or a Shakespeare. Wagner has created a kind of musical prose which flows forever and resists being chopped up into set arias or ensembles. Moreover, the orchestra, instead of tamely supplying a rum-tum-tum accompaniment to the singers in the Italian manner, lives its own complex life and illuminates the narrative at a level which anticipates the Freudian and Jungian unconscious. Wagner generated over a hundred germinal themes, or *Leitmotive*, which symbolise objects, concepts, motivations, personalities; these melt and merge and are transformed as the orchestral flow surges and subsides and recovers and overwhelms in what Wagner called perpetual melody.

The orchestra that he needed defeated conventional opera houses. He called for eight harps in *Das Rheingold*, as well as a phalanx of anvils. New instruments were invented so that each section of the orchestra could form its own self-contained family: heckelphones as well as English horns to drive the oboe tone down to the depths; high trumpets and bass trumpets; a contrabass trombone. Sax in Paris (father of the saxophone) fashioned the Wagner tuba, which helped to blend trombones and horns. Massed strings were divided into shimmering rainbows of sound. Orchestral players all over the world had to learn to become virtuosi. My father used to tell me of his being present at a rehearsal of the Hallé Orchestra in Manchester under Hans von Richter, who had worked with Wagner. The first horn player said that Siegfried's horncall in *Götterdämmerung* was unplayable. This plaint was translated for Richter, who knew no English, and he put out his hand for the horn, fitted to it a mouthpiece he took from his pocket, played the passage flawlessly, then handed the instrument back. From then on there were no more complaints about unplayability. This re-education of musicians was going on everywhere, and it was all in the service of the great musical message of *The Ring*.

Music had, up to Wagner's time, been more decorative than expressive. True, Beethoven dragged the art of sound into regions of morality and philosophy in that Ninth Symphony, which Wagner always regarded as his own starting-point. But with *The Ring* the urgency of the philosophical message turned music into a language more subtle and various than that of even the epic poets. The time would come when Richard Strauss, who cut his teeth on Wagner, could create symphonic poems which made verbal language supererogatory. In the late twentieth century, composers are still trying to free themselves from the Wagnerian heritage. Wagner died a century ago, but we have only to listen to the opening of *Das Rheingold*, where the very groundbass of Nature is heard, hardly distinguishable from the voice of the eternal river, to be seduced into feeling that *this* is what music is about, and Mozart and Haydn and even Beethoven were merely playing parlor games. It is an illusion, but a very powerful one. Wagner was the most dangerous of magicians.

The Nazis have done a lot of harm to Wagner, exaggerating an antisemitism which was nothing more than resentment at the success of the operas of Meyerbeer, who just happened to be a Jew, and seeing in his transformation of the Nibelung myth the glorification of the Aryan. But Wagner is bigger than all the political ideologies, and his realistic pessimism, curiously contradicted by the sheer glory of his orchestral sound, is more in tune with our own age—which has seen *The Ring* enacted on the stage of world politics—than with the facile triumphalism of both the fascists and the communists. He is a very modern poet and composer, as much present in Eliot's *The Waste Land* as in Joyce's *Ulysses*, and his centennial is not an antiquarian celebration: it is an acknowledgment that Wagner is a living force and probably an eternal one.

—1982

THE LITERATURE OF THE BRITISH FROM 1900 TO 1982

❖

The British were originally the Welsh. But now they are also the English, Scots, and Northern Irish, as well as the citizens of Australia, New Zealand, Canada, and various smaller territories dotted over the globe. The language of the British is English. The language of the Americans is English. Some Americans—notably Henry James and T. S. Eliot—turned themselves into British citizens. Some British citizens—notably W. H. Auden and Christopher Isherwood—turned themselves into Americans. Evidently it is not easy to draw the line between what is British and what is not. W. B. Yeats, conceivably the greatest English language poet of the twentieth century, was a citizen of the Republic of Ireland and did not like to be termed British. James Joyce, conceivably the greatest English language novelist of the twentieth century, was not only an Irishman but a quintessential Dubliner, but he retained a British passport to the end of his days, a circumstance which put him into some danger when, living in Paris as he was, the Germans invaded France in 1940. It is best for us not to be too pedantic in our divisions when we discuss the literature in English that has been produced in the present century.

It is convenient for historians of that literature to relate its various phases to the reigns of the British monarchs. Victorian literature has a quality somewhat different from the literature of the reign of King Edward VII (1901–1911). In Victoria's reign there was general agreement about the beliefs, desired conduct, and social aspirations of British citizens. There was an established Protestant Church, a fixed division between the classes of society, and a large and growing British Empire. But, in the middle of the nineteenth century, Karl Marx's *Das Kapital* and Darwin's *Origin of Species* were already challenging traditional social and religious beliefs, and, at the end of the century, there was a good deal of confusion and doubt as to the future of Empire, Church, and the social system. With the war against the Boers in South Africa, it was made clear that the monolithic Empire was not so strong and tranquil as it had formerly appeared. Socialism was on the rise. Not everybody went to services of the Church of England on Sunday. That Church was being assailed not only by atheists and agnostics but also by Catholic converts. The Edwardian era in literature was characterised by various attempts to find new faiths, new aspirations. There was a qualified optimism that was badly assailed by the loss of the *Titanic* in 1912 and the outbreak of a destructive war in 1914.

Thomas Hardy bridges the gap between the Victorians and the Edwardians. He did not believe in a beneficent God, only in an indifferent or possibly malevolent force which he called Nature, in an evil destiny for mankind which could not be countered by the exercise of free will. He was a thorough pessimist. In his best-known novel *Tess of the Durbervilles* a simple country girl ends on the scaffold, the mere sport or plaything of the "President of the Immortals." In his last novel, *Jude the Obscure*, three young children commit suicide because they cannot bear to think of the future. Against this Rudyard Kipling, the poet of Empire, drummed out his belief in the "White Man's burden," the responsibility of the white races to educate the coloured, the necessity for a world confederation in which Anglo-Saxon culture should bring all men to the light. But G. K. Chesterton and Hilaire Belloc wanted to see England restored to Catholic Europe and a new crusaders' cross raised against the growing forces of barbaric materialism.

H. G. Wells and George Bernard Shaw (an Anglo-Irishman, a Dubliner like Yeats and Joyce) saw a future in rationalism, the growth of socialism, the implementation by a progressive State of programmes of educational reform which would produce a new and enlightened race. From Nietzsche Shaw borrowed the concept of the *Übermensch*, which he translated as Superman, and from Henri Bergson the notion of Creative Evolution. A better world would evolve if only men and women, through reason and imagination, helped the *élan vital* to produce it. Wells, a trained scientist, believed that human hope lay in science. He believed in the possibility of a Utopia and even called himself a Utopiographer. The impact of two World Wars dashed his hopes, and he ended by saying that *homo sapiens* was finished, that the time was coming for the emergence of a new species. Shaw, in old age, no longer talked of the Superman, having seen the *Übermensch* in action in Buchenwald and Auschwitz. Optimism was a dangerously unrealistic philosophy for the twentieth century.

Two novelists who belong to the Edwardian age and yet are more congenial to our own age than either Shaw or Wells are, though they wrote in English, essentially European. Joseph Conrad, a Pole, thought in French. Ford Madox Ford, whose original surname was Hueffer, was of partly German blood and wholly French in his view of the fictional art. Both men looked back to Flaubert rather than to Dickens or Fielding. Conrad, a master mariner, emphasised the essential loneliness of man battling with the sea or the problems of right behaviour. Heroism was possible but, since God no longer existed, sanctity was not. In *Heart of Darkness* Conrad showed himself aware of the existence of evil, a traditional theological property which Shaw and Wells denied. Ford, in his great tetralogy *Parade's End*, presented the need for a new kind of courage in facing a world falling into barbarism. The Edwardian values of decency, even quixotry, an ethic without a theological base, are enshrined in his hero Christopher Tietjens, a member of a defunct ruling class who strenuously maintains his code of honour in a world which has lost honour.

Compared with these, Arnold Bennett and John Galsworthy are very minor novelists, despite their greater popularity. Galsworthy can do little more than record the decay of the old Whig property-owners and, though he wishes to show the need for a new morality, with a new sexual freedom, he lacks the courage and eloquence to formulate a positive philosophy. He is himself a member of the class whose death he records. Bennett has had more to say to the generation of writers which began to appear after 1945. A man of lowly social origins, he fictionalises the fight of the ambitious provincial against the entrenched culture and authority of the old ruling class.

Up to his death in 1916, Henry James, an American who ended as a British citizen, provided for all ambitious novelists a pattern of devotion to the art of fiction which owed much to France. If the world was, according to the American Henry Adams (whose autobiography appeared in 1907), falling into a state of entropy, and if the American future which was also the world's future exhibited a gross mechanistic materialism which the man of sensibility had to reject, where was the writer to find his themes? Only in Europe, replied Henry James, with its decadent but subtle culture, only in the European mind and its concern with the immediacies of the personal relationship. What such women writers as Elizabeth Bowen and Rosamund Lehmann and, indeed, Virginia Woolf learned from Henry James was the importance of the human microcosm, the limited cultivated society in which its fulfilment can be found, the personal relationship—not, to quote E. M. Forster, the world of "telegrams and anger." Forster himself, a somewhat timid Edwardian who did not dare expose his homosexuality nor plead for its acceptance, was a humanist of the Jamesian kind.

The American Ernest Hemingway found a new creed in the animality of man—man the hunter and fighter, equipped with a primitive sense of honour but no capacity to articulate it. If the human intellect could produce the horrors of the first great technological war, then the human intellect was dangerous, and its language was dangerous too. Prose should concern itself with physical immediacies. D. H. Lawrence was, in a sense, Hemingway's English counterpart, concentrating on instinct and emotional conviction and jettisoning the reason and the intellect. In Hemingway man is the lone Conradian besieged hero with a gun. In Lawrence man is a sexual creature, finding his creed in his loins, eventually, as in *The Plumed Serpent*, prepared to formulate a new world religion of instinct, imagination and, above all, sexuality. In *Lady Chatterley's Lover* sex, which symbolises Nature, triumphs over an oppressive mechanical civilisation. Lawrence was, in effect, reverting to the philosophy of William Blake (1757–1827), who denounced reason as the devil and elevated instinct and imagination to the level of godhead.

Conceivably the two greatest literary events of the twentieth century occurred in 1922, with the publication of *The Waste Land* by T. S. Eliot (an American) and *Ulysses* by James Joyce (an Irishman). English poetry had sunk to a feeble condition of weekend nature worship, with a style and diction removed from true human language, and it had responded hardly at all to the innovations of Gerard Manley Hopkins, the Jesuit priest whose poetry, though written before 1889, no publisher had dared to issue before 1918. Hopkins developed a freer rhythm and a bolder language than was to the taste of the Noe-Georgian poets (a somewhat contemptuous term used for the versifiers on the reign of George V), and so did the Irishman W. B. Yeats. But it was the American Ezra Pound who had shown, in 1917, the most potent new direction for English poetry, as also Eliot with, in the same year, his volume *Prufrock*. Poetry was to use the language of everyday life and imagery appropriate to the machine age. *The Waste Land* remains the best manifesto of modernism in poetry— a triumph of concision, eloquence, colloquialism, symbolism, cinematic cutting, collage of existing literature as well as popular song, all in the service of a kind of purgatorial philosophy: civilisation was decaying, man was growing impotent, salvation lay in the injunctions of a Sanskrit Upanishad: "Give, sympathise, control."

Joyce's *Ulysses* presented the new fictional direction. Joyce and Virginia Woolf had hit simultaneously upon the need for the human mind to present itself immediately to the reader, as on a psychoanalyst's couch, with thought and feeling uncensored and unshaped but contained in a mythical envelope which controlled the narrative movement of the monologue. Joyce takes a single day in Dublin—16 June 1904—and the unexciting experiences of three main characters have imposed upon them the framework of Homer's Odyssey, whose various episodes—the Sirens, the Cyclops, the Lotos-Eaters and so on—suggest subject matter for thought and feeling, as well as for symbols and the actual style of the narrative prose. Ordinary man is revealed as quite as heroic as Odysseus, though comically so, and style imparts the interest which, in traditional fiction, would reside in the plot.

The age between the wars comes to an end with Joyce's *Finnegans Wake*, in which the author's interest in the deeper regions of the human mind leads him to the kingdom of sleep. The book is a dream of world history and it is couched in a new language, a comic mixture of all the tongues of Europe. Fictional experimentation could not well go further. To many readers *Finnegans Wake* mirrored the European chaos to come, but others saw in it a secret blueprint for rebuilding a civilisation that was on the brink of destroying itself.

In comparison with Joyce and Eliot—and one might add the Ezra Pound of the massive *Cantos*—most writers in England during the period of *l'entre deux guerres* were bourgeois, conventional, and timid. The general public read William Somerset Maugham and crime novelists like Agatha Christie and were fearful of writers who were too frank about sex or probed the human psyche too deeply. Aldous Huxley, whose sensibility was European and whose novels and essays were exhibitionistically erudite, shocked with his *Point Counter Point* (which now seems a very unshocking novel) and his forecast of a beneficent totalitarian future in *Brave New World*. W. H. Auden, Stephen Spender, and Cecil Day Lewis were young poets from Oxford who tried to shock readers of the 1930s into a realisation that the old régime was dying and a revolution was on its way. But they derived their verse technique from the Jesuit poet Gerard Manley Hopkins. Eventually Auden abandoned his revolutionary stance and joined the Anglican Church (though he had first to become an American citizen cut off from the nightmare of totalitarian Europe) but achieved a body of poetry of lasting value and may be considered the true heir of T. S. Eliot. Dylan Thomas, a Welshman, combined Freudian and Biblical imagery in a kind of eloquent surrealism that reminded the English how much they needed the mad fervour of the Celts.

England needed not merely the Celts but also the Europeans—Arthur Koestler, for instance, whose *Darkness at Noon* imported to English letters the true nightmare vision and inspired George Orwell to take seriously the political situation in Europe. He fought in the Spanish Civil War and produced *Homage to Catalonia*. In 1949 came the ultimate nightmare of *Nineteen Eighty-Four*, a strangely un-English novel whose violence and intellectual stringency are totally divorced from the liberal and empirical tradition which had fed most writers from Shakespeare to Dickens. During the war the English discovered Franz Kafka, the great prophet of nightmare, and Rex Warner produced works like the allegorical *The Wild Goose Chase* and *The Aerodrome*, in which the Kafkaesque vision is diluted with English wit and compassion. After the war, with Orwell's *Nineteen Eighty-Four* leading the way, the British began to think seriously of the novel as a vehicle for thought and speculation: it was no longer the mere entertainment that had sufficed for the twenties and thirties. Graham Greene and Evelyn Waugh, who had been converted to Catholicism before the war, viewed human conduct from a theological aspect. Waugh's trilogy *Sword of Honour* looks at the Second World War in terms of ultimate morality, seeing that war (as Ford Madox Ford saw its predecessor) more as a symptom of moral breakdown than as a cause of it. Greene is more concerned with the conflict between official atheism and individual faith (*The Power and the Glory*), the contiguity of sin and sanctity (*The Heart of the Matter; The End of the Affair*), and the need to reconcile *politique* and *mystique*, (*The Comedians* and *The Honorary Consul*).

C. P. Snow and Anthony Powell, mindful of the tradition of massiveness that had animated the nineteenth-century masters, produced, in *Strangers and Brothers* and *A Dance to the Music of Time*, fictional histories of their own time in many volumes. Women novelists began to be important—Iris Murdoch, Doris Lessing, Muriel Spark—and the incredible achievement of Ivy Compton-Burnett began to be noticed: she, for many years, had been foreshadowing the French structuralists in a series of novels which dealt with morality as an aspect of family structure, coolly, objectively, wittily, to the general indifference of the British public.

British society began to change with the overwhelming victory of the Socialist Party in 1945. The British Empire disappeared, and certain novelists saw as their duty the recording of that ambiguous structure. Paul Scott wrote about nothing but India; Anthony Burgess produced a trilogy on the twilight of British rule in Malaysia; Gerald Hanley concentrated on Africa; West Indian novelists like Samuel Selvon, Edgar Mittelholzer, and V. S. Naipaul told England about the nature of colonial life in the West Indies. There was a great temptation for the British novelist to confine himself—or, more particularly, herself—to themes like suburban adultery, to evade the big world themes and the challenges of experiment which were animating European writers like Günter Grass and Nathalie Sarraute. In other words, English literature wished to be parochial. Lawrence Durrell, in his *Alexan-*

dria Quartet, avoided a parochial theme and style but could not divest himself of a certain English insularity—the juvenile excitement of a schoolboy seeing strange things in exotic North Africa.

In the 1950s, perhaps as a product of the new English socialism, the voice of the working-class began to be heard in literature. London had been for too long the centre of literary endeavour, and the upper middle class had established the tone and content of all the arts. Young men from the provinces, born outside the ranks of privilege, demanded attention, and they got it. The British theatre, for instance, had been concerned only with light entertainment suitable for a drowsy middle-class audience, but the feeble complacency of the bourgeois *drame* was shattered by the irruption, in 1956, of John Osborne's *Look Back in Anger*, which brought the articulate rage of the provincial working-class dispossessed, newly educated by the socialists, to the appalled notice of the London bourgeoisie. In fiction, Kingsley Amis's *Lucky Jim* also spoke up for the working-class provincial who, having received an education at one of the new "redbrick" universities, demanded from life certain basic rights—enough money to buy beer and cigarettes and take out to dinner a woman born in a milieu superior to his own. Hypergamy—marrying into the upper class—was the theme of John Braine's *Room at the Top*. Alan Sillitoe's *Saturday Night and Sunday Morning* presented the factory worker as tough, intelligent, hedonistic, and not at all subservient to his masters. The British novel had at last become democratised.

The post-war age demanded many kinds of emancipation. Provincial brands of English had to be considered as valid as the upper-class dialect of the Southeast (an area which contains London and Oxford and Cambridge), and the Liverpool Poets were not only bought and read but even became bestsellers. The division between serious and popular music was questioned, and the Beatles—a singing group from Liverpool that had begun its career in Hamburg—were given not merely respect but adulation. Science fiction, formerly regarded as puerile nonsense, was practised as a serious branch of literature, and names like J. G. Ballard and Brian Aldiss and Michael Moorcock were accorded the sedulous attention of serious literary critics.

Women, too, were asking for attention not as feeble adjuncts of men but as human beings in their own right. An influential book by Germaine Greer, *The Female Eunuch*, asserted not merely the division between the sexes but the hostility between them. In fiction the new phenomenon of the aggressive female was presented in the novels of Brigid Brophy and, more spectacularly, in such a *magnum opus* as Doris Lessing's *The Golden Notebook*, where not only the emancipation of women is urged but also the emancipation of homosexuals. Miss Lessing, having been born in Rhodesia (now Zimbabwe), was also powerfully aware of the rights of the downtrodden black race. The black voice was heard more stridently in America, however, as was the voice of the homosexual (in, for example, Gore Vidal's *The Pillar and the City*), and the black and the homosexual conjoined in novels like James Baldwin's *Giovanni's Room*.

From about 1968 it may be said that books and plays and poems produced in Great Britain had ceased to be assessable in terms of philosophies and political movements. It is possible to look at the novels of William Golding and John Fowles as highly individual artefacts, like the poems of Thom Gunn and Seamus Heaney (a citizen of the Republic of Ireland who disclaims a national tradition and, writing in the language of the British, forms a part of British literature), and to see the vitality of the British theatre as a phenomenon of language and psychological insight rather than, as with *Look Back in Anger*, an expression of social disquiet. But the British of the British Isles are strongly aware that their literature lacks universal appeal, experimental verve, and the sheer greatness it knew in the age of Shakespeare or Swift or Dickens. The great writers (and Nobel Prize-winners) belong to America. If the Australian Patrick White received the Nobel Prize, it was more of a tribute to an emerging postcolonial culture than a signal of the discovery of genuine greatness. Canada feels even more strongly than the mother country its failure to produce a literature of world significance, though possibly the novels of Robertson Davies are beginning to receive serious attention outside the narrow world of Toronto.

Looking around at the literary achievements in the English language that have glorified this century, an English critic has to accept that most of them are not the work of Anglo-Saxons of the motherland. Eliot and Pound were Americans, Conrad a Pole,

Ford Madox Ford a half-German and an adoptive Frenchman, Dylan Thomas a Welshman, Hugh MacDiarmid a Scot (perhaps not really qualified as an English language poet, though perhaps a great one, since, like Robert Burns, he elected to write in Scots dialect), Yeats and Shaw and Joyce and Flann O'Brien, perhaps Joyce's true successor, all Irishmen. But ultimately a literature is not a matter for nationalistic or racial pride, since it is made out of a language, and a language becomes the property of anyone who decides to write in it. Samuel Beckett is an Anglo-Irishman, but he has become one of the glories of contemporary French literature.

At this moment of writing, or concluding, it must unfortunately be said that bookshops in Germany, as also in France, America, and Scandinavia, do not necessarily provide the best of English literature. The best-known names are probably John le Carré, Len Deighton, Jack Higgins, Ken Follett, Alistair Maclean, and other specialists in the fiction of adventure or espionage. To decide why such books are inferior to, say, Golding's *Rites of Passage* or the almost totally neglected *Balkans Trilogy* of the late Olivia Manning, involves aesthetic arguments which are irrelevant to a brief survey like this. But literature is the exploitation of language, of human ambiguity, of action and its motivation, and of the texture of human day-to-day living. If Englishmen forget what literature is, they have only to return to William Shakespeare to find all the above parameters fulfilled. And Shakespeare, like all the authors I have briefly considered and the great number I have had to neglect, is still part of contemporary British literature.

—1982

All About Alice

❖

Lewis Carroll, who wrote *Alice in Wonderland* and *Alice Through the Looking-Glass*, was, in private life, Charles Lutwidge Dodgson, a professor of mathematics at the University of Oxford. He Latinised Lutwidge to Ludovicus or Lewis and Charles to Carolus or Carroll, and, under this name, produced the first Alice book in 1865 and the second in 1872. He produced other books as well, mostly on difficult mathematical subjects. Queen Victoria, enchanted by the Alice books, asked for all of Mr. Carroll's publications and was bewildered by the delivery of treatises on trigonometry and the binomial theory. Lewis Carroll was also the first of the great photographers, and his studies of children—especially of little Alice Liddell, who was both the heroine and the first reader of the two great books—have a charm and a mastery of technique envied by the Nikon-snappers of today.

He also loved little girls and did not like them to grow into big ones, though he was vague about the moment of change. He tried to kiss big seventeen-year-old young ladies and was surprised that their mothers should protest. His love of girls, which he was too innocent to interpret sexually, had perhaps something to do with his desire to remain a child himself. Although he practised the adult art of mathematics, which children hate because it is too abstract, he did not really wish to have the responsibilities of an adult. He never married, he was deeply and innocently religious, he liked to be cut off from the dangerous outside world. He was happy to be enclosed by the walls of an Oxford college and to tell stories to the little daughter of Dr. Liddell, the great Greek scholar. But the publication of the two Alice books brought him fame. There was something in them which touched strings in the adult imagination and yet pleased and continues to please children. Carroll was a greater man than he knew.

Both the Alice books are fantasies, aspects of the love of nonsense which was prevalent in England in the Victorian age. There was no nonsense in the rest of the world. When, in the early years of the twentieth century, France began to discover the delights of nonsense, this was called surrealism, and it was regretted that the British were too old-fashioned to produce surrealist writers or painters. But the British had already produced their own surrealists in the staid age of Victoria, and of these perhaps Lewis Carroll was the greatest.

Surrealism consists in destroying the logic of ordinary life and substituting a kind of logic of the unconscious mind. Alice's adventures take the form of dreams in which bizarre things happen, but these things are based on a more serious approach to language than we can permit ourselves in waking life. By language I mean, of course, the English language in which Carroll wrote; many of his dream-jokes are impossible to render into other tongues. If there is an insect called a butterfly, it seems dreamily logical to have a bread-and-butterfly, and Carroll's illustrator, Tenniel, draws us one of these. The flower known as a dandelion is a dandy lion, hence it can roar. There is a school in which the lessons get shorter every day: the lessons "lessen." If your watch stops, the dreamworld says that time has stopped. The watch of the Mad Hatter and his friends the March Hare and the Dormouse has stopped at teatime, so they must go on taking tea forever.

One of the characters who appears in the looking-glass world is Humpty Dumpty, who is a talking egg. His name not merely describes him: it *is* him (or he). An egg has a hump above and a dump below. He is the most dangerous, and yet the most persuasive, philosopher of language imaginable. He says "There's glory for you," and he explains that "glory" means "a fine knockdown argument." Alice protests, but Humpty Dumpty says "It's a question of who is to be master, you or the word." Words, in other words, can mean what we want them to mean or else what the logic of dreams wants them to mean. Their normal everyday meaning doesn't apply when we pass through the looking-glass.

Alice's world is a world full of eccentric English Victorians disguised mostly as animals. Like real grown-ups they can be very rude or pompous to a child like Alice, but in her dreams Alice can answer back without being punished for her effrontery. She is temporarily living in a kind of Garden of Eden, in which total liberty seems to be possible—in Wonderland Alice can change her shape and size merely by drinking from a bottle that says DRINK ME—but liberty is circumscribed not by notions of right and wrong but by mad logic. In the songs she hears or sings herself this mad logic seems to disappear, but there is substituted for it the spirit of parody, which implies an existing logic in the waking world. Alice knows very well a song that goes

> *Twinkle twinkle little star,*
> *How I wonder what you are,*
> *Up above the world so high*
> *Like a diamond in the sky.*

This becomes

> *Twinkle twinkle little bat,*
> *How I wonder what you're at,*
> *Up above the world so high,*
> *Like a teatray in the sky.*

Why bat? Why teatray? For that matter, why is a raven like a writing desk? We feel that if we dig deeply enough we shall find our answers, but there is no time for digging, except for apples. If, in French, potatoes are *pommes de terre*, they are apples in the earth, and digging is quite in order.

It is the very English eccentricity of the denizens of Wonderland and the Looking-Glass world that endears them to us. The White Rabbit, the Ugly Duchess, the Queen of Hearts, the White Knight, Tweedledum and Tweedledee, all marvellously drawn by Tenniel, are also very fully characterised by Carroll. They speak as we would expect them to speak, and they are full of an appalling self-will and vigour. But the men are less vigorous than the women. It is a child's world of petticoat government in which the women—mothers, sisters, governesses—are near and magisterial, as well as wantonly cruel, while fathers are more distant, nicer, and busied with their own eccentric affairs.

But finally the appeal of the Alice books is to the creative imagination, by which space and time can become plastic and language itself diverted from the everyday course of straightforward communication. There is a strange poem, which Humpty Dumpty kindly explains to Alice, that sums up the possibilities of the dreaming world. It is called "Jabberwocky" and it begins

> *'Twas brillig, and the slithy toves*
> *Did gyre and gimble in the wabe.*
> *All mimsy were the borogoves,*
> *And the mome raths outgabe.*

"Slithy" in both slimy and lithe, to gyre is to girate, to gimble is both to gambol like a lamb and to turn like a gimlet or corkscrew. Humpty Dumpty calls these "portmanteaux words," because, like portmanteaux, several things can be crammed into them. James Joyce saw the possibilities of this Jabberwocky language and, in his great novel *Finnegans Wake*, which presents an adult, not a child's, dream, he used the technique. What, with Carroll, began as a joke ends, in Joyce, as the most serious attempt ever made to show how the dreaming mind operates.

But we leave it to the psychologists and literary critics to find in the Alice books great profundities and profound ambiguities. The Freudians have seen sexual symbols in them, which Carroll's innocent conscious mind could not be aware of, and the Marxists have seen images of social tyranny and revolt. We are wisest if we become children again and use the books to recapture a lost innocence. We must learn to identify ourselves with a girl in a Victorian frock whose hair is long and golden and whose manner has the self-assurance of a product of the Victorian ruling class.

To be honest, Alice is not a very nice little girl. She is far too sharp and bossy and proud. She lacks humility, but—and this is an aspect of the British imperialist spirit—she also lacks fear. It requires great courage at the trial of the Knave of Hearts, with the Queen shouting "Off with her head!" for her to cry: "You're

nothing but a pack of cards!" and to see the chaos of the mass
of pasteboard that, a minute ago, was an imperialist society whirl-
ing about her head. She is transported to mad colonial territories
and retains something of her sanity. She is very British and very
Victorian, but she is also admirably and universally human.

—1982

FLANN O'BRIEN A PREFATORY WORD

❖

He was, as Murphy the sailor in *Ulysses* said Simon Dedalus was, all Irish. Some would add, as Simon Dedalus's son of his father added, all too Irish. I refuse to attempt to define Irish in the sense or nonsense used there and also here, though perhaps the meanings are different, but I would say that the trouble with a lot of writers who are not Irish is that they are not Irish. It is sometimes best to approach essences through their negations. Flann O'Brien is not Walter Pater, Edmund Gosse, Norman Douglas, C. P. Snow, nor even A. E. (he, anyway, was George Russell). He is best, like God, defined tautologously.

That was not his real name. This writer, so elusive of any decent man's assessment, can at least be nailed down to an anagraphical record. He was born Brian O'Nolan in 1911. One of three brothers from Tullamore, of a family learned in the Irish and other, lesser, languages, he went to Dublin and had a hard time—memorialised in *The Hard Life*—at the Christian Brothers' School in Synge Street, and then an easier hard time at Blackrock College. He completed his education at University College, where he wrote a master's thesis on "Nature in Modern Irish Poetry." Joyce, who was also, though a good deal earlier, at UCD, did not get so far academically, and Joyce rejected what O'Nolan embraced—a thorough knowledge of the Irish tongue, Old as well as Modern. O'Nolan was a good student and a flame of high audibility in the College Debating Society. He wrote fine essays and had great humour. But he did not have Joyce's artistic vocation, expressed in silence, exile, and cunning. He did not give up all for literature nor run away with a girl from Finn's Hotel. He married decently and settled to the life of a bourgeois Dubliner. Literature and journalism were hobbyish sidelines conducted during a career spent in the service of the Irish bureaucracy. In the civil service he rose high and, being of high wit and terrifying articulacy, could make his juniors tremble. He wrote a few books in English—*At Swim-Two-Birds*, *The Hard Life*, *The Dalkey Archives* and *The Third Policeman*. He wrote a play for the Abbey Theatre called *Faustus Kelly*. He wrote a novel in Irish—*An Beál Bocht*, translated by Patrick C. Power as *The Poor Mouth*. Under the pseudonym Myles na Gopaleen (Myles of the Little Ponies) he contributed—with the generic title *Cruiskeen Lawn* (The Little Overflowing Jug)—an extravagant weekly humorous column to the staid *Irish Times*. He was known by three names, but he probably had more. He was too big, though little, to be content with one persona. He drank a great deal and died on All Fools' Day in 1966.

His first book, and probably his best, indeed possibly one of the seminal books of the twentieth century, was *At Swim-Two-Birds*. This came out in 1939, the year of *Finnegans Wake*, and Joyce himself, tortured by near-blindness, read it and admired it. Graham Greene, reading for Longmans, as good as demanded its publication: "I read it with continual excitement, amusement, and the kind of glee one experiences when people smash china on the stage." Dylan Thomas said: "This is just the book to give your sister if she's a loud, dirty, boozy girl." Flann O'Brien repudiated the work in later life, calling it "juvenile blather." In many ways it is, or, put another way, it breathes the insouciance and exuberance of youth. It is a novel that denies the possibility of the novel, which is brash when it is not French. The French *anti-romanciers* have seen in it a premature annunciation of their own practice, but Flann O'Brien was less concerned with avant-gardism than with having a good time. There is a narrator who is writing a book about a man called Trellis, who is writing a book about other people, who are writing various books about a man called Trellis. There is also the giant Finn:

> When the seven companies of my warriors are gathered together on the one plain and the truant clean-cold loud-voiced wind goes through them, too sweet to me is that. Echo-blow of a goblet-base against the tables of the palace, sweet to me is that. I like gull-cries and the twittering together of line cranes. I like the surf-roar at Tralee, the songs of the three sons of Meadhra and the whistle of Mac Lughaidh. These also please me, man-shouts at a parting, cuckoo-call in May.

And so on. The collocation of varying styles—mock-heroic, dead-pan educated shabby genteel, low Dublin—goes back to the "Cyclops" episode in *Ulysses*, but Flann O'Brien is less imitating Joyce than being, like Joyce, Irish.

Brian O'Nolan, or Myles, drinking at the Bailey said that Joyce had the edge on him when it came to rendering the speech of the Dublin streets. He used to cite: "Eh, mister, your flies is open, mister," as showing Joyce's superior ear: he himself, Myles or O'Nolan, would not have thought of that extra "mister." But Myles did well enough in those *Cruiskeen Lawn* near-monologues at the busstop:

> The brother says the seals near Dublin do often come up out of the water at night-time and do be sittin above in the trams when they're standin in the stables. And they do be upstairs too. Begob the brother says it's a great sight of a moonlight night to see your men with the big moustaches on them sittin upstairs in the trams lookin out. And they do have the wives and the young wans along with them, of course.
>
> *Is that a fact?*
>
> Certainly, man. The seals are great family people, always were. Well then the brother was showin me two queer lookin men with black and white feathers on them and black beaks, out sittin there in the water.
>
> *Two birds?*
>
> Two of the coolest customers I ever seen, didn't give a damn about us although we went near enough to brain them with the oars.

And (again) so on.

What is (again) less Joycean than pure mad Irish is a double obsession: to notate the stream of speech exactly but not to give a damn about the tyranny of the space-time continuum. In *The Dalkey Archives* we meet St. Augustine and also James Joyce, working as a bar curate in Skerries and writing little pieces for the Catholic Truth Society but denying the authorship of *Ulysses*, a very dirty book. In *The Third Policeman* the denial of the Newtonian universe comes very close to accepting the reality of hell, but let that pass. In *The Hard Life* physical properties like weight and mass are airily refashioned. Discontinuity, of personality as much as of events, is of the Flannian essence. The reality is language, including a subsidiary syntax of Dublin streets, which a new Chomsky may yet prove to be the ultimate deep structure.

The aim of all the writing is ludic. It is, to be more precise, to disturb through the playing of games (O'Nolan was a great chess-player who liked to disturb by winning). One of the games is called Keats and Chapman, a disturbing idea in itself. It depends not on realms of gold and a translation of Homer but on a Sherlock Holmes-Watson relationship and an anecdote whose justification is a bad pun. "This thing is a genuine disease," wrote Flann O'Brien to Timothy O'Keeffe. By God, he was right.

> Keats was once presented with an Irish terrier, which he humorously named Byrne. One day the beast strayed from the house and failed to return at night. Everybody was distressed, save Keats himself. He reached reflectively for his violin, a fairly passable timber of the Stradivarius feciture, and was soon at work with chin and jaw.
>
> Chapman, looking in for an after-supper pipe, was astonished at the poet's composure, and did not hesitate to say so. Keats smiled (in a way that was rather lovely).
>
> "And why should I not fiddle," he asked, "while Byrne roams?"

I will not say more. Once you start looking too deep you're in trouble. I will say only that Myles or Flann had the finest literary equipment of the post-Joyce age but, discouraged perhaps by the example of the master, refused to be serious with it. He was weak on big structures and he distrusted them anyway, working as he was for a big structure called the Irish State. He was the funniest man of his time, but he was writing in an age that did not much care for humour. Even *At Swim-Two-Birds* timed itself to appear when the world did not see much to laugh at. The war killed it, but it came back again. It kept coming back again, and perhaps now it is back for good. The same is true of the lesser books and the journalism. One of the hopeful signs of the mess of the world we are living in may be that we are recovering our sense of humour, having lost our capacity to hope. If that is so, then this great Dubliner is returning most opportunely. He was too wise to be optimistic, too quirky to be everybody's meat, too subtle for the stupid, too learned for the mob. He is a clean Rabelais and an unwhimsical Sterne. But he is finally himself, or hisselves. And, thank the heavens, he is all too Irish.

—1982

ARTIST'S LIFE

❖

There is a waltz by Johann Strauss with the above title, and it is lighthearted, lilting, and (as it used to be possible to say before sodomites appropriated the term) gay. It has to be a fairly delimiting title, suggesting the second act of *La Bohème* not the last one, and of course the music is entirely inappropriate for the reality of life for most painters, poets, composers, and novelists. I speak as a novelist, but I have been a poet and composer also. Only colour-blindness prevented me from being a painter as well. Apparently I was born to be an artist of some sort, which is another way of saying that I was born not to find in that Strauss waltz anything other than a tonal mockery of an elected wretchedness brightened by occasional flashes of creative elation.

It is not easy for the artist to live in a capitalist society, and the condition for his living in a communist society is that he ceases to be an artist. Evidently it is necessary, before I go any further, to define art. Art is the disposition of natural material—sounds, colours, shapes, words (which are not quite natural)—into forms which shall please because they surprise. The surprise is the disclosure of some new truth about life apprehended by a highly individual consciousness. New truths about life, though intended to give pleasure, do not, however, always do so—at least not until they have ceased to be entirely new. Freshness of vision often seems subversive of an existing philosophy or religion or morality or political system. Subvert communist or fascist philosophy in a work of art, and the communist or fascist government under which the artist lives will quickly starve him or imprison him or liquidate him. In a capitalist society he will not be imprisoned or liquidated, but he will certainly starve. Neither the public nor the ruling party wants the powerful original vision: it upsets the bourgeoisie by making it revaluate its view of reality, and the political men—whatever their persuasion—always find it dangerous. As

T. S. Eliot once wrote, "humankind cannot bear very much reality."

If an artist is to live at all—even on the very fringe of subsistance—he must compromise. He must put a shade on his bright light. Many English writers have learned not to be ashamed of compromise because they have the example of William Shakespeare before them, or behind them. Shakespeare made money and became a gentleman and a landowner, but he also wrote the greatest drama of all time. We see how great this drama is now, 365 years after his death, but his contemporaries saw him as a competent purveyor of low laughs and lurid melodrama. Shakespeare accepted the dramatic forms that were popular in his day, but he cunningly added to them the powerfully individual vision which the public could take or leave, just as it chose. He gave the public what it wanted, and he added the free gift of high art, which it probably did not want.

A contemporary Shakespeare would probably be working in the cinema or in television, producing competent entertainments which, on closer examination than most audiences would prefer to give, would be revealed as strikingly new revelations of life which came too soon to be easily understood. Certainly a contemporary Shakespeare would not be starving in a garret writing unsaleable poems or unproduceable plays. Alas, very few artists today possess the Shakespearean stature. Serious artists must do two things: produce their art in secret for no money and earn their living doing something which cannot be called art. There are poets in all countries gaining their bread from teaching in schools, writing advertising copy, labouring lightly as governmental functionaries, and doing their real work at the day's or the week's end. Unfortunately, expenditure of labour on a living leaves insufficient energy to perform the poet's task well. Poetry, like any other art, should be a fulltime job.

Let me now consider how I have earned my living as a writer during the last twenty-five years. I have divided my time and energy on art and sub-art. By art I mean the serious novel, not always easy to read and certainly not easy to write. By sub-art I mean journalism, the writing of film and television scripts, the provision of prefaces for other people's books (you see me now at work on sub-art), and occasional lecturing and even teaching.

Whatever poetic gift I have or had has been diluted into the composition of song-lyrics for the Broadway stage. I am aware that I might have written better novels—and certainly longer novels—if I had been able to give all my time to the fictional art, but I accept the need for compromise. I also accept the need for hard work. I write these words on the first day of spring, and I look back to less than a third of a year in which I have written a ten-hour television script about the agonies and triumphs of the early Christians, a six-hour television script on Attila the Hun, about ten book reviews and half a dozen newspaper articles. I try to write at least one thousand words every day, including weekends, and I have not been able to survive by writing less. I am not proud of this fecundity, accepting it merely as a condition for staying alive. I am, however, desperately ashamed at not having done any work at all this year on a novel. After all, my trade is that of novelist, and it is a trade which I have not been permitted to work at. I might add that a good deal of time has been given up to work which is not writing at all—appearing on television in talk-shows, publicising the foreign publication of certain of my books, assisting at an international book fair. There has been no time at all for writing letters, and the writer who wants to live has to be the worst correspondent in the world.

I call myself a typical novelist of my time, which means that I am not in the best-selling category. There are very few best-sellers, and even fewer of them produce what can be dignified with the title of art. The public wants thrills from sex or violence baldly displayed in ill-chosen words or, preferably, adapted to the television screen. It does not want art, and therefore art has to be subsidised. It can be subsidised by the practice of sub-art, or it can receive subventions from kind patrons. The day of the private Maecenas seems to be over, and probably James Joyce was the last novelist to benefit from the generosity of a patron, (matron, rather: her name was Harriet Shaw Weaver) in the private sector. What can the state or the municipality do? My own country, Great Britain, has an Arts Council which gives a little money to those arts which most spectacularly are shown not to be able to function at all without subvention—ballet and orchestral music. Poetry gets a little money, and novelists occasionally receive prizes. But the queue for such patronage is long, and prizes are

capriciously given. Few are satisfied, and some—like myself—
strongly resent the State's interference in the practice of art. The
artist, like the furniture-maker or dentist, should be self-sufficient.
He does not mind being poor, but he does feel uneasy at being in
debt to the very machine which is dedicated to the pulverising of
individuality. The state only pretends to like the artist, and what
it gives it gives grudgingly.

In Soviet Russia, provided the artist is mediocre enough and
fully prepared to toe the party line, there are no problems. But it
is sadly significant that the only good artists that Soviet Russia
has produced have had to seek exile, suffer contumely, or accept
a kind of compromise that Shakespeare would not have well understood—that, for instance, of Dmitri Shostakovich, whose individual vision is too often obscured by the clouds of "social
realism." The state and the artist never get on well together, and
the state has bigger guns than the artist. The artist has to be free—
free to starve, if necessary.

We would all like to believe that some day, when the masses
have been educated to like something better than Harold Robbins
or Judith Krantz, the highly original artist will be honoured by
wealth and not only by begrudged state medals. But this is not
likely to happen. Art is precious, like diamonds, but unlike diamonds it does not have a scarcity value to which the market can
respond. The artist must take Metro-Goldwyn-Mayer's hypocritical motto—*Ars Gratia Artis*—and leave the mink coats and the
Mercedes-Benz to the purveyors of trash. He cannot threaten the
non-paying public with the withdrawal of his labour, like a rail
or electrical syndicate, for the non-paying public does not greatly
need his labour. Indeed, it would be happier without it. For the
serious artist does not satisfy needs—instead, he creates values.
Values, to the world at large, have—alas, alas, and again alas—
no value at all.

—1983

ELGAR NON È VOLGARE

❖

One of the great mysteries about music is that, though it speaks an international language, it remains obdurately insular. Israel resents having to listen to Wagner, and Beethoven seems to the French to be all too Teutonic. Some composers do not travel at all: like certain wines, they demand an insular palate. This seems to be true of some of the composers of my own country, England, who, despite the few kilometres of sea separating Dover from Calais, have never really entered Europe. Italians will perhaps listen to Henry Purcell and Benjamin Britten, but there is a whole body of composers in between these two who are either unknown or known for the wrong reasons.

Take Sir Edward Elgar. Born in 1857, dead in 1934 (along with two other composers not well known in Europe—Gustav Holst and Frederick Delius—and possessing, like them, a not very English-sounding name), he came at a time when English music was in bondage to the Germans. Handel had come over from Hanover with George I, who never spoke one word of English, and German-speaking Queen Victoria had decreed that Felix Mendelssohn was the new Handel. It was difficult for an English composer to write in an English style—a style that should declare its continuity from the time of a composer like Purcell or, earlier, Byrd or Orlando Gibbons or Lawes. Quite apart from the tradition of religious oratorio in the German manner, there was another German whose influence lay heavy on English music— Richard Wagner, whose orchestral sonorities were so seductive that no young composer could evade them. The musical academies of Britain taught young men to write in a "European," which meant a German, manner. Elgar did not go to an academy: he was self-taught and earned his living as a violinist and the director of an orchestra in a lunatic asylum.

When he came to compose his "Enigma" Variations for orchestra in 1899 it was evident that here was not merely a new voice but a distinctively English one, despite the quotation from Tasso at the end of the score: "Bramo assai, poco spero, nulla chieggio." The Englishry lay less in the orchestral sound and the harmonies—both of which owed much to Wagner—than in a peculiar humour and a peculiar self-doubting passion. The English are a humorous people, and they are frightened of expressing their emotions, though this does not mean that they are devoid of passion. In the "Enigma" Variations Elgar is concerned with the gentle passion of friendship. He presents his theme and then presents it again with a single climax: he is expressing his love for his wife, and this declaration of affection had better be disposed of quickly so that he can get on to less embarrassing avowals. In each variation a close friend is depicted, quickly and economically. We hear an organist friend who played in Worcester Cathedral exercising his fingers. We hear another friend who had a bulldog named Dan, or, rather, in the manner of Hogarth's self-portrait, the dog is placed in the foreground and it is he we hear plunging into the river Severn and then shaking himself dry. When Elgar comes to a final self-portrait (under the initials E. D. U., which stand for the *Edu* or *Eduardo* his wife always called him) he alternates self-mockery with the briefly grandiose. We are hearing, probably for the first time, a quality we have to call Edwardian.

Two years after this composition was first presented, King Edward VII came to the British throne. Edward Elgar, soon to become Sir Edward Elgar, was born to express the peculiar quality of the new royal epoch. It was expansive, concerned with the glories of empire, and seemed to have an unlimited confidence in the future. Elgar composed a symphony in 1908—No. 1 in A flat major—which summed up the era. There are massive soaring melodies in which horns and trumpets and trombones, playing, according to their preference, in flat keys, provide images of imperial grandeur. We are often, perhaps too often, in Westminster Abbey, attending a royal coronation. The quality of Elgar's melodic invention is such that the opening theme of Schumann's "Rhenish" symphony has been described as Elgarian. But there are other qualities, including one of extreme tenderness that seems to have something to do with a response to the English spring. The music, however one describes it, is not European. It is bluff, pragmatic, often elusive, eloquent, ashamed of its eloquence, but not afraid to give the direction *nobilmente*. The symphony is hardly known in Europe, though there was a time when it was much performed in Germany under Hans Richter, to whom it is dedicated. I once saw and heard it performed on Italian television, but the pleasure was impaired for me by the yawning of the first trumpet, who was apparently bored by the work.

The second symphony—in E flat major—was composed in the last year of Edward VII's reign and, when performed in 1912, was obviously intended as a poem of regret at the passing of an epoch. 1912 was the year of the sinking of the *Titanic*; two more years would bring the First World War. The work is full of neurosis. The heavy brass tries to recall the glories of the reign that is gone, but the themes are distorted and become ghostlike. The work ends in a sunset glow of resignation. This is the work that Europe ought to hear. It is more sophisticated than anything by Mahler, it is wholly professional, it is probably the last of the great symphonies.

Unfortunately, Elgar has become known in Europe solely for the trio of a march he wrote. It is a good march, and the melody of the trio is magnificent, but it is not what Elgar is really about. He noted that Johann Strauss and Richard Strauss, had glorified the Viennese waltz, and he proposed doing the same for the military march—hence the group of orchestral marches entitled "Pomp and Circumstance." The title is ironic. It is a citation from a speech made by Othello on his discovery that Desdemona has been unfaithful to him. "Farewell, the pomp and circumstance of glorious war." These marches by Elgar seem powerfully extrovert, but if one listens carefully there are the harmonies of self-doubt, of a neurosis kept under control, of a potential hysteria. They are a profound psychological document, and one that says as much about the state of England as about the composer himself.

Consider the nature of this composer in his maturity. He had received great honours from the state, but he had little money. He was a Catholic purveying the doubts and glories of a Protestant kingdom. He was a man of passion frightened of that passion, a neurotic pretending to be John Bull. In his later days he pretended not to be a musician at all: with his field-glasses and top hat he spent much of his time in the royal enclosure at the horse races. He knew that his fellow-countrymen were philistines. Like the Europeans themselves, they knew him only for a particular tune—one to which the words "Land of Hope and Glory" (ridiculously chauvinistic) had been set. By the year of his death the music of Europe had succumbed to a neurosis which could express itself only in the hysterics of atonalism. Schoenberg was purely neurotic; he had abandoned the ordered structure represented by tonality. Elgar had kept his neurosis under control. Mahler had not, nor had Berg and Schoenberg and Webern. Stravinsky had taken up the posture of the pasticheur and the mocker. Elgar had presented civic order, imperial élan, but he had been aware of the qualifying doubts, the tropical neurosis, the malaria, and the sand-fly fever. In this respect he was very much like his contemporary Rudyard Kipling.

Europe ought to listen to one of Elgar's later works, the symphonic study called "Falstaff." If it is too "English," then Verdi and Boito are too English too. T. S. Eliot pointed out that Sir John Falstaff is not merely an ox of a man, swinishly drunk and greedy, a thief and a coward. There is nobility in him, an immense wit and an unquenchable intelligence, and a great deal of self-doubt. He grows old and his nose becomes "as sharp as a pen." Verdi and Boito knew all this, and Elgar knew it too. Elgar's portrait avoids the Rabelaisian and perhaps over-stresses the nobility. But he sets the portrait, which Verdi and Boito could not do, against a background of the Worcestershire countryside which nurtured him and which Verdi and Boito knew not at all. How music can express the *physical* quality of landscape is a mystery, and only English music seems to have done it.

The music of Elgar is, after all, available on discs and cassettes, but I doubt if Ricordi in Milan is much interested. I think it is up to the adventurous music-lover with innocent ears to give the music of Elgar a trial. If I love this music, it is not because I am a chauvinistic Britisher. It is the only music I know that presents in all honesty the complex *Weltanschauung* of the early part of our century. It does not snivel like Mahler, and it does not scream like Schoenberg. It maintains a gentlemanly dignity, and it scorns to cry in public. But its heart is large.

—1983

❖

Barcelona, Gaudí's city, is a very satisfying visual experience. It is a place of treed avenues, firm street-lines, and elegant contemporary architecture. When a commercial block is thrown up, its façade is often tastefully lozenged with Aztec-type abstractions. There is the example of Picasso, who started his painting career on the Calle de Avino (that's where the Demoisellesd'Avignon come from) and later decorated the façade of the Barcelona College of Architects with a frieze of kings and children and horsemen, in the infantile style of the ultra-sophisticated. But, apart from mere decoration, no Catalan architect dare go too far in either dull boxiness or fussy neo-baroque: he has behind him and in front of him, not to say above him, the warming example of Gaudí.

Gaudí's masterpiece is the still unfinished church of the Sagrada Familia or Holy Family. There is nothing in the world like it. Some have called it Disney whimsicality raised to the level of soaring nobility. It could also be termed metaphysical conceit humanised with crockets and pompoms. It is scrawl and mysticism, vision and fancy, an evanescent dream hammered into sempiternal solidity. New York knows Gaudí: it even has a chapter of the Amigos of the great mad sane genius. Probably only Spain could have produced him; most probably only Barcelona.

Gaudí started work on this improbable cathedral in 1884, and the work was still proceeding when, in 1926, he was run over by a street car and killed. The difficulty of getting the whole structure completed since his death has mainly been due to Gaudí's unwillingness to plan in toto. He approached the work rather in the manner of a novelist, letting new notions flower as he proceeded, and not even the close collaborators who survived him have been able to guess at his final vision. Spain, as the world knows, is a Catholic country, and it was once aggressively Catholic, as

England remembers, but Barcelona has long been given to republicanism, socialism, anarchy, and various kinds of Godlessness, so that there is a very ambiguous kind of civic pride in these flying towers and the flowery sculptural façades out of which, like visual hosannas, they soar. But never in the whole history of ecclesiastical architecture has there been so idiosyncratic, indeed eccentric, a creation, and collective collusion in the stone and concrete hymnody can easily be excused, even by an atheist: Gaudí was one of Barcelona's great men, say the Catalanians, and here is one of the great things he did; we don't share his faith, but we let him dance in our sky; this is a city of energetic individualism, and it is always possible to see that as Gaudí's true credo. Besides, the bulk of his work is secular.

Like, for example, the Casa Batlló, with its balconies like carnival masks, its lizardy rooftiles, its little ogre's tower, its second-floor picture-windows framed in stone vulvae. The stark rectangular is anathema to Gaudí: hard stone must appear not merely soft but edible. Roughcast walls are stuck all over with big fairy money pieces, pillars ape limbs, stone overhangs drip like stalagmites. *Edibility* will always do as one of the Gaudí keywords. Those great towers of the Sagrada Familla are long rolled waffles, formminated, crunchy, with pinnacles of crisp sugar.

His secular masterpiece is the Parque Güell, whose architectural fancies took Gaudí from 1900 to 1914 to erect or exude. You start off on your visit to it by looking at a gingerbread pavilion for the concièrge, spiked and nippled and fox-eared. Then you see roadways and walls of undulant pebblework in jigsaw patterns. Stairways are of azure and gold, very dreamlike, with dribbling guardian dragons. There are colonnades whose ceilings erupt into large boils, lanced by multifaceted columns. There are stone seats like circular railroads, the backrests all frozen kaleidoscope. Viaducts imitate caverns. Pillars and roofs are dragon-scaly with stones stuck on to brick. It's a huge park, once the property of the great rich family Güell but now a playground for the people. But you don't play; you drink black coffee and Fundador and you gape at the exposed curlicues of Gaudí's brain.

Histories of architecture are often very dubious about Gaudí. He is sometimes cautiously described as an art nouveau man, and it is implied that there is something indecent about constructing a Cathedral in art nouveau style. Architecture is a matter of imagination, we are told, and Gaudí is all fancy: nothing could be fancier than art nouveau. But Gaudí was, I think, obsessed with a dilemma that no longer touches the designers of office-blocks and residential highrises. The dilemma is how to reconcile the curvilinear with the rectilinear. Or, putting it another way, how to make a building seem more than a submission to the geometrical datum of length, breadth, and height. The mediaeval builders of cathedrals knew that God was big and that a tiny temple was an insult. They also knew that God was a circle and they tried to exploit the arc while accepting the necessity of rectilinear height. Gaudí found arcs and full circles everywhere—in coins and curls and breasts and eyes. The curvilinear led him back to nature, to the desire to create stone and concrete structures which seemed to have sprung from the hand of a miracle-working giant. Mention the word "giant" or "miracle" and you enter the realm of the fairy tale. The fairy element in Gaudí—gnome, dragon, magic cave—seems, to many, to diminish him; this looks like child's stuff, and the term Disneyesque is not misapplied. But it is precisely the quality of childlike wonder, the acceptance of magic and miracles, that makes Gaudí what he is. Other architects compel admiration; Gaudí demands love as well.

—1984

ORSON WELLES:
THE ARTIST AS BRICOLEUR

❖

There are two ways of making a work of art: that of the engineer and that of the bricoleur. In the cinematic field, Stanley Kubrick may be regarded as a creator unhampered by lack of resources, equipped indeed with an excess of both time and amenities, able to convert his vision into an artefact whose polish dazzles the eyes and sometimes obscures the essential message. On the other hand, Orson Welles is a film-maker who has suffered from lack of money, the pressure of time, and the need to substitute ingenuity, or genius, for the more orthodox properties which only time and money can buy. In his seventieth year, we celebrate his frustrations as much as his triumphs.

If I call Kubrick an engineer, it is in the sense that neither money nor skill may be spared in the erection of his structures. You cannot afford to improvise a skyscraper or a Brooklyn Bridge. The testing of stresses and the adjustment of struts and rivets takes time, and Kubrick spends much time on exactitude of lighting, scenic effects, and the rhythm of speech and action. In the making of his *Barry Lyndon*, so one of the principal actors told me, he took two weeks to rehearse a banquet scene of about three minutes' screen duration. This actor had to stand and make a speech. After about fifty repetitions he stood and said, involuntarily: "Ladies and gentlemen, this is ridiculous." Whereupon Kubrick said, "You seem to have forgotten your lines." Such exquisite care in preparation does not prevent Kubrick from making errors. In *A Clockwork Orange* he gave his hero two surnames—Delarge and Burgess (a tribute to the original author)—but only I seem to have noticed.

Orson Welles is a bricoleur in the sense that he has had to substitute imagination for amenity. The tradition goes back to his early work in the New York theatre, where he had to use

whatever material was available in those days of impoverish-
ment we term the Great American Depression. Thus, producing
Danton's Death, he was unable to fill the stage with a Paris
mob howling round the guillotine, so he bought a hundred or
so Hallowe'en masks (the kind of thing American children wear
on All Soul's Day), strung them together, and, with lighting,
noise, and music, gave a very vivid surrealistic impression of a
crowded stage. This is very much the way of the bricoleur. In one
of his late films, *Othello*, he was unable to present the murder of
Roderigo in a crowded street because he had no money to pay for
costumes, so Roderigo was stabbed to death naked in a crowded
bathhouse.

There is a kind of creative joy in making art out of inadequate
materials or even out of the technical deficiencies there is no
money to rectify. Jean Cocteau, another great bricoleur, made a
masterpiece, *Le Sang d'un Poète*, out of odd scraps of footage. In
the cutting room, the final sequence of another of his films was
seen to be ruined by a fault in the camera: the scene shook,
wagged, wavered. Cocteau was unperturbed. He merely added a
line of "voice-over" commentary: "And so the caravan of life jogs
on its way."

It was an awareness of the limitations of the American radio
audience that elevated the young Orson Welles from mere New
York *enfant terrible* of the theatre to the position of a national
figure. His Mercury Theatre company presented a thirty-minute
drama programme on one channel, while the other channel regaled a very large public with the Edgar Bergen show—Bergen
being a highly popular ventriloquist. Bergen always had a guest
artiste, usually a singer, and it was during the singer's performance that listeners would idly switch channels to hear what the
rival radio company was doing. Welles knew this. He knew that
a vast number of such listeners would thus miss his opening announcement—"The Mercury Theatre presents . . ."—On the occasion that brought him to fame he was broadcasting his own
adaptation of H. G. Wells's *The War of the Worlds*. Listeners
tuned in to hear an authentic news-reading voice announce that
the Martians had landed in New Jersey. Many believed that this
was actuality, not drama. Announcements about the progress of
the Martian invasion were interspersed with rather sedative dance

music which increased tension, and, being boring, gave the impression of a great deal of time passing. A half-hour seemed like an eternity. There was panic in New Jersey and a few deaths from heart failure. The widower of a woman who so died tried to assassinate Orson Welles some years later.

The tour de force of the *War of the Worlds* broadcast established Welles as a great tricheur. We see it now as a typical example of the technique of bricolage: using what is available, in this case the philistinism of a radio audience which preferred a ventriloquist to serious drama. The technique cost nothing, but its effects were devastating.

It was the fame accruing from this exploit that gained for Orson Welles together with the Mercury Theatre company he directed— an opportunity that now seems incredible. He was invited to Hollywood by the RKO company and given *carte blanche* to make a film. The resentment felt by plodding veterans in the film game, who had never been given such an opportunity, was intense. Everybody waited to condemn the film that Welles wrote, directed and graced with his own immense, if eccentric, acting ability. Massive condemnation came from the newspaper tycoon Randolph Hearst, who saw that the central character of *Citizen Kane* was unequivocally based on himself and proposed drastic retribution.

That Welles was able to get away with so libellous a project depended on the total independence on which he insisted—no prying on the parts of the studio heads, full control of the postproduction phase, the completed work thrust into the world without warning of its content. Its content is now well-known. The film depicts the decline and fall of a newspaper tycoon who tries to turn his mistress into an operatic star, despite her lack of talent. Randolph Hearst turned his mistress Marion Davies into a film star (she did not lack talent). The Gothic monster of a house that Kane builds—Xanadu—has its counterpart in Hearst's San Simeon, crammed with the artistic spoils of the world and inexpressibly vulgar. The film sets out to be an inquiry into the significance of the name Rosebud, which finally turns out to have been painted on Kane's childhood sled. In fact, Rosebud was the affectionate term that Randolph Hearst applied to Marion Davies's pudenda.

Hearst's response to the film was manic. He threatened to expose the secret sexual lives of the heads of all Hollywood's studios, using public morality to destroy the film industry. But his own sexual position was shaky. The lawyers warned against libel actions. The film was shown but was not well appreciated—indeed, it was not well understood. Forty-five years after its appearance it is still not well understood. Its techniques were highly advanced for their time and have not yet won general acceptance in the art of popular cinema. The film is not linear in its approach to narrative: it treats time as space and jumps insolently and rapidly from past to future and back again. There seems to be a mockery of orthodox film procedure. We are often made aware that a camera is present, that what looks like action presented direct to the audience is in fact presented indirectly: what the audience is viewing is film within a film. There is an effect of alienation: actors do not pretend to be characters; they are palpably actors consciously taking parts. The technique is Brechtian, but Welles at that time knew nothing of Brecht. It is no wonder that the film lost money and put Welles's future as a cinema director in doubt.

A man concerned with experimentation had better not work in Hollywood, which is dedicated to the bland, the safe, the unsubversive. It has been Welles's tragedy to have chosen a medium that needs heavy box office returns to justify its existence. He should have been content with the living theatre and, in a sense, he has been. But his view of theatre is somewhat cinematic: he likes the speed of film, the sense of seamless flow. Film, to him, is the apotheosis of theatre, and, since *Citizen Kane* he has been obsessed with its possibilities. Unfortunately, few of those possibilities make box-office sense. The film industry is still in the hands of lawyers and accountants who are timorous of art.

Welles's second film, *The Magnificent Ambersons*, got out of his dictatorial hands. He was sent to Brazil on a vaguely governmental assignment, connected with Roosevelt's "Good Neighbour" policy, which began as a filming of the Rio carnival but turned, typically for Welles, into an examination of dictatorial tyranny. In his absence the studio turned a very unorthodox film of epic proportions into a piece of bland banality. The film represents a fusion of engineering and bricolage. Welles used a complicated and expensive crane to film a ballroom sequence. At the same time he rejected the technique of the reverse shot, preferring to have a camera whizzing from speaker to speaker in impatient rapidity. The studio did not like this. It was as scared of film innovation as it was of the declamatory theatrical techniques that Welles imported. The film we were permitted, and still are permitted, to see is not the film Welles made. After making it, Welles had no further faith in the great Hollywood studios.

His subsequent career has, nevertheless, looked like a capitulation to the forces of commercial cinema. He has been seen in many films produced and directed by other men, a reluctant actor who acts magnificently when he considers a good performance worth the trouble. Welles the actor has been seen as Mr. Rochester in *Jane Eyre* and as Harry Lime in *The Third Man*, where he improved Graham Greene's script with a notable addition. "Renaissance Italy was rife with assassination and treachery, but it produced Leonardo and Michelangelo. Switzerland has known peace and democracy, but what has it achieved? The cuckoo clock." The odd cameo parts he has taken—a few days work for $100,000—have represented only a means of gaining money to finance his own films. In such films as he has been able to make out of his own pocket, the old instinct of the bricoleur has served him well. He has been able to afford a star for a day or two but no longer. He has exploited their faces in close-up shots while getting men and women picked up casually on the streets to provide their back views. He has made a hundred extras look like a Napoleonic army.

In making his film of *Macbeth*, he prepared for it by presenting the play first as a stage production, then rapidly transferring this to the studio of a production company better known for cheap Westerns than for high art. Films, he proved, can still be made cheaply. Welles's *Macbeth*, whose bricolage makes it look highly experimental, compares very well with Laurence Olivier's expensive but orthodox *Hamlet*. His last great work, *Chimes at Midnight*, shows him as a magnificent Falstaff in a remarkably realised mediaeval England that is really modern Spain. He triumphs with the resources of an empty purse. And yet the triumphs are appreciated only by the few. His offerings are not good box office.

In his seventieth year—ebullient still, enormous, with a laugh that is either Gargantuan or Democritan—he merits our homage.

He brought an alert and adult mind to a medium which still prefers to be childish. The money-spinning films of our day are brilliant toys but no more—*Star Wars* and *E.T.*, *Raiders of the Lost Ark* and *Indiana Jones*. When an acceptable director makes an adult film like *Apocalypse Now*, it costs far too much. Too many of our directors know how to waste money; too few know the skills acquired from enforced economy. We have to regret that the medium which he was born to rule has for the most part rejected him. It is not an uncommon story in the annals of art. But we have to be thankful for *Citizen Kane*. It is a miracle that it was made at all and it is itself a miracle.

—1985

❖

I first published the novella *A Clockwork Orange* in 1962, which ought to be far enough in the past for it to be erased from the world's literary memory. It refuses to be erased, however, and for this the film version of the book made by Stanley Kubrick may be held chiefly responsible. I should myself be glad to disown it for various reasons, but this is not permitted. I receive mail from students who try to write theses about it, or requests from Japanese dramaturges to turn it into a sort of Noh play. It seems likely to survive, while other works of mine that I value more bite the dust. This is not an unusual experience for an artist. Rachmaninov used to groan because he was known mainly for a Prelude in C Sharp Minor which he wrote as a boy, while the works of his maturity never got into the programmes. Kids cut their pianistic teeth on a Minuet in G, which Beethoven composed only so that he could detest it. I have to go on living with *A Clockwork Orange*, and this means I have a sort of authorial duty to it. I have a very special duty to it in the United States, and I had better now explain what this duty is.

Let me put the situation baldly. *A Clockwork Orange* has never been published entire in America. The book I wrote is divided into three sections of seven chapters each. Take out your pocket computer and you will find that these add up to a total of twenty-one chapters. Twenty-one is the symbol of human maturity, or used to be, since at twenty-one you got the vote and assumed adult responsibility. Whatever its symbology, the number twenty-one was the number I started out with. Novelists of my stamp are interested in what is called arithmology, meaning that number has to mean something in human terms when they handle it. The number of chapters is never entirely arbitrary. Just as a musical composer starts off with a vague image of bulk and duration, so a novelist begins with an image of length, and this image is expressed in the number of sections and the number of chapters into which the work will be disposed. Those twenty-one chapters were important to me.

But they were not important to my New York publisher. The book he brought out had only twenty chapters. He insisted on cutting out the twenty-first; I could, of course, have demurred at this and taken my book elsewhere, but it was considered that he was being charitable in accepting the work at all, and that all other New York, or Boston, publishers would kick out the manuscript on its dog-ear. I needed money back in 1961, even the pittance I was being offered as an advance, and if the condition of the book's acceptance was also its truncation—well, so be it. So there is a profound difference between *A Clockwork Orange* as Great Britain knows it and the somewhat slimmer volume that bears the same name in the United States of America.

Let us go further. The rest of the world was sold the book out of Great Britain, and so most versions—certainly the French, Italian, Spanish, Catalan, Russian, Hebrew, Rumanian, and German translations have the original twenty-one chapters. Now when Stanley Kubrick made his film—though he made it in England—he followed the American version and, so it seemed to his audiences outside America, ended the story somewhat prematurely. Audiences did not exactly clamour for their money back, but they wondered why Kubrick left out the dénouement. People wrote to me about this—indeed much of my later life has been expended on xeroxing statements of intention and the frustration of intention—while both Kubrick and my New York publisher coolly bask in the rewards of their misdemeanour. Life is, of course, terrible.

What happens in that twenty-first chapter? You now have the chance to find out. Briefly, my young thuggish protagonist grows up. He grows bored with violence and recognises that human energy is better expended on creation than destruction. Senseless violence is a prerogative of youth, which has much energy but little talent for the constructive. Its dynamism has to find an outlet in smashing telephone kiosks, derailing trains, stealing cars and smashing them and, of course, in the much more satisfactory activity of destroying human beings. There comes a time, however, when violence is seen as juvenile and boring. It is the repartee of the stupid and ignorant. My young hoodlum comes to the revelation of the need to get something done in life—to marry, to beget children, to keep the orange of the world turning in the rookers of Bog, or hands of God, and perhaps even create something—music, say. After all, Mozart and Mendelssohn were composing deathless music in their teens or nadsats, and all my hero was doing was razrezzing and giving the old in-out. It is with a kind of shame that this growing youth looks back on his devastating past. He wants a different kind of future.

There is no hint of this change of intention in the twentieth chapter. The boy is conditioned, then deconditioned, and he foresees with glee a resumption of the operation of free and violent will. "I was cured all right," he says, and so the American book ends. So the film ends too. The twenty-first chapter gives the novel the quality of genuine fiction, an art founded on the principle that human beings change. There is, in fact, not much point in writing a novel unless you can show the possibility of moral transformation, or an increase in wisdom, operating in your chief character or characters. Even trashy bestsellers show people changing. When a fictional work fails to show change, when it merely indicates that human character is set, stony, unregenerable, then you are out of the field of the novel and into that of the fable or the allegory. The American or Kubrickian *Orange* is a fable; the British or world one is a novel.

But my New York publisher believed that my twenty-first chapter was a sell-out. It was veddy veddy British, don't you know. It was bland and it showed a Pelagian unwillingness to accept that a human being could be a model of unregenerable evil. The Americans, he said in effect, were tougher than the British and could face up to reality. Soon they would be facing up to it in Vietnam. My book was Kennedyan and accepted the notion of moral progress. What was really wanted was a Nixonian book with no shred of optimism in it. Let us have evil prancing on the page and, up to the very last line, sneering in the face of all the inherited beliefs, Jewish, Christian, Muslim, and Holy Roller, about people being able to make themselves better. Such a book would be sensational, and so it is. But I do not think it is a fair picture of human life.

I do not think so because, by definition, a human being is endowed with free will. He can use this to choose between good and evil. If he can only perform good or only perform evil, then he is a clockwork orange—meaning that he has the appearance of an organism lovely with colour and juice but is in fact only a clockwork toy to be wound up by God or the Devil or (since this is increasingly replacing both) the Almighty State. It is as inhuman to be totally good as it is to be totally evil. The important thing is moral choice. Evil has to exist along with good, in order that moral choice may operate. Life is sustained by the grinding opposition of moral entities. This is what the television news is all about. Unfortunately there is so much original sin in us all that we find evil rather attractive. To devastate is easier and more spectacular than to create. We like to have the pants scared off us by visions of cosmic destruction. To sit down in a dull room and compose the *Missa Solennis* or *The Anatomy of Melancholy* does not make headlines or news flashes. Unfortunately my little squib of a book was found attractive to many because it was as odorous as a crateful of bad eggs with the miasma of original sin.

It seems priggish or pollyannaish to deny that my intention in writing the work was to titillate the nastier propensities of my readers. My own healthy inheritance of original sin comes out in the book and I enjoyed raping and ripping by proxy. It is the novelist's innate cowardice that makes him depute to imaginary personalities the sins that he is too cautious to commit for himself. But the book does also have a moral lesson, and it is the weary traditional one of the fundamental importance of moral choice. It is because this lesson sticks out like a sore thumb that I tend to disparage *A Clockwork Orange* as a work too didactic to be artistic. It is not the novelist's job to preach; it is his duty to show. I have shown enough, though the curtain of an invented lingo gets in the way, another aspect of my cowardice. Nadsat, a Russified version of English, was meant to muffle the raw response we expect from pornography. It turns the book into a linguistic adventure. People preferred the film because they are scared, rightly, of language.

I don't think I have to remind readers what the title means. Clockwork oranges don't exist, except in the speech of old Londoners. The image was a bizarre one, always used for a bizarre thing. "He's as queer as a clockwork orange" meant he was queer to the limit of queerness. It did not primarily denote homosexuality, though a queer, before restrictive legislation came in, was the term used for a member of the inverted fraternity. Europeans who translated the title as *Arancia a Orologeria* or *Orange Mécanique* could not understand its Cockney resonance and they assumed that it meant a hand grenade, a cheaper kind of explosive pineapple. I mean it to stand for the application of a mechanistic morality to a living organism oozing with juice and sweetness.

Readers of the twenty-first chapter must decide for themselves whether it enhances the book they presumably know or is really a discardable limb. I meant the book to end in this way, but my aesthetic judgement may have been faulty. Writers are rarely their own best critics, nor are critics. *"Quad scripsi scripsi"* said Pontius Pilate when he made Jesus Christ the King of the Jews: "What I have written I have written." We can destroy what we have written but we cannot unwrite it. I leave what I wrote with what Dr Johnson called frigid indifference to the judgment of that .00000001 of the American population which cares about such things. Eat this sweetish segment or spit it out. You are free.

—1986

The Brotherhood

❖

The British, meaning the English, Irish, Scots, and Welsh, have never had either taste or skill in the visual arts. Their abilities have lain mostly in literature, which is essentially an auditory enterprise. There have, of course, been exceptions, but these have generally been highly eccentric: Turner, Hogarth, Blake. One goes to Italy to look at pictures, but not to London, Cardiff, *Edinburgh*, or Dublin. The lack of taste was well exemplified in my own home when I was a child. My stepmother would occasionally send me out to buy new second-hand reproductions when everybody was sick of looking at the old ones. The new ones were always bought with less selectivity than if they had been cabbages. If they were better than the old ones, it was because they were less mildewed and the hooks were firmer. Nobody liked them much, but you had to have pictures on the walls. The pictures were all the same—scrupulously exact transcriptions of the external world, a scene from a costume melodrama, a literary anecdote or a trite moral point.

In other words, they were all in the tradition of Sir John Everett Millais—debased Pre-Raphaelitism. A young man's revolution had yielded at last to the requirements of the Royal Academy, which meant to the sabbatarian piety and mechanistic mysticism of the middle class. The true horror of the age of Queen Victoria lies in the fastening together of the well-made machine with the sick soul, the breeding of the chimera of an engine animated by stock moral responses. The Pre-Raphaelites began by revolting against the tradition of Raphael, whom they did not well understand. They thought that Raphael was all unnatural posturing. They wanted to get back to live nature. But fidelity to nature meant turning the artist into a copying machine, and the need to hold nature on to the canvas meant the imposition of the extrinsic: postures derived from literature first, later from pious moral tracts.

For the exact transcription of nature, with not a leaf out of place, involves the rejection of contrived visual patterns, and it is by these that the artist justifies his existence. In the very first phase of Pre-Raphaelitism, before the members of the brotherhood went their own ways, it seemed possible to achieve such patterns, so long as the literary theme was regarded as a mere pretext for painting. Millais took a story from a poem by John Keats, in which a young man named Lorenzo falls in love with a girl called Isabella. The girl's brothers eventually cut off Lorenzo's head, but this has not yet happened in Millais's picture. What we see in that picture is a brother of Isabella's thrusting out a leg to kick her dog, presumably in protest at the budding love affair. But the meaning is lost in the aesthetic pleasure we derive from the way in which the leg seems to hold up a whole table-load of eaters, who are curiously flattened. The canvas is a small formal miracle, full of conflict, distortion, and ironic humour. If this is Pre-Raphaelitism, one is grateful for it.

But it is not quite Pre-Raphaelitism: it is close to Rossettianism, which is not quite the same thing. Dante Gabriel Rossetti, British despite his name, was one of the founder-members of the Pre-Raphaelite Brotherhood and, since he was also a poet, its most articulate propagandist, could not go back all that easily to nature, meaning the Italian clarity that existed before Raphael, allegedly, made everything brown as though roasted. Rossetti was fired by a vision and also somewhat weak on perspective. He was drawn more to the ardour of art than to the arduousness of craft. There is nothing amateur about the work of Ford Madox Brown, Holman Hunt, and Millais, but Rossetti's paintings look like a literary man's *violon d'Ingres*.

Yet, because Rossetti had the poet's intensity of vision, *The Girlhood of Mary Virgin* and *Ecce Ancilla Domini* are superior in art, though inferior in craftsmanship, to Holman Hunt's *Early Britons Sheltering a Missionary from the Druids* and Millais's *Christ in the House of His Parents*. The Hunt and Millais are not really much more than the sum of their parts. Hunt has to tell us that the Britons are Christian converts; untitled, his picture could just as well be of a divinity student being welcomed to a cup of tea by people who have just come from a fancy dress ball dressed as Early Britons. In the Millais picture, the infant Christ has hurt his hand on a nail, and the symbolism is a little obvious and embarrassing. The Rossettis, on the other hand, breathe a devotional quality which is no mere formality, despite the archaic quaintness.

Rosetti was literally a Pre-Raphaelite in that he looked back to Giotto, but the movement was not intended to jettison everything that had been learned since thirteenth-century Florence. But when we think of Pre-Raphaelitism we cannot help thinking of conscious archaism. Men like Ford Madox Brown and Charles Collins were too ready to succumb to its allure—Brown's *Wyclif Reading His Translation of the Bible* is very early Florentine, and Collins's *Convent Thoughts*, in which a nun carrying lilies (with, lest we miss the message, SICUT LILIUM in ornamental script above) stands on the verge of a lily pond, is a little sickly and insincere. But the lilies are not heraldic: they are real. John Ruskin, referring to the *alisma plantago* of the picture as well as the lilies, wrote: "As a mere botanical study . . . this picture would be invaluable to me, and I heartily wish it were mine."

This comes from a defence of the Brotherhood that Ruskin wrote to the *Times*, replying to an attack so virulent that only an established critical reputation could counter it. The attack alleged that the Pre-Raphaelites had "an aversion to beauty in every shape, and a singular devotion to the minute accidents of their subjects, including, or rather seeking out, every excess of sharpness or deformity." This meant that St. Joseph's feet should look fresh as if from the chiropodist, not dirty as from a morning in the workshop. It also meant that it was blasphemous for the young Christ to hurt his hand on a nail. Ruskin praised the Pre-Raphaelites on the ground that, "as far as in them lies, they will draw either what they see, or what they suppose might have been the actual facts of the scene they desire to represent, irrespective of any conventional rules of picture-making." It was not what we would call an aesthetic defence, merely a defence against the attack perennially levelled at all new art: "This is a distortion: life is not like that." So the road to respectability was opened up to these young painters. They became acceptable to the Royal Academy and Millais was given a knighthood by Queen Victoria.

It is strange that Ruskin, who defended so powerfully the right of the Pre-Raphaelite Brotherhood to depict life as it really was, should himself have rejected a very important, perhaps the most important, aspect of it. For, as is embarrassingly well-known, he married a girl we all remember as Effie, and the marriage was not consummated. This was because Ruskin discovered that women had pubic hair, a fact he had not previously known. We talk of art as the mirror of life, but in the pubic region art had taught Ruskin nothing. After an annulment, Effie married Millais, who presumably was not shocked by pubic hair. But it was probably Effie who persuaded him to become rich and respectable through the retailing of highly saleable prettiness and banality.

Perhaps the great gulf between the artist and the mere critic is exemplified by this story of Effie's (and everybody else's) pubic hair. The Pre-Raphaelites were not shocked by anything, nor were they afraid of anything. There is something very compelling about the young Millais setting up his easel in a real carpenter's shop, the equally young Holman Hunt daring pneumonia on winter nights in order to make an accurate copy of lunar shadows. One goes back to them with love whenever one of our art students starts whining that nobody will buy the canvases he has ridden over with a paint-wet bicycle.

—1988

WHY WERE THE REVOLUTIONARIES REACTIONARY?

❖

Revolutions lead to steel whips, salt mines, and great writers in prison. Nevertheless, the term "revolutionary" continues to carry the noblest of connotations; "reactionary" has, whether in art or politics, the monopoly of the bad. It has been remarked that the revolutionaries in literature have usually been reactionary in politics. My recent ruminations on T. S. Eliot's centenary lead me to ask whether that dictum applies to him, and, if so, whether that should affect our attitude to his work as a poet.

Behind the literary revolution initiated in London by T. S. Eliot and Ezra Pound stood an *eminence grise* whose philosophical and poetic career was cut short by a bullet in Flanders during the First World War. This was T. E. Hulme, who taught that "the humanist's belief in the perfectibility of man is wrong . . . and the reason for this is a failure to recognise original sin. Life is essentially tragic and futile. . . ." Of course, there were older and more distinguished pessimists than Hulme—St. Augustine and Schopenhauer, for example—but it was Hulme who was the mentor of the modernists. The great progressive vision had, in England, been spread by H. G. Wells and Bernard Shaw and the Socialists, but Eliot and Pound, as also W. B. Yeats, rejected it. Rejecting it, they seemed prepared to embrace such vile doctrines as fascism and endorse such vile practices as genocide. T. S. Eliot, who was, like Generalissimo Franco, a Christian gentleman, was on the wrong side in the Spanish Civil War. Ezra Pound, who adored Mussolini, was on the wrong side in the World War that followed, and that was a far more serious crime.

These artistic revolutionaries who were also political reactionaries believed passionately in art as a vision of order. Here they differed from the socialist George Orwell, who merely saw literature as a mode of political communication. Unlike Orwell, they did not see how art and the common people could be compatible. Art must decay, they believed, without a sustaining elite or aristocracy; therefore, in politics, they had to lean towards authoritarianism—for Eliot, the Conservative Party, the monarchy, the Church of England. For Pound, the Corporate State. For Yeats, the poor clamouring at the gate of the rich but held off by men with weapons. These three, and others like them—Wyndham Lewis and Evelyn Waugh, for instance—were no doubt misguided in thinking that one type of society must necessarily breed better art than another. Art has its own authority, and this is altogether parallel to the political order. Conversely, they had no right to wish to impose the hierarchical structures of their art on a society that—*pace* Eliot's *The Waste Land*—was no more a welter of brutish values than any segment of the Golden Age it pleases poets to invoke.

Eliot seems to have been antisemitic, and Pound certainly was. Since the Nazi Holocaust, antisemitism has become criminal, but neither Eliot nor Pound could foresee the Hitlerian Final Solution. There was a lot of mild antisemitism about before the war, and it is enshrined in some of Eliot's poetry. He has a thumbnail sketch of a detestable Sir Ferdinand Klein and an even more detestable Bleistein. He sees a decaying Venice: "The rats are underneath the piles. The jew is underneath the lot." "My house is a decayed house," the narrator of *Gerontion says*, "and the jew squats on the window sill, the owner, spawned in some estaminet of Antwerp." This makes unpleasant reading. But it makes unpleasant reading for a Catholic to have to have John Milton inveighing against the Pope—"the triple tyrant"—or, for that matter, to have to listen to the news on the BBC's Overseas Service being prefaced with the tune of "Lillibullero," which drove the Catholic King James II out of his kingdom. Racial or religious prejudice is not the worst crime in the world. To kill a race or to persecute a religion is a different matter.

It remains a great mystery to some that the finest literature of this century should be associated with political reaction. There are Marxist critics who can find good only in literature based on revolutionary politics. When, many years ago, I lectured on literature for the Workers' Educational Association, a very left-wing

organisation, I was instructed by my superiors that I must find
no good in Eliot or Pound. Jean-Paul Sartre was forced by his
Marxism to declare John Dos Passos the greatest American writer
of the twentieth century. The aesthetic issue doesn't count. A
writer cannot be good, we are told, unless his politics are beyond
reproach. But it would appear that politics are an irrelevance in
literature, just as theology is. I cannot tolerate John Milton's reg-
icidal puritanism, but I worship his poetry.

Still, if the reactionary political stance of a writer like Eliot or
Pound implies willingness to accept fascism rather than an easygoing liberalism, then this casts doubts on the humanity of his
art. For art, certainly literature, has to be judged in terms of human values: it promotes properties like love, tolerance, redemption. It is impossible to imagine a literature based on hate and
damnation. When I taught in America, certain of my black students brought me poems about the desirable castration of white
men. I was sincerely reviled for not approving of them. Literature
does not work in that way. It cannot base itself on sectarian prejudices. A Nazi poetry is a contradiction in terms. Literature assumes that all mankind is one, occasionally rejoicing but mostly
bewildered and suffering, certainly mortal. Literature thus puts
politics in the right place: as a system for maintaining minimal
order and looking after the drains. Politics is not important
enough to be a theme for literature.

All art would be music if it could—divorced from human concerns, concentrating on structure, mysteriously exciting and then
tranquillising emotion, but not saying anything that can be tran-
scribed into words. Even Wagner's *Parsifal*, which has a grossly
antisemitic programme, rises above its subject and becomes an
ennobling experience. George Steiner once expressed wonder that
a concentration camp commandant could spend the day consign-
ing Jews to the incinerator and then go home to weep tears of
pure joy at the Beethoven played by his eldest daughter on the
piano. Evidently, music has the power to attack the human spirit
at deeper, or higher, levels than are represented by the dirty work
of a political system. Unfortunately literature, being made out of
words, touches the world of degrading enactments, but this entails
the responsibility of its practitioners—and readers—to keep it
away from politics.

We need not be surprised, then, if the sensible critic refuses to consider the reactionary politics of Pound, Eliot, and the rest as having much relevance to the work they wrote. Pound's *Cantos* rage against usury, which they see as an abomination created by international Jewish banks, and Eliot's *Four Quartets* call for a Christian resignation in the face of the horrors of history, but the value of these works resides in the rhetoric—a rhetoric devised to suggest where the just society might be located. But the creation of that just society has nothing to do with politics.

—1988

SHAKESPEARE THE POET

❖

We know why Shakespeare wrote *Venus and Adonis* and *The Rape of Lucrece*. Not, in the manner of a Keats or Shelley, to express what his inner heart was telling him to express, but in search of social and financial advancement. This sounds cynical, but the situation of a young man from a provincial town, trying to make his way in the London of the 1590s, demanded a realistic approach to life which only a later, more sentimental, age could condemn as having little to do with artistic idealism. Shakespeare dedicated both poems—very fulsomely, almost cringingly—to the young Earl of Southampton in the hope that the handsome nobleman, cherished by the Queen, a close friend of the brilliant Earl of Essex, might become his patron. This, of course, does not invalidate the poems as art. It reminds us that writers have to live.

It reminds us also that Shakespeare's primary way of earning a living—as an actor, a member of the troupe known as the Lord Chamberlain's Men, as a patcher of old plays and a furnisher of new ones—did not, at that phase of his career, seem altogether satisfactory. Actors were inferior beings, mere entertainers, and, in the sonnets, Shakespeare disparages the craft of the stage: "I have made myself a motley to the view." He wished to be known as a poet and perhaps to show himself the superior of Christopher Marlowe, whose long narrative poem *Hero and Leander* had made the exquisites of the Inns of Court swoon with delight. That he succeeded we know from contemporary evidence. *Venus and Adonis* was a bestseller, even by the standards of the poets of our own time.

When I first read the poem at the age of fourteen I too swooned with delight, or rather with concupiscence. The lines are crammed with sensuality. I wanted to be Adonis, wooed by this gorgeous goddess of love. Later I learned to see in the work a possible autobiographical element—the young Will wooed by the some-

what older Anne Hathaway in the woods of Warwickshire. That
the whole narrative was set in the English countryside would perhaps earn, from fellow-poets who had studied the classical authors at Oxford or Cambridge, a certain scorn: where was the
Hellenic landscape, where were the asphodels? But the poem is
dear to me precisely because Shakespeare is disclosing his English
country origins and, more than that, identifying with nature in a
manner that shows what Keats called "negative capability"—the
magic of identification with a snail or a hunted hare. It is poetry
of a kind that could not easily be written today. It approaches
epic, though Coleridge said that Shakespeare could never have
tackled his own Odyssey or Iliad: he would have died of plethora
of the imagination. And the whole concept of poetry on which
the work is based is different from our own. You took a narrative
theme in those days and a set verse form and then you went to
work, wondering what lyric sparks would be struck from the flint
of laborious engagement. Nowadays poetry has become almost
totally egocentric and it is not expected to tell a story.

The Rape of Lucrece has never been as popular as its home-
grown, earth-smelling, sexy original. Here sex becomes distasteful, an act of violence, and the austerity of both the theme and
its treatment seems to point to Shakespeare's decision to hide the
country boy in himself and join the stern classicists who possessed
the university degree he did not have. It is a fine poem but it does
not proclaim joy. "Light and lust are deadly enemies," says the
poet, and the light goes out. It is mature art, but it is not the
"sweet Master Shakespeare" celebrated by Francis Meres. Meres
also said that the sonnets were "sugared," but nothing less sac-
charine could be imagined. With this third body of non-dramatic
poetry Shakespeare is not seeking patronage and fame. He is, in
Wordsworth's phrase, unlocking his heart. And, with that univ-
ersalising gift he had in such abundance, he is unlocking our
hearts too.

I both admire and deplore the sonnet form that Shakespeare
decided to use. The only true sonnet form is the Petrarchan, which
brings in the tide with an octave of lines rhyming ABBA ABBA
and then sends it out again with a seset rhyming CDC DCD or
something like it. With English pragmatism Shakespeare saw that
English did not have enough natural rhymes to accommodate the

form. What he calls sonnets have fourteen lines, true, but the effect is not at all sonnet-like, and the final clinching couplet has the force of an often highly moral or intellectual epigram. Nor are they, in the Italian and French traditions, somewhat conventional poems of love. They astound by being addressed to a man and yet not seeming to be homoerotic. A dark woman enters the sequence and her effect on the poet is so devastating that the Petrarchan tradition of courtly address shrivels into the mere versa-game that it is.

Twenty-odd years ago I was summoned to Hollywood to write the script of a huge film on Shakespeare's love-life. The film, as you would expect, was never made, but my scenario survives. A great deal of it is based on the story told in the sonnets. The dowager Marchioness, Southampton's mother, wishes her son to marry and so commissions the young man's poet-friend to propagandise for the holy state in verse. But Southampton does not wish to marry. A dark woman, a fine player on the keyboard instrument of the time, the virginals, enters the poet's life, and he praises her blackness with a kind of defiance: the Queen was fair-skinned and red-haired, and dark women were considered ugly. The sexual turmoil into which the poet is thrown is expressed in the incredible sonnet beginning "The expense of spirit in a waste of shame," with its phrase "Had, having and in quest to have," which sounds like the panting of a lustful animal. Then the dark lady—who I am convinced was black, one of the negresses who were not uncommon in the London of the time—is stolen by the poet's friend. Southampton does not marry, but he discovers sex.

A genuine autobiographical sequence then, with Shakespeare's beating heart almost surgically exposed. He never wished the poems to be published, so far as we know, and the printed book was an act of piracy. It is not easy for me to express my emotional and intellectual indebtedness to at least two of these sonnets—the one on the diminishing returns of sex, which I have already cited, and the one about power and corruption that begins "They that have power to hurt and will do none." But all the sonnets, even those blatantly propagandist ones at the beginning about the necessity for beauty to breed, are of great imaginative strength. We gain an image of a mature personality, sufficiently sure of itself to be playful at will, knotty, ambiguous, candid in its portrayal of self-doubt ("Desiring this man's art and that man's scope"), vulnerable, above all passionate.

Here, anyway, in this great sequence, and in the two vivid narrative poems, we see Shakespeare fulfilling an artistic impulse very different from the one that produced the plays. The plays, of course, are themselves poetry, but they are not poetry all the time. The poetry is released by dramatic circumstance, in sharp spurts of tension or sudden insight. It is always Shakespeare speaking, but Shakespeare in disguise. In the "pure" poems, and above all in the sonnets, there is no mask, no costume. We are living in an age in which the arbiters of literary aesthetics, especially in Paris, have been telling us to view poems as artefacts divorced from the personality of the creator. Indeed, we are told to think of art as creating itself. There is truth in this, as so much creation springs from an unconscious over which the mere wielder of the pen has less control than he thinks. Nevertheless; we are all romantic enough to wish to idolise the artist, and one artist above all. "We ask and ask—thou smilest and art still," said Matthew Arnold in his sonnet to Shakespeare. This is not altogether true.

What, ever since my youth, I have found in Shakespeare the pure poet is myself. I do not mean that, as a writer, I could ever approach Shakespeare in talent. I mean that my own nature, which is no more than human nature, is revealed in his work, and above all in the sonnets. If we can talk of art as having a *use*, then the use of Shakespeare is the clarification of what human nature is like. We are all Will, and sometimes "Will in overplus." This supreme wordmaster found the words to tell us so. And what astonishing words they are.

—1988

THE ORIENTAL DISEASES OF FICTION

❖

When I lived in Malaya, I encountered three diseases peculiar to the Eastern tropics. Two of them were monopolised by the Malays, the other by the Chinese. The primary Malay disease, which is known in the West and has even exported its native name, is called *amok*. The sufferer, or *pengamok*, broods for some time over a wrong, real or fancied, and then takes his revenge on as much of the entire world as he can. He runs amok (the saying has been borrowed by the Western languages) and kills indiscriminately in the hope that he will himself be killed. A Malay student of mine stole a military pistol, shot five people, and then was himself shot by the Malay police.

The second Malay disease is called *latah*. This may be defined as morbid mimesis, in which the sufferer is infinitely suggestible and will try to turn himself into anything that is suggested to him. Many of the suggestions are cruel. I have seen a sufferer who was easily convinced that he was a bicycle: he pedalled away until he dropped in exhaustion. Another was persuaded that the bolster on his bed—commonly known as an *isteri Belanda* or Dutch wife—was really his own Malay wife, and he behaved towards it accordingly, evincing profound jealousy when someone tried to take it away from him.

The Chinese disease is known as *shook jong*. It is very frightening. The sufferer, if male, believes that his penis is shrinking into his belly, and he tries to prevent this from happening by fastening it to his testicles—or even his thigh—with a sharp knife. He believes that his *yang* or masculine element is being assailed by the female *yin*. Women also can suffer from the disease, in which instance they are convinced that they are being attacked by the forces of the *yang* and that the female aperture is closing. They use the knife not for fastening but for cutting.

None of these diseases features in any of the literatures of the

East. There has been more than one Western novel entitled *Amok*, as well as a memorable French film, but neither *latah* nor *shook jong* has found celebration in art. The curious thing is that the three diseases can serve as very revealing metaphors for certain Western impulses in art, especially the art of fiction. It may be said, for instance, that all fiction is *latah* in that it deals in mimesis. The novelist enters into the life of beings distinct from himself and, at his most manic, becomes an animal or even an inanimate object. Jack London turned himself into a dog in *The Call of the Wild*. Charles Dickens is always willing to make a candlestick behave like a human being, a London fog take on the properties of a prehistoric animal, Mother Nature herself become a brewer of beer (*A Christmas Carol*, second page). Knowing that such mimesis is really a disease, we are impelled to the frivolous theory that what the East does in life the West does in art.

Amok, of course, is less a disease of the novelist than of the satirist, especially if he is as manic as Jonathan Swift. In his *Gulliver's Travels*, Swift begins by trying to diminish humanity, including himself, blows up humanity into monstrous giants to demonstrate both the physical horror of the race and its pretensions, finally makes horses the rational creatures of the earth and human beings mere bestial Yahoos. Gulliver himself, or Swift, is a Yahoo. If he fails to extinguish the vile race it is because death is too easy a punishment. That he has run *amok* in this frightening book no one will doubt.

A great deal of our television entertainment is based on the principle of *amok*. It is closer to the Malay variety than to the Swiftian because it presents killing without perceptible motivation. The final shoot-out, the act of multiple vengeance is often the point of the story, and psychological complexity would be alien to a plot intended to stimulate in a void. It is the gun or the knife that stimulates the telespectator and not the reason for its use. Introduce a true Malay motivation and the result would seem comic. The Malay *amok* I knew was motivated to murder because he had been asked to deliver a message in the rain and had been severely rebuked for not wishing to do so. The *amok* massacre is all act and no (under Western eyes) acceptable motive.

Shook jong is most clearly demonstrated in the work of specialists in machismo. The writer doubts his own masculinity and has, with the blunt knife of his prose, to convince himself and his readers that his penis is not retracting into his scrotum. We find this in Ernest Hemingway, whose posthumous *The Garden of Eden* proclaims his essential femininity, and also in such best-selling writers as Harold Robbins, who may be said to practise on the sub-Hemingwayan level. There is a good deal of the *shook jong* in Alberto Moravia, especially in *Lui*. Feminist writers exhibit the other side of the *shook jong* coin, though they assert their sexual identity by taking the knife to men, attacking the *yang* element in its most convenient incarnation.

That literature (and perhaps every other art) is essentially morbid is somewhat fancifully implied by the above observations, which must not, of course, be taken too seriously. In his book *The Wound and the Bow*, the late Edmund Wilson dealt with specific authors in whom the morbid element was sublimated into high art: Charles Dickens and Rudyard Kipling. Dickens cannot forget that his father debased his son by being shut up in a debtor's prison: sooner or later, even in a joyous work like *The Pickwick Papers*, the author homes to the cell and the bars and the humiliation. Kipling could not forget the hell of his childhood, and he has to punish the *kuch-nays* like Aunt Rosa by turning them into the "lesser breeds without the law" which the British Raj will discipline. At the end of his book, Wilson presents the mythical Philoctetes as the type of the artist. His wound will not heal; it festers and infects the air. Philoctetes must dwell alone, removed from his fellows, but he has to be called upon in times of crisis. He may have a wound, but he is skilful with the bow. The artist is diseased, but society occasionally needs him.

But is all art really morbid? I have practised the art of the novel for thirty years. The need to become a novelist sprang out of morbid circumstances. I had been given a year to live because of a mistaken medical prognosis and there was no work I could undertake in my pseudo-terminal year except that of the writer of fiction. I was in an extreme Philoctetean situation. Whether my vocation is morbid in the profounder sense I still do not know. D. H. Lawrence said: "We purge our sickness in books." He demonstrated the whole spectrum of Oriental diseases in his work—the savage *amok* of the hater of his own country, the *latah* of a poetry which could identify the poet with everything from a snake

to a figtree, the *shook jong* of a precarious masculinity. I think I
have written professionally because there was nothing else I could
profitably do, and that in itself may be a disease. Thomas Mann
had a theory of artist's guilt. The artist is guilty because he is
playing no part in the useful work of the world—banking, brick-
laying, medicine. The world will get on well enough without art,
and the artist suffers from a sense of his uselessness. To be useless
is to be diseased.

The sense of this is perhaps a *maladie du nord*. In Sicily and
its extensions (such as Turin and the United States) the Mafia
practises what may well be an art, in the sense of a clear aim and
the deployment of a number of well-defined techniques. It would
be more accurate to speak of a Mafia culture. That this culture is
based on *shook jong* can easily be demonstrated. Masculinity has
to be asserted, and the assertion is undoubtedly morbid. There is,
among mafiosi, a powerful, if unconscious, doubt of sexual identity. This partly explains the essential health of Sicilian literature,
from Pirandello to Lampedusa. If the artist is surrounded by an
unhealthy society, he can cut himself from it and be a kind of
Philoctetes without a wound. In other societies, the disease of the
artist affirms the sanity of his environment. There is something
consoling about this.

—1989

PLAYING HAMLET WITH HAMLET

❖

Let me explain my title. When I was a boy in my native Lancashire, I frequently heard the expression "I'll play Hamlet with thee, lad." This was an adult threat levelled at naughty boys. It meant that the threatener would fall into a posture of madness and do great harm. Clearly the reference was not to the hero of Shakespeare's tragedy but to the original Scandinavian myth of the prince who avenged the death of his father by murder and arson. This prince went genuinely mad, not like Shakespeare's Hamlet, who merely pretends dementia. There was nothing implausible about the survival of a Scandinavian legend among the unlettered folk of the English North. The Danes ruled there for a long time. I sometimes heard "Hamlet" pronounced as "Amloth," which is the original form of the name.

Stage and film directors are playing Amloth with *Hamlet*. I will not catalogue the various travesties of the great tragedy that have either been proposed or already passed into the annals of theatrical madness. *Hamlet* on ice, on roller skates, as circus, as Wild West melodrama, as Oedipal comedy, as feminist propaganda— the list of possibilities is pretty long. The play admits of so many absurd interpretations because of both its universality and its ambiguity. It contains everything, and it is crammed with contradictions.

T. S. Eliot tried to teach us that the play is an artistic failure. He asserted that Shakespeare was, at the time of writing it, trying to express various personal dilemmas and failing to find an "objective correlative"—that is, an artistic mode which should be the dramatic equivalent of a highly complex set of emotions. *Hamlet*, said Eliot, lacks coherence. There is no real excuse for the prince's failure to exact revenge for the murder of his father. He delays because Shakespeare has to fill up five acts somehow. The love affair between Hamlet and Ophelia does not convince. Hamlet's

pretense of madness is unnecessary. Above all, said Eliot, Shakespeare had failed to relate the material he was given—the story
of Amloth in the history of the Dane Saxo Grammaticus—to the
more sophisticated preoccupations that were swirling in his brain
in the year 1601.

The excavations in London which have unearthed the site of
the Rose playhouse are relevant to our broodings on *Hamlet*. In
1601 there was at that theatre a revival of Thomas Kyd's play
The Spanish Tragedy. This was without doubt the most popular
play of the age. The rather crude rhetoric of Kyd was, for this
revival, polished by Ben Jonson, who also added extra dialogue
of his own. The Globe playhouse, a literal stone's throw away
from the Rose, feared heavy competition from its rival, and we
cannot doubt that Richard Burbage, the leading actor at the
Globe, urged his friend and colleague Shakespeare to tidy up and
sophisticate another play by Kyd. This was *Hamlet, Revenge*, a
tragedy which has totally disappeared. It seems to have been
based on the old Danish legend as fictionalised by a certain Bel-
leforest. So, with a new *Spanish Tragedy* playing at the Rose, and
a new *Hamlet, Revenge* playing at the Globe, London's South
Bank was getting its fill of Kyd in the acting season of 1601.

We see now what Shakespeare's problem was. He was given a
crude play with all the ingredients that endeared *The Spanish
Tragedy* to the London public: a ghost, madness, revenge. But
Shakespeare was, at that time, not greatly interested in those de-
lapidated properties. He had other things on his mind. His father
had recently died, the death of his son Hamnet (a name which he
probably pronounced as Amblet) was a green memory, the Essex
rebellion had failed ignominiously and Essex had been executed,
the succession to the English throne was in doubt, he had been
reading Montaigne in Florio's translation, he was getting old and
probably thinking of death, he was undoubtedly stricken by the
new skepticism which wondered whether there was really a life
after death. Memories of his father mingled with memories of his
boyhood in rural Stratford, and one particular memory had been
brought back to life by the very title of the play he had to work
on. A young girl named Kate Hamlet had drowned herself for
love in the river Avon and been forbidden Christian burial. The

static world of *The Spanish Tragedy* was dying: there was no certitude in religion; revenge solved no problems; ghosts were either hallucinations or mischievous uncovenanted powers. Life, lacking its eschatological substructure, was stale and unprofitable. There was a lot of melancholy about, and its probable cause was inflation: there was no certainty even in money. To impose the sensibility of a manic depressive like Hamlet, very much a modern man, on the structure of a primitive revenge play was to court artistic disaster. Hence T. S. Eliot's conclusion that *Hamlet* is a bad play.

It may well be that the art we prize most is grossly imperfect. We are repelled by perfection and for that reason reject the plays of Racine. Oriental carpet-makers used to introduced crudities into their designs so as not to blaspheme by rivalling God, who alone is the author of perfection. Imperfection is all too human, and *Hamlet* is a very human play. Its looseness of structure, its shakiness of motivation are compensated by a wit and a rhetoric that have affected all the literatures of the West and modified more languages than English. As for the Danish prince himself, he is the first character in the whole of world literature to reveal the inner workings of his mind and to invite not just empathy but identification. We all think we are Hamlet, even if we are women. Sarah Bernhardt played the role with a wooden leg and no sense of sexual incompatibility.

One factor that impels directorial ingenuity is the absence of anything we can call a definitive text of the play. There is a very bad quarto apparently put together by a guest actor who, not being a regular member of Shakespeare's troupe, felt no guilt at selling his patchwork to an eager printer. This bad quarto had to be driven out of circulation by a good quarto which is authentic Shakespeare. But the version of *Hamlet* we find in the 1623 First Folio is somewhat different from its predecessor of twenty years before. It is also very long. We rarely see a complete *Hamlet*. Clearly, Shakespeare was so obsessed by the need for the "objective correlative" to his emotional and intellectual state that he went beyond what was possible in the "two hour traffic" of the stage. He undoubtedly expected directorial cuts, and he still gets them. I, when a professor of drama at a male college, put the whole play on and took two nights to do it. I also needed two Hamlets, since no single one of my students was willing to learn the entire role.

This production was in modern dress, not because of any innovative desire but because there was no money for period costumes. It works as well in modern dress as in Renaissance doublets. My Hamlet was able to smoke cigarettes on stage. He was also able to come on reading Schlegel's translation and begin his great soliloquy by sneering *"Sein oder nicht sein—ja, dass ist die Frage."* That soliloquy is too well known. It is agony for an actor to try to draw new nuances from it. The whole play is too well known. This partly explains the need to present it on skates or in a fantasticated Third Reich or in the nude. Directors are desperate to seek fresh modes of presentation. It will not really work on film, despite Laurence Olivier's desperately truncated version. Despite, too, the four-hour travesty I once saw in Hindi, with, following Indian cinematic custom, at least ten songs. A dusky Hamlet intoned "To be or not to be" in a wavering cantilena with drums and pipes.

It will not work on film because it has no real locale. We are not really in Denmark. There is no castle, there are no battlements. We are on a stage on the South Bank of the river Thames. The visiting actors discuss with Hamlet the state of the London theatre, hit hard by the Shirley Temples of the day, the child actors of the indoor playhouses. They look at the flag flying over the Globe, with its representation of world-carrying Hercules. The first gravedigger sends the second for a "stoup of liquor" from Yaughan's, the Danish beer shop not far from the Globe. Hamlet is all too aware of his audience. He delivers his soliloquies to the dirty ears of the lower orders and the clean ears of the gentlemen who sit on stage. He mocks these latter by saying "My tablets—it is meet I set it down." The young intellectuals of the town were always copying good lines into their notebooks, ready to deliver them as their own at later supper parties. Hamlet may say "Now I am alone," but he never is.

There has only ever been one great Hamlet—Richard Burbage, for whom the part was written. He had the advantage of being schooled in the meaning, tempo, and intonation of his lines by their author. Every actor wants to take on the role, but he foresees that neither he nor his audience will be satisfied. Dustin Hoffman came to the London theatre to play Hamlet, but he has had to be content with Shylock in *The Merchant of Venice*. The difficulty of producing a superb *Hamlet* explains why actors and directors hopelessly continue to try. It is a baffling play made of great scenes highly satisfying in themselves but not really capable of cohesion the one with the others. We look forward to the soliloquies, the ranting First Player, the play within the play, the final fencing bout, but as single items and not as aspects of a well-structured whole. The nearest parallel to *Hamlet* is a film by Charlie Chaplin, in which the parts are superior to the totality. It is great theatre but, with T. S. Eliot, we have to doubt whether it is a great play.

—1989

GRAHAM GREENE: A REMINISCENCE

❖

I first met Graham Greene in 1957. I had just returned from Malaya and had been asked, by one of his friends in that newly independent protectorate, to take him some silk shirts specially made in Kuala Lumpur. I delivered them to his Albany flat, and we then had lunch together. A rumour was later to put it about that the silk shirts had opium pellets sewn into the cuffs, but this was not, I think, true. Greene and I had in common a devotion to opium, well satisfied in the Far East. We were also both Catholics but this did not, despite the old Marxist gibe, represent a cognate addiction. It was a Friday when we met, and so we ate fish for lunch. He mixed me a powerful martini first. He had, in those days, the vast collection of whisky miniatures which he was soon to dramatise in "Our Man In Havana." These were decor, and were not to be broached.

I had just published my first novel, *Time for a Tiger,* and Greene graciously asked me to sign his copy. We were both published by Heinemann in those days, and I do not doubt that Greene got that copy free. He considered my Malayan fiction to be amusing but lacking in profundity. He had no doubt that he was the only living novelist equipped to deal with the questions of mystique and politique which inflame those regions where dictators arise and white men go to pieces. Of my later work he had no considered opinion. He did not read it because he did not like it, or it may have been the other way round.

I was, in my later dealings with him, to be aware of a certain distrust. This, I think, had something to do with religion. He was a convert to Catholicism, like his friend Evelyn Waugh, and he was undoubtedly conscious of the gulf that separates a convert from a cradle Catholic like myself. I belonged to a different culture, more Continental than British, and had neither Waugh's rigidity nor Greene's pedantry. Waugh was the better convert of the two, and his theological objections to *The Heart of the Matter,* which I still think to be Greene's best book, were brilliantly valid. There was no doubt which of the two had the better brain.

Greene was fascinated by sin, while Waugh merely abhorred it, and he had some notion that it was holier to sin than merely to do right. In his first Catholic novel, *Brighton Rock,* he set up a curious opposition between a secular system of conduct, with right feebly sparring with wrong, and an eschatological code, in which good wars with evil. Evil was somehow noble, and the Catholic gangster Pinky, who improbably says "Credo in unum Satanum," is at least, to quote Eliot, man enough to be damned. Greene never liked my objections to his ethical distortions. He was not happy to be corrected. He put carrots into a Lancashire hot pot in *The Human Factor,* and he promised to emend the solecism in a later edition, though he never did. He used "Gibraltese" for "Gibraltarian" in another novel, and this was a reprehensible error. I should have pointed neither out. He was touchy about such things.

Greene was, I used to feel, born for exile. We had that in common, and it was not unconnected with our common faith. This took both of us to the Mediterranean, he to Antibes, myself to Italy and then Monaco. We were, in a manner, neighbours. I was unhappy about the menage he conducted, since he lived with another man's wife, but, as he grew older, he developed a highly idiosyncratic version of Catholicism, which could even accommodate a probable absence of the deity. What worried me most about him was his capacity to reconcile a spiritual system with a materialistic one. Communism, to him, was the politique which matched the Catholic mystique. He is explicit about this in his *The Comedians*: communism may have blood on its hands, but that is better than the bowl that Pontius Pilate washed in. It seemed to me that he was evading certain complex moral issues by travelling to regions where the problem of establishing the good society was over-simplified. It was easy to be on the side of the revolutionaries if their task was to eliminate a godless dictatorship. Haiti, Panama, Argentina were his preferred settings for rather simplistic human dramas. These were often resolved in a manner that struck me as sentimental. Waugh always avoided sentimentality. Greene could, figuratively at least, weep at the

thrusting of the Christ-child's head in the filthy straw or the tin-
kling of a medallion falling from the body of a dead sinner.

Our last meeting took place eleven years ago. We met in his
small apartment on the rue Pasteur. I was anxious to probe his
literary rather than theological roots. As for these latter, I still
maintained that he was a Jansenist who found corruption in the
natural order, but he was adamant in his denial of this. He was
still reading what James Joyce would have called light theology,
but he endeared himself to me by concentrating much of his reading time on the works of Ford Madox Ford, whom, like myself,
he considered to be the finest, and certainly most neglected, novelist of the century. But his devotion to Ford was the cause of
new dissension between us. He had edited *Parade's End* for the
Bodley Head and, unforgivably in my view, eliminated the final
novel of the tetralogy. There was a curious, but not uncharacter-
istic, obtuseness in his assumption that Ford's own disparagement
of *Last Post* was to be taken seriously. His literary judgments
were not trustworthy: this he admitted.

The Edwardian era that Ford graced was Greene's literary Ithaca. He deeply admired Conrad, and he saw himself in some measure as Conrad's successor—prober of human motivation under
exotic skies. But he was aware that he had elected to serve a genre
inferior to what *Nostromo* and "The Heart of Darkness" represent. His novels were popular in a double sense. They sold many
copies and were made into mostly mediocre films. They also exploited well-tried plot devices and did not dare the expansion that
Ford and Conrad assumed to be necessary for a panoramic view
of life. Greene admitted that none of his novels was "great." He
accepted the judgment of the Nobel committee that he was too
popular to be worthy of the accolade which traditionally goes to
the worthy but ill-selling. At seventy-five he said to me that he
was looking forward to a greater prize than the Nobel. What
prize? Death.

He may have said that he wanted that final benison or malison,
but there was no doubt that he was enjoying life—he was tall, fit,
clear-eyed, lover of an attractive Frenchwoman and of French
wine. Part of life's pleasure was the daily quota of two hundred
words—no more, no less—in a minuscule hand. He prided himself to me (and the pride is transferred to the novelist hero of

The End of the Affair) on the exact word-count he could inscribe on the title-page of a new typescript. Two hundred words a day left most of the day for living. Living could mean being combative. The "J'accuse" he levelled at Jacques Medecin, Mayor of Nice, showed the fighting spirit of a man undisposed to tolerate injustice. He paid dearly for what was taken to be a libel, but the payment was only in money, of which he had plenty, though this was not manifested in opulence or sybaritism of lifestyle. "Il n'est pas facile," said a prominent Niçois to me. Nor was he. I regret that our relationship collapsed because of a prickliness that seemed, at the time, unworthy but was merely a symptom of encroaching age.

I was asked on a French television programme how old Greene now was, and I overestimated his age by a couple of years. This drove him into a fury whose excess was not matched by the exquisite small handwriting in which it was couched. Later I was indiscreet to a reporter about the Greene menage. The fury now modulated to an urgent recommendation that I see a doctor. But I was aware that there was an antipathy not easy to analyse, expressed in a "saying of the week" in a Sunday newspaper. I had interviewed him and shown him the text of the interview. He had approved but now publicly said: "He put words into my mouth which I had to look up in the dictionary."

I sustained my cautious affection. He cared about writing and he wrote well. I never gave him a review less than almost fawningly laudatory. Though he lived abroad and thus officially disqualified himself from the right to high honours, he received the Order of Merit and was humble about it, remembering that it had been awarded to Henry James. He always showed, when it was necessary, a becoming humility and was always aware of himself as a sinner and as a popular writer. He admitted to the exploitation of the Catholic faith for sometimes sensational ends. But he was convinced, justly, that the wrongs of the world could only be properly judged sub specie aeternitatis.

I asked him once what Auden meant by the phrase "How Graham-Greenish" and what was the exact location of Greeneland. He saw that such journalistic shorthand expressed a discardable superficiality—the seedy exile driven to drink under the palms, occasionally visiting a native brothel, conscious of the world's—or God's—abandonment. The whisky priest of *The Power and the Glory* is this, but, being a Catholic minister of the faith, he is far more. The carious world of Greeneworld is that of fallen man, the desperate Adam unsure what his sin was but certainly convinced of guilt. Redemption seems to be a different story altogether. In other words, Greene's theme was Original Sin, a concept not popular in our relativist societies. The astonishing thing is that he was able to make popular fiction out of it.

At our last luncheon together I asked what he missed most about England. "Sausages," he said. There was not enough bread in the garlicky French variety. He died a sort of Catholic, a sort of cosmopolitan, a very considerable writer, certainly an Englishman.

—1991

CRAFT AND CRUCIFIXION—
THE WRITING OF FICTION

❖

Counting the number of my published novels listed on the shameful page of blazoned achievement opposite the title page of my newest book, I see that I have produced thirty as well as a volume of short stories. This, I am told, is too many. If I had written fewer I would have written better, though this is a hypothesis difficult to prove. I spent ten years working on my longest novel, and an Italian reviewer said *"Troppo."* When I began writing fiction professionally—that is, not as an evening or weekend hobby—I thought of a novel as a construct of between 70,000 and 80,000 words and the maximum time to be spent on its composition as about six weeks. The weeks contained seven days and the days about six hours. But such novels as I produced under these conditions I felt, and still feel, to be disgracefully brief. It is not possible to define a novel except under some such rubric as "a work of fiction long enough to be sewn rather than stapled," but the tradition of considerable length established by Cervantes and followed by Richardson, Fielding, Dickens, Joyce, and the American busters of blocks is not to be discountenanced by such slim productions as those of, say, Anita Brookner. A novel ought to be panoramic. Many of the novels written today would be regarded by Henry James as long short stories.

True, even *War and Peace* was achieved by a process of serial accumulation. That was the nineteenth-century way, best exemplified in this country by the novels of Dickens. If we went back to the fortnightly serial we would produce picaresque monsters whose progress could be monitored by the response of their readers. But we must accept the limitations that are imposed upon us by such factors as the price of books and the diminution of reading time (there was no television in the age of the postcenal family reading aloud), and, while we should be doubtful about the propriety of publishing novels of 40,000 words, we should regard 100,000 words as an acceptable length.

It seems coldblooded to consider a work of art in such quantitative terms, but the measuring rod is an aspect of the process of artistic preparation. The painter starts with a canvas of a particular size, the symphonist used to give himself four movements and a playing time of between forty and fifty minutes, the height of Michelangelo's David was determined by the block of marble that arrived from the quarry. Before starting a novel, the novelist should have a notion of its probable length, and this entails foreknowledge of the points at which its climaxes, minor and major, should arrive and its dénouement ensue.

The shape of a novel, like that of a symphony, is conditioned by its length. But to speak of a shape, a form, a structure, is to introduce the notion of artifice, which means artificiality. Whether we like it or not, a novel is essentially artificial. It is artificial in having a beginning, a middle, and an end. Real life is all middle, also muddle. The task of the novelist is to suggest that a slice of life has a shape, and shape is determined by a theme. Every novel is about something, and this something can sometimes be inscribed on the back of a postage stamp. A novel is sometimes no more than an extended anecdote. Its plot, no matter how complicated, is reducible to a simple statement. *Madame Bovary* is about *bovarysme*. *Great Expectations* is about great expectations. *Pride and Prejudice* is a very fair summary of content. Amis *père* shows in what way Jim is lucky. Amis *fils* wrote about money and could find no other title.

The artificiality of fiction is usually condemned when it presents a property not much found in real life—that of coincidence. Dickens is regarded as a prime offender, but it may be that without coincidence the novel cannot properly exist. Characters appear, disappear, then appear again, but in a manner so obviously contrived that we know that we are outside the stringencies of real life. The nearest analogue to this process is to be found in symphonic form, where it is against the law to introduce a theme only to discard it. Characters, though they must appear to have free will (and the novel may be seen as a kind of testament of free will), are essentially manipulable, as musical themes are, and they submit to fictional structure, however much they seem to fire and power that structure.

A novel being a work of literature, and literature being defined as the exploitation of language to an aesthetic end, language itself may be seen as one of the characters of fiction. In that class of fiction which appears to be a verbal form of cinema, language may be transparent and almost discardable: to this class belong most bestsellers. We can call this Category 1 fiction. Opposed to it is Category 2, in which language is trickier. Joyce's *Ulysses* is the most notable example of a novel in which language (as in the "Oxen of the Sun" episode) actively obstructs the narrative. The work begins with the word "stately" and ends with "yes," so that initial and final letters are reversed to form a kind of book-ends. For that matter the first chapter begins with a mock mass, in which false blood flows, and the last chapter ends with the heroine lavishly menstruating. Most novelists would regard this as taking the externals of the form too far, but few would see it as wrong to make the lighting of a cigarette in the final chapter balance the puffing of a fag in the first.

As a practising novelist—though not one who is likely to practise very much longer—I find myself closer to opaque Joyce than to transparent Jack Higgins. This ensures unpopularity, but one cannot evade the calls of one's temperament. The Joycean approach undoubtedly has something to do with musical training, and I wrote a symphony before I wrote a novel. The symphony contained traditional elements of repetition and balance, but it told no story. The orchestral score was two hundred pages long, and it seemed an easier prospect to produce a like number of pages of narrative than to labour at another clotted web of notes. As a novelist I am a symphonist *manqué*. In the early 1970s I wrote a novel entitled *Napoleon Symphony*, in which the events of the Corsican's career were directly related to the movements of Beethoven's *Eroica*. This was difficult to do and did not please, though it brought me a commission to compose a genuine symphony. An earlier book of mine, *The Worm and the Ring*, had been an attempt to present Wagner's music drama in the form of a modern novel. This followed an early effort at relating a modern narrative to the structure of Virgil's *Aeneid*. Obviously I had had

Ulysses in mind. I still feel that I am cheating the reader, though the reader would prefer to be cheated, if I do not build a novel on the template of a known myth.

In my most recent novel, *Any Old Iron*, the three main characters were intended to relate to the Dante, Virgil, and Beatrice of the *Divine Comedy*. The heroine was named Beatrix; her two brothers were respectively Reginald Morrow Jones, whose name is easily corrupted to Vegetable Marrow, which recalls Vergilius Maro, and Daniel Tetlow Jones, an improbable Dan T or DanTe. The final chapter pursued the pattern of the *Inferno* pretty exactly, though nobody noticed. Nobody was intended to regard it as essential to notice. Probably this desire to thicken the texture of fiction through underlying myth and/or ambiguous language derives from a musical background. Words are monodic, and one would prefer them to be harmonic or even contrapuntal. This urge to musicalise fiction to the limit led Joyce to write *Finnegans Wake*, in which every semanteme is polysemic.

Let me come now to the actual mechanics of writing my kind of novel. I do not think that the physical action of generating fiction can easily be separated from the mental processes involved. One may create poetry or music in the head, but fiction, like sculpture or painting, requires the hand. When music or poetry submits to handling, then it needs the pen. Fiction requires the typewriter or the word-processor. It always required it, even when only the dipped quill was available. The word-processor is perhaps dangerous, because the ease of correction makes prose-production lazy. With a typewriter one has to hear a sentence or phrase in one's head before committing it to paper: that ensures a sufficient elegance and reminds one that the novel, like the epic, is an auditory art. To write a novel with a pen is hard work, and the expense of muscle gives one the illusion that one has written more than one actually has. Three pages of typed quarto should add up to about a thousand words. That is probably enough work for one day.

Enough work if enough paper has been irritably crumpled and thrown away. The three completed pages, impeccably typed and requiring the minimum of corrections, ought to be what is eventually submitted to your editor and, one hopes, the printer. At least, that is my way, and it owes something to the preparation of orchestral scores. A score cannot have deletions and corrections; it must be readable and playable.

Of course, one brings to the typewriter and the virgin sheet rolled into it more than one's fingers. One knows the names of one's characters and roughly what they propose to do within the segment of life one has allotted them, but one does not know very much more. The physical appearance and, perhaps more important, manner of speech spring, or uncoil, out of the typing fingers. The room in which they are sitting, or street they are walking on, can as easily be made out of an arbitrary page of your dictionary as from memory or fancy. Thus: "There was Mechlin lace on the chairs and cases of medals were displayed on the sideboard. Sticky bottles of medicine sat on Medea's side-table, and one had spilled on to a big though tattered book on the Medicis. A vase by the window had been stuffed, improbably, with a leguminous plant with clover-looking leaves, perhaps medic. There was a mock-mediaeval tapestry on the wall, representing a troop of Canterbury pilgrims, not Chaucer's. The colour scheme of the room resembled the first faeces of a newly born brat," and so on. (The first faeces is known as meconium, which also means poppy-juice.)

The three-page daily stint (more at weekends, when the telephone rings less) represents a strictly mechanical, or journeyman's, approach to novel-writing. The structural aspects of the work are, of course, not mechanical at all. A novel is divided into chapters, and, if one visualises one's final typescript as a wad of three hundred folios, each containing about four hundred words, then it will be helpful to think in terms of, say, thirty chapters of ten pages each, though this must be the roughest of guides. In my view, the number of chapters in a novel ought to have an arith-mological significance—that is to say, a symbolism in respect of theme or character. I wrote a novel called *A Clockwork Orange* which had twenty-one chapters—twenty-one being the symbol of legal maturity at the time of writing—and was angry when the American publisher cut the final chapter, thus destroying the arithmology. A later novel, *Earthly Powers*, was planned to have eighty-one chapters, eighty-one being the age of the narrator-hero, but I miscounted and found I had eighty-two. This concern with the symbolism of number is mediaeval—important in Dante, for instance—and was still to be found in Milton's *Lycidas*, whose eleven sections remind the attentive reader that 11 is the sign for resurrection after death.

A novel makes itself as it goes along, most of the basic work being given to the unconscious mind. It is inadvisable to plan too much in advance, to know, for example, precisely what is going to happen in Chapter 29. E. M. Forster, writing *A Passage to India*, had no idea what was to happen after the incident in the Malabar Caves. In 1957 my first wife gave me a brief story from real life which started a novel off—the title was *The Right to an Answer*—but left me pleasantly in doubt as to how it would proceed and conclude. The story was of two English married couples—Mr. and Mrs. A, Mr. and Mrs. Z—who played the weekend game of swapping spouses. Unfortunately the game was taken too seriously by Mr. A and Mrs. Z, who fell in love and thus disrupted two marriages. A character entered the fiction from nowhere—a Mr Raj, a Singhalese ignorant of the principles of English adultery, who resolved the unfinished tale bloodily. This I had not expected when I commenced writing, but I knew something would emerge out of the unconscious. Novelists have to have this kind of confidence in the unknown.

Let us now consider the writing of a novel which has not, and never will be, written. There are sometimes baffling, necessarily unconscious, obstructions to the construction of a work of art, and here we have an example. Tennyson wrote a poem beginning "It is the miller's daughter, and she is grown so dear, so dear/ That I would be the jewel that trembles at her ear." Schubert composed a song-cycle entitled *Die Schöne Müllerin*, sometimes translated as "The Maid of the Mill." What was there, I wondered, about miller's daughters that they should be so attractive? The answer probably is that, in a poor village, the girl who could afford to wear ear-rings was a prize catch. The miller, gold-thumbed and cheating, was wealthy enough and his children were well-fed. I thought of a novel with the title "It Is the Miller's Daughter", and under this flimsy *donnée* trembled some basic structure about bread (flour, miller) and water. Water, why water? I did not know.

But the story was set, certainly, in a French village, probably

on the Belgian border. A young man, Pierre, an agricultural la-
bourer, lives with his grandmother, who feeds him on soup that,
she says, has simmered non-stop ever since the reign of Louis XIV.
History, then, is suspended in fragments in hot water. Cold water
comes from the village well, the centre of the community's activities, where women meet to draw water in their buckets and gossip, young men meet young girls, songs are sung, dances danced,
and male trials of strength performed. Pierre hopelessly loves Marie, the miller's daughter, but her three hulking brothers beat him
up whenever he approaches the millhouse.

One day a representative of the central government arrives to
inform the villagers that their well water contains an insidious
poison and that, by governmental order, the well must be boarded
up and officially sealed. Water in future will come in carts and
will be guaranteed pure. Pierre's grandmother mutters at this,
finds the new water tasteless, and orders Pierre to get their sup-
plies in a bucket from a stream some miles distant. To Pierre's
astonishment, this stream is patrolled by uniformed men and ac-
cess to it forbidden. On his bewildered way home, he meets by
chance the miller's daughter and declares his love. She is unhappy
at home, and it has been proposed by her father that she marry
a man she greatly dislikes, an elderly farmer with money and
drunken, brutal habits. Pierre asks Marie to run away with him
over the border. They will marry, he will work, they will be poor
but happy.

They cross the border, install themselves in a small town, paying rent to the landowning keeper of a tavern, and Pierre works
as a mechanic in a garage. Their rent is wantonly increased, he
loses his job, they are threatened with eviction while Marie is six
months pregnant, and Pierre goes to the tavern to beg compassion
and leniency from Grosdieu, his landlord. Grosdieu is unsym-
pathetic. He is a huge man, large drinker and colossal eater,
boaster, bully, loud of voice, illogical, rather like the Jehovah of
the *Book of Job*. He has a single resident in his upstairs accom-
modation, a Herr Geist who is perpetually typing and from whose
open window fall odd sheets of what looks like neatly worded
nonsense.

Grosdieu has a son, Manuel, very different from his father,
compassionate, sentimental, even maudlin, with melting brown

eyes and trembling lips. He is too good to live, and he very nearly dies. He looks after the bar of the tavern. In the cellar there is a stock of very old and exclusive burgundy which is worth a fortune. An oenophile is always asking if he may buy it—money no object—and M. Grosdieu says no. But the plight of Pierre and Marie fires Manuel to make a midnight arrangement with the would-be purchaser: he drags the wine up from the cellar in the dark. But his father hears what he thinks is a burglar, comes downstairs from his bed, and nearly kills Manuel.

M. Grosdieu is from then on a changed man. He has built a new house on a hill, and he and Manuel live there, leaving the running of the tavern to Pierre and Marie. Herr Geist is still typing away, letting sheets of gibberish fall from the window. Pierre and Marie go on a visit back to their native village. Pierre, encouraged by the sacrifice of Manuel, who was to sell the rare wine only in order to provide rent-money for the pair, is determined to unseal the well and to give the villagers back their liquid centre of life. But what happens on their return? Have the villagers been turned into zombies by the treated water administered by the government? Has the well dried up? Stories are always damnably difficult to complete.

One can see why this material cannot be novelised. The actions do not spring out of the temperaments of the characters. The narrative is an imposed one, and it is fabular or allegorical. It is known totally, from outset almost to the end, and there is no pleasure in composing a novel in which everything is predetermined. This should be a great lesson for the tyro novelist, who is welcome to do what he or she will with the above material. This is the kind of lesson I am prepared to give, for I do not think there are any other lessons.

Courses in creative writing are popular in American colleges, but they are mostly useless. What can one teach except what should have already been taught: syntax, the use of a dictionary, a basic knowledge of the progress or retrogress of world fiction? There are tricks that can be imparted, but most students, who are over-serious, despise trickery. Would-be novelists should listen to a great deal of symphonic music, finding there the principles of development, climax, and dénouement. They must read, and particularly they must read dictionaries. If they want to write best-sellers they must forget about literature.

They must learn craft, also craftiness (artfulness too), and be prepared for crucifixion. They will get this chiefly from reviewers, who are rarely novelists themselves, though they have tried the form and failed at it. Reviewers will tell them what they have done wrong, but they are always unable to tell them how to do right. As for the great world that rolls outside the Ptolomaic preserves of the reviewers, that contains comparatively few readers of books. Those that do read them will usually be silent about what they have read, though they may complain to the novelist if he has gone wrong on a point of botany, French cuisine, or the technique of whisky blending. The novelist is on his own, and, even when he gets to heaven, he will probably be coldshouldered by Flaubert and Proust. But God, who is the supreme novelist, may love him. After all, he has permitted his crucifixion.

—1991

STREGA IN DO MAGGIORE

❖

The Anglo-Saxon musical world seems at present to be inundated with new recordings of the *Symphonie Fantastique* of Hector Berlioz. The renewal of interest in the work may have something to do with the work of the musician-antiquarian Roger Norrington, who insists on using the original instruments and instrumental techniques for composers even so recent as Brahms and Wagner. Richard Strauss will be next. With his version of the *Symphonie Fantastique*, Norrington has reverted to very rustic-sounding oboes and clarinets, and his strings have little vibrato. He has an ophicleide rasping away in the bass. The work sounds romantic but naive; all modernity had been expunged. But the *idée fixe* still sounds clear and chilling, high above the orchestra. The witch who once haunted Berlioz has not been exorcised. Her name was Harriet Smithson. It was she who convinced Paris that Shakespeare was conceivably a great poet.

The actor-manager Samson Penley put Shakespeare on the stage in Paris in 1822, though little could be heard over the crash of hurled sabots and little seen through the rain of eggs, coins, and cabbages. The sight of Desdemona being smothered appalled Parisians brought up on the classicism of Voltaire, and they cried: *"A bas Shakespeare! C'est un lieutenant de Wellington!"* Honest anglophobia got mixed up, in a thoroughly French non-Cartesian way, with an aesthetic which, as Stendhal very clearly saw, was fast disappearing. Romanticism was awaiting its cue, but Penley gave that cue a little too soon.

In 1827, Paris, which had now become unreasonably anglomaniacal, what with volumes of Scott and Byron on salon tables and Windsor soap and lavender water by the washbowls, was ready for a company whose actors were drawn from the theatres at Covent Garden, Drury Lane, and the Haymarket. *Hamlet*, with Kemble in the lead, was billed for 11 September at the Odéon, and—despite the mockery of the *Courrier des Théâtres*: "Parnassus drowned in the Thames" . . . "Moliere traduced by the English"—the occasion was anticipated with interest and even eagerness.

It was Harriet Smithson as Ophelia who set Paris on fire. The daughter of an acting family of no great note, English by blood but Irish by birth, she was already established in Britain as a useful all-round actress, graceful and beautiful but of no great talent. To the French, unaccustomed to an uninhibited style of acting that the English had long taken for granted, she was a revelation. By the time Harriet spoke her final lines "And peace be with all Christian souls, I pray heaven. God be with you," there was hardly a dry eye in the theatre. Men reportedly stumbled weeping out of the auditorium unable to watch further.

Practically the entire French romantic movement was in the audience: Hugo, de Vigny, Delacroix, de Musset, Deschamps, Sainte-Beuve, Barye, Huet, Boulanger, Gautier. There was a young musician there too, Hector Berlioz, who was later to say:

> Shakespeare, coming upon me unawares, struck me like a thunderbolt. The lightning flash of that discovery revealed to me at a stroke the whole heaven of art, illuminating it to its remotest corners. I recognised the meaning of grandeur, beauty, dramatic truth.

He was only twenty-three, not merely dangerously young but also dangerously susceptible, and he had difficulty in separating the impact of Shakespeare from that of Miss Smithson. She was, of course, unattainable, a goddess, the Muse, while he was merely a struggling composer spurned by his philistine family. But it is no exaggeration to state that the thunderflash of the vision of Harriet-Ophelia turned him, almost overnight, into the greatest romantic composer of the age. He tried to purge his obsession into music and produced the *Symphonie Fantastique*—a brilliant, wild, botched confection in which Harriet, rarefied into the Beloved and desecrated as the Evil One, floats transfigured as the first ever leitmotif over orchestral noises intended to match the verbal impact of Shakespeare. This was in 1830, merely three years after the death of Beethoven. Music was forced into changing into something desperately new.

With the catharsis of art, the obsession with Harriet might have ended. Berlioz fell for the pianist Marie Moke, more poetically known as Camille, and proposed marriage. But Camille deserted him for the Monsieur Pleyel of the pianofortes, and Berlioz Shakespearianly cried out on high heaven, purchased a gun, proposed a *Hamlet*-like massacre. He calmed down, seduced a girl on the *plage* at Nice, and wrote the *King Lear* overture. There the whole story of tempestuous passion might have ended had not Harriet reappeared in his life. She was back in Paris, unsuccessful in repeating her former triumphs, and, by chance, attended that remarkable concert of December 9, 1832, in which the *Symphonie Fantastique* and *Le Retour à la Vie* (a weird romantic hotch-potch of music and monologue) were presented. The risen composer wooed the falling star with a symphony orchestra of great size. At length they married. It was a great pity.

It is always a great pity when myth has to melt into the Monday of quarrels over ill-made coffee and unpaid bills. Berlioz was first an enchanted husband, then a contented one, then a disillusioned one. Harriet was a bad housekeeper and an imperfect mother. She never spoke French adequately. She grew fat and drank too much. Berlioz was unfaithful and she whined with jealousy. At length, having lost the power of speech, she fell into a decline and died. Though Berlioz mourned: "I loved Ophelia. Forty thousand brothers/Could not, with all their quantity of love,/Make up my sum," he had the honesty to admit that his true residual emotion was pity—pity for a decayed body and a failed vocation. Disillusioned with the too too solid Harriet, he never became disillusioned with Ophelia or Juliet. The fire of that first vision remained with him and produced the best Shakespeare music in the repertory.

It is a sad but illuminating story. There remains a residuum, Harriet as the posthumous embodiment of the romantic spirit, at least to the French. Did she inspire Hugo and Musset and Fantin-Latour? When Rimbaud wrote *"O belle Ophelia! Belle comme la neige!"*, he was helping in the process of turning a drowned girl driven mad by grief into one of the central icons of romanticism. She is in the paintings of Delacroix, bare-breasted, wide-eyed, recognisably Harriet. The French had to discover Shakespeare sometime, and they discovered him that evening of September 11,

1827, his spirit, passionate but not really erotic, incarnated in a dark-haired Irish girl. Turn on the compact disc player and, in a few bars in C major, she is back with us.

—1993

First Novel

❖

In the 1930s I was a published poet of modernist tendencies. In 1940 I won a large prize for a short story. Nevertheless, my ambitions were never really literary. I wanted to be a great composer.

This ambition continued until 1953, when, as an English master at Bambury Grammar School, I had a few musical works locally performed but no hope of national acclaim. Devising the libretto for a possible opera, I discovered a capacity for writing dialogue which went beyond the strictures of musical form. It induced me to write a novel; this did not indicate a switching of ambition: it was merely a relief from the scratching of musical notes.

At that time I rather admired the work of Graham Greene. He was published by William Heinemann, and so it was to Heinemann that I sent the typescript of this first full fictional effort. To my surprise, I received a letter from Roland Gant, the Editor in Chief of the establishment, inviting me to visit him.

Schoolmasters in those days were so badly paid that I could not raise the rail fare to London. But it happened that at the time I had applied for a post in Malaya and was summoned to a meeting at the Colonial Office. I was sent a travel warrant and so was able in the same day to confront two new futures—one as a colonial officer, the other as a published novelist.

Gant liked my novel. He found it funny. This rather surprised me, as I had always seen myself as a creature of gloom and sobriety. He said, however, that it was not suitable as a first novel: it had the quality of a second novel. Would I now kindly go home and write a first novel and present it for the consideration of Heinemann?

I did this. The novel was entitled *The Worm and the Ring*; it had a dank Midlands setting and was suffused with Catholic guilt. Gant was extremely annoyed and very reasonably rejected the novel. As there was to be no first novel from my pen, there was to be no second novel either. Both typescripts were doomed to languish.

The fictional ambition was not to be fulfilled then, but the colonial one was. I went to Malaya as an education officer but had the novelistic ambition newly thrust upon me. Malaya had to be recorded before the British abandoned it to self-rule. I felt that Somerset Maugham had never done this adequately and not even Joseph Conrad had known the inner working of the Malay mind sufficiently well to delineate it. I got down to the planning and plotting and eventual composition of my *Malayan Trilogy*, later to be entitled, following Tennyson, *The Long Day Wanes*. Heinemann was the publisher. That original contact had borne fruit, though of an unexpected tree.

When I was invalided out of the colonial service in late 1959, I was forced into being a professional novelist in order to keep my wife and myself. With the kind of novels I wrote, and still write, this was not easy. My advances were much the same as what D. H. Lawrence had received in 1912, and my royalties were negligible. It was necessary to write much and to publish much in order to attain an income of something like £300 a year. It was inevitable that I try to publish those two rejected novels of 1953. The typescript of *The Worm and the Ring* was grossly disfigured by its tropical residence, so I retyped it and daringly submitted it to James Michie at Heinemann. This time it was greatly liked; Roland Gant thought it was masterly.

There remained the other novel, the genuine first. This was entitled *A Vision of Battlements*, and its setting was wartime Gibraltar. The title had a double reference. It meant the great Rock itself; it also meant one of the symptoms, according to a family medical dictionary, of migraine. I suffered from migraine throughout my army service, but medical officers never considered it a genuine ailment. I suffered it especially in Gibraltar—something to do with the heat of the sun, the stress of duty, above all sexual frustration.

A Vision of Battlements could have been autobiographical, but was not. Its hero is an army sergeant named Richard Ennis, who resembles his creator only in his army rank and his musical ambition. In North Carolina in 1971, a university professor gave a learned lecture on this book (now, evidently, published) and discovered that the name of my hero was a palinlogue: *R. Ennis* is *sinner* backwards. It signified the load of Catholic guilt which I have never been able wholly to eliminate from my work. But this was entirely unconscious wordplay: I had chosen the name Ennis because it was Celtic for an island and stood for isolation; it was also as close as I could get to the name of Virgil's hero Aeneas.

In fact, I had followed James Joyce in using a classical matrix to support my first lengthy exercise in fiction. The Virgilian references were often merely facetious. In the very first paragraph Ennis announces himself as belonging to the Arma Virumque Cano Corps, instead of the Army Vocational and Cultural Corps, a thin disguise for the Army Educational Corps. Ennis has to have a love affair with a Gibraltarian Dido, widowed in the Spanish Civil War. He has to pay a visit to hell, which is Franco's La Linea. As Aeneas has his faitful Aehates, Ennis has his faithful Agate, a homosexual ballet dancer. The Virgilian references are not all pure fancy. Aeneas the Trojan has the task of founding the Roman empire. The Catholic and half Irish Ennis has two tasks—one imposed upon him by the British Army, the other springing out of his own musical ambition. In an age of chaos he wishes to create great music that mirrors the cosmos. The army tells him to teach the troops how, through freshly developed democratic techniques, to build a Utopia.

This is not a bad novel. Written at the age of thirty-five, with a background of wide reading and a certain verbal talent, it had to have some virtues. Why then did I not rush it into the hands of Heinemann and request its publication as my nth novel? Well, I was overloading Heinemann with freshly minted fiction, from *The Doctor Is Sick* to *A Clockwork Orange* and old stuff had to be nudged out. In 1964 I sold *A Vision of Battlements* to Sidgwick & Jackson whose fiction list at the time was very skimpy. It was proposed that the Victorian custom of publishing illustrated fiction should be revived, and my novel appeared with comic illustrations by Edward Pegram. This turned out to be not a good idea: the text was diminished by the drawings and the book not taken seriously. It was never paperbacked and so failed to reach a genuine reading audience.

The situation in the United States was different. There the book appeared without illustrations and was taken seriously by *Time* magazine. It reached a paperback audience and ended up as a subject for university dissertations. I was in New York last December and found copies of the work around. In Britain it was permitted to sink like a stone.

I should very much like to see the book back in print.

Indeed, there are a number of books of mine that I should like to have introduced to new audiences. Roman poets like Horace could, when they wrote, boast of having achieved something *aere perennius*—more lasting than brass. In Shakespeare's sonnets we find the same proud blazon. Nowadays an author of any seriousness accepts that his/her work must be liquidated in order to make room for the mere phantom books of Jeffrey Archer, Barbara Cartland, and those devisers of best-selling adjuncts to television commercials. This is unjust, and injustice can be partially remedied by the occasional reprint. My wartime vision still has something to say to the world.

—1993

ANNIVERSARIES AND CELEBRATIONS

Like Joyce, Burgess was extremely fond, perhaps superstitiously, or even mystically so, of anniversaries. At any rate, as this selection of short pieces indicate, he seldom declined the opportunity to celebrate a favorite writer, composer, or book. National anniversaries are also reexamined, especially when they concern a crucial turning point or milestone in England's history ("Domesday" and "God Struck with His Wind," for example). Then there are the quick portraits of great figures of the theater or the cinema, Laurence Olivier, Charlie Chaplin, Marilyn Monroe. As usual, Burgess is drawn to these personalities for several reasons: for their allure, for their skill, but perhaps most of all for their iconic power to transcend the merely human, and to bring to focus an entire epoch.

JOYCE AS CENTENARIAN

❖

James Joyce was born in 1882, on February 2, the Feast of Candlemas or the Purification; Igor Stravinsky was born in the same year, on June 17 the day after Bloomsday. The Irishman and the Russian alike became Parisians. In 1913 Stravinsky's *Le Sacre du Printemps* caused a riot at the Paris Opera House. In 1922 Joyce's *Ulysses*, publishable only in Paris, caused a world-wide riot. The two men, who apparently never met, were fathers of revolution in the arts. One hundred years after their nativities, there are people around who say that they can't stand this modern stuff, meaning what they have heard or heard of or seen of one or the other or both. But Joyce and Stravinsky are no longer modern; they are as much classic artists as Goethe and Beethoven. Yet it is their function to continue to disturb.

I leave the celebration of Stravinsky to the musicians. In commemorating Joyce's centenary, I have to approach him not merely as a reader or as a fellow writer working, to some extent, in his shadow, but as one who, while still a boy, recognised a temperamental kinship. I was brought up in a lower middle class Catholic Irish ambience in Manchester. Dublin where Joyce had the same kind of upbringing, was closer to us than London, and not merely geographically: it was a Catholic capital, while London was a heretical one; it was the port where our relatives embarked to pay us visits, usually with illegal Irish Sweep tickets stuffed in their bloomers. Joyce was dim of sight and given to music; so was and am I. I began to lose my faith at the age of sixteen, and it was then that I first read *A Portrait of the Artist as a Young Man*. The great sermon on hell scared me back to conformity, but I could not resist the slow but ineluctable divestment of the peel of faith, and it was to *A Portrait* that I frequently returned to find a magisterial justification of my apostasy.

Of course, according to Joyce, you were really only permitted to abandon the Church if you found a spiritual substitute for it, and it was only art that provided such a substitute. In art, which to Joyce meant literature, you could find priests and sacraments and even martyrs but art gave you your reward in this world, not just a promise of pie in the sky. So, since I could not be a good Catholic, I had to become some sort of an artist, and I fought against the English side of my upbringing to learn to understand how holy art really was. To the Protestant English, art has always been a somewhat amateurish affair: you don't build a book as you build a bridge; you let it accumulate, like hash. The rigour of Joyce was something new, and his devotion to literature was somehow unclean and Parisian. Oscar Wilde, another Dubliner, had ended up in Père Lachaise, and he had always been burbling about how art was above bourgeois morality. Look where art, meaning pederasty got him.

When Joyce produced *Ulysses* it was promptly banned everywhere except Paris. This, to the bourgeoisie, confirmed the equation of art and dirt. No British or American printer had been willing to risk jail by setting up the abominable text, and it had had to be given to a printer in Dijon who knew no English. The book was published by the American owner of a Paris bookshop, and it was sent through the mails to such as relished highly wrought literature, or dirt. Winston Churchill bought it, but Bernard Shaw did not. It was seized by the customs authorities at New York and Folkestone and sequestered or burned. The ban was still in force when, in 1934, my history master smuggled the Odyssey Press edition out of Nazi Germany and lent it to me.

The sexual candour of *Ulysses* is nowadays nothing in comparison with the multiple orgasms of Miss Jackie Collins or the fretful impotence of Mr. Harold Robbins. The mouthfuls of obscenity uttered by Privates Carr and Compton in the nighttown episode is kid's stuff, even to maiden lads who see Mr. Pinter's plays on television. And it was clear, even to a lubricious seventeen-year-old like myself, that the sex and obscenity were aspects of a programme of realism very remote from pornography. Joyce had taken a day in Dublin—June 16, 1904—and set down in their uncensored entirety the thoughts, feelings, and acts of three not quite representative Dubliners. Leopold Bloom, the advertising canvasser of Hungarian Jewish origin, eats breakfast and then visits the toilet. He has a satisfactory movement, a dose of cascara having eased his slight constipation of the days before. On the beach later in the day he is erotically excited by the sight of a girl's lifted skirt, and, while the fireworks of the Mirus bazaar let off sympathetic whizzes and bangs he masturbates. Towards the end of the book Molly Bloom menstruates. The outrage of menstruatrices like Virginia Woolf and masturbators like E. M. Forster was considerable, though decently contained in Bloomsbury locutions. One would have thought that Joyce, and not Sir John Harington, had invented the water closet.

Joyce set down life as he honestly saw it, and it did him no good. The Bloomsburyites did not like what they termed coarseness, and they were not pleased either with Joyce's comic-epic glorification of the lower middle class. *Ulysses* was considered by communists to be a reactionary book, and Joyce was plaintive about it. "There's nobody in any of my books," he said, "who's worth more than a hundred pounds." But the reactionary charge, raised also against Eliot's *The Waste Land*, which appeared in the same year as *Ulysses*, had more to do with the parade of erudition, and a technique that did not lend itself to easy intelligibility, than with the subject-matter.

Erudition is easily obtained: it is available in public libraries and it costs nothing; nevertheless, since neither the workers nor the middle class particularly want it, it is regarded as an unwarrantable imposition in a novel: a novel should be *a good read*. *Ulysses* is not *a good read*. Joyce plays terrible tricks with the English language. He separates out like curds and whey, its component Latin and Teutonic elements. He parodies every writer from the Venerable Bede to Thomas Carlyle. He turns one chapter into a textbook on rhetoric. Another is made to behave like a *fuga per canonem*. The last chapter has no punctuation marks. And, when these games are not being played, he gives us stretches of raw thought and feeling in the form of *monologue intérieur*:

> O sweety all your little girlwhite up I saw dirty bracegirdle made me
> do love sticky we two naughty Grace darling she him half past the bed
> met him pike hoses frillies for Raoul to perfume your wife black hair

heave under embon *señorita* young eyes Mulvey plump years drawers
return tail end Agendath swoony lovey showed me her next year in
drawers return in her next her next.

But, as we know now sixty years after the publication of *Ulysses*,
the difficulties of experimental writing like that are not so great
as they seem. If we have read the book attentively up to this
masturbatory point, we shall recognise every motif of the ungram-
matical flow. Joyce loves mysteries but does not like them to go
on too long. He hides the keys in drawers which themselves have
no keys. He is not always easy, but he is never impossible.

There was a time when Joyce excited rage for making the prose
style get in the way of the narrative. Nowadays we are more
inclined to take pleasure in the manner of his exalting—through
myth and symbol—ordinary people into epic heroes, even if exaltation means also shoving them up onto a music hall stage and
making them go through a comic act. The real Ulysses of Homer
has a rock hurled at him by a one-eyed giant man-eater. Bloom,
the new Ulysses, is assailed by a drunken Irish chauvinist who
can't see straight enough to hit him with a Jacob's biscuit tin.
Bloom, reviled as a Jew and mocked as a cuckold, ends neverthe-
les as a king in Ithaca, whose location is No. 7 Eccles Street. He
is also ourselves, and we too endue the crown of absurd glory.

The world has forgiven Joyce for the excesses of *Ulysses*, but
it is not yet ready to forgive him for the dementia of *Finnegans
Wake*. Yet it is difficult to see what other book he could well
have written after a fictional ransacking of the human mind in
its waking state. *Ulysses* sometimes touches the borders of sleep,
but it never actually enters its kingdom. *Finnegans Wake* is
frankly a representation of the sleeping brain. It took Joyce sev-
enteen years to write between eye operations and worry about
the mental collapse of his daughter Lucia. He got little encouragement, even from Ezra Pound, that prince of avant-gardistes;
his wife Nora merely said that he ought to write a nice book
that ordinary people could read. But clearly *Finnegans Wake*
had to be written, and Joyce was the only man dedicated or
mad enough to write it.

It is about an innkeeper, in Chapelizod, just outside Dublin,
who seems to be called Mr. Porter. In his dream he becomes Hum-

phrey Chimpden Carwicker, the Nordic Protestant invader of
Catholic Ireland, a man who carries the hump of a kind of incestuous guilt on his back, expresses his guilt in a stutter, and turns
himself into the whole generality of sinful man. His wife Ann is
all women, and she is also Anna Livia Plurabelle, the river Liffey,
and, by extension, all the rivers in the world. Her consort, who
stitches his initials HCE into the text like a monogram, is the great
archetypal builder Fir and also all the cities which he builds. Their
daughter Isobel is all temptresses. Their twin sons, Kevin and
Jerry, or Shem and Shaun, represent the eternal principle of opposition—sometimes Cain and Abel, sometimes Napoleon and
Wellington, sometimes (God help us) Brutus and Cassius disguised as Burrus and Caseous or butter and cheese. Identities shift,
space is plastic, time is the year 1132, which is no time at all,
merely shorthand for the circular process of fall and resurrection
(to count eleven on our fingers we have to make a new start;
thirty-two feet per second per second is the rate of acceleration
of falling bodies). The narrative is cyclical and never ends. The
language is a Babylonish dialect of Joyce's own invention, made
out of all the tongues he had learned in exile and regarded as
suitable for recounting a universal dream.

There must be many people, and they of the most literate, who
opened the book and groaned wretchedly at what they found:

> . . . nor yet, though venissoon after, had a kidscad buttended a bland
> old isaac: not yet, though all's fair in vanessy, were sosie sesthers wroth
> with twone nathandjoe. Rot a peck of pa's malt had Jhem or Shen
> brewed by arclight and rory end to the regginbrow was to be seen
> ringsome on the aquaface . . .

It looks like nonsense, but it isn't. Joyce never wrote a line of
nonsense in his life. Here is Jacob, who is James or Shem, the
younger son or cadet, but also a cad, putting on a kidskin and
duping his bland-blind old father Isaac into giving him his blessing, and also Parnell wresting the Irish leadership from Isaac Butt.
Susannah, Esther and Ruth are present, all loved by older men
(as HCE loves his own daughter), as well as Stella and Vanessa
(who both had the name Esther) loved by a Jonathan Swift who
is Nathan and Joseph in one. And then Shem and Shaun, cloudily

refashioned into the sons of Noah glued together, await the brewing of whisky at the rainbow's end. There's too much here, of course, but to complain of excess is a little ungrateful. Most writers don't give us enough.

Clearly, Joyce, though a man of the people, did not set out to be a popular writer. Nevertheless his centenary is being celebrated with rather more enthusiasm than, in 1970, the literary world accorded Charles Dickens, who did set out to be popular. The celebration will achieve its greatest intensity in Dublin, where there are still people who call Joyce a blackguard and revere his father as a great gentleman (compare the situation vis à vis Lawrence *père et fils* in Eastwood, Notts). It is very hard not to celebrate Joyce in Dublin, in any year and on any day of the year, because, like Earwicker-Finnegan himself, Joyce has created Dublin. He has turned it into a place as mythical as Dante's Inferno, Paradiso, and Purgatorio all in one. At the same time he has stressed its physicality and given the stamp of an enhanced reality to its streets, pubs, and churches. When we drink Guinness in the Bailey or Davy Byrne's, we are borrowing Joyce's taste-buds, and when we walk on Sandymount strand it is in Joyce's broken tennis shoes. Joyce couldn't live in Dublin, but he couldn't leave it alone. His obsession with the minutiae of its life and its speech forces all who read him to become Dubliners themselves. No other writer has so made the soaking in of a locality the primary condition for understanding his work.

Ulysses begins in a Martello tower which still stands. The Odyssey of Bloom can be checked with a map and timed with a stopwatch. Even *Finnegans Wake*, the most recondite and rarefied book ever written, has a precise mise en scène: Chapelizod, south of the Phoenix Park, where Earwicker's pub may be identified with the Dead Man (so called because customers would roll out of it drunk to be run over by trams). Solidity of place is matched by the solidity of character. Leopold Bloom is so three-dimensional than no amount of linguistic tomfoolery can obscure him. Earwicker's sad stutter sounds clearly through all the mazes of dream. There are some celebrants of Joyce who can ignore the tortuosities of style and concentrate solely on the flesh and blood and their confining geography. Unfortunately, there are far more who revel pedantically in the style, the structure, and the symbolism. The secret of appreciating Joyce lies in not letting him go too much to one's head. He is not, after all, John Jameson.

Joyce has been posthumously lucky in having the best biography of our century devoted to him. This is Professor Richard Ellmann's book, a wonder of fact, wit, and qualified affection. Ellmann is entitled to draw our attention to such ingenuities as the asymmetrical book-ends of the opening and closing words—"stately" and "yes." He is similarly entitled to show that Buck Mulligan's mock-transubstantion at the beginning of the work is contradicted by Molly Bloom's real menstruation at the end. But there are too many scholars—and they will be in Dublin in force on 16 June this year—who treat both *Ulysses* and *Finnegans Wake* as mystical codices, showing no interest in the Ascot Gold Cup (which comes around Bloomsday) and little taste for Guinness. Joyce is, so this centennial ought to show, probably at last becoming the property of the people and not the thesis-writers.

To other, unscholarly, writers like myself, Joyce is the novelist's novelist, although neither *Ulysses* nor *Finnegans Wake* can properly be termed a novel. If fiction is the art of fitting the sensations and emotions of life into a structure which shall have some of the shapeliness and autonomy of a piece of music, then Joyce is all our daddies. We can study him on the structural level, finding the principles of symphonic development cunningly exemplified in the "Oxen of the Sun" and "Circe" sections of *Ulysses*, and on the nuclear level of the phrase. These are pieces of distinguished writing:

A wise tabby, a blinking sphinx, watched from her warm sill.

The bungholes sprang open and a huge dull flood leaked out, flowing together, winding through mudflats all over the level land, a lazy pooling swirl of liquor bearing along wideleaved flowers of its froth.

He foresaw his pale body reclined in it at full, naked, in a womb of warmth, oiled by scented melting soap, softly laved.

Under their dropped lids his eyes found the tiny bow of the leather headband inside his high grade ha.

For "ha" read "hat." Sweat has erased the *t*. John Gross has pointed out that other fictional characters have conventional headwear: only Bloom has a ha. Yet we have here less literary eccentricity than a concern with reality. Joyce's language is always anchored to its referents. At the same time it achieves a certain melodic independence, reminding us that Joyce was a tenor who, if he'd stuck to singing, would have outsung Count John Mc-Cormack.

The man himself, improvident, given to drink, exiled, silent and cunning, vocal, convivial, devoted to his family, lacking in what Hampstead would call good taste, lanky, seedily elegant, half-blind, dead untimely at fifty-nine, lives on in anecdotage, but the essence of his personality—eccentric and yet conventional—is totally contained in his works. His preoccupations are there—the social stability which finds its best expression in the lower middle class family, language as man's supreme achievement. He has left his voice to the world under the hiss and scratches of a pre-electric recording, reciting parts of his two greatest books with skill but a sacerdotal intonation that was perhaps to be expected. Intended for the Jesuit priesthood, he built a church of his own, an ecclesia on Eccles Street. His books are confessional, leaving out no sins but making no excuses. His eucharistic function is the conversion of quotidian bread into beauty, which Thomas Aquinas defined as the pleasing. He does not please Mrs. Barbara Cartland nor Lord Longford, but he reminds us that life is a divine comedy and that literature is a jocose and serious business. He has left us in *Finnegans Wake* a little prayer which sums up his attitude to life. It is a very reasonable attitude.

Loud, heap miseries upon us yet entwine our arts with laughters low!

—1982

GREAT SCOTT?

❖

The one hundred and fiftieth anniversary of Sir Walter Scott's death is being overshadowed by the centenary of James Joyce's birth, and there is, among the more rarefied of the literary, an assumption that the fictional values that Joyce represents are a negation of all that Scott stood for. In other words, Joyce took the novel-form seriously, while Scott regarded it merely as a rag-bag. Scott's primary vocation, it is accepted, was poetry, and he turned away from that art when he realised that he could not beat Byron at it. The novel was a *pis-aller*, diffuse pageantry without the poetic lift and, eventually, something that had to be churned out to pay debts. In *A Portrait of the Artist as a Young Man*, there is an adorer of Scott who seems to be the imbecilic product of incestuous coupling. In *Ulysses* Scott's Wardour Street posturings come in for very heavy parody. The novel as art—meaning Flaubert, James, Conrad—could not merely not learn anything from Scott; the Scottian method, or lack of it, was fictional death. In my student days, the techniques of close verbal analysis found in passages from Scott's novels admirable negative lessons: here was how not to write. And yet the achievement of Scott, diminished by some of his followers, was more than merely literary. For a vast European audience he embodied the rediscovered magic of the North. He was the pure Romantic while Byron was the polluted one. Pope John Paul I's brief pontificate began with a tribute to the influence of Scott on his own life and thinking: his novels were highly moral, and they made the moral conflicts of life thrilling: morality was high adventure. He did not speak of Scott as a poet and, except for the anthology piece about proud Maisie, Scott's first vocation has been largely forgotten. Yet Robert Graves remembers Thomas Hardy expressing admiration for the Iliad and saying: "Why, it's almost in the *Marmion* class."

Here are some lines from *The Lay of the Last Minstrel*:

Breathes there the man, with soul so dead,
Who never to himself hath said,
This is my own, my native land!
Whose heart hath ne'er within him burn'd,
As home his footsteps he hath turn'd
From wandering on a foreign strand!
If such there breathe, go, mark him well;
For him no Minstrel raptures swell . . .
High though his titles, proud his name,
Boundless his wealth as wish can claim,
Despite those titles, power and pelf,
The wretch, concentred all in self,
Living, shall forfeit fair renown,
And, doubly dying, shall go down
To the vile dust, from whence he sprung,
Unwept, unhonour'd, and unsung.

The lines are, I think, well known in the way that any simple
rhetoric expressive of a stock emotion becomes well known. It is
political language and it used to be beloved of politicians. Combine its general sentiments with a specific reference, and Scott may
be regarded as a founding father of Scottish nationalism:

O Caledonia! stern and wild,
Meet nurse for a poetic child!
Land of brown heath and shaggy wood,
Land of the mountain and the flood,
Land of my sires! what mortal hand
Can e'er untie the filiallband
That knits me to thy rugged strand!

The sentiment is greater, one would say, than the poetry, or rather
the poetry is banal enough for the sentiment. But when even a
minor poet—Thomas Moore is another Celtic instance—can find
words for a popular velleity, then his literary importance is swallowed up in something far closer to life than literature can ever be.

    This is, I suppose, a kind of heresy. But it is important to re-
cognise that there is a kind of maker about whom one does not

make literary judgments. Conan Doyle created Sherlock Holmes (and he was, as *The White Company* reminds us, a man much in the Scott tradition), and he is a creation that renders judgments on the way Conan Doyle uses words or frames plots altogether ofiose. Scott created something far bigger than Sherlock Holmes. He created a regional feeling, a mode of patriotism, and for his readers outside Scotland an image of that country which, over-romanticised though it might be, shifted the focus of post-enlightenment sentiment from the South to the North. It is true that, with the growth of anti-Napoleonic feeling in the German states, and the national ardour behind the work of the brothers Grimm, there was already a new concern with the history and legends of the North (Wordsworth and Coleridge read the German authors; Scott translated them; his later compatriot Carlyle became an adoptive German), but Scott's energy, imagination, and authority were to ensure Scotland's incarnation of the properties of romance.

And, quite apart from the native content of his poems and novels, Scott was the first writer to convert the past into a location, a sort of bigger Scotland for free wandering. He created the historical novel, and this may be regarded as another extra-literary achievement. For the strictures usually made against Scott's literary methods in the novels—the falseness of the dialogue, the naiveté of the sentiments, the artificiality of the plots—are of small validity when we consider that history has, for the first time in literature, become a living substance, a spatial entity. We know we are in the presence of the past, because nobody speaks like a person of the present: " 'Slay him not, Sir Knight,' cried the Grand Master, 'unshriven and unabsolved—kill not body and soul. We allow him vanquished.' " That, of course, is from *Ivanhoe*. But there is little fault to be found with the récit, which is usually vigorous and without affectation:

> He descended into the lists, and commanded him to unhelm the conquered champion. His eyes were closed. The dark red flush was still on his brow. As they looked at him in astonishment, the eyes opened—but they were fixed and glazed. The flush passed from his brow, and gave way to the pallid hue of death. Unscathed by the lance of his

enemy, he had died a victim to the violence of his own contending passions.

It is the Wardour Street English of Scott's novels that has most earned him disdain, but the problem of conveying ancient modes of speech has never been satisfactorily solved. Too strict an allegiance to archaism detracts from immediacy and credibility, but Shaw's willed anachronisms and Edwardian colloquial in *Caesar and Cleopatra* result merely in a fancy dress ball, while Scott does seem to present the strangeness, or "unpresentness", of the past. Even when, as in *Old Mortality*, it is only a century away from his own birth:

> "I will pledge you with all my heart," said Claverhouse, "for here is a black jack full of ale, and good it must be, if there be good in the country, for the Whigs never miss to find it. My service to you, Mr Morton," he said, filling one horn of ale for himself, and handing another to his prisoner.
>
> Morton raised it to his head, and was just about to drink, when the discharge of carbines beneath the window, followed by a deep and hollow groan, repeated twice or thrice, and more faint at each interval, announced the fate of the three men who had just left them. Norton shuddered, and set down the untasted cup.
>
> "You are but young in these matters, Mr Morton," said Claverhouse, after he had very composedly finished his draught; "and I do not think the worse of you as a young soldier for appearing to feel them acutely. But habit, duty, and necessity reconcile men to everything."
>
> "I trust," said Morton, "they will never reconcile me to such scenes as these."

A fault in Scott, exemplified even in a brief extract like the above, that is more psychological than stylistic is the tendency to a simplistic manicheeism, with the good and the evil not merely opposed but frozen into unchangeable postures. That brief speech of Morton shows what kind of young man he is, and we know from the tone that he will not change. Few of the characters in the novels undergo the torments of division, and the weakness of psychological unsubtlety is only to be condemned if we view the works in terms of Tolstoy or Dostoevsky, and not as moral allegories presented on a wide historical canvas. It was the allegorical aspect probably that appealed to the late Pope.

One of the graver charges that have been levelled at Scott is a falsification of history in the service of entertainment. It is a charge not much made today, since history—especially in the works of Americans like John Barth and E. L. Doctorow—is increasingly being regarded as plastic material for aesthetic reordering. But it was alleged that Scott's fictional method had a bad effect on Carlyle, whose *French Revolution* sometimes reads like a novel and hence invites the rejection of soberer historians. I do not think this charge can be upheld. Scott recognised the division between pure history and the historical romance. His life of Bonaparte is scrupulously exact, and even the *Tales of a Grandfather*, which invite the looser approach of the novel-reader, are genuine Scottish history. We have to remember that the publication of the *Waverley* novels stimulated a genuine antiquarian interest, with the founding of learned societies like the Bannatyne and Abbotsford clubs which devoted themselves to the exhuming of Scotland's forgotten past. As a historian Scott was restrained and Hume-like. As a novelist he was a novelist.

In trying to assess Scott's achievement in an age that finds his works diffuse, artificial, and ethically simplistic, we are drawn more to recording his influence than to approaching him for the pleasures of art. His influence was wholly bad in America, at least Mark Twain said so: even *Uncle Tom's Cabin* tended to make present injustices seem remote and historical when the Scottian afflatus came over Mrs. Beecher Stowe. If Scott could be divested of his own language, as in France and Italy, he was able to assert a massive force on writers like Hugo, de Musset, and Gautier. Only an artist separable from his technique could affect other arts. We can, and not at all fancifully, see Scott's influence in the paintings of Diaz, Dupré, Corot, and Millet. He provided innumerable libretti for romantic operas. But, in the land of *Lucia di Lammermoor*, he taught Manzoni to write *I Promessi Sposi* (which Scott thought superior to his own work). He had the power to loosen shackles. He was a revolutionary force. But finally, perhaps, his function was to influence others and not himself to produce great art.

For perhaps his two volumes called *Minstrelsy of the Scottish Border* are worth all his poetry, and his power to revivify the Scottish past through suggestion greater than a capacity to modify the ethos of his own time. He remains a writer still difficult to judge, since we seem to lack the critical techniques for assessing him. T. S. Eliot found it difficult to relate Rudyard Kipling's undoubted importance to any existing aesthetic canon, and, if he had dared to notice Scott, he would have found the same problem. To the Scots, Scott's greatness is not in doubt, but it has more to do with romantic nationalism than with literature. Many use Waverley station, but probably few read *Waverley*.

—1982

RUDYARD KIPLING AND
THE WHITE MAN'S BURDEN

❖

Joseph Rudyard Kipling died in Sussex, England, just fifty years ago. To my generation, fighting in Spain, carrying cards of membership of the British Communist Party, preparing for Armageddon, he was one of the enemy. He had taught imperialistic ideals that we all rejected. He was a racist who had no doubt about the civilising mission of the white man. His poetry was either slangy or full of pretentious biblical phraseology. His stories were the work of a man suffering from an unclean attitude to both women and Americans. He was a curious mixture of the extrovert and the neurotic. We did not read him, but we could not always avoid him. A vast number of his phrases had, as with Shakespeare and the Bible, crept into common speech. He had modified the English language. To those of us who read T. S. Eliot and Ezra Pound he was nevertheless part of the discardable past. It was not until T. S. Eliot revalued him during World War Two that we were disposed to take another look at him. Eliot described greatness in him but could not define the greatness. The consensus of the Anglo-Saxon world today is that he is an inescapable but disturbing presence. We who resented him in our youth are inclined to be warily respectful of him in our old age. We read him and he worries us.

Kipling was born in Bombay in 1865. His father was curator of the Central Museum at Lahore in northwestern India. His uncle was the pre-Raphaelite painter Burne-Jones. There was in the young Kipling a concern with art, and the craftsmanship that precedes art. When we read his stories we observe a scrupulousness of construction, an obsession with the right rhythm and the right image, that point back to the practice of such painters as Holman Hunt and Dante Gabriel Rossetti. And yet the early writing of Kipling seems to have nothing to do with art. He worked for seven years as a sub-editor for the *Civil and Literary Gazette* in Lahore, writing little stories and verses to fill up space. His audience was at first local and restricted, but it was not long before he found the whole of the English-speaking world ready to listen to him.

He was listened to because he was the first English writer to tell the truth about India. The British knew that India was there, the jewel in the crown, the vast sub-continent that made Queen Victoria an Empress, but they knew little about it. Kipling told the truth, unglamourised, about the sweat and fever, the infant mortality, the life of the British garrison troops. He eulogised the British soldier, despised in peace, a hero in war, but he showed him as he was, blasphemous, drunken, immoral. He told the truth in stories and verses, and the verses had the rhythm of the street barrel organ and the vocabulary of the barrack-room. He was not an intellectual writer; he lacked the vague grace of the *fin de siècle* poets; he sounded sometimes like the journalist he was. But no writer, except Shakespeare and James Joyce, has so thoroughly exploited the resources of the English language.

If he told the truth about contemporary India, he told it equally about the life of the American seaboard (he lived for years in Maine with his American wife), Antioch under the Roman Empire, the working of a railway engine, the working of Shakespeare's mind when considering the 1611 translation of the Bible. He had a passion for exactitude of detail, a lust for the terminology of trades. He was no scholar, but his instinct for historical truth, which he arrived at by intuition, sometimes made fools of the scholars. When he placed a particular Roman legion on Hadrian's Wall, the scholars said he was wrong. Later they discovered that he was right. It was intuition that enabled him to penetrate into the soul of the animal kingdom. *The Jungle Book* has delighted Italian children as much as British ones. It is good fun, admirable fantasy, but it is also profoundly serious.

What Kipling looks for in the jungle is the law that sustains it. What he looked for in the British Empire was a principle of service and order that could be developed into the philosophy of a world civilisation. The Empire was not there for the white man's exploitation of the barbarous natives. The white man was there to serve the principle of order and to suffer in serving it. When Kipling spoke of "the white man's burden" he was thinking of the small sweating functionaries who gave their brief fever-racked lives to the betterment of creatures who were "half-devil and half-child." In 1936, while Kipling was dying and Mussolini and Hitler were ranting about the responsibility of the superior races to civilise (meaning exterminate) the lesser breeds, it was too easy for progressive intellectuals to disparage the imperialist mission. But where Rome failed, thought Kipling, Britain might succeed in spreading the light of reason and order in the dark places of the earth.

The British Empire was dismantled after the Second World War, not without pain and bloodshed. Some think it was dismantled too hastily. But the liberated territories have best succeeded in promoting order and achieving prosperity when they have remembered the lessons of Kipling: the need to abolish "dirtiness and mess," the duty of tolerance, the acceptance of the Hellenic virtue of reason. Empire was not just lofty philosophical ideas. It was also impartial justice, well-made roads, hospitals with clean scalpels, dynamos, and a railway system. The poet of Empire was also the poet of the new technology.

There is a poem by Kipling which is well known even in Italy. It is called "If." It propounds virtues which seem impossible—"If you can keep your head while all about you/Are losing theirs and blaming it on you. . . . If you can fill the unforgiving minute/With sixty seconds worth of distance run . . ." It is a catalogue of the virtues to be found in the good infantry officer or the good colonial administrator. Fulfil them, and you will be "a man, my son." It is glib, demagogic, all too appropriate to a Spartan civilisation trying to administer an empire. But it is only one side of Kipling, the side of the higher journalism. The other side shows that he was well aware of the power of the darkness, the unwillingness of the jungle to submit to the order and tidiness of a book. Some of his stories deal frighteningly with the tortuous darkness of his own mind. He knew neurosis, he even knew madness.

Too dim-sighted to participate in the active life of the soldier or the district commissioner, Kipling nevertheless, with that powerful intuition of his, could penetrate into the life of action which sustains a civilisation. The soldiers knew that he understood them, and they go on knowing it. Regretfully, the poets and novelists of India accept that nobody understood their own country as well as Kipling. The intellectuals who once despised him are at last bringing their tribute of respect. He was honoured too early—he received the Nobel Prize in 1907—but perhaps only now are we beginning to understand him. He speaks to the common man with disarming simplicity. But he addresses the darker places of the soul with complexity of a Dantesque or Shakespearean order. He was a great man and he merits our respect. Perhaps even our love.

—1986

DOMESDAY

❖

With the return of Halley's Comet, some Anglo-Saxons may be tempted to look at a copy of the Bayeux Tapestry, which shows that heavenly body bright above the battle of Hastings in 1066. Comets in those days foretold the deaths of princes, and an English prince—King Harold—was due to be killed by an arrow shot into his eye by the Norman invaders. William of Normandy, the bastard duke who claimed title to the English throne, conquered the English and has been known ever since as William the Conqueror. By the English we do not mean the bastardised race of today, which contains a good number of the bloods of Europe and is disposed to accept Asiatic and African blood as well, but the mixture of more or less racially pure Germanic tribes which invaded Britannia, drove the Celts into the Welsh hills, and settled to a life of pastoral tranquillity on some of the richest agricultural land of the world. Their main components were from Frisia—the Angles—and Saxony—the Saxons—and they did not expect, until 1066, that they were to be converted into Anglo-Normans.

1066 was a bad year, not only because of the coming of the Normans, but because the Danes were conducting battles in the East of England, and King Harold faced enemies on two flanks. He had two ferocious and efficient hordes to contend with. They were both of northern blood, but while the Danes spoke Danish, the Normans had learned French, which they spoke in their own rough way, very different from the smooth tongue of Paris. The Anglo-Saxons, who spoke Anglo-Saxon, were plunged into a linguistic agony. They tried to communicate with foreigners, and they simplified their tongue in the process. If English is a grammatically simple language today, that is because it desperately shed its grammar—of which the first component to disappear was the gender system—in a desperate effort to be understood on two fronts. English became what it is still is: not a true language, like Italian, but a creole.

It also became the language of a subject people, since William the Conqueror and his barons imposed Norman French on the country. It was the language of government, education, the polite arts. In time it began to mingle with the Anglo-Saxon tongue, and the process was initiated that was lead to the peculiar mixed status that English has today among the world's languages. English is mostly a Latin language, with some ancient fragments of Germanic vocabulary and a simple grammar that is a very poor relation of the grammar of Martin Luther and Günter Grass. That it has produced a rich literature may have something to do with its being mixed and disdaining the formalities of grammar. That this literature is chiefly comic may have a lot to do with the Laurel-and-Hardy confusion of its two disparate elements.

In 1086, this new Norman England got its first big book. It was not in Anglo-Saxon, and it was not in Norman French. It was serious enough to be written in the great international language Latin, and it still survives. In 1986, the British bring it out of its closet to the public view. They celebrate the nine hundredth anniversary of what is known as Domesday Book. This is an astonishing document, and the ink on it as nearly as clear as when it was first written. It is a comprehensive survey, in almost painful detail, of the wealth and resources of the newly conquered country. It has an ominous title. *Domesday*, in its modern form *Doomsday*, means the Day of Judgment, when Christ shall return to the earth in thunder and with archangelic trumpets to separate the sinners from the saved. This was not the title that William the Conqueror, who had little of either poetry or religion in his Norman soul, bestowed on the book. It was given to it by those who suffered from what the book signified. It signified confiscation of land and goods, and against this royal confiscation there was no appeal any more than there would be against the final judgment of Jesus Christ. *Domesday* still rings terribly in Anglo-Saxon ears.

The book is a model of bureaucratic enterprise. William the Conqueror found in the England he took over an advanced administrative system, with the country divided into a network of administrative areas called shires (to be translated into Norman French as counties), which persisted as the basic pattern of English organisation until the county boundaries were needlessly revised in 1974. These counties had their own system of administration, as they still do, but they were subject to the central administration of the king in London. The counties had wealth—chiefly in wool—and this wealth was expressed in the silver of a royal coinage. As the Japanese were delighted to take over a well-organised civil service when they conquered Britain's Eastern Empire, so William the Conqueror was pleased to assume control of a well-ordered land whose wealth was perhaps the greatest in Europe.

He needed this wealth in the later days of his reign. The North of England, I am glad to say (since it is my own province) was rebellious to Norman rule, chronically so. In 1085 King Cnut of Denmark and King Olaf of Norway prepared massive invasion fleets. Norman England was in trouble. Fortunately or not (much depends on how much Norman blood one possesses: I have practically none) the invasions did not materialise, but the Conqueror saw the need to maximise his revenue for the purpose of organising the means of defence. This meant knowing, in as much detail as possible, how much wealth—in land, sheep, cattle, gold, and silver—his subjects possessed. It meant establishing a feudal order in which the king saw landowners as royal tenants. It meant the swearing of feudal oaths of loyalty: the oaths of the tenants in the town of Salisbury, sworn in 1085, are still on record.

The survey recorded in *Domesday Book* was begun at Christmas 1085. The whole of England (with the exception of those northern counties which had not yet been brought fully under control) was divided into seven circuits. These circuits, which contained groups of counties, had each three or four royal commissioners assigned to them, and their task was to verify the information already available about the resources of men, land, livestock and money, and to test this information in courts of law. Take the Worcester circuit in the English Midlands. This was travelled by Remigius, the Bishop of Lincoln, with a clerk and two monks in attendance, and three important laymen: Henry de Ferrers, Walter Giffard, and Adam FitzHubert (*fils d'Hubert*). These are all Norman names. In Cambridgeshire, we meet some Anglo-Saxon ones: Osmund the small, Fulcold a man of the Abbot of Ely, Baldwin the cook, Edwin the priest, Wulfric, Silac, Godwin of Fulbourn. The Anglo-Saxons shrugged their shoulders and worked with their Norman overlords: they had little alternative.

To give some notion of the thoroughness with which the *Domesday* survey was made, here is part of the inventory for the manor of Southwell in the county of Nottinghamshire. "Land for 24 ploughs. Archbishop Thomas (of York) has 10 ploughs in lordship and 10 freemen, 75 villagers and 23 smallholders who have 37 ploughs. A fishpond and a ferry . . . The men-at-ams have 7 ploughs in lordship and 35 villagers and 26 smallholders who have 21 ploughs . . . To Southwell belongs meadow, 188 acres; woodland pasture 8 leagues long and 3 furlongs wide; arable land 5 leagues long and 3 wide. Value before 1066–£40. Now £40 15 shillings." It was said that King William the Conqueror knew precisely how many red deer he had in the ample forests of his realm, and he loved every one like one of his sons or daughters. He had no sons or daughters. That was one of his problems.

Domesday Book has been touched by many hands, and, being parchment not paper, it has responded to the grease in human skin very kindly. The Latin is clear, though it contains a damnable number of abbreviations. Inevitably it is many volumes, like a metropolitan telephone directory. These volumes are kept in an ancient chest of studded iron, and they are taken out every few centuries to see if they need re-binding. The book does not represent a mere antiquarian glory. It remains as a proof of ancient landholding, rights and boundaries, and it has been cited in court actions several times during the twentieth century. It is a vital source book for understanding the peculiar make-up of English society. So, while Halley's Comet reminds the English of the death of an English prince in the only war of invasion ever fought on their soil, and the subsequent conquest by a foreign power that, in time, was gently absorbed by the conquered, so the year 1986 reminds them of a nine-hundred-year-old enactment that remains unique in the annals of Europe. The Geneva colloquies between Reagan and Gorbachov may have postponed Doomsday (or the end of the world) indefinitely. A book once as terrifying as *Domesday* will offer itself to the gaze of the curious in Mrs. Thatcher's 1986. An iron lady will envy the power of an iron man.

—1985

LORENZO

❖

David Herbert Lawrence was born on September 11, 1885, and thus is a subject for centenary celebration in those countries which read him and value him. Italy is one such country. Translations of Lawrence helped to foster a concern with developing the Italian novel along the lines of what is termed "modernism." Lawrence himself spent a great deal of his life in Italy and Sicily, earning an Italianate version of his name, Lorenzo. He would have died in Italy had he not been persuaded to take his terminal tuberculosis to the sanatorium Ad Astra in Vence. In Vence he died and in Vence he was buried. His widow, Frieda Lawrence, uttered a simple valediction over his grave: "Goodbye, Lorenzo." When his remains were removed to Taos, in New Mexico, where Mrs. Mabel Luhan had donated a ranch to the Lawrences, she again bade farewell to Lorenzo. It is in order for Italians to call him that and consider him to be one of their own writers. I ought to add that Lawrence worked hard for Italian literature and gave up some of his brief life to translating little-known Italian novelists into English. His most notorious work, *Lady Chatterley's Lover*, was published by Orioli in Florence. There was a symbiotic relationship between Lawrence and Italy; it would be in order for Italy to grant him the centennial homage which his own country seems unlikely to give, for Lawrence has never been popular in England.

Consider his life, which ended in 1930 not long after his forty-fourth birthday. He was born in Eastwood, a small mining town in the country of Nottinghamshire, the son of a coal miner. This ought to make him a proletarian writer, except that writing is essentially a bourgeois art and Lawrence lived at a time when it seemed natural to aspire to bourgeois values. His mother had certain ideals of refinement and middle-class success, while his father—massive, muscular, a speaker of dialect hardly able to write his own name—belonged to a dying tradition of uninhibited

299

masculinity which did not think in political terms. It was enough to hack coal in the mine, get drunk in the local pubs, snare rabbits, grow vegetables in the cottage garden, and beget children with the minimum of sexual finesse. Moreover, Lawrence was less a product of industrial England than of that area—long since disappeared—where the life of the coal miner and the life of the farmer met. Lawrence belongs to pastoral England, and he is one of the greatest of England's nature poets. James Joyce was a city boy and hated flowers. Lawrence was surrounded by fields and was not far from the Sherwood Forest where Robin Hood had proclaimed the virtues of Anglo-Saxon anarchy in the face of the Norman rulers.

At the University College of Nottingham, where Lawrence had been sent on a scholarship, there was a well-known philologist named Professor Ernest Weekley. He was married to a German aristocrat, Barnness Frieda von Richthofen, daughter of a distinguished military family and cousin of the man soon to be known as the Red Baron, the greatest aviator of the First World War. Lawrence had lunch with the professor and fell in love with his wife. The love was reciprocated, and the two ran off together, first to Germany, then to Italy. He was penniless, she had abandoned her three children as well as her husband. They were to live a nomadic life together, in Europe, Cornwall, Sicily, Capri, Ceylon, Australia, eventually in New and Old Mexico. He lived in a condition of voluntary expatriation all his brief career, writing, writing, writing, propounding a new philosophy of sexuality, denouncing British puritanism and hypocrisy, making himself extremely unpopular with his fellow countrymen. Italy, which has never been puritanical and whose hypocrisy takes more open and engaging forms than is the case in England, gave him various homes. It never persecuted him. British persecution of Lawrence represents one of the most shameful episodes in the whole history of world literature.

Persecution began with his first important novel, *Sons and Lovers*, which represents with excruciating candour the emotional fixation a mother and a son develop for each other. It was not banned by the British state, but it was banned by the libraries, especially in Lawrence's home county. The book was too frank, too honest. Only the Freudians, of whom there were few at the time, saw the importance of the novel as an Oedipal document; only a few littérateurs saw the poetic strength of the writing. Official persecution came with the publication of *The Rainbow*, which was attacked as a monstrous parcel of raw pornography in the press and condemned to be burnt in the courts of law. That was during the First World War, when Lawrence and his wife were living in Cornwall. Clearly, according to the official mind, no man who could write pornography could be a patriot, especially when his wife was a cousin of the Red Baron, and the Lawrences were suspected of sending signals to the enemy (they were living on the coast; Frieda Lawrence would hang her washing out to dry; this was assumed to be a semaphore message to U-boats). It is no wonder that he began to loathe the British state. Although he was tubercular, and had been so since his childhood, the military authorities insisted on calling on him for medical examinations, chiefly to jeer at his body and pull at his beard (a beard was also unpatriotic, except in the navy).

After the war his writings were still considered dangerous. The novel *Women in Love* was attacked as both libellous and pornographic. His theories about the importance of the sexual impulse in human life were regarded as indecent. But with the publication of *Lady Chatterley's Lover* shortly before his death the greatest storm broke on him. His letters from Italy to England were opened, illegally, by post office officials. The police walked into an exhibition of his paintings in London and confiscated thirteen of them as obscene. (At the same time they confiscated a volume of the drawings of William Blake who, dead in 1817, was considered to be one of Britain's artistic glories.) The filthy aura of *Lady Chatterley's Lover* spread over everything he did. He was a dying man, but the dogs of hypocritical puritanism tore at him till the end.

Lady Chatterley's Lover remained a proscribed book for thirty years after Lawrence's death. In 1961, Penguin Books, the respected publishers of paperback literature, deliberately provoked a court case—*Regina versus Penguin*—which resulted in the lifting of the ban and the inauguration of a period of liberty of expression for writers on sexual subjects. Those of us who had complained of the banning of a great work of literature were intensely relieved because we were now free to tell the truth about the book—it was not great; it was the work of a writer long past his best; its use of base words to describe the sexual act was misguided. But Lawrence was right when he said that sex had too long been cloaked in euphemism or suppressed altogether as a subject for literature. *Lady Chatterley's Lover* exalted the rediscovery of sexual tenderness by a woman who had lost it. She found it not with her husband, who had been paralysed in the war, but with her husband's gamekeeper. The book seemed to condone adultery and, later, divorce. It was not popular with good Catholics. But the liberal-minded hailed it as a landmark in the history of the novel: at last sex had been granted in literature the importance that it has in life.

Lawrence, or Lorenzo, is mainly known as the author of *Lady Chatterley's Lover* and not as the great poet and original thinker he really was. The sexual element in his work, though important, is less important than the more fundamental Laurentian philosophy. This teaches the importance of the non-mental element in human life. The brain, the intellect, the reason has ruled too long; it is time to remember the instincts, the glands, the "dark gods of the loins." Man has cut himself off from the natural world through the exercise of the generalising powers of the brain: we live more and more in a universe of abstractions and machines, less and less with the trees and flowers and animals, all of which are closer to us than we like to admit. It is better to be an anonymous alley cat than Aristotle or St. Thomas Aquinas. Lawrence blamed a great deal of the cult of the abstract, which produced logic and science, on Plato, who taught that universals inhabited a higher order of reality than the materials of the phenomenal world that surround us. Lawrence denied the importance of the Kantian noumenon, which is unknowable, and said that the phenomena are enough.

His rejection of reason and science went too far. He would not accept that the earth went round the sun and that sunset and sunrise were illusions. "I don't feel it *here*," he said, when the truth of Larwinian evolution was demonstrated to him. "*Here*" meant his guts, his solar plexus, his nerves and glands. But it was necessary for him to exaggerate the instinctual and the physical in a world which science and technology were driving mad. He had seen one world war and feared, rightly, that there would be another, and he saw how science was increasingly in the hands of the destroyers. The disease which racked his body might, in a less obstinate man, have led him to exalt the non-physical, the spiritual, the separable soul, but in his very last book, *Apocalypse*, he proclaimed "the glory of living in the flesh" and praised the living gods of the Mediterranean world, not the great abstraction Jehovah, which the West had taken over from the Jews. He was essentially a pagan. He was also a puritan: he could not easily overcome the Cromwellian nonconformist tradition which he had sucked in with his mother's milk. The combination of puritanism and paganism is not a bad one. It is a dualism which works. It may be said even to have been absorbable by the Church of Rome in its better days. It is a doctrine which prevents paganism from going too far and brings the honey of pleasure to moralistic rigour. Whether we want it or not, it is what Lawrence taught. His own countrymen, needless to say, do not want it.

They do not want Lawrence, even a hundred years after his birth. Visiting the pubs and shops of Eastwood, earlier this year, I found that nobody liked him. He ran away with a foreign woman who was not his wife. He put the members of various local families in his novels and showed them up in a bad light. He preached the importance of the erotic life; could anything be more reprehensible? The Bloomsbury group that for so long ruled English taste disliked him intensely. He was a working man who had not been to Oxford or Cambridge: what right had he to turn himself into one of England's most important novelists and poets? The same, of course, could be said—and indeed *was* said—about William Shakespeare, another son of the English Midlands who had not been to a university and yet dared to quote Ovid and imitate Plautus and Seneca. The class struggle goes on in Britain, even retrospectively, and Lawrence is involved. Italy, which is blessedly immune from such trivial concerns, can honour Lawrence as a great writer who, quite by accident, was also the son of a coal miner. They can even canonise him. San Lorenzo. He is probably still praying for us: forget God and go back to the gods; remember the vitality in your loins; live. That above all: *live*.

—1985

QUIET PIONEER

❖

Arthur Annesley Ronald Firbank died sixty years ago just after his fortieth birthday. This means that those who admire him must suggest, though diffidently, a centenary celebration. Like Oscar Wilde, Ronald Firbank was a homosexual Catholic, though his conversion to the faith came early, while Wilde's was reserved to his deathbed. There is a good deal to be written about the relationship between Catholicism and British homosexuality. Probably those of sexual inversion, with their tradition of theatrical display, find something appealing in the extravagance of Church vestments and ceremonies. There are even, in Britain, autocephalic churches with innumerable archbishops, nearly all of whom are homosexuals. There is an English term, very hard to translate and of unknown etymology—"*camp*," which signifies display of a baroque kind and has a strong homosexual connotation. Firbank was a "camp" writer.

He was, like Wilde, a dandy, a drinker of absinthe, and an habitué of the Café Royal on Regent Street in London. This bar-restaurant still exists, but it has lost the reputation it possessed in the period 1880–1916. It was French in character, and was the haunt of Wilde, Whistler, Max Beerbohm, Frank Harris and even George Bernard Shaw (who drank water, not absinthe). D. H. Lawrence affected to despise the place, and he satirised its aesthete habitués in his novel *Women in Love*, but he chose it for his farewell dinner before opting for final exile. Firbank sat there, much stared at by the gross and unaesthetic, offering money to stockbrokers and bookmakers to go away and leave him alone. He had come too late to be a genuine Oscar Wilde figure; he was aware that his dandyism was out of date; his homosexuality was not, as with Wilde, contradicted by a fighting physique and a large capacity for witty insult. His life was lived in his writings.

His writings were not much appreciated in his own lifetime. He had money enough to be able to pay for the printing and publishing of his own work, which was avant-garde in style and vaguely perverse in content. His volume of stories, *Odette d'Antrevernes*, appeared as early as 1907, and the novels *Vainglory, Inclinations*, and *Caprice* all belong to the period of World War One. They all suggest technique and sensibility appropriate to a later age. *Valmouth*, which he published in 1919, is a fantasia set in an exotic watering-place dominated by a black masseuse named Mrs. Yajnvalkya, and its content is too perversely erotic even now to find a wide audience. It was only with *Prancing Nigger* in 1924 that a publisher was prepared to finance his work. This, a study of life in the West Indies whose tropical heat and weird manners come entirely from Firbank's imagination, contains Firbank himself in the character of an orchid, "a dingy lilac blossom of rarity untold." It is an unreal novel, and yet its narrative style was to have an immense influence on such realistic novelists as Evelyn Waugh, Ivy Compton-Burnett, and Muriel Spark.

Firbank's last finished work was *Concerning the Eccentricities of Cardinal Pirelli*. It came out two years after its author's death in Rome, where, like John Keats in 1821, Firbank had repaired with ravaged lungs in the hope of a cure in the mild southern air. It sums up Firbank's quality, with its worldly ecclesiastics, its totally invented Spain, its harmless enormities (such as the baroque baptism ceremony for a dog), its strange scheming aristocratic ladies, its ever-present hint of sexual perversities, which do not in fact take place. While Oscar Wilde's *The Picture of Dorian Gray* contains real sin, *Cardinal Pirelli* flirts with mere naughtiness. The homosexual temperament of its author is manifested in an exquisite manipulation of language, a certain wit, a passion for the external properties of the high life. There is no philosophy, except for the Wildean metaphysic of the importance of the surface. Where morality appears, it has more to do with the sit of a necktie than with human behaviour. There is a dowager in it who talks much of the "morale" of the perfect brassière, the *soutien-gorge* in the mind of God.

His works went out of print, but, in the sixties, an inquiry in the columns of the *Times Literary Supplement* which asked how many readers would welcome a reprint of his novels brought a surprising response. Four thousand people wished to read him again, or for the first time, and this made a single-volume reissue of his major novels a viable commecial venture. Now his importance as a literary pioneer is widely recognised, even in Italy.

Why is he important? Some critics believe that he did more than James Joyce to liberate fiction from its heavy burden of nineteenth-century realism. He did not believe in the massive artefaction of a *Middlemarch* or a *War and Peace* or a *Bleak House*. Whatever had to be said could be said briefly. Fiction depended on the concentration of language and the use of poetic imagery. The mechanism of a plot should not hold the forefront of a narrative. When things happened, they had to happen obliquely, between the chapters, between even the paragraphs. One of his major technical innovations was the device of the party (cocktail or dinner), in which many voices could be heard, all easily recognisable through some trick of rhythm or some verbal obsession, apparently talking about nothing while some unnoticed word or phrase pushes the plot forward.

Evelyn Waugh said that Firbank "negligently stumbled" upon his technical innovations. He doubted his intelligence. Martin Seymour-Smith, in his mammoth *Guide to Modern World Literature*, finds room to say of him: "He was a pathetic and yet genuinely agonized trivialist, a chic fugitive from life who hid, in aestheticism, what his giggling response to terror could not neutralise; his substanceless fiction attracts fellow-homosexuals—and writers whose roots are in, or half in, the Nineties." The 1890s still fascinate, with their dandyism, elegant perversity (as in Aubrey Beardsley), paradoxical wit, and their climax of nemesis as manifested in the trial of Oscar Wilde for sodomy. If D'Annunzio has little to say to modern Italian writers, Wilde retains his influence, from Joyce to Anthony Powell. It was Firbank who sustained the Wildean into the 1920s and gave it a modernistic chic that meant much even to Aldous Huxley, the stone-eyed mescalin saint who ended in most unfirbankian mysticism.

Prancing Nigger (its rather gross American title: Firbank preferred the British one, *Sorrow in Sunlight*) may be regarded as important in a way removed from that of mere technical innovation. It helped to make black things chic. It is no exaggeration to state that the Paris adoration of all things negro—with Josephine Baker as a black goddess—that flourished in the 1920s owed a good deal to Firbank. The cult of *négritude* had nothing to do with the explosion of "black power." Blackness was a kind of *décor*, jazz was a new and piquant form of elegance in which, as in the paintings of the Douanier Rousseau, the jungle was tamed and considered rather charming. To see Josephine Baker's lithe body gyrating was not to savour the rank meat of tribalism: the Parisians received their Africa through the alembic of Dior and the *Shocking* of Schiaparelli. Behind the exotic thrills lay the the over-civilised *frissons* of Firbank.

You may, if you wish, ignore Firbank. But you cannot ignore his influence. When you read a British novel in which the narrative is carried by the dialogue and not by any discernible *récit*, you are in a Firbankian ambience. Such dialogue tends to be highly allusive, peppered with the slang of the younger members of the ruling class, and an expensive perfume exudes delicately out of it. It dates quickly, but that is part of its charm. Many of the perverse fashions of the illiterate, from the mini-skirt to punk, have a Firbankian quality. It is a great deal to survive as an adjective.

—1986

GOOD GLUCK

❖

Christoph Willibald Gluck died in 1787, but it's unlikely that this bicentennial will arouse the same enthusiasm as George Frederic Handel's three hundredth birthday did in 1985. Gluck was not the sort of composer whose life would make a thrilling film. He lacked the Falstaffian ebullience of Handel, the romantic disorder of Beethoven, and the enigmatic mixture of refinement and vulgarity that made up the character of Mozart. Nor is he known for much more than a couple of operas that do not draw the crowds as *Otello* and *Tosca* do. This year there will probably be a dutiful trotting out of *Iphigénie en Aulide* or *Orfeo* in the opera houses of the world, but there will be a sense of disappointment in audiences accustomed to the rhodomontade of Verdi or the lachrymosity of Puccini, to say nothing of the apocalyptical thunder of Wagner. Gluck always seems a little too bland. He lacks salt and pepper.

The truth is that without Gluck some of the developments of romantic opera would not have been possible. Opera, after all, should not be gymnastic vocal display from tenors and sopranos who have lost their figures and have never cared much about acting. Opera should be the apotheosis of drama, like *Wozzeck* or *Lulu*. We should feel that we are watching comedy or tragedy tuned to the highest possible pitch, in which music is the servant of human conflict and reconciliation. Before Gluck's time it had not been like that. Opera-lovers were lovers of the human voice, especially if the range was phenomonal and castrati could purvey a perverse thrill with incredible *roulades* and stratospheric tremolos.

The fact that Gluck, by the standards of Mozart and Wagner, was not much of a musician was something of an advantage to his concept of opera. He felt no compunction to show off musi-

cally. He had a fine melodic gift, but his orchestration was thin,
his bottom lines were unadventurous, and he had no great gift
for counterpoint. When he came to London the great Handel said:
"Gluck know as much contrapunto as my coke." That last word
may mean "cook" or something more vulgar. Gluck could not,
like Bach or Handel, dash off a convincing fugue. There was a
certain meagreness about his music. He entertained Londoners by
playing on the musical glasses (glasses filled with variable
amounts of water and struck with a little hammer), and that was
rather different from Handel thundering away on the full organ.

We cannot explain the thin musical endowment by referring
to the thinness of his musical education. His father Alexander,
who became head forester to the Duchess of Tuscany in Reichs-
stadt (now Liperec) in northern Bohemia, tried, like many fathers
of musical geniuses, to suppress his son's talent, probably revealed after a few local lessons in violin and perhaps cello. The
boy ran away from home at the age of thirteen and tried to
earn his living by playing on one instrument or the other. In
Prague, where he had the chance of a formal musical education,
he preferred to teach himself the elements of composition and
to learn about opera by going to it. He escaped the domination
of German style by listening to Vivaldi, Albinoni, Lolli and
Porta, whose works filled the Prague Opera House. He went,
inevitably, to Vienna, only apparently to come under the influence of another Italian, Sammartini. It was not till he was
twenty-seven that, in Milan, he composed his first opera,
Artaserse, with a libretto by Metastasio.

Metastasio was the poet of the imperial court, and he wrote
innumerable libretti, not many of which have survived. But he
part-fathered over eight hundred operas in the sense that his libretti were used again and again by a variety of composers. This
situation implies a kind of homogeneity in the opera world, a lack
of powerful individuality on the musical side. We cannot imagine
Verdi being satisfied with a second-hand libretto or, for that matter, one not tailored exactly to his musical style. Metastasio, who
considered himself a great man, regarded the musical settings of
his stiff and heroic dramas as a mere tribute to the action or
inaction. He was closer to Gluck in this than Gluck himself per-

haps realised. But if, in the mature Gluck, the drama came first, it was through a fusion of music and words and not the predominance of the latter.

The eighteenth century was a great period of travel for musicians who had not secured sinecures in princely or archiepispocal courts. Gluck went to London, where Handel, despite the gibe about his lack of contrapunto, gave him professional support. Gluck even put on an opera before the Duke of Cumberland. *La Caduta del Giganti* was a political opera in that it was a vocal compliment to the Duke's massacre of the Jacobite Scots at Culloden in 1745. Then Gluck travelled the German princedoms until, nearly forty, having caught gonorrhea but still made a prosperous marriage, he settled in Vienna. It was there that he wrote *Orfeo ed Euridice*, to a text not by Metastasio but by Calzabigi. Paris and Vienna became the twin foci of his mature experiments in opera. He wanted to outlaw the baroque, though the baroque was partly in his nature and had been exemplified in most of his operas, few of which we now hear. The baroque was display and decoration. The new, reformed, opera was action, drama, psychology, character.

If we listen carefully to *Orfeo* we will hear how Gluck made a virtue out of the simplicity imposed on his music by his comparative lack of skill. He exploited his weaknesses. Music did not get in the way of the direct impact of the drama. With Gluck we begin to see that librettos will in future have to be written for one composer only and that the wholesaling of a poet like Metastasio belongs to the utilitarian past, the age of purely decorative music. Gluck's musical slenderness is really an athletic property: it goes along with a forceful energy; at the same time, as we know from the Dance of the Blessed Spirits in *Orfeo*, it is not incompatible with an almost heavenly serenity. Compare the vision of Hades and the vision of Elysium, put side by side in Act Two of *Orfeo*, and the breadth of Gluck's genius cannot be in doubt.

In the melodic field, perhaps only Mozart and Handel share with Gluck the ability to convey an almost unbearable emotional poignancy in a major key with the simplest of harmonies. This can be heard in Orfeo's aria "Che faro senza Euridice," which is one of the universally known and loved melodies, and in "O malheureuse Iphigénie," sung by the heroine of the opera named for her. He is not afraid of invoking the antique—as in the instrumentation of *Orfeo*—and this produces a mythical remoteness which does not war with the emotional immediacy. The opening storm scene of *Iphigénie* shows how he could attack the audience with a pictorial directness which, without doubt, Wagner was to recall in the opening of *Die Walküre*. Wagner learned a good deal from Gluck.

So did Mozart, who attended all the rehearsals of the Vienna production of *Iphigénie*. The ballet music in Gluck's *Don Juan* left its mark on *Don Giovanni*, and so perhaps did Gluck's trombones. The March of the Priests in *The Magic Flute* is suprisingly similar to the chorus "Chaste fille de Latone" in *Iphigénie*. As opera-goers know Mozart better than Gluck, these debts tend to be missed.

But it was the two great figures of early romantic opera, Berlioz and Wagner, who acknowledged the greatest debt to the forester's son from Reichstadt. *Les Troyens*, long neglected, especially by the Paris for which it was written, is at last being accepted as Berlioz's masterpiece. Gluck taught Berlioz how to deal with myth, how to reconcile the sense of classical remoteness with the immediacy of human passion. He even influenced the orchestration of that prince of orchestrators—the menace of a horn call, choral unisons against seething textures of instrumental sound. Wagner owed to Gluck the concept of continuous musical action, driving out the convention of opera as a set of separate arias and ensembles divided by dry recitative.

The question is always arising, even now: which is the important part of opera—the words or the music? Should the composer bow to the drama or accept a formal scheme of musical numbers? Richard Strauss's opera *Capriccio*, set in the time of Gluck, is one of the magisterial examinations of the problem. It may be said that the problem was solved for the first time by Gluck, in whom the claims of drama and music are exactly balanced, and there is an artistic compromise wholly satisfying to the aesthetic sense. It is the beauty and skill of the Gluckian solution which makes him an important figure in the world's music and, in this bicentennial year of Gluck's death, compels our homage.

—1987

UNRAVELLING RAVEL

❖

This year we commemorate the fiftieth anniversary of the death of Maurice Ravel, a very French musician (his father's background was Swiss and his mother's was Basque). Although the actual date of his death was December 28, the French are starting their celebrations early. They think highly of him—far more highly than they think of their colossus Hector Berlioz. Perhaps Berlioz, with his vast orchestras, symphonic rigour, and epic conceptions, sinned against the French canon of good taste. Ravel was elegant, exquisite, and none of his works go on too long— except perhaps for *Boléro*, which lasts little more than fifteen minutes but seems to go on forever.

Conceivably, Maurice Ravel was the last of the twentieth-century composers to combine serious musicality with the ability to make himself popular. He disdained serialism, stuck firmly to the tonal, and actually produced tunes. *Boléro* as nobody can deny, contains a tune—indeed, it contains nothing else but a tune, repeated *ad nauseam* on all the melodic instruments while the basses thrum out an incessant do sol sol and the drums hammer away in a slow crescendo at a figure which never once changes. Ravel himself disparaged the work. Having composed the tune, he said, all he had to do was to give minimal instructions to a group of music students and leave the construction of the score to them.

We, the mere listeners, tend to disparage *Boléro*. But when we hear that pianissimo rhythm on the side-drum and then the first statement of the theme on the flute (somewhat Basque, a filial tribute) we respond, against our will, to its curious magic. It is not, of course, a bolero at all. A bolero is fast. This is more like a sarabande danced in the desert. A hot wind blows through the work. We feel a burning sun on the back of the neck. I am not being fanciful. One of the curious aspects of Ravel's music is its capacity to evoke non-musical reality. It seems to describe things. Nobody can understand quite how this is done.

In the early days of the talking cinema there was a film called *Bolero* (no acute accent: the name of the work was quick to be degallicised). It featured George Raft and Carole Lombard and it was set in the Paris of the First World War, a long time before *Boléro* was actually written. Raft's great ambition was to open a night club in which, in partnership with Miss Lombard, he was to dance to *Boléro*. But the war got in the way. Raft in the trenches was accompanied by the rhythms of *Boléro* transferred to the guns. He survived, and his night club, which had no room for a symphony orchestra, resounded to his dancing feet and huge negroes battering jungle drums. You could, it seemed, do anything with *Boléro*, and Ravel never complained. There was even a dance band arrangement in which I remember hammering away at the piano part until my fingers bled.

Ravel, although he wrote a good deal of abstract music, was happiest when he could evoke the outside world—the world of nature, ancient history, fairy stories. *L'Enfant et Les Sortilèges*, with its libretto by Colette, is surely the one perfect opera of all time. The staging is fantastic: cups and saucers that dance, a whole forest that sings, Watteau shepherds and shepherdesses stepping down from their frame to rebuke the naughty child who treats things and animals badly and is taught, by Nature herself, the necessity of love and compassion. This could have been sentimental, but the citrous sharpness of the music keeps an ironic distance from the subject. There is wit. If there are any tears, they are ours, and they are compelled by the sheer beauty of the sound.

This concern with expressing the exterior world makes Ravel an impressionist. He is usually spoken of in the same breath as Debussy, the first and greatest of the musical impressionists, who used the orchestra to describe the moods of the sea and the wind, the passage of the clouds over the night sky, and, in his piano *Préludes*, a great variety of subjects, from Mr Pickwick to footsteps in the snow, from a girl with yellow hair to a firework display ending with an ironic echo of the *Marseillaise*. We may legitimately doubt whether music is capable of describing the outside world. It is, after all, only a succession of sounds which possess their own logic, withdrawn from reality. But give a piece of

music a title—*La fille aux cheveux de lin* or *Poissons d'Or*—and
we are only too eager to see that outside world with our ears.
What both Debussy and Ravel disdained to do was to express
emotion. Emotion was Germanic, romantic, somewhat dangerous. It was too close to the id, condemnable by both St. Augustine
and Sigmund Freud. Wagner's *Meistersinger* Overture could excite an urge to fight for Germany, but nobody listening to Ravel's
La Valse has ever wanted to fight for the Austro-Hungarian
Empire. Or, hearing the baroque pastiches of *Le Tombeau de
Couperin*, has shed tears for the demise of Louis XIV's France.
Ravel's music keeps its distance from the didactic and the pornographic. It is exquisitely static.

And, as I say, it is popular. George Gershwin learned from it
when writing his *Rhapsody in Blue*. The British composer-critic
Constant Lambert condemned the *Rhapsody* as snobbish, disdaining the demotic roughness of the jazz on which it was based
and proud of its French lessons. But probably both Ravel and
Gershwin were right to see whether jazz themes could yield to
sophisticated symphonic treatment. In the Hollywood film about
Gershwin's life Maurice Ravel is actually portrayed nodding with
approval at Gershwin's ragtime rhythms. It was a fairly accurate
portrait: elegant, slight (he did not carry enough avoirdupois to
get into the French army), something of the dandy.

My own knowledge of Maurice Ravel is somewhat limited, but
I cherish certain stories told to me by our British composer, the
late Ralph Vaughan Williams. Ravel was the most exquisite or-
chestrator who ever lived, and Vaughan Williams went to him in
Paris to learn how to improve his own orchestration. Ravel said:
"Write me a little minuet in the style of Mozart," and Vaughan
Williams replied: "*Monsieur*, I did not travel this distance to write
little minuets in the style of Mozart." Ravel was impressed by this
British bluntness and taught his very mature pupil the technique
of orchestral *pointillisme*. Vaughan Williams invited him to London to eat steak and kidney pudding in a restaurant near Victoria
Station. Ravel was entranced by the dish and, every weekend,
took the Channel boat to eat steak and kidney pudding. The
heavy diet did not diminish his delicacy

Shortly before his death, Cambridge University awarded Ravel
the honorary degree of Doctor of Music. The French do not well

understand doctorates. They think that the only doctors are doctors of medicine, and Ravel was extremely puzzled by his new distinction. In London his exquisite ballet *Daphnis et Chloe* was performed, and one of the dancers sprained her ankle. Ravel was distressed and said: "*Mademoiselle*, you have injured yourself dancing to my music. *Hélas*, I cannot cure you, complete doctor though I am."

He was a man of great delicacy and large compassion. The piano concerto he composed for Paul Wittgenstein (brother of the philosopher) is an instance of this. Wittgenstein had lost his right arm in the First World War and it was evident that he would have to abandon his career as a concert pianist. But Ravel wrote his concerto for the left hand only, and Wittgenstein made a new name for himself. The work seems to me to be very difficult even for two hands.

It is right to think of Ravel fifty years after his death and to listen closely to his music. He is regarded by some—on the evidence of *Boléro* and *Pavane pour une Enfante défunte* and *Ma Mère Oye*—as a rather lightweight composer. He lacks Beethoven's clumsiness (always a sign of sincerity) and is at the opposite pole to Teutonic portentousness. But he remains an exemplar of French culture at its best. He will not be played much during France's revolutionary bicentennial in 1789. That was, when you come to think about it, a very unfrench event. From the French we expect delicacy, wit, refinement, artistic images of high civilisation. We get them from Maurice Ravel.

—1987

GOD STRUCK WITH HIS WIND

❖

I have just returned from Madrid, where I asked many young Spaniards what centennials we were celebrating in 1988. Many knew about 1788 and the birth of Lord Byron, which was gratifying to a Celtic Englishman like myself, but none associated the year 1588 with any special event. I fear that the same may be true of my own countrymen, who might now be accepting the religious rule of the Vatican if 1588 had not severed England definitively from Europe. 1588 was the year of the defeat of the Spanish Armada.

King Philip II of Spain was the avenging arm of the Counter-Reformation. He had been married to Queen Mary of England, who had briefly restored Catholicism to her country after the split with Rome engineered by her father King Henry VIII. The restoration of the old faith had been affected with blood and fire, and it did not last long. Indeed, it sealed with the martyrdom of the recusants an English decision never to be Catholic again. But the widower Philip II believed he could force England back into the fold. Or, to be more accurate, he thought that Protestant England could—like the Netherlands—become enslaved to the Spanish Empire.

For no war has ever yet been fought on a purely religious issue. It worried Philip II less that the English should be Protestants than that they should be pirates. English pirate ships, under men like Drake and Hawkins, were sacking Spanish galleons laden with gold from the Latin New World, and all with the connivance and, indeed, tacit encouragement of Queen Elizabeth I. This had to be stopped. It seemed a pity that King Philip II was not receiving more than the purely formal blessing of the papacy, but the Pope did not greatly like King Philip II. He was a distressingly humourless man who saw nothing absurd about putting his empty armour on parade and making his troops salute it.

In 1588 Philip sent his invincible fleet of 130 ships, massive, top-heavy, but undoubtedly magnificent, from Lisbon to the English Channel or Manche. It met 197 much smaller ships under the command of Howard, Effingham, and Drake. The Spanish Armada anchored off Calais, but it was efficiently burned by English fireships. God blew with his wind, according to the medal later solemnly struck, and the Spanish were scattered. History was now presided over by two Gods, one of whom was an Englishman. What remained of the Armada escaped round the North of Scotland and the West of Ireland, suffering heavy losses from storm and shipwreck on the way. Only about half of the invincible Armada got safely home.

I was asked by a journalist in Madrid if there was any Spanish blood in my family. It was a facetious question, but it could be given a serious answer. A number of Spanish sailors, shipwrecked on the west coast of Ireland, settled there and married into the country. The Irish segment of my family had strong Spanish colouring, but this has been qualified in myself with the paler tints of Scotland and Anglo-Saxon England. Naturally, my family, being Catholic, regretted the failure of King Philip II to subdue the heretical English. Speculation still continues about what kind of a country England would have been if Whitehall had been converted into a baroque Escorial.

There are two novels—*Pavane* by Keith Roberts and *The Alteration* by Kingsley Amis—which address themselves to this intriguing subject. Roberts's novel shows Queen Elizabeth I dying of a heart attack at the moment of the launching of the Spanish Armada. Immediately the Catholic elements of England disrupt the country, sabotage the English fleet, and welcome King Philip II ashore. This is less important to Roberts than a fantasy about how England would have been today if it had been cut off from the spirit of free Protestant enquiry. He envisages a kind of neolithic civilisation without Newtonian physics, without, indeed, electricity, but he ends with a thoughtful coda: perhaps the Church, knowing that scientific investigation would culminate in nuclear fission, was wise to persist in a kind of holy obscurantism. But perhaps, only perhaps.

The vision presented by Kingsley Amis is substantially the same as that of Roberts, though it is more humorous. England, like the

rest of the civilised world except for a small Protestant pocket in
New England, is Catholic. The Church controls all fields of intellectual endeavour. Jean-Paul Sartre is a cardinal, like Berlin-
guer, and Picasso has specialised in sacred art of a wholly
representational kind. Even James Bond has become Father Bond,
a sniffer out of Islamic plots emanating from Istanbul. Something
mysterious and unspecified has happened to the heresiarch Anthony Burgess.

These books are jokes, mere entertainments, but they rest on a
question that is being asked every day, and not only in Brussels
and Strasbourg—how far can England (as opposed to Ireland,
Scotland and even Wales) be regarded as a member of the European community? The perhaps laudable intention of King Philip
of Spain was to drag England back into Christendom. He was
not the first man to try it, nor was he the last. In the reign of
King Henry VIII of England, that much-married monarch, separation from Rome had been impelled by the need for the king to
divorce and marry a woman who would bear him a son, which
the barren Catherine of Aragon could not. The Protestant Church
of England could be regarded as a kind of morganatic gift to his
second queen, Anne Boleyn. But the tide was running in the direction of a dismemberment of Catholic Europe, and England saw
herself as an Atlantic island severed from the European land-mass.

One man, the King's Chancellor, Sir Thomas More, was beheaded for his refusal to accept that there was now an English
Church, with a secular monarch at its head. The Church of Rome,
always reluctant to canonise English martyrs, was slow to glorify
Sir Thomas into Saint Thomas, but now—thanks partly to the
film *A Man for All Seasons*—he is universally accepted as a great
witness for the cause of Catholic, or European, unity. It might be
more realistic to see him as a man looking backwards, a thinker
of anachronistic temper, trying to sustain a position that was already out of date. For England, the island kingdom protected by
a navy, was already looking west, trying to bridge the Atlantic
river. With Oliver Cromwell, a mercantile empire began to be
built. It had nothing to do with Europe.

Napoleon tried to restore England to the European family, as,
in his own eccentric way, did Adolf Hitler. Both failed. But God's
wind blows curiously, and, in spite of the recalcitrance of the

great realist General de Gaulle, England eventually found herself to be a member of the European Economic Community. Before this millennium ends, a submarine tunnel will restore the island to the maternal land-mass. But England speaks the language of the United States and still looks west. And, irony of ironies, Iberia still looks west also. Buenos Aires is the arbiter of the Spanish language, as Rio de Janeiro is of Portuguese. Perhaps the great historical secret was always to look west and east at the same time, Janus-fashion.

That year of a lost Armada, 1588, seems now very remote, but it is worth recalling. It confirmed the death of one empire and the rise of another. And it is a reminder of the futility of most great endeavours. Do not hurry history, or God. Wait patiently, and everything will be peacefully delivered. As for religion, the whole of what used to be called the Christian world is effectually united in the worship of the gods known as consumer goods and the fear of the devil called AIDS. History is only dates, which are very adventitious things. This brief celebration of the invincible Armada is little more than an obeisance to round numbers.

—1988

CELEBRATING T.S. ELIOT (I)

❖

How quickly, it seems, our modernists slide into the past. We have had centennial celebrations of James Joyce, Igor Stravinsky, and D. H. Lawrence which, affirming that these artists are now classics, did not mitigate the hostility of the reactionaries. There are people around who, hearing *Le Sacre du Printemps*, shudder and declare that they can't stand this modern stuff. This is despite the fact that that revolutionary work belongs to 1913. Similar shudders are provoked by *Ulysses* and *The Waste Land*, both of which appeared in 1922. But when a modernist achieves his hundredth birthday he ought, by rights, to be accepted by the orthodox. Argument as to his merits and adverse reaction to his innovations alike should be at an end. If he continues to shock, it is only in the sense that Shakespeare and Dante and Cervantes shock—as, indeed, all great art, however antiquated, shocks. The shock derives from the exquisitely exact enunciation of eternal truths which we do not like to hear.

But the shocks of modernism were, and to some extent still are, more seismic than those administered by the art of tradition. It is something of an anomaly to speak of modernism as a thing of the past, and to accept that we are living in the age of postmodernism. It is even more of an anomaly to think of Marinetti's futurism as having the smell of old lavender or moth balls. We face a problem of terminology which denies the ability of language to deal with time. It is absurd that "modernist" should be a historical term, but it is clear that the explosive confrontation of a self-conscious artistic novelty and a worn-out tradition occurred only once in the history of literature. The sense of a thing's being totally new, totally "modern," arose uniquely at a particular time, and that modernity still clings to a period now historically remote.

I am concerned with paying a centennial tribute to Thomas

Stearns Eliot, so I had better confine myself to the explosion in poetry which he helped to ignite. This explosion startled the literati of London when they should have been most, but in fact were least, ready for it. The Great War of 1914–1918 was three years old, and the world had already changed when Ezra Pound published his "Homage to Sextus Propertius" and T. S. Eliot his *Prufrock and Other Observations*, but English poetry was stuck in the mud of a genteel tradition. Even the young war poets, faced with devastating experiences which no man had ever known before, could only express their own psychic explosions in the language of bourgeois gentility. Everybody's favorite poet at that time was Rupert Brooke, dead at the Dardanelles, who wrote patriotic sonnets of an embarrassing evasiveness. The atmosphere of the comfortable rentier life, with tea on the lawn of the weekend cottage, adhered to the poetry of the time. Pound and Eliot, both Americans, attempted to smash this English tradition.

Eliot was born in St. Louis in 1888, but his family belonged to New England. He was drawn to Europe, as his compatriot Henry James had been, by a nostaglia for a richer and more complex civilisation than America could provide. America was obsessed by material values and, in matters of art it was, like all revolutionary societies, desperately old-fashioned.

Modernism could not possibly arise in a country concerned with conservation, whether of wealth or ideas, and modernism had to be considered essentially a European movement. Eliot's important American contemporary, William Carlos Williams the doctor-poet, spoke out against modernism as "un-American." So it was. It was a cisatlantic phenomenon nourished by a sense of decay, pessimism, total disenchantment with the notion of progress, recognition of man as an imperfect creature. To the England of 1917 it was new. In Europe it was not.

It has been pointed out all too often that Eliot owed his capacity to innovate to the poets of continental Europe. Names like Jules Laforgue, Tristian Corbière, Mallarmé and, behind them all, Baudelaire are invoked. With equal justice the name of Guido Gozzano must be mentioned. Gozzano's quality is "Eliotian" in the sense that it is colloquial, sceptical, nostalgic. The image of the poet that it conveys is of a creature less vatic than divided, unsure of himself, certainly all too human and imperfect. The image is more important than the thought. "Imagism" is, of course, one of the movements inside modernism. Ezra Pound was the first to employ the term. Emotion was to be conveyed not by direct statement but by the finding of some physical image which should be the equivalent of the emotion, its—to use Eliot's term— "objective correlative." This was a reaction against empty rhetoric, "great thoughts," ready-made sentiments.

In Eliot's poem "The Love Song of J. Alfred Prufrock," the argument is expressed as a string of images. It begins:

> Let us go then, you and I,
> When the evening is laid out against the sky
> Like a patient etherised upon a table . . .

That was very shocking to the conservative. There is rhyme there, which is traditional enough, but, as the poem proceeds, we see that it comes in no prescribed pattern and that the lines are of variable and arbitrary length:

> Let us go, through certain half-deserted streets,
> The muttering retreats
> Of restless nights in one-night cheap hotels
> And sawdust restaurants with oyster-shells . . .

In other words, we are into the world of *vers libre*. But it is the images which are shocking: they are not, according to poetic tradition, acceptable images. They do not derive from nature but from the urban experience, and the urban experience at its most sordid or frightening. It was ungentlemanly of Eliot to introduce *hôtels de passe* and filthy restaurants; it was indecent of him to invoke the terror of the operating theatre. What is sordid is also faintly humorous, and humour had no place in tradition. Even Byron's magnificent *Don Juan* could not be termed true poetry, since it makes the reader smile. Poetry was a desperately serious business, and here was Eliot being apparently facetious.

But the poem is serious enough, far more serious than Rupert Brooke's war sonnets. It is the monologue of a man who, we assume, is rather like Eliot and not unlike Guido Gozzano. As no movement in art can ever be completely original, and as attempts to tidy up the history of art in neat compartments are always doomed to fail, we need not be surprised to find this type of monologuising character somewhat earlier in the poetry of England. For instance, there is Arthur Hugh Clough's long poem *Amours de Voyage*, written in 1849, with its epigraph *"Il doutait de tout, même de l'amour"*—which would do as well for Eliot's Prufrock's poem. Clough presents the monologue of a young Englishman who is in Rome at the time of the revolution of 1848 and cannot make up his mind about anything-Rome itself, the young lady he is pursuing, revolutionary politics. Of the city itself he says:

> *Rome disappoints me much; I hardly as yet understand but* Rubbishy *seems the word that most exactly would suit it.*

Of political action he muses:

> *I do not like being moved: for the will is excited; and action Is a most dangerous thing; I tremble for something factitious, Some malpractice of the heart and illegitimate process;* We are so prone to these things, with our terrible notions of duty.

There is the modernist touch, sixty-eight years before Eliot's Prufrock, but J. Alfred Prufrock is the first fully developed portrait of what we may term modernist man—cultivated, timid, sexually unsure, hypersensitive, a failure as a fully integrated human being (as we all are), candid, even indiscreet. He does not like the modern age, and this makes him modernist instead of modern. It seems we must accept that modernism is based on the rejection of modernity.

—1988

Celebrating T.S. Elliot (II)

❖

The modernists did not like the modern age. Eliot's *The Waste Land*, which we may regard as epitomising modernist poetry, is, on one level, a denunciation of modern commercial civilisation. If the work may be said to have a topography, this is to be found in the city where, while he was preparing to write the poem, Eliot worked as a foreign trade official of Lloyd's Bank. In that ancient part of London that borders on the Thames, Eliot could see signatures of a dead and glorious past cohabiting with all the sordour of an inglorious present. For in the City of London Sir Christopher Wren built his incomparable churches—St. Magnus Martyr, St. Mary Woolnoth, St. Paul's Cathedral itself—which were, in Eliot's day, surrounded by grim warehouses and vulgar temples of trade. On the Thames, now sweating oil and tar, Queen Elizabeth I and the Earl of Leicester once rode in a gilded barge. A romantic past and a sordid present clash throughout the poem.

The modern world is to Eliot the waste land of ancient legend. It is dry and infertile. It needs the revivifying rain that never comes and which it does not really want. The first lines of the poem— "April is the cruellest month, breeding/Lilacs out of the dead land"—sum it all up. April is cruel because it brings new life, and the modern world is committed to death. Water is the enemy, because it flushes the earth to fertility. The poem echoes with the voices of those who died of too much water—the drowned Ophelia, Phlebas the Phoenician sailor. Physical love is sterile and this sterility is summed up on two levels—that of a working-class woman who has suffered her latest abortion, that of Tristan and Isolde which ended in a *Liebestod*.

But there is a paradox here. The Wagnerian hero and heroine are at least glamorous, with the glamour that belongs to the dead romantic past whose passing the poet deplores. Queen Elizabeth

I is glamorous too, but her love affair with the Earl of Leicester was sterile. The Phoenician sailor who died of too much water is also glamorous, but he was drowned on a maritime trade mission. There is no didactic opposition between the glorious past and the sordid present: the two are intertwined. When the poet sees the morning crowd rushing to work over London Bridge, the lines of Dante come to mind—"So many, I had not thought/death had undone so many." London is the "unreal city" but it is also the Christian hell. Yet this hell can become confused with purgatory. To become worthy of the invigorating rain that will flush the land, we must all be purged, and the dead world of our modern degradation may be the preordained place of salvatory suffering.

If the poem describes the waste land over which the Fisher King of Arthurian legend presides, it also hints at the need for Parsifal, the blameless fool, to find the Holy Grail, which held Christ's blood, and the lance which pierced Christ's side. But Jessie L. Weston, who wrote *From Ritual to Romance*, taught Eliot that the Grail and the lance are sexual symbols, and that it is impossible to separate religious regeneration from the theme of fertility. Towards the end of the poem the "dry sterile thunder without rain" is transformed into the vocable DA, which is, in Sanskrit legend, the thing that the thunder says. But DA stands for three words: *Datta, Dayadhvam, Damyata*, meaning "Give, sympathise, control." Through the breaking-out from the prison of self we come to the vision of the waste land regenerated. But what does "control" have to do with it?

Eliot illustrates the key-word *Damyata* with the following lines:

> *The boat responded*
> *Gaily, to the hand expert with sail and oar*
> *The sea was calm, your heart would have responded*
> *Gaily, when invited, beating obedient*
> *To controlling hands*

We seem to have entered a highly personal region, where the masterfulness of the male, controlling the female in a sexual encounter, is wistfully evoked as a thing wished for but not possessed. If we examine the poem closely, we will see that there is a lot of failed sex in it, invitations to physical love proferred but rejected through impotence or timidity. There is a girl carrying hyacinths, symbols of fertility, in whose presence the poet-narrator cannot speak, and his "eyes fail, looking into the heart of light, the silence." And then comes the line from *Tristan*—"*Oed und leer das Meer.*" Tristan and Isolde did not hold back from physical love beside the waste and empty sea. Nor does the "house-agent's clerk," ugly and carbuncular, who assaults the typist in her dingy flat. But the poet is scared of sex, as the whole modern world is scared of fertility.

Since Eliot's death, there have been many unseemly probings into his sex life, or lack of it. There was in him a good deal of the New England fear of physical love that characterised Henry James. It would be indiscreet to refer to his second marriage, which came late but seems to have bestowed a measure of sexual fulfilment, but his first marriage—to the neurotic and eventually demented Vivienne—is fully recorded as a disaster. It has even been made the theme of a very painful stage play—*Tom and Viv*—which has shocked and titillated. There was a lack of blood in Eliot (his doctor confessed that his was the thinnest blood he had ever examined) and *The Waste Land* is a testament to his bloodlessness in its very expression of horror at the sordid material vulgarity of the modern world. At the same time there was an inevitable desire to come to terms with that world, to be vulgar with the vulgar.

All human beings are walking anomalies, and Eliot's poem owes its modernism to his willingness to deal in ambiguities. Ophelia is dead, but her death from too much water makes her more alive than the modern woman who welcomes her latest abortion. Phlebas the drowned Phoenician is a watery saint but also a sordid bearer of commerce. Phoenician commerce produced the alphabet. The magnificent church of St. Mary Woolnoth was built out of the money of the wool merchants. The poem is not simple.

Indeed, it was the poem's lack of simplicity that shocked a literary public accustomed to the simplistic. The language is pure enough, but it is highly allusive. There are quotations from Dante, Wagner, the Elizabethans, and (highly shocking) popular song. We have Dante in Italian, Verlaine in French, Wagner in German, the Upanishads in Sanskrit. There is no moralising, only a con-catenation of images which follow each other with the rapidity of a film. If one meaning is contradicted by another, the poem still holds together as a unity through its power as rhetoric. It is this rhetoric that has permitted the poem to survive. As a boy of fourteen I read *The Waste Land* in the public library, was entranced though mystified, and, being unable to afford to buy Eliot's poems, learned that particular poem by heart. It was the best tribute to its power, and *The Waste Land* remains, sixty-six years after its appearance, the best tribute to the potentialities of modernism.

—1988

LORD OLIVIER

❖

William Shakespeare, a humble actor, did a bold thing when he
turned himself into a gentleman. His coat of arms had the motto
"Non Sanz Droict," a somewhat low-keyed claim to something
less than nobility, but the claim was made on the grounds of
moderate wealth rather than the sources of that wealth—writing
plays and acting in them. It was unthinkable that an actor could
become a knight. Garrick and Kean went unhonoured by the
monarch. It was only with Henry Irving, who looked and sounded
more like an archbishop than an actor, that an actor could receive
the accolade proper only to a magnate or a politician. Nowadays
every actor becomes a knight sooner or later: even Charlie Chaplin—though he was in extreme old age—became Sir Charles.
Laurence Olivier got his knighthood early—in 1947, at the age
of forty. In 1970 he was elevated to the peerage. He was the first
actor to enter the House of Lords, and the simple-minded tend to
take this ennoblement as an index of his greatness as an actor.
He was a remarkable actor on both stage and screen; he was also
an admirable director in the two dramatic media. As for greatness,
one is not quite sure what the term means. Is it not for originators
only to be great, not mere interpreters?

Put it another way—did Olivier rise above all his contemporaries in this matter of dramatic interpretation? Some will be
doubtful. The best Hamlet of the century was either Ernest Milton's or Sir John Gielgud's. Olivier's is better known because he
turned *Hamlet* into a film. His Richard III, which also survives
on film, is remarkable, but it is a lesser role than Hamlet. His
Henry V, eternised in one of the best British films ever made (and
one wonders at the necessity of making another film out of Shakespeare's blatant exercise in chauvinism) is unsurpassable. It is a
role of some nobility, but one had better not enquire too deeply
into the ethics of a brutal campaign consummated at Agincourt.

It has fine patriotic lines, unsubtle humour, and some plausible soul-searching. It is essentially a physical role, and some have said that Olivier was essentially a physical actor.

He was blessed with a handsomeness that shone in all camera-angles, and a robust physique that was marred only by thin legs. When, in 1939, he appeared as Heathcliff in the film of *Wuthering Heights*, he had a brooding masterful quality that melted all female hearts. When he took the leading male role in *Rebecca*, he came close to being the heart-throb of what used to be called the shopgirl romance. There was always that tendency in him to approach the vulgarity of a masculinity untempered by moral or intellectual doubt. When, again on film, he played Lord Nelson to Vivien Leigh's Lady Hamilton, he brought brilliant physical panache to the role but did not seem to probe the soul that lay hidden behind the historical icon.

Perhaps to his credit, he never became a real film star. He was given an Oscar in 1979 as a tribute to a distinguished career in the cinema, but no one performance ever swept the board. It was different for Vivien Leigh, who became his wife: she was Scarlett O'Hara in *Gone With the Wind*, perhaps the major female role in the whole history of film. He had all the gifts except charisma. This is undoubtedly because the cinema was not his primary art. He was responsive enough to the camera, but he found it hard to think in terms of the quick shot or to mend into smoothness the broken rhythms in which the film director deals. When he was directing himself on film he preserved the wider curves of a stage performance, and, indeed, his three Shakespeare films were born out of his own stage productions: the cinematic elements are more applied than idiomatic, though the application was made with great cunning.

As a remarkable stage actor he must live, like his predecessors, in the records of those who saw him, particularly at the Old Vic in the post-war years. For that matter, the true talent of Vivien Leigh shone best under Olivier's stage direction: her, and his, *Titus Andronicus* made genuinely major drama out of Shakespeare's cynical exercise in *grand guignol*. Vivien Leigh's promise was never wholly fulfilled: she died young after suffering physical and mental breakdown which her husband stoically recounts in his brief autobiography. When Olivier turned Joan Plowright into

Lady Olivier, he tied himself to an actress with less glamour but more solid skill. It was a good marriage.

In the theatre Olivier essayed most of the classic parts on which the fame of an actor rests. It is believed that he made some errors. His Othello, for which he deepened the bass register of his voice by half an octave, was falsely founded on a conception of how a West Indian would behave if promoted to a Venetian generalship: there was not enough of the Moor in the interpretation. There was, and this was generally true of most of his interpretations, not enough of an intellectual content. He had an over-simplistic view of Hamlet, which he blatantly reduced—in the opening voice-over of the film version—to the story of "a man who could not make up his mind." He had toyed with the Oedipal interpretation of Ernest Jones (the prince does not really wish to avenge the death of his father: he is glad he is dead because he desires his own mother), but he had never gone deeply enough into those historical factors which make Hamlet the first modern man. He looked the part—or rather, with his blond hair, he looked like the Prince of Denmark—but he could never plumb its depths as Ernest Milton had. He was best left to follow his instincts, but instinct has never been enough with a role like Hamlet, Macbeth or King Lear.

Instinct led him to take on a part that was the antithesis of the classical tradition in which he was held to excel. This was the role of Archie Rice in John Osborne's *The Entertainer*, written expressly for Olivier. The film is inferior to the play, but there is enough in the film to remind us of the intense theatricality, in a deliberately limited sense, of what we saw on the stage. Osborne is lamenting the decay and death of a very British tradition—that of the popular music hall and its "low" or vulgar comedians. Archie Rice, the aging comic with his appalling routine and ghastly songs, playing twice nightly to an ever-dwindling audience, stands for an England in a state of moral collapse, clinging to the rags of a popular culture which has already disappeared, aware of being a living ghost and unable to keep a gape of horror out of his professional leer. Olivier was superb in the role. In it he paid tribute to a demotic form of theatre whose last exponent—the comedian Tommy Trinder—died only a day before Olivier himself.

The range, then, was wide. It was not wide enough to encompass boulevard comedy of the kind in which, as actor and dramatist, Noel Coward excelled, but it could cope with Ibsen, Chekhov, and Tennessee Williams—always more than competently. As Olivier advanced into old age, he gracefully accepted the roles appropriate to elegant decrepitude. Unlike some Hollywood actors who had better not be mentioned, he never dyed his hair or had a face-lift in order to force himself into the ludicrous travesty of a *jeune premier*. He who had been the hero for so long became the villain in films like *Marathon Man*. It was in this that Dustin Hoffman, undoubtedly a star, showed his fear of Olivier's professionalism by bullying him into endless strenuous rehearsals that emphasised the old actor's physical decay. Olivier never complained. He never threw tantrums when faced with the less than Shakespearian lines of *The Jazz Singer* or *The Betsy*. An actor's job was to act. It was always a nerve-racking job. Night after night, before his entrance, Olivier would vomit into the fire bucket.

His transmutation into a peer of the realm had to do with his all-round services to the theatre rather than purely his skill as an actor. Accepting the directorship of the National Theatre, he tried to fix standards of professionalism and dramaturgical values which should be a model to the world of the English-speaking stage. On the whole he succeeded in providing a model of technical excellence for young actors to follow, and new plays for the National Theatre have never sunk to the drivelling level acceptable in the purely commercial theatre. He was the best possible man to preside over a state enterprise, and it is right that one of the playhouses that make up the complex on the South Bank of the Thames should have been named after him even when he was still alive.

De mortuis nil nisi bonum, but it is only fair to Olivier's memory to stress his imperfections when compared with some of his contemporaries who, achieving knighthood, would not have been considered worthy of receiving more. If animal instinct and physique may be considered as possessing intelligence, it is there that Olivier's intelligence must be sought. Sir Michael Redgrave, who was probably a better actor, has to live on in his children Vanessa, Lynn, and Colin and a few run-of-the-mill films which only his performance saved from mediocrity. His intelligence, and even scholarliness, were exemplary, but his animal spirits were comparatively feeble. Sir Ralph Richardson, Olivier's partner in so many Old Vic ventures, Buckingham to his Richard III, gave the impression of projecting sobriety through mild drunkenness. Sir Alec Guinness has severe vocal limitations. Richard Burton had the finest stage voice of the century, despite the ravages of drink and tobacco, but ruined himself through neglecting what should have been his primary medium, the stage. Olivier's voice was not miraculous—he was never a great reader of poetry—but it was under excellent technical control. Where he beat his contemporaries was in physical presence. He spoke through his body. One of his last performances was as the dying Lord Marchmain in the televisual *Brideshead Revisited*. There comes a moment, the climactic moment of the story, when the old man, breathing his last, affirms a Catholic faith long in abeyance by heavily making the sign of the cross. It is simple. It could have been ludicrous. But, without a word spoken, it brings a sob to the throat of even a watching atheist. If acting can ever be considered great, this is probably great acting.

There are plenty of considerable actors around on the English-speaking stage, some of them skilled equally in film (Glenda Jackson has two Oscars; Ben Kingsley, never previously seen in the cinema before *Gandhi*, won one with ease), but Lord Olivier probably represents a tradition already finished. For good or ill, few young actors regard theatrical achievement as their major goal. Television and cinema provide the real fame and money. The techniques of both media are increasingly infecting the traffic of the stage. Stage actors are growing wooden, as though gripped by the camera lens, and are forgetting how to project their voices. Even the thespian standard speech of which Olivier was a fine exponent is giving place to substandard dialects deemed, in this democratic age, suitable for a prince of Denmark. Olivier belongs to an important past, and we must regret that so little of it can be preserved. The films are something, but they are not enough. Olivier was much more than his films. It was in the theatre that the olive tree bore its juiciest fruit.

—1989

GERARD MANLEY HOPKINS 1844–1889

❖

It is just a hundred years since the death of Father Hopkins SJ, and about sixty years since I first read him. Those were the days when to read *Ulysses* was to break the law. Modernism was dangerous, and one of the marks of modernism was strangeness of language. Hopkins, like Joyce, had bizarre compound words like *beadbonny* and *fallowbootfellow*: he seemed to be dragging the Germanic roots of English out of freshly dug earth. Yet how could a Jesuit priest, dead in the same year as Robert Browning, be a modernist? By an accident, the fact of his not being published until 1918, he was forced into joining that tide of literary innovation on which Eliot rode, also, Pound, above all James Joyce. Robert Bridges, the closest friend of Hopkins, had, I still think, done wrong in delaying the publication of Hopkins's small poetic *oeuvre* until the end of the Great War. Young poets died in that war, and they would have been glad to take that thin volume of Hopkins into the trenches. But the world, according to the highly conservative, not to say timid, Bridges was not ready for the Hopkinsian hand grenade, and it is true that the 1918 edition of his work was slow to sell out. I read the second impression of 1930. I read it on the Channel packet coming back from France, a schoolboy tremulous at having stuffed the Odyssey Press edition of *Ulysses* (two paperback volumes) into his waistband. I still cannot read Hopkins without the sensation of daring proper, at that time, to reading *Ulysses*.

Joyce had formed his own style by the time Hopkins was first published. There was no possibility of the great Jesuit's influencing the great ex-Jesuit. Joyce was seven when Hopkins died. Yet he died in Dublin, at the University College where Joyce was to take his B.A. Asked in late life what he thought of Hopkins, Joyce said that he was a kind of English Mallarmé (sure proof that he hadn't read him). The two writers were on the same sort of track in total independence of each other. Joyce sought those flashes of revelation which he called "epiphanies." Hopkins spoke of "inscapes" and "instresses." Both meant that ordinary experience had the capacity to startle, in sudden unsought explosions, with a vision of truth. The expression of truth couldn't be entrusted to the weary clichés of conventional verse or prose: language itself had to startle.

One way of startling was to exaggerate the Teutonic element in English, complete with the eschewal of those timid hyphens which make some English compound words look like items in a child's primer. Hopkins's windhover, or kestrel, is dappledawndrawn. Oxford is, or was, larkcharméd and cuckooechoing. John Milton's method of making new in *Paradise Lost* was to exaggerate the Latin heritage of English. His elephants are endorsed with towers; spring is vernal. The Hopkinsian way looked more eccentric than the Miltonic, chiefly because speakers of English don't like to be reminded of the brutal Anglo-Saxon base on which the Latinised Normans built. And yet the Anglo-Saxon element is native, radical. William Barnes, the Dorset clergyman who was a contemporary of Hopkins, was not wrong in wishing to call an omnibus a folkwain. A telephone works no better than a farspeaker. Anglo-Saxon went in for heavy headrime (or alliteration). This was one of the items in the Hopkinsian battery. ". . . Treads through, prickproof, thick/Thousands of thorns, thoughts." The thorns and thoughts are the same. Not until Joyce's *Finnegans Wake* would it be possible to say "thornts." But Hopkins was on the way to this kind of counterpoint—one word doing the work of two, even more. And he was always ready, in the interests of verbal freshness, to expand usage. Self, selves—why not "selve" as a verb? If a thing "selves" it speaks itself, says what it is. A bell selves, so does a snowstorm. And a thing that selves shows its "sakes," its individual marks, a bird's plumage, a bell's harmonics.

To Hopkins, who was almost blindingly devout, God's glory showed itself in the intense variety of the physical world, especially when such variety was present in a single member of it. Hence his laudation of "pied beauty"—"Glory be to God for dappled things." Dapple was a kind of tension of opposites, nothing flaccid, everything dynamic—"fickle, freckled." His poetic

practice broke away from the flaccidity of the regular Tennyson-
ian or Emersonian line—"Come down, O maid, from yonder
mountain height." The English language had allowed itself to be
shackled into a verse-system borrowed from the Latin languages,
which don't go in for the hammer blows of the native Saxon.
Hopkins seems to have invented a new kind of prosody he called
"sprung rhythm." What he was really doing was restoring a native practice that the Normans drove out—the counting of
stresses, not syllables.

The line "Morning, evening, noontime, night" is regular and
traditional. Not too many syllables, nor too few. Four stresses,
the down, left, right, up of the conductor's baton. But why
shouldn't we have "Morn, eve, noon, night"? Why not "In the
morning, during the evening, sometimes at noontime, always at
night"? Always four beats and as many, or as few, syllables, as
you wish. The rhythm springs out of the beat, not the syllable
counting. Hence the name sprung rhythm. And so Hopkins wrote
sonnets—his tribute to traditional regularity—which are perfect
examples of the form except for the number of syllables:

> I caught this morning morning's minion, king-
> Dom of daylight's dauphin, dappledawndrawn falcon
> in his riding . . .

No trouble with the first line, as regular as anything in Wordsworth. But for the second line we have to dig out the stresses,
finding them on "daylight's," on "dauphin," on "dappledawndrawn," on "falcon," on "riding." There's a lot of hurry there,
as in ordinary speech. Hopkins knew that it was all too easy to
let such verse sink into prose, but the charged language, the heavy
headrime, the ecstasy of expression keep the vehicle airborne.

The difficulty of reading Hopkins and getting the sprung
rhythm right has always troubled poetry-lovers who have no musical ear. Ideally his verse should be set out in musical notation,
with crotchets, quavers, bar-lines. Hopkins, like Joyce, was a musician (he wrote a song in the 1860s which employs quartertones).
He saw where poetry and music came together; he tried notating
his poem "Harry Ploughman" in a quasimusical form; he recognised, with a sigh, that readers of books are not necessarily read-

ers of scores. The difficulty of reading him correctly remains. He
was a poet who could not compromise. There was no compromise
in his religion either. His family was heartbroken when he left
Anglicanism and turned Catholic. His fellow-Jesuits didn't understand him. He knew the dark night of the soul. He died young
of typhus. He knew no fame in his lifetime.

His fame, in this centennial year, remains limited. The difficulty
of understanding his language and his technique confines him to
university departments. *The Wreck of the Deutschland*, his masterpiece, is not likely to be filmed. His Jesuit theology puts un-
believers off. The English object to his apostasy from Anglicanism;
the Irish are unhappy about his fear of the consequences of Home
Rule. Even his co-religionists are dubious about his ecstatic excesses. But, whether we like it or not, his influence subtly pervades the
practice of all who are forced to take language seriously. I should
imagine he is on the shelves of most Madison Avenue copywriters.
Phrases like "gash gold vermilion" must tempt advertisers in
Vogue. He was ready to teach the world the idiom of ecstasy, but
we reserve ecstasy to the latest state-of-the-art acquisition. We live
in an age of dilution. Hopkins brews the powerful liquor of faith.
In God, also in language.

—1989

Two Hundred Years of the Bounty

❖

The National Maritime Museum at Greenwich has organised an exhibition to celebrate the bicentenary of the most famous naval mutiny in history. The fame has, of course, much to do with a film made by Hollywood in the 1930s, in which Charles Laughton played the part of Captain William Bligh, who allegedly ruled the *Bounty* like a maritime Caligula and deserved to be deprived of his command by mutineers and set adrift in an open boat. As is often the case, fictionalisation obscures truth.

Bligh, a mere naval lieutenant, was put in charge of a ninety-foot ship and ordered to collect breadfruit plants in the Pacific. These were to be cultivated as cheap food for slaves. It was an ignoble mission, and the British Admiralty gave it a low priority. The ship was too small, there were too few regular officers and no marines at all. The marines, whom Kipling was to call a sort of a hermaphrodite, soldier and sailor too, had the task of controlling restive or riotous ship's crews. If there had been any marines on board the *Bounty*, there would certainly have been no mutiny.

Why did Bligh's crew mutiny? By all accounts, Bligh was a highly competent officer, not much given to violence or vindictiveness. But he had a highly cultivated capacity for bad language (this would never have got past a film censor of the 1930s) and a fine line in sarcasm. Sarcasm is one officer attribute that ratings in the navy and private soldiers in the army cannot tolerate. This was as true, as I know from personal experience, in the Second World War as it was in the eighteenth century. Bligh's sarcasm was vented on fellow-officers and petty officers in the presence of their inferiors, but neither vituperation nor sneers would have granted sufficient grounds for revolt. For unrest and grumbling, yes, but not for the ultimate dreadful act which automatically earned the death penalty.

In fact, the outward bound voyage of the *Bounty* was marked by no great unrest or indiscipline. Bligh, like most ship's masters of his time, ordered flogging and cuts in the rations for breaches of good order, but he was never as fearsome as the great Captain Cook who, decent and beloved in his early voyages, became bloodthirsty and intolerable in his later ones. It seems that the revolt on the *Bounty* was instigated not by excessive cruelty but by excessive lenity.

There was no trouble aboard the ship until it arrived at Tahiti. But, once arrived, Bligh permitted naval discipline to relax. His friend and fellow-Manxman Fletcher Christian set up an establishment on shore and became enamoured of a local woman. Following his example, many of the crew took unto themselves native "wives." Life became easy and lazy. Bligh failed to exact the discipline that Captain Cook insisted upon in langorous climates where the fish jumped into one's hand and the coconuts fell into one's lap. Cook would have his men climbing the rigging for the sake of the exercise or organising regattas in the bay. But Bligh permitted six months of illicit sex and lassitude, himself remaining aloof but torpid in his cabin. When the time came to set sail, the crew was resentful. There were tearful farewells to the Tahitian beauties and a great unhandiness in the resumption of shipboard duties.

The event that fired the mutiny was trivial. Captain Bligh had taken, for his own consumption, a supply of coconuts on board and he found some of them missing. The accusation of theft wounded Fletcher Christian deeply. He kept muttering to himself "I am in hell . . . I am in hell"—a surely excessive reaction—and he dreamed of the Tahitian heaven he had left behind. Anxious to return to it, he began to build a raft. But a number of the members of the crew encouraged him to do more—to take the *Bounty* out of the hands of Captain Bligh and set that alleged tyrant adrift with such of the men has had no stomach for mutiny. Out of the crew of forty-six, eighteen elected to go with their captain in a twenty-three feet open launch. This was off the island of Tofua, about a thousand miles west of Tahiti. Bligh had to sail further west, between New Guinea and the northern coast of Australia, to reach the island of Timor, where, he knew, he would find transportation back to England and a summary revenge.

Bligh's competence remains one of the most astonishing features of British naval history. He had to sail 3,600 nautical miles, and this totally without charts. When he got to the Australian coast he was only a few miles out in his computation. Food and water were, of course, the main problem. For forty-two days, the company subsisted on a daily ration of an ounce of biscuit, a morsel of salt pork, and a half pint of water. Bligh meticulously measured these out with an improvised balance made of coconut shells and musket balls. The suffering was intense, but nobody perished. With a sextant, quadrant, compass and log line, Bligh completed his voyage and established himself as one of the great naval commanders of all time.

But what of the mutineers? To return to Tahiti seemed the obvious thing to do—the recovery of the paradise from which, like a cruel Jehovah, Bligh had cast them out. But there was the danger that justice, in the form of an armed frigate, would catch up with them, and this necessitated the search for another island of exile, one not known or wrongly charted. And so Pitcairn Island, a thousand miles southeast of Tahiti, became the refuge of some of the mutineers. It was not much of a refuge. Christian set off with twelve Tahitian beauties and four Tahitian toughs who, furious at being treated like inferior servants of the white man, ran amok at Pitcairn and killed Christian and eleven of his followers.

When Pitcairn was rediscovered in 1808, there was only one mutineer—John Adams—but there were twelve women and a number of children, three of them fathered by Fletcher Christian. One of his descendants, Glynn Christian, is well-known in Britain as a television cook. A cultivation of a civilised cuisine seems to be a kind of genetic response to the inadequate diet of the mutineers.

Bligh, who had started the voyage from Tofua on April 28, 1789, reached Timor in June, and was back in England by March 1790. He spread around a version of the mutiny story that ensured his being treated as a hero. But the recovery of fourteen of the mutineers from Tahiti and their subsequent trial in London enabled the other side of the case to be heard. There were six death sentences, of which only three were carried out. The true instigator of the crime was, of course, missing, but Fletcher Christian's brother Edward, an expert in law, initiated a long process

of posthumous justification and pilloried Bligh for tyrannous conduct and professional incompetence. This latter charge could not,
on the evidence of that incredible voyage from Tofua to Timor,
be at all upheld, despite the later efforts of the cinema. Bligh was
a remarkable commander.

This was acknowledged by Nelson himself. After a number of
voyages, at least one of which was again in search of breadfruit,
after three further mutinies of a minor and easily controllable
kind, after a court-martial on the charge of using bad language,
Bligh engaged in the great naval war against France and fought
battles with distinction. It was for his part in the Battle of Copenhagen that Nelson issued heartfelt congratulations. Bligh was
promoted to vice-admiral and ended a distinguished career as
Governor-General of New South Wales. But the iconography of
the cinema has earned him a place in the pandemonion of villains.
We cannot think of him without the interposition of Charles
Laughton's face and voice. Art is often unfair. History purveys
true justice.

I doubt if it is relevant to connect the greater event of 1789
with this sad act of disaffection. The *Bounty* mutiny came some
months before the storming of the Bastille. And it is doubtful
whether Fletcher Christian read Voltaire or Rousseau. In Rousseau he would have found a kind of confirmation of the existence
of unspoiled paradises in savage parts where "natural man" lazed
around uncorrupted by civilisation. But it was four uncorrupted
Tahitians who shot Christian in the back of the head with one of
his own muskets and then smashed in his face with rocks and
axes. Jealousy and pride grow wild like coconuts and breadfruit.
Man is born in original sin, and this is the true snake in our
tropical Edens. Crews should not revolt and captains should not
provoke them to revolt. The mutiny on the *Bounty* reminds us
that mankind is unregenerable. But the consequence of that revolt,
Bligh's incredible voyage to Timor, also reminds us that our human faults are redeemed by immense skill and fortitude. Man is
a terrible mixture.

—1989

OUR ETERNAL HOLMES

❖

It's just over a century since the first appearance of *A Study in Scarlet*, and the adoration of Sherlock Holmes that began shortly after shows no sign of abating now. At this moment, on the West End stage, there is a Holmes play and a Holmes musical. There is a Holmes series on television, and a send-up Holmes film (far from the first) on the cinema circuit. Holmes can be severely mistreated by his adapters. He is currently being presented as a kind of moronic lay-figure for the exploitation of a Dr. Watson who possesses the true detectional brilliance. He is doing Cockney knees-ups in Mr. Bricusse's loving travesty. A few years ago he was seen as a drug addict in need of the ministrations of Dr. Freud. We await a gay Holmes and a syphilitic Holmes, though a Holmes suffering from terminal AIDS is too anachronistic to be plausible. Do what you will with him, he always bounces back, formidably intelligent, addicted to cocaine and the violin, a Bohemian whom the Establishment accepts, a great Englishman with nothing English about him.

After all, his creator, Sir Arthur Conan Doyle, was himself no Englishman. His blood was Irish and he was born in Edinburgh. He was educated at the Jesuit Stonyhurst College in Lancashire, and it is without doubt the rigorous logic of Jesuit theology that Doyle injected into the arteries of his most famous creation. That image is a just one, since Doyle, like Watson, was a physician. The cold eye of the diagnostician allied to the steely reasoning of a St. Thomas Aquinas makes Holmes what he is. But to the logical brain must be added a profound belief in what we may think of as a rather outdated chivalry—Christianity on horseback. Nobody today possesses the worshipping attitude to women that Doyle maintained all his life and which is ready to emerge in Holmes despite his bachelor asceticism (or perhaps because of it). Doyle's mother suffered from a shiftless husband, sustained a family through long hardship, and earned from her famous son a devotion more suitable for the Blessed Virgin. This he applied to all women. Women, who do not relish worship, have never been great devotees of the sleuth of Baker Street.

If you travel to Baker Street by Underground, you will see the station decorated with a frieze of Sherlock Holmes heads, complete with pipe and deerstalker hat. The Sherlock Holmes Hotel has a doorman dressed in the authentic outfit. No character in fiction outside Shakespeare and Cervantes has earned such immortality and, more, such recognisability. Hispanic illiterates as far back as Cervantes's own time could name the lean knight on the spavined nag when he processed round a bullring. British illiterates know Falstaff, even if only as a pub sign. But Holmes beats them both. And yet Conan Doyle has never been accorded the respect of the literary. His books are quickly dismissed in histories of English literature; his style is never analysed and his psychology never discussed. The popularity of those books has militated against their being taken seriously. T. S. Eliot, the greatest literary authority of our century, was a Holmes addict— he lifted eight lines of his *Murder in the Cathedral* from *The Musgrave Ritual*, totally without acknowledgment—but he never wrote a line in praise of Doyle. The rift in our literary tradition between the popular and the recherché has produced a deplorable double standard, a kind of aesthetic hypocrisy which we'd better do something about expunging. Doyle was a great writer and Sherlock Holmes remains a superb creation.

Why does the adoration continue? Perhaps because we're always in need of an authoritarian figure who can come up with logical solutions to our problems. The problems that face Holmes are pretty limited, being all in the criminal field, but we feel sure that, given the chance, he could sort out the bigger problems of politics and economics. He has an absolute moral sense, a Jesuitical awareness of the boundaries of good and evil, but, though he seems to have no sex life, he is dissolute enough to merit the love we always reserve to imperfection. He smokes excessively (keeping his tobacco eccentrically in a Turkish slipper), and he jabs himself occasionally with cocaine injections. He plays the violin, probably not very well. When he is cruel, he tempers his acidity with humour. He is not a distant Olympian figure; we are permitted, in the disguise of the often fatuous Dr. Watson, to visit him in his humble, and not very tidy, lodgings. He is a Londoner who knows his London as well as Sam Weller; he is not cut off from the common people in Belgravia or Cliveden, and he has very much at heart the right of the common people to a modicum of justice. He is not a snob; he is courteous if pedantic; he is not a product of the British ruling class. Like his creator, he probably had his education at Stonyhurst. His mind works in what we may call a Continental manner. He is not afraid of being either logical or learned. He is not at all a typical product of Victorian England. To create a Bohemian character who works on behalf of British moral stability requires something like artistic genius. This Conan Doyle undoubtedly had.

Shakespeare tried to kill off Falstaff, but Queen Elizabeth wouldn't let him. Doyle tried to kill off Holmes, but the British reading public protested. "The Final Problem" is the story in which Doyle tried to free himself from Holmes forever so that he could get on with the serious work of writing historical novels (of which he was the greatest master after Sir Walter Scott) and studying spiritualism. *The Hound of the Baskervilles* (published in 1902) tells of an adventure in the life of a man already dead. "The Adventure of the Empty House" (1905) revealed that Holmes had, very implausibly, survived his apparent killing at the hands of Moriarty (named after the stupidest boy at Stonyhurst). In 1927, in *The Case-Book of Sherlock Holmes*, the physical immortality of the great detective was taken for granted. Doyle died three years later, but his creation, now out of copyright, walks the world through the manipulation of lesser men. That Holmes can be mauled, travestied, traduced, and yet remain serene and imperturbable is an incredible tribute to his inner strength. Perhaps some epigone of Doyle ought to make him stand for parliament and be called by his Queen to form a government. He would certainly put the country right on a basis of high morality tempered by harmless addictions. But he is too big for any political party. And he would not be happy to leave the cluttered fug of Baker Street for the empyrean of Number 10. After all, he remains, like the best of us, an outsider.

—1989

The Cold Eye of Yeats

❖

This year we celebrate the fiftieth anniversary of the death of William Butler Yeats, Irish poet, statesman, and Nobel Prize winner. The English feel both shame and exaltation at the fact that the greatest writers of the last hundred years writing in English have mostly been Irish. True, Conrad was Polish and T. S. Eliot and Ezra Pound were American, but few will deny that the crown for drama goes to Oscar Wilde and Bernard Shaw, for the novel to James Joyce, and for poetry to Yeats. The English are ashamed that the motherland of the language has not done better, and at the same time proud that a language imposed upon a subject people should have yielded such exceptional results.

But it is always difficult to extricate the Celtic element from the Anglo-Saxon and Norman and Danish when considering the great Irishmen of the century. Joyce alone was thoroughly Celtic, also Catholic, while the others were of mixed stock in which the Anglo-Saxon Protestant predominated. In our own age, another Irish Nobel Prize winner, Samuel Beckett, claims French Huguenot ancestry and, writing exclusively in French, may be said to have returned to his origins. As for Yeats, the name comes from Yorkshire, the man himself had a land-owning background and, though he identified himself totally with the Irish, it was less with the Irish peasantry than with a kind of mythical aristocracy that never had existed and never could exist. His case is a strange one. He had love neither for Catholicism nor for Protestantism, and his life was spent searching for a mythology upon which both an aesthetic and a philosophy could be based. This mythology was only partly Irish.

The poems which gained him the Nobel Prize belonged to the phase in which he was addicted to the "Celtic Twilight" (which Joyce was to mock as the "cultic twalette"). A misty ancient Ireland was evoked, in which remote mythological figures like Cu-

344

chulain and Fergus and Deirdre of the Sorrows and Cathleen ni
Houlihan (suffering Ireland itself) moved ineffectually through a
fog of *appliqué* poetic beauty. But the Celtic myths were not
enough. Yeats was much influenced by the fake pseudo-religions
of the *fin de siècle*: theosophy, Rosicrucianism, and the Order of
the Golden Dawn. Later, his wife was to pretend to receive mystical messages from supernatural beings, all of which Yeats took
with great seriousness. The intellectual life of Yeats was that of a
backward schoolboy. His intelligence was limited. But lack of intelligence, apparently, was no drawback to his becoming a great
poet.

His love life, similarly, was that of an adolescent. He fell heavily
for Maud Gonne, an Englishwoman who hated sex and her own
country with equal virulence and was always ready, during the
Boer War, to organise the planting of bombs on British troop-
ships. She naturally espoused the cause of suffering Ireland. In
Yeats's mythology she was Helen of Troy and Pallas Athene unattainable beauty, the welcome source of sexual suffering—welcome because it produced poetry. The other woman in his life,
apart from the woman he married, was Lady Gregory, who kept
a great house in Coole Park and, for him, symbolised an aristocracy remote from and disdainful of the peasantry. Several visits
to Urbino fed the aristocratic ideal, and Urbino itself changed into
Byzantium, a kind of dream heaven, a holy city symbolic of the
pure soul freed from the mire and torment of the life of the flesh.
Yeats's best poetry was written in late life, long after the Nobel
award, when the agony of ageing (alleviated somewhat by a glan-
dular operation employing the Steinach technique) was set against
the vigour of a mind, and of erotic desires, which the decaying
body derided.

When Ireland became an independent republic, Yeats was
elected a senator. One of his enactments is still with us—the Irish
coinage is among the most beautiful in the world. When a Catholic government proposed banning divorce, Yeats spoke up for
the Irish Protestant interest. It was the Protestants, he declaimed
in the Dail, who had given Ireland what liberty she had—Parnell,
whom the priests had condemned from the pulpit and the confessional, Grattan, Burke, Berkeley, Swift. Not many of these had
Irish blood. His dream was still that of a haughty aristocracy,

with the unteachable and unregenerable Irish poor clamouring vainly at the gates of Coole Park (which, inevitably, the Irish Agricultural Board bought and then tore down).

Yeats, the poet and senator, achieved what every writer has longed for: a place in the community, a national theme, the function of the bard and the prophet. Perhaps only Gabriele D'Annunzio, outside Ireland, has synthesised poetry and political action. If D'Annunzio is associated with the rise of fascism, Yeats may be thought of as impotently totalitarian. He admired Mussolini and even gave his support—albeit briefly—to the short-lived Irish fascist party inaugurated by O'Higgins. One of the disturbing aspects of the poetry of our age has been the manner in which its practitioners have leaned to the authoritarian—Yeats, Eliot, Pound. This undoubtedly springs from the great gulf which subsists between the high artist and the common people. Superior art cannot, we are told, be demotic. The question has been asked by Conor Cruise O'Brien: "How can we like Yeats as a poet when we detest his politics so heartily?" The mystery of the gap between the art and the artist remains, for we do like Yeats's poetry. It may seek to be aristocratic, but its language is the language of ordinary people.

His poem "Easter 1916," which commemorates ambiguously the Dublin revolt which destroyed the Post Office and resulted in innumerable shootings and hangings, begins like a personal letter: "I have met them at close of day/ Coming with vivid faces/ From counter or desk among grey/ Eighteenth-century houses . . ." Yeats's incredible gift was to raise the language of daily speech to high oratory by the sheer control of rhythm. There was nothing of the D'Annunzian about him during that latest and greatest phase of his career. On his grave at Sligo are carved (by his order) the words: "Cast a cold eye/ On life, on death./ Horseman, pass by." There are no horsemen nowadays, only the drivers of Fords and Fiats. Yeats could not resist the aristocratic or cavalier touch. But the injunction to look on both life and death indifferently, unemotionally, sprang out of a life inured to the disappointments of the poet. For poetry changes nothing. "Did that verse of mine send out/ Certain men the English shot?" wrote Yeats, probably hoping for an affirmative answer. The only reply can be a shake of the head. Yeats never even wrote a marching song for the Irish Republic.

Poetry changes nothing because it deals with the unchangeable. It is finally a manipulation of language to produce magic spells which effect no magic. Yeats could not write a single line that was not magical. One not dare enquire too much as to meaning, for meaning is not important. Rhetoric is. The Irish remain the great rhetoricians of the age.

—1989

Powered by all the engines of modern technology, the Oxford English Dictionary has absorbed its four massive supplements into its main body and now stretches shelf-long, the gigantic total picture of the English language, past, present, though not necessarily to come. For languages change, none changes more than English, and even a lexicon so all-inclusive as the OED is, fire-new from the printers, already a picture of the past. The work goes on forever; the OED is an epic achievement, but the final line cannot be written. All we can do at the moment is to marvel at the elegance, the erudition, the labour. Dr. Johnson, who produced his own dictionary more or less single-handed, gives a secondary definition of a lexicographer as "a harmless drudge." On one level that is apt. In an age of destruction that always catches the headlines, a small army of men and women have drudged to conserve. It is heroism, but there is nothing sensational about it. It is quietly, or harmlessly, honourable, and I am here to honour it.

Or rather honour the pioneers. Every lexicographer builds on work already done, and the main work was achieved in the nineteenth century. It was proper that the OED should have its beginnings in an age of massive engineering projects, empire-building, the overturning of history by Marx and of cosmology by Darwin. The OED, in its nineteenth-century form, has rightly been called our Victorian epic and, in the Johnsonian tradition, it was mostly the work of one man. This was a godfearing teetotal non-smoking philoprogenitive polymath Scottish dominie named James Murray.

In Thackeray's *Vanity Fair*, Becky Sharp throws away her copy of Johnson's Dictionary, a parting gift from the Miss Pinkerton who runs a young ladies' academy. It is a gesture in the direction of modernity, for Johnson tried to fix standards of English usage for ever out of a past already dead. A scientific age started after

Waterloo, and it was time even for dictionaries to be objective, up-to-date, descriptive rather than prescriptive. Johnson was quirky and very personal. There was in his Dictionary, however, one thing that the new lexicographers would abandon only at their peril: ample citation to show words at work. One of the glories of the OED is the mass of illustrative quotation which supports definition. It is the reason why the OED is so big.

1876 was a momentous year for dictionary-makers. The only lexica that the Anglo-American world then had were by Noah Webster, Charles Richardson, and Joseph Worcester. Richardson, impressed by Johnson, was full of citation, but he substituted this for definition. Richardson's etymologies were very shaky: he was, for instance, quite ready to derive *hash* from the Persian *ash*, meaning a stew. Webster was good, and still is, but not quite good enough. Harper, the American publisher, wanted to collaborate with Macmillan in London on the production of a new dictionary "like Webster, in bulk, and as far superior in quality as possible." Who should be editor? There was only one man, and that was James Murray.

Murray was a self-made scholar. Born near Hawick in Roxburghshire, he became a teacher at Mill Hill School near London, one of the dissenting academies set up as counterparts to the Anglican public schools. He had a passion for learning which, if it ever needed justification, could find it in the duty to serve God and honour his creation by trying to understand it. He was a man curious about everything, and especially language. He had at least a theoretical knowledge of every language, living and dead. When the exiled Hungarian patriot Kossuth visited Hawick—a town passionate about national liberty—he was met by the town band and a banner inscribed in Magyar—"*Jöjjön-el a' te orszagod*," meaning "Thy kingdom come." Murray had been at work. He learned his languages from translations of the Bible. In old age he could still write down a good deal of Genesis in Chinese characters.

Brought up on the English-Scottish border, Murray was struck while still a young child by the failure of a political boundary to coincide with an isogloss (or frontier between languages). The Sassenachs down there spoke his kind of tongue. Language was a continuum—in time as well as space. Anglo-Saxon and Middle

English lived on, in the guise of "incorrect" speech. Language was primarily speech, not marks on paper. If you were a true philologist, you had to learn first about English as a sound-system, with the sounds always in process of change. Murray learned phonetics from Alexander Melville Bell, and, while he was at it, gave lessons in electricity to the teenaged son Alexander Graham Bell, who then invented the telephone. Graham was to call Murray the grandfather of that marvel. Paternity was reserved for something else, as well as children named Wilfrid, Hilda, Oswyn, Ethelwyn, Elsie, Harold, Ethelbert, Aelfric, Rosfrith, Gwyneth and Jowett. The something else was a dictionary so compendious that Macmillan and Harper took fright. The Philological Society of Great Britain, to which Murray now belonged, forced a concept of 6000 pages on the publishers, who wanted a mere 2000. Anglo-American lexicography was to get into the mainstream of modern philology as practised in Germany. That was Murray's idea. The Delegates of the Oxford University Press took over the project, but even they were to take fright. Not, evidently, forever.

In his house at Mill Hill Murray set up what he called the Scriptorium, and he lined it with pigeonholes. There were never enough. The project grew. No word was to be omitted if Murray could help it. He had to yield to Victorian prudishness, but, in heaven, he is doubtless nodding with approval at the inclusion of *fuck* and *cunt* in the OED of our more permissive epoch. He was angry at Robert Browning for misusing a lot of words, including *twat*. The colossal labour went on in the intervals of schoolmastering, but Murray, hoping for a possible university appointment and more scholarly nourishment than was available at Mill Hill, moved the Scriptorium to Oxford. Oxford was not helpful. Henry Sweet, the great philologist who became Bernard Shaw's Henry Higgins, warned him:

> You must be prepared for a good deal of vexatious interference and dictation hereafter, liable to be enforced any moment by summary dismissal. You will then see your materials and the assistants trained by you utilized by some Oxford swell, who will draw a good salary for doing nothing. I know something of Oxford, and of its low state of morality as regards jobbery and personal interest.

The warning was in order. Scholarly blindness, tyrannous dead-lines, spurts of indifference and unworthy commercialism beset the long journey from A to T (as far as Murray got). But the indomitable dominie pushed on. Somewhat despised by the Ox-onians as a man with no degree (but British degrees in philology didn't exist), he was given a doctorate by Edinburgh University and found the academic cap useful for keeping his head warm. Eventually he was given a knighthood, but he feared that the local tradesmen would put their prices up. He made no money out of his labour, and he didn't want fame. "I am a nobody—if you have anything to say about the Dictionary, there it is at your will—but treat me as a solar myth, or an echo, or an irrational quantity, or ignore me altogether."

In 1884 Murray still had a vision of a four-volume work of 6,400 pages, which would take about ten years to complete. But it took him and his fistful of helpers five years to get as far as *ant*. The first fascicle, published in February 1884, was in some ways a bomb. It indicated not merely the complexity of the un-dertaking but the complexity of the language itself. Murray was a great man for cutting through complexities. At Mill Hill one of the set books had been William Paley's *Horae Paulinae*, a worthy exposition of theological utilitarianism which Murray's pupils found baffling. The great teacher made a synopsis of it and used different types to make Paley's arguments "eloquent to the eye." He brought the same technique to the OED, very satisfying to handle because of Murray's appreciation of the semiology of type—something that the Oxford swells, who had never taught children, were slow to see. He also, devised his own phonetic system, but that has at last yielded to the IPA, or International Phonetic Alphabet, which ought to be the first thing taught in our schools, though it never is.

Murray died in 1915 at seventy-eight. It took another thirteen years—under first Henry Bradley, later William Craigie and Charles T. Onions (to whom the Murray children would deri-sively sing "Charlie is my darling")—to bring out the final vol-ume. That was in April 1928, with 15,488 pages covering more than 400,000 words and phrases. The twenty volumes of the sec-ond, or 1989, edition have 22,000 pages and they define over half a million words, with 2.4 million illustrative quotations. This final achievement (if one may speak of finality in the context of the ever-flowing river of language), the work mainly of J. A. Simpson and E. S. C. Weiner, encloses the astonishing four fat supplements of R. W. Burchfield, which brought the survey of English right up to his, and very nearly our, present day. Slang, jargon, obscenity and the linguistic spawn of a liberated empire—including America—are all there. English is shown as a totality, not merely the property of the literate and literary. The organ has all registers booming, all stops out. There has to be a heaven to accommodate the saintly Murray and enable him to bless the work. In essence, it is all his.

It is also the work of the thousands, anonymous, unpaid and unseen, who contributed the illustrative citations. Murray inherited from the Philological Society two tons of paper slips—headwords with quotations—from all over the Anglophone world. These came in sacks (a dead rat in one, a live mouse with family in another), parcels, a baby's bassinet, a hamper of I's with the bottom broken. He was found with the American consul in Florence, though it had started fifteen years earlier with Horace Moule, Thomas Hardy's teacher and friend. Fragments of Pa were found in a stable in County Cavan, but most of the slips had been used for lighting fires. They all betrayed slapdash amateurishness. Murray had to start all over again, laying down rules, playing the dominie in letters of inordinate length. The work that has gone into the illustrating of the words in the second edition of 1989 builds on the Murray punctiliousness, as does the clarity of definition.

Take Rubik's cube, which was a craze in 1981. "A puzzle consisting of a cube seemingly formed by twenty-seven smaller cubes, uniform in size but of various colours, each layer of nine or eight smaller cubes being capable of rotation in its own plane; the task is to restore each face of the cube to a single colour after the uniformity has been destroyed by the rotation of the various layers." Exemplary. As for illustration, we are all there, journalists, novelists, biographers (for all I know) of the Queen's corgis. I illustrate the word *rhotacismus*. Even solecisms get in, so long as they are ratified by distinguished usage. T. S. Eliot wrote "In the juvescence of the year/ Came Christ the tiger." He was wrong; it should be *juvenescence*. His authority prevails, and we can all dishonour Latin etymology if we wish. The OED bestows the right.

This is not a utilitarian dictionary in the sense that it invites a quick glance to check on a meaning, a pronunciation, an origin. Once open any volume and you start browsing. Evelyn Waugh browsed before going to bed and the next morning wrote about the "curlicues" of somebody's brain. Vladimir Nabokov's *Lolita* is as much about a love affair with the OED as a passion for a nymphet. W. H. Auden learned from it that the truth of a word (*etymon* in Greek) is not synchronic (here and now) but diachronic (covering the whole stretch of its history). If *silly* once meant holy (as it does still in "Silly Suffolk"), in a poem it may carry a flavour of the antique meaning. The word *buxom*, as Auden discovered, has a background of Anglo-Saxon *bugan*, meaning to bend, and has to mean not merely plump and comely but yielding and pliant. It may be said that the OED, stirring the imagination through words, is as much a poem as a source of poems, and hence the longest epic ever written.

But it is not a complete epic, since its subject-matter is not dead and gone like the voyages of Ulysses or the anger of Achilles. Language cannot come to an end like human life. George Orwell was wrong in supposing that the almighty State could legislate for English and produce the unchanging lexicon of Newspeak. Language does not operate solely on the level of conscious deliberation. New words and new usages for old words spring out of the deeper recesses of the brain. I've noticed in England in the last month or so at least two new idioms—"lager lout" for the young city man who gets drunk and offensive after his easy day's work; "steaming" for mugging on underground trains. "Bottle" for strength or stamina is already a little out of date, but it was blazoned on posters of the Milk Marketing Board in the slogan "Milk Delivers Bottle." When I was told, untruthfully, that I was still "wanking," I assumed that this meant masturbating, but it has developed the meaning of lazing, refusing to work. It is difficult for a dictionary to accommodate usages which may disappear overnight, but even a short life ensures that they become part of history.

Here, then, is the history of the English-speaking peoples as embodied in their language. But that language is itself the greatest product of their history and, like so many events and moments in history, it is something thrown off absent-mindedly. The builders of Babel had an intention they tried to fulfill—"Let us build a tower that will reach the skies"—though they were frustrated by a God who perversely punished them by confounding their language. Nobody ever had the intention of inventing English. But the intention to fully record it was an heroic act that we are right to honour. And if, as English speakers believe, God is an Anglophone, there may even be rejoicing in heaven.

—1989

CHAPLIN ON STAGE

❖

This year we celebrate the first centenary of the birth of Charles Chaplin. I have a familial interest less in the days of Chaplin's cinematic fame than in the preceding days when he made a small name in the English music hall. My father was a pianist by profession, not of the stature of Rachmaninov or Rubinstein, but of that lowly order that found employment in theatres and cinemas. He worked very briefly for Fred Karno, an impresario who sponsored both the young Chaplin and the equally young Stanley Jefferson who became Stan Laurel, better known in Italy as the Stanlio of Stanlio e Ollio. Thus my father had the privilege of playing the piano for two potential stars of the cinema who learned their trade through the hard grind of popular stage entertainment.

The music hall is no longer with us, though its ghost survives in some of the variety programmes put out by the RAI. In my father's day, which was also Chaplin's, the major towns of England had innumerable theatres which purveyed a genuinely proletarian art. London alone had thirty-six. The pattern of entertainment was always the same: the audience drank beer, joined in the choruses of popular songs, laughed at the comedians, threw rotten cabbages and rottener eggs at the turns they disliked, and accorded almost divine status to the major performers. These included Marie Lloyd, who, on her death, received the accolade of a long essay by T. S. Eliot. This praised an art which was minor but perfectly controlled and a capacity for articulating in song the preoccupations of a proletarian audience. Another star was Charles Chaplin—not the man we know but his father. The genius of the son owed little to the father, who was dissolute and irresponsible, but the music hall tradition was in the family blood and found expression, before Charlie got to the stage, in the work of Charlie's brother Sidney. Sidney is now forgotten. He had talent but no genius. But it is important, when we consider the achievement of the great man of the cinema, to know that his skills did not spring out of the empty air but out of a family tradition. Even the mother, Hannah (commemorated in the name of the heroine of the film *The Great Dictator*), worked as a singer and dancer before the lunatic asylum and the poorhouse claimed her.

The troupe organised by Fred Karno, which the young Chaplin joined, was kept together by strict discipline and the cultivation of very high standards of comedy. Much of the comedy was visual: words were never very important. It was athletic, acrobatic, and depended for its effect on strict timing. The young comedians, like their forebears of the Shakespearean theatre, had to be musicians as well as acrobats. When we see Charlie on the screen, playing a violin strung in reverse to accommodate his left-handed technique, when we hear the rather sedative music he composed for his talking films, we are not in the presence of an exceptional phenomenon: skill in music was part of the Karno requirement.

When I was in the British army in World War II, a typical piece of military inefficiency was usually greeted by the words "It's a proper Karno." Soldiers of that war had never known Fred Karno's theatre: they were merely reproducing slogans of their fathers and uncles in the previous one. But a song sung on the march in that war (to the tune of an Anglican hymn—"The Church's one foundation") made the comic disorganisation of the British army very explicit:

> *We are Fred Karno's army,*
> *The British infantree.*
> *We cannot fight, we cannot shoot—*
> *What bloody good are we?*
> *And when we get to Berlin,*
> *The Kaiser he will say:*
> *"Mein Gott, mein Gott, what a bloody fine lot*
> *Are the boys of Company A."*

Fred Karno stood for the comedy of disorganisation, the disruption of civic order, and a kind of hopelessness in the downtrodden. But it was a disorganisation that concealed immense theatrical skill, unlike the British army.

The hopelessness of the downtrodden is, eventually, to be expressed in the comic tramp of Charlie Chaplin. But it is a subtle kind of hopelessness in that it is qualified by great skills of survival. The tramp survives because of athletic agility, the ability to outrun his pursuers, the element of luck which seems to show that the universe, despite everything, is on his side. Moreover, the deplorable dress that he wears—trousers and boots too big, jacket too small—is qualified by a bowler hat, which can be raised with courtesy, and a walking stick which symbolises gentility. Chaplin, in that same World War I, became a symbol of survival for the British soldiery. To the tune of "Pretty Redwing" it sang:

> O *the moon shines bright on Charlie Chaplin,*
> *His boots are cracking*
> *For want of blacking,*
> *And his little baggy trousers they'll want mending*
> *Before they send him to the Dardanelles.*

The song is dated exactly—1916—and the disastrous Dardanelles campaign is seen by its victims for the débâcle it was. But Chaplin is clearly going to survive it.

The film that Chaplin made during that war—*Shoulder Arms*— made a perfect identification of the average soldier with the conscripted tramp. The music hall found a new setting: the trenches of Flanders, deep in mud. And the end of the war, it was assumed, would mean a return to Charlie in his ghastly tramp's outfit, the hopeful bowler hat and the genteel swagger cane, the pre-war world with its beer and music halls and proletarian culture. But, though the film world expanded, the music hall died. My father found himself accompanying Chaplin's comedies in the cinema, not the man himself in the theatre. The way was open for the depersonalisation of entertainment, which has found completion in television. Ten years after the 1918 Armistice, the talking films arrived and the universal art of pantomime, fostered and perfected by Fred Karno, had to surrender to it.

When we see a film of Chaplin's we are struck by the primitive cinematic technique, the failure to make the camera move, the poor cutting, the conflation of outrageous burlesque and unacceptable sentimentality. Though we may call Chaplin king of the cinema, we are wrong if we think we are watching anything other than a photographed music hall performance. Chaplin learned his techniques not in Hollywood but in the old music halls, now long demolished, that bordered the river Thames. The same is true of his one-time colleague Stan Laurel or Stanlio. Looking at their performances, we witness the preservation of something long dead, and we have to ask the question: why did it die?

We do not know the answer. It may have something to do with the increasing popularity of the cinema as demotic diversion, with Chaplin himself marking the transition; it may have something to do with the proletariat seeking upward mobility and learning to despise the music hall as the entertainment of the poor. If there are vestiges of the old music hall still around in Britain, they are mostly in the form of a rather supercilious imitation, usually for television. The chairman bangs his gavel and introduces the performers in sesquipedalian language, and the old songs are sung. The verses of the song tell a story, and the refrains, in which the audience joins, are melodious and simple. I know them all, which is a sign of my rapid decrepitude. The ultimate mockery of their simplicity is to be heard in a late film of Chaplin's, *Limelight*, in which a song is sung whose words are no more than "It's spring, spring, spring" repeated. That film stands as a fine memorial to the old music hall, whose demise is seen as tragic. The same may be said of John Osborne's play *The Entertainer*, where a decaying theatre called the Empire stands for the death of Britain's imperial past as well as for its live, hopeless, vigorous proletariat. I regret many things, but I regret none more than the end of the Chaplin world—the world that existed before he sought the bright light of Hollywood and the centennial fame which we celebrate this year.

—1989

EVELYN WAUGH: A REVALUATION

❖

There are writers whom one adores but whom one would not wish to have written more. I would not be happy about the discovery of a Shakespeare tragedy as good as *King Lear* or the epic on the sea that James Joyce spoke of writing after *Finnegans Wake*. Enough is enough already. I feel differently about Evelyn Waugh. I once envisaged paradise as a state in which a new Waugh was brought daily with one's morning tea. Probably an analogy with morning tea, or, better, mid-morning champagne, is right for Waugh. It is the taste I like, and I want the taste renewed indefinitely. All I can do, since Waugh died too young and wrote not nearly enough, is re-read. Perhaps I have over-re-read: it is unseemly to know whole paragraphs of mere prose by heart.

Waugh's prose is elegant, and I recognise that elegance is not suitable for fiction. Elegance, especially of Waugh's kind, which is mock-Augustan, makes for distance from fictional events and characters: the prose style should be involved, as Joyce's is, with what is happening. Waugh seems to be making judgments from above, like a saint of the Church Triumphant. There is something of that in Muriel Spark also: it can be a property of Catholic novelists. It can also make for cruelty. This is from *Decline and Fall*:

> It was a lovely evening. They broke up Mr Austen's grand piano, and stamped Lord Rending's cigars into his carpet, and smashed his china, and tore up Mr Partridge's sheets, and threw the Matisse into his water-jug; Mr Sanders had nothing to break except his windows, but they found the manuscript at which he had been working for the Newdigate Prize Poem, and had great fun with that.

There, true, he is less attempting elegance than a kind of biblical immediacy, but he is totally cut off, he has no pity. And when he kills little John Last in *A Handful of Dust* there is no pity either. The desire to be cold, uninvolved, may be an aspect of the desire to cultivate a Gibbonian style.

What was unlikable about Waugh as a person is also unlikable in his novels. He was a snob; he considered that only the British ruling class was to be taken seriously. In *Brideshead Revisited* he presents a blatantly false historical situation, identifying the English Catholics with the English aristocracy. He could not bear to think that his fellow-worshippers were typically Irish labourers and Soho waiters. He was a misanthrope as well as a snob. He was horrible to people and declared that he would have been worse without the grace granted by his Catholic conversion. The detestability of Waugh the man rubs on to Waugh the writer, and it is redeemed only through two atheological graces: the style and the humour.

The humour is considerable. Waugh is funny. Few comic writers can sustain comedy as he can. P. G. Wodehouse wearies in time: too many tricks are repeated. But, with immense economy and inexhaustible resource, Waugh sustains in the trilogy *Sword of Honour* a comic fresco of immense length. The comedy is totally compatible with high seriousness and even tragedy: it is revealed as a literary quality and not a genre. The account of the débâcle in Crete employs the same Augustan technique as the story of Apthorpe's thunderbox. It is dispiriting in terms of historical truth; it elevates the spirit by reason of its style—exact, clipped, balanced. The wit is never in the service of mere diversion. The theme of this best of our novels about World War II is close to that of Ford Madox Ford's *Parade's End,* a tetralogy (shamefully edited into a trilogy by Graham Greene) which sees World War I as a symptom rather than the cause of social breakdown. Waugh writes of Churchill, Stalin and Roosevelt "presiding over the dismemberment of Christendom." That is precise, even witty. It is also one of the most terrible phrases in all modern literature. Waugh records, from an upper-class English Catholic angle, the dethronement of the qualitative judgment and its replacement by the quantitative one.

My title promised to revaluate. I have done nothing so far except say what we all know about Evelyn Waugh. In his day, on the strength chiefly of the smart brittle side of his work—*Decline and Fall, Vile Bodies, Scoop, Black Mischief*—he was regarded as merely funny, though possessed of a somewhat irrelevant bite (the last of the great wars in *Vile Bodies*, the cannibalism in *Black Mischief*). Things changed with the appearance of *Brideshead Revisited*, which he had to announce as an "eschatological" book concerned with the working of God's grace. Here was a high romantic style, though fun could not easily keep out of it. It had to be treated as a full-blown novel, not as an entertainment, yet it is as a novel that few enlightened readers can accept it. It is a work of propaganda for the Catholic cause, beautiful, moving, but weighted in advance by the author's own convictions. In Henry James the characters have free will; here everything is almost Calvinistically predestined. Lord Marchmain makes the sign of the cross on his deathbed after a life of sybaritic atheism. God wins; God has to win; there is no contest.

Sword of Honour I call the best of the British war novels, aware however that there is not much choice. The viewpoint is limited. Guy Crouchback represents the recusant upper class; the war is a war of officers; the troops who did the real fighting are out there on the margins, cursing in comic accents. There is a little too much contrivance, too much coincidental meeting of the main characters, as though the war were conducted solely by members of Bratt's Club. The virtue of Ford's *Parade's End* is novelistic in the Jamesian or Conradian sense—the subordination of all its elements to a main theme, the eschewal of the *tour de force* or the anthologisable purple patch, even the avoidance of the easy laugh. *Sword of Honour* is unified only through its protagonist and the reality of history. History or autobiography provides a chunk of worn velveteen on which jewels can haphazardly be sewn. It is a gallimaufrey of brilliant bits, a stage show of admirable turns. The writing is wonderful, but it has nothing essential to do with the subject-matter.

But it was never possible to tell a story through wonderful writing. When W. H. Auden said that the novelist must "suffer dully all the wrongs of man" he was in effect denying the novelist's right to write brilliantly or elegantly. Reviewers go wrong when they denounce the "clumsiness" of, say, Kingsley Amis's writing, forgetting that the unwillingness to shape a sentence in the Waugh style matches the acceptance of the shapelessness of daily life. Waugh writes too well for a novelist.

So my adoration of his work persists in the face of his rejection of what I consider should be the nature of the novel. But what is very much in the nature of the novel is a quality in Waugh I have not so far mentioned: a fine ear which catches exactly the tones of British upper-class speech. When he makes a Maynooth priest speak, he cannot avoid caricature ("And how would I be knowing that ye're not a captain, me not being a military man at all"), and his corporals and sergeants are too lower-class to be true ("Now you've been and gone and let me down," moans an instructor to his officer squad). But when we hear Lady Brenda or Lady Kilbannock or Virginia Troy, we know we are listening to the true tones of pre-war Mayfair.

The best tribute I can pay to the Waugh style—in speech or récit—is the fact that I re-read and re-re-read. I expect snobbishness, cruelty, and a grave limitation of outlook, as well as a religious intolerance improper in a convert, but I expect to be delighted too. I dare not skip a line. As for his position in the pantheon of writers in English, I do not think it profitable to assign him a place (better than Greene, inferior to Ivy Compton-Burnett, a mere epigone of Ronald Firbank?). As a manipulator of prose he stands outside his contemporaries—outside, not above. Though his world died, as he knew it would, with the war in which he fought, his language encapsulates it, a grub in amber, and that language will go on living for a long time.

—1989

JAMES JOYCE: FIFTY YEARS AFTER

❖

Joyce had written a great part of his masterpiece *Ulysses* in Zürich during the First World War. In the Second World War he died in Zürich. It had been a difficult business for him and his family to get out of Nazi-occupied France into that neutral place of refuge. Although they were officially citizens of the independent Republic of Ireland, they clung to British passports. Indeed, James Joyce's grandson Stephen, though he hardly knows Great Britain at all, still follows that family tradition. On June 16 1982, during the celebrations to mark the centenary of Joyce's birth, his native city of Dublin made certain half-hearted gestures in the direction of granting civic honours to the greatest of its literary sons—a plaque here, a bust there—but Ireland has never liked him. His publishers were in London, and his patroness, Harriet Shaw Weaver, was an Englishwoman of Quaker convictions. He glorified the English language in his earlier books, and in his last book, so some say, he set out to destroy it. Which country really owns him? He left Dublin, with his Galway mistress Nora Barnacle, in 1904, and lived in Trieste, Zürich, and Paris. He was naturally an exile—*Exiles* is the title of his one and only play—and he has to be considered an international writer because he disowned all nations (except for that strange matter of the British passport). And yet he had only one subject a rather narrow one. All his books are about Dublin.

We may visit Dublin, as some of us do, to search for the ghost of the young Joyce—poor, ragged, myopic, intensely literary, already polyglot—but the city he knew no longer exists. It was one of the most beautiful cities in Europe, despite its vast slum population, but the demolition experts are pulling it down. With its office blocks, boutiques and discos, it is just like any other European city. Its population is over a million, and Japanese electronic firms provide employment. But it is still a bibulous city, where the true life is lived in the pubs, with their Guinness, whisky and fantastic conversation. The men are too drunk to be interested in sex. A Dublin homosexual is defined as a man who prefers women to drink.

The Dublin enshrined in Joyce's books is, then, as dead as the London of *Oliver Twist* or the Madrid of *Torquemada*. The volume of short stories entitled *Dubliners* shows what the city was like in 1904—morally and sexually paralysed but socially pullulant, full of talk and drink. The city is still there in *A Portrait of the Artist as a Young Man*, though the emphasis is on the development of a young soul that is trying to fly against the nets imposed by religion, family, and the nationalism rejecting the vassalage of the British Empire. *Ulysses*, one of the most influential novels of our century, is about a Dublin transformed into an archetypal city, and its hero is the archetypal citizen. Leopold Bloom is not, however, a typical Dubliner. He is half-Jewish. Living Dubliners call on their fathers' memories to deny that there were ever any Jews in their Catholic city. There were, but there were far more in Trieste, where Joyce began to write the book. To combine the images of that Adriatic port and the one on the Irish Sea is to underline the cosmopolitan nature of Joyce's vision. He is writing about the condition of all modern cities. Bloom is all modern men.

It is not, however, the subject matter of *Ulysses* that makes it distinctive. The plot is meagre. Bloom, who has lost his son, finds a surrogate son in the young poet Stephen Dedalus—the hero of *A Portrait of the Artist* and a barely veiled version of Joyce himself. Bloom's wife Molly commits adultery but looks forward to the entry of Stephen into her household—as son, redeemer and probably lover. The book is about the need of people for each other, in the smaller structure of the family, in the larger structure of the city. This simple theme is made universal by the imposition of a timeless myth, that of the wanderer Odysseus in search of his island kingdom. Bloom is Odysseus or Ulysses. His rather banal experiences on a single Dublin day—June 16 1904—are turned into comic parallels of the adventures of Homer's hero. These in turn approach various symbolic methods of underlining the classical parallel, chiefly through style and language.

Thus, Bloom encounters, in a Dublin pub, an Irish nationalist

known as "the Citizen". His Homeric parallel is the Cyclops.
This suggests a literary style known as gigantism, in which language is swollen unconscionably. Everything is exaggerated, in
the manner of demagogic rhetoric or pseudo-sciencific verbiage.
In the chapter where Bloom visits a maternity hospital to enquire
about the parturition of one of his wife's friends, Mrs. Purefoy,
the Homeric parallel is the slaughter by Odysseus's crew of the
Oxen of the Sun. These stand for fertility, and the young Dublin
medical students in the hospital are blaspheming against fertility
by glorifying "copulation without population." The structure of
the chapter imitates the growth of the foetus in the womb. Masculine seed fertilises female womb; masculine Anglo-Saxon fertilises female Latin; we have an entire history of the English
language through the progress of its literature, with Joyce as
master pasticheur.

Style becomes more important than content, but the intense
concentration on language enables Joyce to touch reaches of the
human mind previously inaccessible to the novelist. Language is
not merely complex but unprecedently candid: sexual allusions
abound, and words are used which, in the year of publication,
1922, and for forty years after, were officially taboo. This is why
Ulysses was banned and why Joyce, unjustly, gained the reputation of a dealer in obscenity and pornography.

Ulysses, using the technique of "interior monologue" to uncover
its characters' deepest thoughts and feelings—pre-syntactical and
almost pre-verbal—pushed the fictional examination of the human
consciousness to the limit. Joyce was only forty when the book
was published, and the question was asked: what, having gone so
far, can he possibly do with the rest of his creative life? In fact,
there were only nineteen years of this left, and they were fully
taken up with the composition of an incredible dense and difficult
pseudo-novel called *Finnegans Wake*. Having dealt with the conscious mind, Joyce had now to dive deep into the dream-world.
Finnegans Wake is the record of a single night's sleep. The sleeper
and dreamer, Humphrey Chimpden Earwicker, is the lowly landlord of a pub in Chapelizod, a suburb of Dublin, but he becomes
the whole of male humanity in its paternal manifestation, from
Adam to Joyce himself, while his wife Ann is all mothers, his
daughter Izzy is all temptresses (Eve, Delilah, Lady Hamilton),

and his twin sons Kevin and Jerry are all pugilant male rivals,
from Cain and Abel up to Napoleon and Wellington and beyond.

The language is dream-language or oneiroglot. As time and
space dissolve in dreams, so must words, through which we view
the spat temporal continuum, be distorted so that meaning does
not shatter but become ambiguous. Ambiguity is of the nature of
a dream. Joyce knew that the Freudian and Jungian techniques of
interpretation were not enough. An invention like "cropse" is a
fusion of "crops" and "corps," so that the opposed notions of
life springing from the earth and the dead body being buried in
it are unified. The action of the dream takes place in 1132, a
purely symbolic year, in which 11 stands for resurrection (having
counted ten on our fingers, we start again) and thirty-two for
falling (falling bodies go down at the rate of thirty-two feet per
second per second). "The abnihilisation of the etym" means both
the splitting of the atom and the re-creation of meaning (Greek
Otymon) from nothing (*ab nihilo*).

The work is, to put it simply, an attempt to reconcile opposites,
to affirm life, to insist that nothing dies. It is more than a novel;
it is a kind of vital manifesto. It is tempting to see in it the Catholic James Joyce who very nearly joined the Jesuit order but fore-
sook one kind of priesthood for another—that of art, in which
the dull bread of daily life is converted into the eucharistic host
of timeless beauty. Yet Joyce had left the Church, refused a Catholic marriage to his common-law wife, and denied his two children the benefit of baptism. He lost his religious faith and never
wished to recover it, but the atmosphere of his work is Catholic
European—closer to Dante than to Goethe or even his idol Ibsen.
Bloom, as an agnostic half-Jew, is merely interested in religion as
a binding social force, but his wife Molly, who was born in
Gibraltar, knows Catholicism from its Mediterranean as well as
its Northern Puritan aspects and worships a kind of Franciscan
God. Stephen Dedalus seems never to have recovered from the
frightful sermon on hell that is preached in *A Portrait*, and is
visited by his dead mother who shrieks for his repentance. Despite
the vast number of atheistical professors who specialise in Joyce
studies, it is probably true to say that only a Catholic, believing
or apostate, can fully understood Joyce.

But we celebrate the fiftieth anniversary of his death—as we celebrated, more lavishly, the hundredth anniversary of his death—in a spirit wholly literary. We are living in what is termed the post-modernist era, but we are still the heirs of modernism, and Joyce, along with Pound and Eliot, made shiningly clear precisely what modernism is. Modernism is, from the linguistic angle, the employment of a vocabulary which rings the bells of the colloquial as well as of the traditionally poetic and the new technological. It is concerned with exactness of language, but it knows that it is in the nature of language to carry a load of exploitable ambiguity. Modernism is honest and unaddicted to philosophical formulae for saving the world. It is extra-political and highly sceptical of both totalitarianism and populism. It is difficult, as Joyce is difficult, because it tries to look at humanity as a complexity which only politicians, priests, and subliterary bestsellers prefer to see as simple. The difficulty of *Finnegans Wake* is immense precisely because of its human subject-matter. Modernism dared to dig deeply, but the average man and woman is scared of such courage: it may uncover things it is convenient to ignore.

This summary of Joyce's achievement ignores a quality which we must regard as highly life-enhancing, namely, his humour. Despite the grimness of Dostoevsky, the tragic vision of Dreiser, and the relentless violence of so many contemporary bestsellers, the novel is essentially a comic form. The greatest novel of all time, *Don Quixote*, is a massive comedy, and Joyce learned from it more than he was willing to admit. *Ulysses* reverses the Cervantes situation by making a kind of Sancho Panza into his hero and placing a kind of Don Quixote in a secondary, or filial, position. When Leopold Bloom and Stephen Dedalus walk together after midnight through a deserted Dublin, we are asked to look at a tall thin figure and a shortish plump one. Bloom knows more than Sancho, but his wisdom is of Sancho's order, expressed in banal proverbs; Stephen is the poetic dreamer who needs the common sense of his surrogate father. They subsist in a comic relation, however, and they are supported, or rather opposed, by a huge comic cast of characters. *Ulysses* is one of the rare books that make us laugh aloud. *Finnegans Wake* is full of laughter too, with a language based on the comic possibilities of English. English may be regarded as a comic language in that it has irreconcilable elements—Germanic and Latin—perpetually thudding against each other. Translate *Finnegans Wake* into Spanish or Italian, and this comic element disappears. The miracle is that, though Joyce exploited the possibilities, and impossibilities, of English to the limit, he remains a European writer. He is cocooned in English, but he rises above it.

Like all the greatest novelists he somehow manages to subsist outside his literary medium. Don Quixote and Sancho Panza were riding round the Valladolid bullring in 1605, and they still ride in South American carnival processions. Charles Dickens's characters are recognised even by the illiterate. Leopold Bloom, Molly Bloom, Stephen Dedalus and Humphrey Chimpden Earwicker belong to this classical order. They are so big that they can submit to any amount of stylistic eccentricity or linguistic play and still shine out, full-bodies, three-dimensional, desperately alive. In an age when so many of our writers are pessimistic, it is good to celebrate one who is on the side of life.

—1990

TOLKIEN: A CENTENARY

❖

John Ronald Reuel Tolkien, who was born in South Africa in 1892, practised the remote craft of linguistic scholarship for most of his life but, in 1973, died famous. *The Hobbit*, published in 1937, was a child's fantasy that was to draw adult readers. In 1954 and 1955 he produced *The Lord of the Rings*, which attracted a large cult following, especially among the disaffected young of America. The poet W. H. Auden was to be seen wearing a tee-shirt proclaiming that he loved Tolkien. To love Tolkien was also to love Charles Williams and C. S. Lewis, two British authors who, with Tolkien, made up the triumvirate once known as the Inklings. Tolkien was nominally a Catholic, while the other two were Anglicans. Williams and Lewis were scholars given to popular fantasy with a strong Christian bias. Though English, they were fascinated by the Celtic legends that preceded the Anglo-Saxon culture of England. Tolkien was steeped in the Anglo-Saxon language and its mediaeval derivative, known as Middle English. With my old professor, E. V. Gordon, he produced an edition of *Gawain and the Green Knight* which, in the form in which it emerged from the Manchester University Press, is one of the most beautiful books in the world.

Gawain, an Arthurian narrative poem which continues to fascinate and has been both filmed and operatised (this year, by Sir Harrison Birtwhistle at Covent Garden), shows the influx of a large Norman vocabulary into a structure basically Germanic. Anglo-Saxon was, in fact, as Teutonic as modern German, with three genders, a battery of strong verbs, and a harsh melody that spoke of a cold northern climate and the presence of a turbulent sea. Modern English readers of *Beowulf* and *The Seafarer* approach their ancestral tongue as if it were a foreign language, which it is. The general view is that it needed the softening and civilising that contact with Latin Europe was to grant. Modern

English has as great a Latin vocabulary as Italian; it has simplified its Anglo-Saxon structure to the limit, so that it approaches Chinese in its grammatical spareness. It was Tolkien's eccentricity to hold that Anglo-Saxon never needed the modification of the Latin (and Greek) influx; he regretted that the Norman invasion had taken place. He had a nostalgia for a time when the native Germanic stock of the language was self-sufficient.

He has, at one time or another, shared this eccentricity with other English scholars. In the nineteenth century, William Barnes, a Doresetshire clergyman and a formidable linguistic scholar, insisted on delivering his sermons in the Dorsetshire peasant dialect. He hated words like *omnibus* and strove to introduce the native formation *folkwain*, which is close to *Volkswagen*. Instead of *telephone* he would have preferred *farspeaker*. *Despair* was too French a word; surely the late Anglo-Saxon *wanhope* was sufficient? In James Joyce's *Ulysses* the young Stephen Dedalus is suffused by "agenbite of inwit," which is more intelligible as "mordency of internal consciousness" but carries the stark lack of sophistication of a mediaeval monk's beating his breast and moaning about his sins. In Tolkien's South Africa the wholly Germanic Afrikaans confronted the wild Babel of black jargon. It is not too fanciful to suppose that his devotion to Anglo-Saxon was cognate with an unpleasing racism.

Tolkien's hobbits are humanoids, dwarfish, amiable, plump, fubsy, given to minding their own business but always ready to resist the invasion of beings—human or otherwise—they do not like. They dwell in a land called Middle Earth, a very Anglo-Saxon name, and they are virtuous in a very Christian way. *The Lord of the Rings*, in its very title, goes back to the ring-givers of the old Germanic tribes. The flavour of the book is feudal rather than democratic: the theme is loyalty and the willingness to combat pagan enemies. Clearly it is the work of a scholarly and sophisticated writer, but there is something childish about it, and this childishness is best seen in a total eschewal of the erotic. In an age like the sixties, when sex was bursting out all over among the young, it was strange to find such devotion to a work in which hobbits do not seem to couple and evil has no sexual admixture. Tolkien is wholly clean, like his fellow Inklings Williams and Lewis, and there is something dirty about this cleanliness.

We know little of Tolkien's marital life, except that he left a son named Christopher, who edited his last hobbit book, the *Silmarillion*. Like his friends, he preferred male company and evenings spent on textual discussion and much beer. There was something immature about the three of them, and this is what repels many readers. I have never been able to read either *The Hobbit* or *The Lord of the Rings* without severe distaste. To dislike the non-scholarly work of Tolkien never endeared one to W. H. Auden, who made devotion to Tolkien a criterion of literary taste. To Tolkien's credit, he never approved of this and was a little bewildered by his cult following. He wrote his fantasies as a diversion from serious study, rather as Lewis Carroll wrote the *Alice* books. He received many letters and even valuable gifts from his adorers. Uncritical admiration, as with Auden, is not what an author expects; there ought to be vocal enemies, and Tolkien seems to have had none of these.

The youthful cults of the 1960s take some understanding. There was not only Tolkien but also Hermann Hesse, especially his late book *Das Glasperhenspiel*. Both Tolkien and Hesse dealt in closed worlds which did not touch real life. Tolkien not only presented a Middle Earth with its own laws and customs; he even invented a language called Elvish, complete with a runic alphabet. It was a game, and it may be considered very English. It may even be considered schoolboyish, and it is the closed worlds of English public schools and Oxford colleges that have served to conserve the altogether masculine ethos of so many British writers, with their total exclusion of the world of women. Women are dangerous. They may appear in the novels of P. G. Wodehouse, but always as decent hockey-playing girls who are themselves trapped in a school world not dissimilar from that of their awfully decent boyfriends. The dark mystery of woman, which has it own logic and its fearful eruptions, is alien to so many of our British writers, though not to the French or the Italian. Tolkien loved Anglo-Saxon literature because there were no women in it. The great epic poem *Beowulf* is entirely masculine, all warriors relaxing in meadhalls before going off to fight fearful enemies. Beowulf's supernatural enemy is Grendel, a frightful monster, but Grendel's mother is worse. Being female, she has to be. *The Lord of the Rings* is a tamed, fairy-storyish, version of Anglo-Saxon epic, untouched by the female spirit, which Tolkien did not well understand.

He cannot easily be considered without reference to Charles Williams and C. S. Lewis. Lewis found a female companion late in life, after long devotion to a mother-figure with whom he had no sexual connection, and his introduction to the world of the erotic is painful and embarrassing because so childish. It was at the time of his marriage that Tolkien deserted him. He was not playing the game of being wholly self-sufficient as a male beer-swilling scholar. Perhaps Tolkien's private life is irrelevant to his work, but a certain personal insufficiency is all too evident in *The Lord of the Rings*. To indulge in fantasy is probably shameful. But there rests Tolkien's remarkable scholarship and his devotion to Anglo-Saxon. Auden heard him reciting Anglo-Saxon verse with panache and fervour and was thereafter hooked, as his own verse shows, on its prosody and vocabulary. He never liked the intrusion of the Romance world, which meant yielding to the feminine. But the marriage of North Sea and Mediterranean in modern English is what gives the language its peculiar allure. The allure of Tolkien is one-sided, sexless, and ultimately destructive.

—1991

Virginia Woolf Mortua 1941

❖

The two most innovative English language novelists of this century were born in the same year, 1882, and died in the same year, 1941. Thus we now celebrate the fiftieth anniversary of the deaths, both premature, of James Joyce and Virginia Woolf. Joyce escaped from the European war by fleeing to Switzerland, where he died of peritonitis. Virginia Woolf escaped from it by drowning herself. That war was going badly for her native England, but her suicidal despair had nothing to do with the future of the British Empire. Her despondency is not easy to explain, either, in terms of her literary career. Her last novel, *Between the Acts*, is as remarkable as her first, *Jacob's Room*; her reputation was secure and her marriage was happy. Indeed, Leonard Woolf, her husband, was the rock to the whirlpool of her mental instability. She was never mad, but she was hypersensitive. She inherited an excessive refinement of sensibility from the Stephens family. Her talent was a thin-skinned one. She found much of contemporary literature coarse and gross; her own contributions to it were made out of a desire to refine, sensitise, aerate.

Her refinement was not a throwback to Victorian puritanism. She was never puritanical. She swam naked with the beautiful young poet Rupert Brooke; her sexuality was epicene; she belonged to the most progressive social group of Europe, if not of the world. She was of Bloomsbury. Bloomsbury is, topographically speaking, that district of London which contains the British Museum. It was by chance that it became the centre of intellectual life that owed its ethos to the teachings of the philosopher G. E. Moore, whose *Principia Ethica* seemed to posit a modified hedonism. Any mode of action was justifiable if it gave refined pleasure to the actor and did not entail pain to others. There was a refined homosexual pattern in the lives of certain of the leading Bloomsburyites, especially the biographer Lytton Strachey, the novelist E. M. Forster, and the great economist Maynard Keynes. There was a certain snobbishness, an awareness of superiority. The University of Cambridge was the intellectual mother of the group. When Virginia Woolf first read James Joyce's *Ulysses*, she condemned it as the work of a "self-taught working man . . . an adolescent scratching his pimples." T. S. Eliot's adoration of the book did not make her judgment waver. Eliot, who was a managing director of Faber and Faber in Russell Square, very much Bloomsbury territory, was acceptable to the group even though he was an American. He had the requisite refinement and weak heterosexuality. But Joyce was beyond the pale.

And yet Joyce's innovations in fiction were close in spirit and sometimes technique to Virginia Woolf's own. Virginia Woolf rejected the novel as practised by H. G. Wells, Arnold Bennett, and John Galsworthy. She ought to have seen that Joseph Conrad was of a different pasta to these, more innovative than herself, but Conrad was a Pole, a foreigner, and hence outside the purlieu of her very English taste. Besides, Conrad, like the other Edwardians, contrived plots, and Virginia Woolf was dead against the limitations of traditional narrative. So was Joyce, but she could not see that. Joyce regarded narrative plot as vulgarly journalistic, concerned with the sensationalism of action and climax, and real life was not like that. Virginia Woolf agreed, but believed that she had come to that conclusion on her own. *Mrs. Dalloway*, like *Ulysses*, tells much of its story through interior monologue, but, unlike *Ulysses*, avoids those treacherous areas of the mind where the Freudian id sends its cloacal or lubricious messages. *Ulysses* has all the honesty of a male creation which recognises the importance of the lowlier aspects of the life of the body. In Virginia Woolf the spirit soars above sperm and urine. This was a limitation, one imposed less by her sex than by her gentility. She was too much of a lady to be willing to take in the smells of the back alley or the rubbish in the gutter.

Her view of character as a component of the novel was far ahead of Joyce's and, indeed, approached the phenomenalism of the French *anti-roman*. The personages of traditional fiction did not, in her view, correspond to observed reality. The notion of identity was, to her, highly artificial. In Joyce's novels the characters are so firmly drawn that they excuse the wilfulness of style.

We are prepared to struggle with excessive verbal eccentricity in order to come to terms with Leopold Bloom or Humphrey Chimpden Earwicker. These characters are highly memorable; indeed they seem separable from the fictions in which they are embedded, like Hamlet and Don Quixote. But in Virginia Woolf's *The Waves*, symbolism destroys character as we have previously known it. Or rather, character is shown not to exist. All we have are phenomena.

Some years ago, at the request of a famous British actress, I tried to make a Broadway musical out of Virginia Woolf's *Orlando*. This is a remarkable novel in which the action begins in the London of Queen Elizabeth I and ends in the Mayfair of the author's own time. The chief character, the eponym, starts as a man and ends as a woman. Here, with a vengeance, is demonstrated the fragile nature of human identity. When I envisaged my actress boldly changing her sex against a scenically shifting background, I was elated. Here were great dramatic possibilities. But, re-reading the book, I was infuriated at the lack of action. There was no drama at all. It was all atmosphere.

I am asserting a totally unacceptable masculinity when I contend that the greatest fiction has a forward-moving thrust, a power as of pistons. This is interpreted as phallocentric. Sir Walter Scott referred to it as the "big bow-wow style," but he was capable of appreciating the feminine delicacy of Jane Austen. Our own age is registering a fission, in which, instead of the feline quality of Jane Austen complementing the canine noise of Sir Walter, the masculine novel is condemned by the feminists and the female novel read in glum but unprotesting silence by the males. Virginia Woolf is the feminine novelist *par excellence*. Her sensitivity is exquisite, but a coarse male like myself wishes to drag her into a low tavern for an evening's debauchery. Some of us find her fiction hard going because of the huge areas of life it leaves out. To literary women she has become a matron saint. She has bequeathed a kind of literary bible entitled *A Room of One's Own*.

She pleaded, long before the bursting of the bomb of militant feminism, a woman's right to self-expression. Women needed a competence, a room to work in, the independence of the male scribbler. She never yielded to the traditional assumption that professional writing was a male province. The Brontë sisters had to publish under the masculine pseudonyms of Acton, Currer and Ellis Bell; George Eliot's real name was Mary Ann Cross. Virginia Woolf entered the literary lists as very much a woman. She was even a married woman, and her use of her husband surname was not a disguise but an acceptable convention. That she never became a mother may be glossed as the substitution of books for babies; had she had a child or children it is conceivable that she might have undergone a profound psychic change. She could behave like a submissive *Hausfrau*, cooking the dinner, maintaining meek silence while the men talked after it, but this was unimposed, it was a performance, the thing she wished to do.

She remains, for me, a difficult novelist but a highly approachable literary critic. The volumes of *The Common Reader* disclose what we may term a hermaphroditic sensibility, in which there is no female axe to grind. This has been left to her followers, who coarsen her somewhat by drawing her into a tendentiousness she was too much of a lady to have approved. Nowadays we have feminist publishers, who produce nothing but books for and by women. The Woolfs published too, but they were never partisan. There used to be an Irish sweepstake, in which Irish hospitals were endowed through a lottery linked to the great horse race called the Derby. The Woolfs won a prize in this lottery, and they invested the money in a printing press of a now long superseded kind—a flat bed with manual operation. Out of this venture came the Hogarth Press, which published poets and novelists regarded as uncommercial. Offered the works of Sigmund Freud, they demurred; there were limits to what they could produce in their household cellar. But their enterprise was honourable, helpful, and devoted to literature. Virginia Woolf loved books, if they were sufficiently—in the Bloomsbury sense—refined. Her devotees are less literary. To call her a great woman writer, as those devotees do, is to diminish her. We do not call James Joyce a great male writer. She is a great writer, *tout court*. If I find her fictions hard to read, that expresses my own limitations, not hers. She is one of the makers of the modern soul.

—1991

MARILYN

❖

She died just thirty years ago, in another era, one that was to
close with a presidential assassination. She'd be sixty-six if she
were still alive, no great age, but one well past the sell-out date
of sexual glamour. She died in the flush of her youth and beauty,
which is highly convenient for her myth, though hardly for herself. Apparently, she wished to die, but presumably not just yet.
It is generally accepted that she did not take her own life but was
murdered by the Mafia, or the Mob as Americans call that venerable institution. She was deeply involved, in an amatory capacity, with the President and his brother, the Attorney General. The
Mob hated both, since they had embarked on a plan of purification of the American scene, and they were to eliminate both,
with the elimination of their sex goddess as a warming-up act.
There is something Attic in the whole story: the fall of the house
of the Kennedys, like the house of Atreus. But Aphrodite, being
a goddess, has proved impossible to kill. Marilyn remains one of
our major icons. The Mafia, which originated in a classical island,
should be aware of the Greek tragedy implicit in the whole drama,
but they presumably have more important things to do, like the
blasting of incorruptible Italian judges.

Let us consider Marilyn outside the political context. She was
one of the blonde goddesses of the silver screen, one of two only,
the other being Jean Harlow. The American cinema has produced
many stars of great sexual glamour, from the Gish sisters and Mae
Marsh onwards, but the divine attribution has always been severely limited. Joan Crawford and Bette Davis were great stars,
but they conquered through melodramatic aggression: they lacked
the yielding, vulnerable quality which men see as essentially feminine. Besides, they were not blondes. Joan Crawford had assertive black eyebrows, and Bette Davis has no crinal memorability.
In the chromatology of the American cinema, blondeness is nec-

essary for true divinity. Hedy Lamarr came close to this state, but she was dark-haired and also foreign. Foreignness worries American cinemagoers who, of course, are themselves all foreign immigrants. Marlene Dietrich was blonde enough, but her Germanicity, and her sexual ambiguity, profoundly disturbed. America wanted—and, apparently, we non-Americans wanted too—a blonde goddess born on American soil. There were plenty of blonde actresses with the chthonic qualification, but—Joan Blondell, Doris Day, others—they were too much like one's sister, or the girl next door. Jean Harlow and Marilyn Monroe were different.

Gold is a rare metal, and, despite the fact that it can easily be applied out of a bottle, the gold of blonde tresses is to be considered rare also. The majority of the women of the world have raven hair: it is the primary female banner of the Third World, which is now the Second. It is a northern blessing or curse, this blondness, and with men it is associated with the aspirations of the Nazi Party. The blond Teuton is sheeplike, oxlike only in strength and stupidity. Blonde women developed a fictional mythology in the nineteenth century, best seen in Madame de Staël's novel *Corinne*. Corinne is a brunette of startling dramatic talent, but she loses her man to a blonde girl with only the talent to seduce. The seduction itself is unintentional: men fall for blonde women because they seem childlike, helpless: they need the protection of the fireside. In George Eliot's *The Mill on the Floss*, Maggie Tulliver, the dark-haired heroine, has to contend with an inside fair-haired doll who steals her man. Lucie Manette, the blonde heroine of Dickens's *A Tale of Two Cities*, is also a doll, but her fair hair represents a cool asexual cleanliness which is very attractive to men embroiled in a dirty world. D. H. Lawrence's wife, Frieda, was a blonde German baroness, but she gave the lies to the myth of fair-haired cleanliness. Aldous Huxley's dark wife, Maria, was astonished at the filth of Frieda's domestic arrangements: she had taken it for granted that blondes are clean.

The title of Anita Loos's novel makes a firm American assertion: *Gentlemen Prefer Blondes*. In the film made from this book, Marilyn played Lorelei, the heroine who conquers by being blonde and dumb, but not so dumb as not to know that diamonds are a girl's best friend. Anita Loos followed with *But Gentlemen*

Marry Brunettes, though her later homophobia led her to consider writing *Gentlemen Prefer Gentlemen*. The American blonde was firmly esconced in literature from the 1920s on. Cinematic blondes needed to talk, so they came later. The allure of Jean Harlow (whose hair was termed platinum) was a very American property. She played parts of a lower-class provenance: the patrician blonde was never an American concept. There was an edge of coarseness in her roles, and this made her seem available. Frieda Lawrence's baroness mother told her that, in marrying the son of a coal miner, she had reduced herself to a *Kellnerin*, what the British call a barmaid. It is precisely the barmaid accessibility of Jean Harlow that appealed: her body was luscious and vulnerable, and the vulnerability of her soul was symbolised in the hair of a doll. Dolls have usually been blonde. The Barbie doll, an American artefact, cannot be conceived of as bearing the tresses of Gina Lollobrigida or Sophia Loren.

Marilyn Monroe succeeded Jean Harlow, but the myth of her life was at least as compelling as her screen embodiments; she inhabited a bigger world than Jean Harlow. She married Joe Di-Maggio, a baseball star of immense eminence; she also married Arthur Miller, a great Jewish intellectual and the foremost American playwright of his time. And, of course, she found her lovers in the highest echelons of the State. But her persona was primarily that of the archetypal dumb blonde who turns out to have instinctive gifts which enable her to prevail. Vulnerability, again, is the keynote. In the film *How to Marry a Millionaire*, Marilyn played a girl desperately short-sighted: without her spectacles she walks into walls. This image made her comic, but not pitiably so. Her elegance, the cut of her clothes and the poise of her body, above all the sensual messages she unwittingly gave out (or wittingly: one could never be sure) conspired to arouse a laughter of which she herself was in control.

In the Billy Wilder film *Some Like It Hot*, the vulnerability was still there, but she was not likely to be wounded. She was on the make: her idea of male handsomeness was middle-aged eyes squinting at the columns of the *Wall Street Journal*. She was witty, but the wit seemed to be the bestowal of a guardian angel, not her own. And of course she sang well, with the most seductive body language. The body was a divine bestowal, and it did not lose its exquisite lines when she took heavily to drugs variegated with junk food. Arthur Miller, in his autobiography, noted that men would covertly masturbate in her presence. The body was not flaunted, in the professional manner of a model or showgirl: it was shown off, as it were, distractedly. There was a notorious nude photograph of her, but it was never her total nudity that appealed, in fact or in fantasy. The segmental epiphanies were enough, as in that bewitching shot of her skirt blown up by a puff of air from a grating in *The Seven Year Itch*.

That she was a great comic ought to detract from her divine glamour. She had a quality she may have learnt from Mae West, the blonde seductress who mocked seduction, indeed mocked sex: this was the intimation that she, the true she, was somewhere outside her body, that her body was a kind of glorious impersonation, an image of an archetypal love goddess. There is, of course, nothing more hair-raisingly seductive than this combination of terrible innocence with terrible sexual power. By all accounts, she was not greatly interested in the sexual act. She never seduced any man to bed and, once in bed, found little satisfaction in the act of love. Such revelations, naturally, do not affect her image in the slightest.

Her image remains, and no amount of analysis can properly explain continued potency. It ought to be a tragic image but is not. If Marilyn had been beautiful, there might have been a quality of high Greek poignancy, but tragedy is not a property which goes with mere prettiness. For, though her beauty of body was undoubted, her face had no classic lines. It had a snub nose, and it had the cheery, even cheeky, playfulness which we regard as an attribute of the American girl—open, free, a little combative. It remains a slangy face, essentially plebeian. It was not a face that could have come out of Greece or Italy. It was an American face that exuded American optimism—alas, terribly misplaced. But, since America dominates our age, it is proper that its chief sexual icon should come from that land of promise. Promise unfulfilled, like Marilyn herself.

—1992